D1191532

Deliberative Democracy and the Institutions of Judicial Review

In this book, Christopher F. Zurn shows why a normative theory of deliberative democratic constitutionalism yields the best understanding of the legitimacy of constitutional review. He further argues that this function should be institutionalized in a complex, multilocation structure including not only independent constitutional courts, but also legislative and executive self-review that would enable interbranch constitutional dialogue and constitutional amendment through deliberative civic constitutional forums. Drawing on sustained critical analyses of diverse pluralist and deliberative democratic arguments concerning the legitimacy of judicial review, Zurn concludes that constitutional review is necessary to ensure the procedural requirements for legitimate democratic self-rule through deliberative cooperation. Claiming that pure normative theory is not sufficient to settle issues of institutional design, Zurn draws on empirical and comparative research to propose reformed institutions of constitutional review that encourage the development of fundamental law as an ongoing project of democratic deliberation and decision.

CHRISTOPHER F. ZURN is associate professor of philosophy at the University of Kentucky. The recipient of a Humboldt Fellowship in 2004, he has published articles on deliberative democracy, judicial review, critical theory, feminism, moral theory, and aesthetics. One of his articles on democracy and judicial review was chosen as one of the ten best philosophy articles published in 2002 by the editors of *Philosopher's Annual*.

Deliberative Democracy and the Institutions of Judicial Review

CHRISTOPHER F. ZURN

University of Kentucky

CAMBRIDGE
UNIVERSITY PRESS

CAMBRIDGE UNIVERSITY PRESS
Cambridge, New York, Melbourne, Madrid, Cape Town, Singapore, São Paulo

Cambridge University Press
32 Avenue of the Americas, New York, NY 10013-2473, USA

www.cambridge.org
Information on this title: www.cambridge.org/9780521867344

First published 2007

Printed in the United States of America

A catalogue record for this publication is available from the British Library.

Library of Congress Cataloging in Publication Data

Zurn, Christopher F., 1966–
Deliberative democracy and the institutions of judicial review/
Christopher F. Zurn.
p. cm.
Includes bibliographical references and index.
ISBN-13: 978-0-521-86734-4 (hardback)
1. Judicial review – United States. 2. Constitutional courts – United
States. 3. Legislative power – United States. 4. Executive power – United
States. I. Title.
KF4550.Z9Z87 2007
347.73′ 12–dc22
2006020511

ISBN 978-0-521-86734-4 hardback

Contents

Acknowledgments   *page* vii

1   Introduction   1
   A. An Old Chestnut is Actually Two   2
   B. Pathologies of ad hoc Triangulation   8
   C. Functions and Institutions   25

2   Majoritarian Democracy and Minoritarian Constitutionalism   31
   A. Judicial Review as Substantially Legitimate Protection of Minority Rights 32
   B. Judicial Review as Procedurally Legitimate Protection of Democracy 39
   C. Moving Beyond Aggregative Majoritarianism and Minoritarian
     Constitutionalism   63

3   From Majoritarian to Deliberative Theories of
   Constitutional Democracy   68
   A. Deliberative Democracy: Four Axes of Analysis   68
   B. Constitutionalism: Four Central Elements   84
   C. Constitutional Democracy?   103

4   Deliberative Democracy and Substantive Constitutionalism   106
   A. Keepers of the Substantive Flame of American Exceptionalism 107
   B. Guardians of the Moral Law in the Forum of Principle 113
   C. Are Substantialist Defenses of Judicial Review Self-Defeating? 124

5   Disagreement and the Constitution of Democracy   130
   A. Democratic Precommitment to Judicial Review: Freeman 131
   B. Deliberative Majoritarianism and the Paternalism of Judicial Review:
     Waldron   141
   C. Upshot: We Need a Theory of Democratic Constitutionalism 161

6   The Seducements of Juristic Discourse as Democratic
   Deliberation   163
   A. A Division of Labor between Juristic Deliberation and Populist
     Aggregation?   164

B. *Actual Juristic Discourse in the United States System of*
Constitutional Adjudication   184
C. *Legal Principles and Moral-Political Reasoning*   207

7   Constitutionalism as the Procedural Structuring of
    Deliberative Democracy   221
    A. *A Provisional Summary: Criteria for an Adequate Theory of*
    Constitutional Review   221
    B. *Guardians of the Conditions of Procedural Legitimacy: Habermas*   227

8   The Institutions of Constitutional Review I: Design
    Problems and Judicial Review   253
    A. *The Problems of Designing Institutions of Constitutional Review*   253
    B. *Independent Constitutional Courts in a Concentrated Review System*   274

9   The Institutions of Constitutional Review II: Horizontal
    Dispersal and Vertical Empowerment   301
    A. *Self-Review Panels in the Legislature and Regulatory Agencies*   302
    B. *Mechanisms for Interbranch Debate and Decisional Dispersal*   305
    C. *Easing Formal Amendability Requirements*   312
    D. *Establishing Civic Constitutional Fora*   323

    Bibliography   342
    Index   355
    Table of Cases   366

Acknowledgments

I have been thinking about the ideas in this book for several years. My original interest in the topic of judicial review was sparked by a conversation with Martino Traxler in 1998 about Habermas's approach to constitutional interpretation. As often happens, Martino made what seemed at first to be a rather straightforward objection, one that should be answerable in due course through, perhaps, a few minor adjustments of leading concepts: wouldn't judges using a proceduralist theory of constitutional interpretation need to rely on contextually specific and contested ethical values in order to adjudicate constitutionally specified social and ecological rights, thereby violating their proceduralist mandate? My first approaches to answering this objection were all unsatisfactory and, as time went on, I found myself needing to delve ever more deeply into basic questions about the proper normative conception of constitutional democracy itself, and about how to institutionalize a legitimate practice of constitutional democracy, before I could adequately address issues of how judges should interpret constitutional provisions. Some of the fruits of that thinking were first published in 2002, and this book represents my sustained efforts over the years since to come to terms with those basic normative and institutional questions.[1] Unfortunately, an adequate response to Martino's concerns about adjudicative methods, if there is one, still awaits further work.

I would like to thank many people for helpful comments, conversations, and criticisms of various claims and arguments presented in this book: Amy Allen, Ken Baynes, Jim Bohman, Jean Cohen, Brian Cubbage, Will Dudley,

[1] Christopher F. Zurn, "Deliberative Democracy and Constitutional Review," *Law and Philosophy* 21 (2002). Though this book largely reproduces the normative arguments made there, it introduces a more complex characterization of the distinctions involved in debates about deliberative democracy and constitutionalism (see especially Chapter 3), significantly expands the scope of those normative arguments, and substantially changes the speculations concerning various institutional reform proposals considered there.

Oliver Eberl, Rainer Forst, Nancy Fraser, Pablo Gilabert, Robert Goodin, Roger Hartley, Martin Hartmann, Joe Heath, Felicia Herrschaft, Jaeho Kang, Avery Kolers, Frank Michelman, Kevin Olson, David S. Owen, Max Pensky, Konstanze Plett, Doris Provine, Bill Rehg, Emmanuel Renault, Gerald Rosenberg, Christian Rostbøll, Martin Saar, Giovanni Saavedra, Larry Sager, Thomas Schmeling, and Hans-Christoph Schmidt am Busch. I owe a special debt of gratitude to Vic Peterson who has, for some six or seven years, read just about every one of my drafts on these topics and has given detailed and insightful criticism, comment, and advice on them – it has been an exceptional gift to have a sympathetic yet challenging reader willing to give such time and attention.

I have benefited immeasurably from the sure counsel and philosophical acumen of Tom McCarthy throughout my scholarly development. Whether advising me on the ins and outs of academic careers or critically evaluating my ideas, Tom has gone above and beyond the simple duties of a doctoral advisor, becoming rather a long-term mentor and friend. I also would like to thank Jürgen Habermas not only for his inspiring theoretical work but also for always being willing to engage in argumentative discourse oriented toward the right and the true.

This bulk of this book was written during my year as an Alexander von Humboldt Fellow at the J.W. Goethe-Universität in Frankfurt – without this financial support, this book simply would not have been possible. My host, Axel Honneth, provided a generous and supportive environment in which I could pursue my work on this book, without becoming hermetically sealed solely in its own orbit. In particular, the multiple deliberative fora he sustains in Frankfurt and his remarkable interactive demeanor have nourished my broader intellectual interests and shown me what authentic intersubjectivity means in practice. My thanks also to the Department of Philosophy and the Dean's Office of the College of Arts & Sciences at the University of Kentucky who provided both material support and very welcome flexibility in times of need.

It is hard for me to adequately recognize the care and support I have received from the members of my immediate and extended families over the years, most especially that of Michelle Saunders and Finn Saunders-Zurn. As an insufficient acknowledgment of all they have done for me, let me simply dedicate this book, with all of my love, to Michelle and Finn.

1

Introduction

Is judicial review democratic or antidemocratic, constitutional or anti-constitutional? Should electorally unaccountable judges in a constitutional democracy be able to declare unconstitutional, and so overturn, the laws and decisions made through ordinary democratic political processes? At its most basic, this problem of where to place the powers of constitutional review appears to revolve around fundamental tensions between two of our most important political ideals – constitutionalism and democracy – and between various ways of realizing these ideals in political institutions and practices. If courts perform constitutional review, how can this be squared with democratic ideals? How can the people be sovereign if their direct representatives can't make the laws that the people demand? Alternatively, how can the democratic process be kept fair and regular without constitutional controls on elected politicians? Wouldn't constitutionally unhindered officials attend only to the demands of majority preferences at the expense of the rights of individuals and minorities? Can the distinction between ordinary law and the higher law of the constitution be maintained over time if elected politicians are responsible for both? Can the distinction between making law and applying law be maintained over time if judges do both in their role as expositors of the constitution? Should the constitution be a part of the political process, or an external check on that process? And, finally, who decides: who decides what the scope of constitutional law is, who decides what a constitution means, who decides whether ordinary laws violate the constitution?

One central premise of this book is that such questions are best answered in the light of a philosophically adequate and attractive theory of constitutional democracy, one that can convincingly show how constitutionalism and democracy are not antithetical principles, but rather mutually presuppose each other. Political philosophy, then, plays a crucial role in understanding and justifying the function of constitutional review in terms of its fundamental role in a well-functioning democracy. But pure normative theory alone is insufficient to settle questions about how best to design institutions to carry out that function. Whether constitutional review is best performed as part of the normal appellate court system (as in the United States), or in independent constitutional courts (as in many European nations), or in more politically accountable branches such as parliaments (as in many British commonwealth nations) – these are questions that require judgments sensitive to the empirical conditions of institutions, politics, and law as we know them, and to the different legal, political, and historical contexts evinced in various constitutional democracies. Thus a second central premise of the book is that an adequate theory of judicial or nonjudicial review – a theory that proposes specific ways to institutionalize the function of constitutional review – needs also to be attentive to the results of legal scholarship and comparative studies of democratic institutions. The types of questions posed here – concerning the legitimacy, institutional location, scope, and adjudicative aims of constitutional review in constitutional democracies – must be addressed, then, through a combination of normative and empirical research: political philosophy, comparative political science, and jurisprudence.

More specifically, this book argues for a theory of constitutional review justified in terms of the function of ensuring the procedural requirements for legitimate democratic self-rule through deliberative cooperation. Proceeding from the premises of deliberative democratic constitutionalism, it claims further that constitutional review is best institutionalized in a complex, multilocation structure including independent constitutional courts, legislative and executive agency self-review panels, and civic constitutional fora. It proposes that such institutions would work best in a constitutional context encouraging the development of fundamental law as an ongoing societal project of democratic deliberation and decision. Recognizing that specific institutions of constitutional review should be tailored to different political and legal systems, it claims that such institutions should, in general, be oriented toward broadening democratic participation, increasing the quality of political deliberation, and ensuring that decision making is reasons-responsive and thereby democratically accountable.

A.   AN OLD CHESTNUT IS ACTUALLY TWO

The central issue this book addresses then is the tension commonly felt between democracy and the institution of judicial review. Although there are many ways of formulating exactly what this tension consists in – and, of course, of formulating responses to it – two formulations in the American context stand out as canonical: Alexander Bickel's and

Judge Learned Hand's. I want now to briefly indicate what these two formulations are in order to show that they are not equivalent: they depend on different conceptions of the ideals of democracy, of democratic decision making processes, and of the relationship of judicial review to those ideals, and processes.

1. The "Countermajoritarian Difficulty" with Judicial Review: Bickel

The root difficulty is that judicial review is a counter-majoritarian force in our system.... When the Supreme Court declares unconstitutional a legislative act or the action of an elected executive, it thwarts the will of representatives of the actual people of the here and now; it exercises control, not in behalf of the prevailing majority, but against it. That, without mystical overtones, is what actually happens.... The essential reality [is] that judicial review is a deviant institution in the American democracy.[1]

According to Bickel's formulation, democracy is essentially rule by current majorities, and the American political system is fundamentally a democratic one. Furthermore, the current majority whose will is supposed to rule are the current citizens of the United States, and that will is most manifest and forceful as reflected in the will of the directly elected representatives of the people: elected representatives, the elected president, and all those who are directly authorized by these elected representatives. Because national judges in the United States are not elected but appointed, and once appointed serve for life terms, there is no direct electoral control over them, and precious little indirect control. When a court strikes down a legislative act or executive action as unconstitutional then, it acts in a countermajoritarian, and therefore antidemocratic, way. Thus, "judicial review runs so fundamentally counter to democratic theory ... in a society which in all other respects rests on that theory."[2] Of course, Bickel does have a series of arguments to show that even if countermajoritarian, judicial review is nevertheless an overall good in the American political system (I discuss these arguments in the next chapter), but what I am concerned with here is the basic normative conception of democracy that underlies the countermajoritarian formulation of the objection. In short, democracy is taken to be a preeminent value of politics; the ideal of democracy is rule by present majority will; that will is effected through the democratic process of electing representatives who in turn pass laws and administer

---

[1] Alexander M. Bickel, *The Least Dangerous Branch: The Supreme Court at the Bar of Politics*, second ed. (New Haven, CT: Yale University Press, 1986), 16–18.
[2] Ibid., 23.

policies; judicial review of those laws and policies is countermajoritarian and so undemocratic.

2.   The Paternalist Objection to Judicial Review: Hand

Although Bickel quotes approvingly Judge Learned Hand's objection to judicial review in his discussion of the countermajoritarian difficulty, I believe that the latter's concerns are of quite a different kind than Bickel's:

> For myself it would be most irksome to be ruled by a bevy of Platonic Guardians, even if I knew how to choose them, which I assuredly do not. If they were in charge, I should miss the stimulus of living in a society where I have, at least theoretically, some part in the direction of public affairs. Of course I know how illusory would be the belief that my vote determined anything; but nevertheless when I go to the polls I have a satisfaction in the sense that we are all engaged in a common venture.[3]

To begin with, the rhetorical reference to Platonic Guardians conveys a quite specific set of antithetical attitudes towards practices of paternalism. An individual is treated paternalistically when she is forced to do something against her own will and where that something is asserted or justified as being in her own best, real, or true interests by another who claims to know better what those interests are than she herself knows. Paternalism is opposed to self-rule, to self-government, to autonomy. It is important to note here that the problem is not so much the coercion involved, or even the coercion against one's present will – although coercion is a necessary part of paternalism – but, rather, the fact that the person controlled has no significant part in the decision-making processes of the guardian even though the matter centrally concerns her own interests.

When the idea is extended into the political realm of the government of a collectivity, paternalism is opposed to democratic self-government. The individual treated paternalistically becomes the collective group of democratic citizens, who are forced to do something against their own manifest will and where that something is asserted or justified as being in their own best, real, or true interests by others who know better what those interests are than they themselves do. Clearly with the change in scale from individual to collectivity, the decision-making processes involved are more complex socially and institutionally, and it may be harder to say what exactly counts as manifesting the will of the citizenry. Yet Hand's formulation gives us crucial criteria here: democratic processes

---

[3] Learned Hand, *The Bill of Rights* (Cambridge, MA: Harvard University Press, 1958), 73–74.

must be those in which each citizen has an inexpungeable role in the mutual determination of collective decisions and each must be able to understand her or himself as part of a common venture of self-rule. The issue is not the impact of one's vote on the outcome – in large collectivities like modern nation-states individuals' electoral impact may well be miniscule – but, rather, the degree to which the decision-making processes accord individuals the capacity to understand themselves as collective authors of the law that each is subject to. And that self-understanding is accorded precisely where each has a role in mutual and collective processes of practical reasoning together in order to decide the terms of their common political life.[4] Finally, insofar as the decision-making processes of courts exercising constitutional review do not allow citizens to understand themselves as involved in a common venture of self-government with their fellow citizens – appointed, life-tenured judges using legal methods for decision do not generally consider the people's own opinions about where their best, real, or true interests lie – those processes are objectionable because paternalistic. On this formulation, then, the ideal of democracy concerns the self-government of a collectivity; democratic processes must somehow allow each citizen the equal satisfaction of being engaged in a common venture of self-government with others; judicial review, as it doesn't allow this, is paternalistic and so undemocratic.

We have then two quite different formulations of the old chestnut concerning the tension between democracy and judicial review, each drawing on different conceptions of the ideals of democracy, their proper realization in democratic processes, and the relation of those ideals and processes to the institution of judicial review. Democracy as majority rule versus democracy as self-government; representative reflection of the desires of the majority versus facilitation of consociation among citizens on terms arising from the mutual exercise of practical reason; countermajoritarianism versus paternalism. In short, Bickel's objection to judicial review rests on a vision of democracy as majoritarian aggregation; Hand's on a vision of democracy as deliberative consociation. As this book moves in Chapter 2 through the traditional defenses of judicial review and into Chapters 3 to 7 through more recent defenses of and attacks on judicial review, it will be moving

---

[4] For those who think that this reads too much into Hand's phrases about "some part in the direction of public affairs" and "a collective venture" I would refer them to the parable of democracy he puts forward at Learned Hand, "Democracy: Its Presumptions and Realities," in *The Spirit of Liberty: Papers and Addresses of Learned Hand*, ed. Irving Dilliard (New York: Alfred A. Knopf, 1960 [1932]), 99–100, in which explicit references are made to mutual reckoning, listening to the concerns of others, and collectively consociating through the pooling of wishes. Note also that Hand's parable connects paternalistic guardianship to infantilization.

from the terrain of aggregative to deliberative conceptions of the meaning, import, and institutional bases of democracy.

3. Reopening the Chestnuts

The set of problems revolving around the relationship between judicial review and democracy make up a well-worn *topos* – in jurisprudence especially, but also in allied fields of political philosophy, political science, and comparative law. One might wonder what is to be gained from returning to that ground. There are three broad types of reasons for the thought that it is worthwhile to take up anew the questions about how to institutionalize constitutional review. First, many treatments of judicial review tacitly presuppose particular normative ideals of democracy and constitutionalism, without fully noting how much argumentative weight these particular ideals carry. When, for example, some juris-prudential treatments argue for a specific method for interpreting constitutional provisions, crucial claims and arguments often turn on foundational normative premises about how to understand constitutional democracy, rather than strictly jurisprudential concerns. Often these implicit assumptions are in fact embedded within the nationalist limita-tions of the theory. So, for example, although American legal academics have taken a lead role in the revival of thought about the legitimacy, scope, and methods of judicial review, they have often simply assumed that the arrangements that give the Supreme Court of the United States supreme authority to carry out the function of constitutional review are increasingly universally shared arrangements, or are at least universally justifiable. They then proceed to develop theories with universal intent that in fact are only appropriate to the contingent historical legal and political context of the United States. The sketches of the ideals of democracy and constitutionalism employed in some recent juris-prudential positions in the next section of this chapter are intended to indicate the argumentative pathologies that arise when specific normative conceptions of democracy and constitutionalism are instrumentalized to the need to justify United States arrangements for constitutional review as the best of all possible arrangements.

Second, a central claim of the book is that the complex of issues sur-rounding the questions concerning how to institutionalize constitutional review look quite different once one sees them from the perspective of new developments in political philosophy over the last generation. On the one hand, deliberative theories of democracy have arisen that intend to supplant older models of competitive elitism or corporative pluralism. Deliberative theories stress the normative significance, and the empirical relevance, of discussion and debate for generating convincing public reasons for collective decisions and state action. Rather than viewing democracy as the simple aggregation of a majority's private preferences, deliberative democrats tend to see it as a way of structuring wide cooperative participation by citizens in processes of opinion formation and decision. They thereby provide, to my mind, a more compelling picture of the ideals and actual practices of democracy.

On the other hand, constitutional theory has moved away from natural law inspired accounts – those stressing the constitutional protection of a substantive list of metaphysically grounded prepolitical individual rights – and turned instead to accounts of constitutionalism as the procedural structuring of political processes, where constitutional rights are seen as one part of the procedural requirements that warrant the legitimacy of democratic decisions. I argue that a deliberative conception of democracy and a proceduralist conception of constitutionalism belong together, and that this combination – deliberative democratic constitutionalism – is, in comparison with more traditional models, both more attractive normatively and more compelling empirically in modern societies marked by deep and apparently intractable moral disagreements.

Chapter 2 schematically presents variations on the traditional model of constitutional democracy employed in the United States – what I call majoritarian democracy constrained by minoritarian constitutionalism – and indicates some of the normative and empirical deficiencies of the model, deficiencies that motivate a move beyond it. Chapters 3 through 7 then present a series of competing conceptions of deliberative democracy and constitutionalism, using the specific arguments presented by each conception for and against judicial review as a way of focusing attention on the interactions between normative ideals and considerations about appropriate political institutions. This examination supports the conception of deliberative democratic constitutionalism I put forward by drawing on the insights, and avoiding the deficiencies, of the various competing conceptions.

Third, I argue that the resulting conception can helpfully guide and inspire the design of responsive and competent institutions for realizing the function of constitutional review. Political philosophy alone, however, is insufficient to carrying out such design tasks: we need rather to combine the insights of normative theory with productive directions in recent empirical, comparative, and legal scholarship. In a sense, the result of the arguments in Chapters 3 through 7 is a robust conception of deliberative democratic constitutionalism that can provide a strong justification for the *function* of constitutional review, but not for any particular way of *institutionalizing* that function. It is the task of Chapters 8 and 9, then, to try to mediate between the ideal and the real, between norm and fact, by proposing a series of reforms in current institutions that carry out constitutional review. Only by attending to the burgeoning fields of scholarship focused on courts, political institutions, constitutional design, and democratic deliberation can one properly support particular institutional designs. The relationship between normative and institutional issues is not a one way street however. Not only do normative ideals help shape appropriate institutional designs, but the differences in performance manifested by various arrangements in the world of politics, law, and institutions as we know it in turn help to specify the determinate content of, and thereby support the cogency of, the normative ideals – that is, the ideals of deliberative democratic constitutionalism. In the worlds of politics and law, good ideals and institutions are not drawn from some conceptual heaven, but are the determinate results of historical learning processes and reflections on such.[5]

B.   PATHOLOGIES OF *AD HOC* TRIANGULATION

Part of the motivation for reopening the old chestnuts is a certain dissatisfaction with the normative conceptions of democracy and constitutionalism that underlie much of the most interesting recent work in American constitutional jurisprudence. Many of the impressive insights in this scholarship – concerning, for instance, the historical transformations in American judicial doctrines of constitutional construction, what current doctrinal innovations could plausibly carry forward worthy political ideals while fitting together with existing doctrinal touchstones, what kinds of structural and institutional innovations could improve democracy in the United States, what interpretive methodologies judges should adopt, the proper role of the Supreme Court in relation to other branches and subnational regional governments, and so on – are simultaneously accompanied by political philosophical conceptions that distort democracy or contort constitutionalism. The speculative thesis I explore here briefly is that these distortions and contortions are, in an important sense, determined by the argumentative context faced by American legal academics. The idea is that such scholarship must triangulate between three types of argumentative constraints: the normative ideals of constitutional democracy, the facts of how constitutional review is institutionalized in the United States, and the relations between firmament and favorite Supreme Court precedents. Because some of these constraints are more constraining than others – in particular, as the ideals of democratic

---

[5] Said differently, the best one could hope for methodologically is a merely analytic separation between the justification of a normative political scheme and the institutional designs intended to put that scheme into practice, as the two are dialectically interconnected. For, in actual fact, our considerations of what general normative schema is most justifiable is formed against a background sense of what kinds of institutional realizations have and have not been successful over time and in various contexts. Reciprocally, institutional innovations can change our sense of what the real meaning and import of the various general principles and values are that are normatively schematized.

constitutionalism are most open to contestation – the variable elements end up getting instrumentalized to the more fixed constraints. To make this speculation clear, I first explain briefly what the three types of constraints are, before turning to some selective examples of the argumentative pathologies that arise from them.

1. Three Argumentative Constraints

The first constraint involves the need to refer favorably to the ideals of democracy, constitutionalism, and constitutional democracy, and to refer to them as preeminent or superordinate political ideals. In modern Western societies these are powerful ideals, and in the United States they play a particularly salient role in citizens' sense of their collective identity, as the collective members of a particular nation-state. In United States legal contexts – not only in the legal academy but also in political and judicial arenas – they have an especially pronounced salience. To put it another way, it would be seriously beyond the pale for a legal elite – whether a judge, a politician, or a law professor – to put forward a substantive claim or theory that outright rejects democracy, constitutionalism, or constitutional democracy as ideals government ought to live up to. Changes in the intellectual milieu also have intensified attention to the ideals of democracy, in part because of the demise of a felt consensus on substantive principles of justice tied to the tradition of natural law, and in part because of the rise of attacks on the American judiciary – as an antidemocratic imperium – in the wake of tumultuous social changes and legal adaptations to them after the end of World War II. However, because these abstract political ideals can be considered essentially contested concepts, they provide a great deal of maneuvering room in jurisprudential argumentation.

The next constraint – what might be called institutional panglossianism – is, by contrast, much more fixed. The idea here is that the established institutions and practices of the United States political system are to be accepted as, in the main, unchangeable social facts, and that any comprehensive constitutional jurisprudence should be able to justify their main structures and features as being close to "the best, in this the best of all possible worlds." In the context of constitutional law, this tendency is particularly pronounced with respect to the peculiar American system for the institutionalization of constitutional review. A theory of constitutional jurisprudence that seriously doubted the basic legitimacy, for instance, of the role of the Supreme Court of the United States in interpreting the constitution or in producing a body of controlling constitutional doctrine through the development of case law, would be a theory destined to have little impact where it matters for the legal academy: both among other academics and among judges engaged in that precedential development.

Surely theories are allowed to raises questions around the edges – perhaps concerning different ways of amending the constitution or ways of changing ordinary political structures or jurisprudential strategies in order to alter the balance of power between courts and other political organs – but the basic legitimacy of the Court and a great deal of its actual work product must be accepted as facts of American political life, and as unavoidable facts for constitutional jurisprudence.[6] To be relevant and influential, a theory must accept these facts; to be comprehensive it must further offer some way of justifying it from the point of view of the theory's preferred normative conceptions. Michael Perry nicely encapsulates the fact-value amalgam of institutional panglossianism, putting the point explicitly as a question of patriotism:

Judicial review has been a bedrock feature of our constitutional order almost since the beginning of our country's history. Nor is it a live question, for us [the people of the United States now living], whether judicial review is, all things considered, a good idea. It would be startling, to say the least, were we Americans to turn skeptical about the idea of judicial review – an American-born and -bred idea that, in the twentieth century, has been increasingly influential throughout the world. For us, the live questions about judicial review are about how the power of judicial review should be exercised.[7]

---

[6] One might object here by pointing to a number of recent works in jurisprudence that facially challenge the legitimacy of judicial review as currently practiced in the United States – two of the most prominent are Larry D. Kramer, *The People Themselves: Popular Constitutionalism and Judicial Review* (New York: Oxford University Press, 2004), and Mark Tushnet, *Taking the Constitution away from the Courts* (Princeton, NJ: Princeton University Press, 1999). I am not claiming that such positions are literally an intellectual impossibility, or that they have not actually been defended. The claim is rather that, to the extent that a constitutional jurisprudence seriously questions current American institutions and practices of judicial review, it risks becoming irrelevant and uninfluential. Clearly this is a predominately sociological claim that I cannot empirically support here. Indirect evidence is found in the rhetoric of the opening lines of a review of Kramer's book in a preeminent legal journal: "Larry Kramer has written an awesome book, and we mean 'awesome' in its original and now archaic sense. *The People Themselves* is a book with the capacity to inspire dread and make the blood run cold. Kramer takes the theory *du jour*, popular constitutionalism (or popular sovereignty), and pushes its central normative commitments to their limits. *The People Themselves* is a book that says 'boo' to the ultimate constitutional authority of the courts and 'hooray' to a populist tradition that empowers Presidents to act as 'Tribunes of the People' and has even included constitutional interpretation by mob," Larry Alexander and Lawrence B. Solum, "Popular? Constitutionalism? A Book Review of *the People Themselves* by Larry D. Kramer," *Harvard Law Review* 118, no. 5 (2005): 1594.

[7] Michael J. Perry, "What Is 'the Constitution'? (and Other Fundamental Questions)," in *Constitutionalism: Philosophical Foundations*, ed. Larry Alexander (New York: Cambridge University Press, 1998), 120.

The basic institutional arrangement of constitutional review is, then, not something up for grabs here, no matter what one's preferred conceptions of political ideals are. After all, everyone is copying our arrangements, so they must be the best possible.[8] The main issue is, rather, to develop a theory of constitutional interpretation that will serve those ideals within the given institutional order.

This brings me finally to the third constraint: the sorting of Supreme Court cases into firmaments and favorites. Given that theories of constitutional jurisprudence are oriented mainly toward explicating and justifying a particular mode of constitutional interpretation, each theory will have to work from and incorporate two lists of cases. On the one hand, there is the widely accepted list of firmament cases: those decisions that are acknowledged in the legal community as unimpeachably correct or erroneous. *Marbury*, *McCulloch*, and *Brown* are all firmament cases correctly decided; *Dred Scott*, *Plessy*, and *Lochner* are all firmament examples of cases wrongly decided.[9] Firmament cases are ones that a jurisprudential theory must be able to explain and justify as rightly or wrongly decided. A theory goes beyond the pale when it entails the endorsement of an erroneous firmament or the rejection of correct firmament. The list of favorite cases, on the other hand – comprising positive and negative judgments on the outcomes of select nonfirmament cases – is specific to the particular theory and constitutes the central core around which the originality of the account of constitutional interpretation is built. The idea here is to illuminate in a new way areas of settled constitutional precedent in a manner that can normatively guide judicial

---

[8] The claim that everyone is copying United States judicial review is empirically false at relevant levels of specificity: most constitutional democracies that have some form of judicial review have not arranged it on the model of the United States, many constitutional democracies have systems of constitutional review that include nonjudicial branches in the process, and many constitutional democracies have no formally structured procedures for judicial review. Investigating some of this diversity becomes essential in Chapters 8 and 9 when I turn to the questions of institutional design. Before then, it is worth keeping in mind Railton's observation: "There is an intolerable degree of parochialism in explanations of the survival and growth of liberal democracy in the United States that place great credit in the Constitution, the Supreme Court, the two-party system, or 'the genius of American politics,' while ignoring that other nations have made similar progress though lacking these features," Peter Railton, "Judicial Review, Elites, and Liberal Democracy," in *Liberal Democracy*, ed. J. Roland Pennock and John W. Chapman, *Nomos XXV* (New York: New York University Press, 1983), 167.

[9] *Brown v. Board of Education*, 347 U.S. 483 (1954), *Dred Scott v. Sandford*, 60 U.S. 393 (1857), *Lochner v. New York*, 198 U.S. 45 (1905), *Marbury v. Madison*, 5 U.S. 137 (1803), *McCulloch v. Maryland*, 17 U.S. 316 (1819), *Plessy v. Ferguson*, 163 U.S. 537 (1895). Obviously the list of firmament cases changes over longer stretches of time: *Plessy* was a firmament correct case before being overruled by *Brown*; moving *Lochner* onto the correct list has very recently become a possibility, at least among some legal academics if not the courts.

decisions in the future.[10] These two lists of cases then are the building blocks around which different judicial methodologies are built and justified: originalism, textualism, structuralism, minimalism, neutralism, pragmatism, proceduralism, interpretivism, rationalism, and so on.

Although the articulation and justification of an interpretive methodology against rival versions is possibly the central task of American constitutional jurisprudence, I will not be frontally addressing those debates here, either in this chapter or throughout the book. My interest is squarely focused on the questions of the relationship between normative conceptions of constitutional democracy and the institutional design of constitutional review. From this latter point of view, it is important to note that much of the debate about interpretive methods has centered on how best to relieve the tensions felt between democracy and the United States institutions and practices of judicial review. The strategy then is to square actual judicial practices with the ideals of democracy and constitutionalism. The main reason I do not treat these interpretive debates is that, inferentially, they put the cart before the horse, as it were. If the concern is about the legitimacy of a judicial institutionalization of the function of constitutional review, then a preferred conception of how judges should interpret a constitution cannot supply reasons for or against the legitimacy of judicial review. If we do not assume that judicial review is a fact of life – if in fact the very question is whether we should accept or reject this particular institutional structure – then a claim that one judicial methodology is more democratic than another cannot answer to concerns about the democratic legitimacy of the institution in the first place. Perry's "live questions … about how the power of judicial review should be exercised" may be the central ones given the constraints of institutional panglossianism, but answers to those 'live questions' cannot be used to justify that panglossianism. Answering the democratic criticism of the institution of judicial review with a method for judicial interpretation simply begs the question at issue.

---

[10] Ely adds an important argumentative constraint on jurisprudence that I have not stressed here: the general academic requirement for an "original contribution to scholarship." "Law teachers are caught in something of a whipsaw here, in that academia generally rewards originality, whereas the law generally rewards lack of originality – that is, the existence of precedent. The tension thus created probably helps account for the common scholarly slalom in which the author's theory is said to be immanent in a series of decisions, though no prior academic commentator has even come close to apprehending it," John Hart Ely, "Another Such Victory: Constitutional Theory and Practice in a World Where Courts Are No Different from Legislatures," *Virginia Law Review* 77 (1991): footnote 55, 583.

2. Distorting Democracy

One *ad hoc* strategy for justifying American-style judicial review then – recommending a democratic mode of interpretation to the courts – begs the question at issue. Another *ad hoc* strategy is more promising, however: that of employing a persuasive redefinition of democracy. The idea here is to accept U.S. judicial review as it is, and exploit the more malleable argumentative constraints of the normative ideals of democracy and constitutionalism in order to show that, despite appearances, judicial review is not a "deviant institution in the American democracy" as Bickel claims. Here the inferential direction is more cogent: explicate and defend the most compelling account of the ideals of constitutional democracy, show how those ideals can be best realized in a particular set of political institutions and structures, and conclude that U.S. judicial review sufficiently approximates those justified institutions and structures.

There is then nothing inferentially wrong with this strategy – in fact it is the same basic strategy employed in this book. The proof, however, is in the pudding: namely, in the degrees to which the conception of constitutional democracy proffered is cogent and compelling, to which that conception convincingly supports proposed institutional designs, and to which United States institutions do or don't accord with the preferred institutions for constitutional review. If argumentative pathologies arise here, they are caused by the particular character of American institutions. For if we accept the argumentative constraint of institutional panglossianism, then the conclusion of the argument is predetermined, and the premises must be instrumentalized to that conclusion. If in fact one is skeptical, like Bickel and Hand, about the extent to which judicial review can actually be considered a democratic institution, then one should expect distortions in the ideals of democracy and constitutionalism that the theory uses to justify its particular institutionalization in a specific national political system. In this and the next section I want to sketch the underlying ideals of democracy and constitutionalism found in some American constitutional jurisprudence as a way of supporting my speculative thesis that argumentative pathologies arise from the particular argumentative constraints. It is important to stress that I will be largely ignoring much of what is most valuable and interesting in this work – the advice given to United States judges – in order to focus on the question of the legitimacy of judicial review. I should stress further that these are somewhat polemical sketches, intended mostly to motivate the move beyond the argumentative constraints of nation-state specific jurisprudence.

The most straightforward instrumentalization of democratic ideals to the justification of American judicial review is to be found where democracy is simply redefined as equivalent to the extant American judicial system. Consider, for example, one articulation of what it would mean to have a "democratic" form of constitutionalism:

Modern constitutionalism in the western democracies has generally involved the idea of a civil society organized and governed on the basis of a written body of "constitutional" law. A "democratic" constitution embodies a conception of the fundamental rights and obligations of citizens and establishes a judicial process by which rights claims may be litigated. The function of a judiciary is to interpret the constitution and to authorize the enforcement of its decisions. Pragmatically, it seeks to strike a "delicate balance" between the rights and freedoms of "the governed" and the exigencies of effective government.[11]

According to this formulation, the difference between constitutionalism as such and *democratic* constitutionalism is that only in the latter are individuals' fundamental rights guaranteed, and guaranteed by an independent judiciary. It is hard to see exactly what is specifically democratic about such a practice of constitutionalism, at least on a minimal understanding of democracy. For democracy seems to have something to do with the direction of governmental decisions by citizens, and perhaps could be capaciously defined as a form of government in which all citizens have some significantly equal opportunities to influence, in some way or another, the actions of government. Perhaps the formulation above would be better rewritten in lines with the classical understanding of liberal political arrangements: "a 'liberal' constitution embodies ... " Then of course judicial review would be justified as liberty protecting, but this does little to still democratic skepticism of the institution.

Chemerinsky provides a much more frank acknowledgment of the bald strategy of redefining democracy to accord with American judicial review:

To clarify analysis and arguments [in a "defense of judicial activism"], "democracy" should be redefined. Analytically, altering the definition is unnecessary.... However, democracy is an incredibly powerful term in this society.... In essence, there are two choices: abandon the term democracy as the major premise in analysis or redefine it to portray accurately the nature of government embodied in the Constitution [of the United States]. Because the former is improbable, the latter is essential. Altering the definition of democracy has important implications in determining a role for the Supreme Court and ascertaining the proper approach to judicial review.[12]

---

[11] Alan S. Rosenbaum, "Introduction," in *Constitutionalism: The Philosophical Dimension*, ed. Alan S. Rosenbaum (New York: Greenwood Press, 1988), 4.

[12] Erwin Chemerinsky, "The Supreme Court, 1988 Term – Foreword: The Vanishing Constitution," *Harvard Law Review* 103 (1989): 76.

Once democracy has been redefined to accord with the realities of one particular nation-state's constitution and its historically particular governmental institutions, then one can get past the pesky problem of institutional legitimacy and on to the real tasks of recommending to the Court preferred modes of constitutional interpretation.[13] Alleviate the democratic worry about judicial review rhetorically by simply calling what we happen to do around here full democracy, and move on to the "live questions."

The bald redefinition strategy then, although admirably frank, will do little to overcome the democratic objections to judicial review. A different approach might be termed the denigration strategy.[14] Here democracy is portrayed in such an unattractive light that, although one may admit that judicial review conflicts with democracy, it doesn't amount to such a worry since no one could really support democracy in the first place. I think we can espy this strategy, ironically, in one of the most virulent attackers of the work product of the Supreme Court of the United States as a form of antidemocratic despotism. Consider Bork's radically anticognitivist account of constitutional democracy. The key phrase throughout is "value choices" and the major issue of constitutional democracy is whose value choices are to be authoritative and in what areas of governmental decision. According to Bork, the American model of constitutional democracy "assumes that in wide areas of life majorities are entitled to rule for no better reason that they are majorities. We need not pause here to examine the philosophical underpinnings of that assumption since it is a 'given' in our society."[15] In other areas of life, however, "value choices are attributed to the Founding Fathers"[16] and these are the particular areas of control placed beyond the value choices of present majorities. Judicial review, then, should be as far as possible exercised to implement the actual value choices made by the founding fathers. Any judge that goes

---

[13] To be sure, Chemerinsky's overall strategy is somewhat more complex than portrayed here. He proposes, on the one hand, to attend only to the countermajoritarian objection to judicial review and, on the other, to "extract" the major normative ideals of the American system from the Constitution and claim that democracy is not central to that system. The idea is then that the U.S. Constitution is the definition of normative and institutional rightness and, although it is rightly undemocratic, jurisprudes should throw a rhetorical bone to those who want it to be.

[14] Waldron has consistently attacked this denigration strategy, in particular by considering the asymmetries in jurisprudential attitudes towards the comparative competence and work product of legislatures and judiciaries, celebratory in the one case and fully skeptical in the other. Jeremy Waldron, *Law and Disagreement* (New York: Oxford University Press, 1999). I consider in more detail Waldron's arguments against judicial review in Chapters 4 and 5.

[15] Robert H. Bork, "Neutral Principles and Some First Amendment Problems," *Indiana Law Journal* 47 (1971): 2–3.

[16] Ibid.: 4.

beyond those value choices is imposing her own value choices on the majority, and is thereby illegitimately exercising power. To the objection that a judge – or for that matter any other person – might be able to give a convincing reason or justification for her value choices, Bork's repeated response is clear: there are only facts about actual decisions by persons, and none of these decisions have any cognitive content:

> There is no principled way to decide that one man's gratifications are more deserving of respect than another's or that one form of gratification is more worthy than another.... Equality of human gratifications, where the document does not impose a hierarchy is an essential part of constitutional doctrine.... Courts must accept any value choice the legislature makes unless it clearly runs contrary to a choice made in the framing of the Constitution.[17]

I do not intend here to enter into meta-ethical considerations about emotivism, subjectivism, decisionism or other radically skeptical forms of noncognitivism, some combination of which are clearly playing the leading roles in Bork's arguments. For those so skeptically inclined, this book is not for you. I do however want to point out the denigration strategy involved here. If democracy is nothing more than the satisfaction of the unvarnished subjective desires for gratifications of contingent present majorities, and other past supermajorities have made value choices (according to their own subjective gratification preferences) to put certain gratifications out of the reach of future gratification-seeking majorities, then a system of judicial review is unobjectionable from the point of view of democracy because ... well, democracy is basically worthless.[18] Why exactly anyone would want to live under either a democratic system of unreasoned majoritarian decisionism or a constitutional system of unreasoned supermajoritarian decisionism goes wholly unexplained, as does any thought about how or why the exercise of governmental coercion in the light of those facts of "value choice" could be seen as legitimate by citizens and subjects. Nevertheless, on this wholly desiccated and hollow "conception" of constitutional democracy, there can be no democratic objection to judicial review (properly performed of

---

[17] Ibid.: 10–11.
[18] Although I said I would avoid meta-ethical considerations, one should stop to wonder exactly what moral or general normative grounds Bork could invoke to support his central jurisprudential claim in the article: namely, that judges *should* adopt a *principled* manner of decision making with respect to the constitution. As Apel would put it, this simultaneous denial of the justifiability of any normative recommendations and assertion of particular normative recommendations commits the fallacy of a "performative self-contradiction," Karl-Otto Apel, "The a Priori of the Communication Community and the Foundations of Ethics," in *Towards a Transformation of Philosophy* (London: Routledge & Kegan Paul, 1980).

course), since objections involve reasons and in the realm of value choices there simply are no convincing reasons of any sort.

A much more typical denigration strategy does not start with extreme normative skepticism but, rather, attempts to explain the worth and attractiveness of constitutional and democratic ideals by showing how they are carried out in practice and embodied in actual American political institutions. Because the central argumentative move is to demonstrate the gap between political ideals and their actual realization, it is perhaps better to call it a deflationary strategy. In particular here, a robust conception of democracy is counterposed to the actual workings of representative institutions in the United States and, in the light of their failure to live up to the ideals of democracy, judicial review is justified as better fulfilling those ideals. The variations here are numerous, and I will be investigating many of them throughout Chapters 4 through 7.

One good place to start is Ronald Dworkin's conception of democracy as that system of government that gets the right answers according to substantive criteria of equality amongst a nation's members. His conception of democracy:

> *denies* that it is a defining goal of democracy that collective decisions always or normally be those that a majority or plurality of citizens would favor if fully informed and rational. . . . Democracy means government subject to conditions – we might call these the "democratic" conditions – of equal status for all citizens. When majoritarian institutions provide and respect the democratic conditions, then the verdicts of these institutions should be accepted by everyone *for that reason*. But when they do not, or when their provision or respect is defective, there can be no objection, in the name of democracy, to procedures that protect and respect them better.[19]

Because I will deal with Dworkin's arguments at greater length in Chapter 4, I wish only to note here how the deflationary strategy will work given this robust conception of democracy. In short, actual electorally accountable political institutions, such as legislatures and executives, will be shown to be deficient in the extent to which they support the democratic conditions of equal status. So the institutional design question becomes: what institutions would best ensure these equality conditions? By definition, any institution – no matter how its decision-making processes are structured and no matter how or in what ways it is or is not responsive to the demos – that best secures equal status will count as democratic. For Dworkin the special qualities of the judiciary for reasoning according to principle will then provide a way of reconciling

---

[19] Ronald Dworkin, *Freedom's Law: The Moral Reading of the American Constitution* (Cambridge, MA: Harvard University Press, 1996), 17, emphases added.

judicial review with democracy. For there could be no democratic objection even to rule by actual Platonic guardians, if in fact those guardians better secured the substantive conditions of democracy than could those institutions more traditionally associated with democratic politics. Because democracy requires getting the right answers on fundamental questions, any political institutions that do so are by (re)definition democratic.

A somewhat different deflationary strategy focuses not upon judges' superior capacity for moral reasoning per se, but rather on the special suitability of the language of judicial opinions for exemplifying democratic conversations about the basic structures of society. Chapter 6 looks at three different variations on this theme. One variation put forward by Rawls starts with an account of the ideals of democracy in terms of the need for citizens to find a specifically political language that is not partial to any of the competing ethical worldviews that different citizens find compelling and motivating.[20] Democratic citizens should then adhere only to the limits of this political language when deliberating about and deciding upon the fundamental terms of their political consociation.

In a democratic society public reason is the reason of equal citizens who, as a collective body, exercise final political and coercive power over one another in enacting laws and in amending their constitution. . . . The limits imposed by public reason do not apply to all political questions but only those involving what we may call "constitutional essentials" and questions of basic justice.[21]

---

[20] One might object here that Rawls is a poor example to use in support of my general thesis about the argumentative constraints faced by United States jurisprudes – after all, he is a political philosopher. Three brief comments are in order. First, as I explain in Chapter 6, Rawls does not take himself to be engaged in institutional design, and his comments about the United States Supreme Court are intended to be illustrative of philosophical points, not a justification for the claim that judicial review is an indispensable institution. Second, however, Rawls's theory of democracy, such as it is, is almost entirely carried by his discussion of public reason, and he consistently thinks of public reason as the reason of judges. This suggests that he takes democracy as an ideal that must be incorporated into his theory, and that he has a way of making that incorporation fully consistent with the actual institutions of the American political system as given, including judicial review. (It is notable here that Rawls's discussion of judicial review quickly moves from abstract considerations concerning "a constitutional regime with judicial review" to a more parochial set of "remarks on the Supreme Court" John Rawls, *Political Liberalism*, paperback ed. [New York: Columbia University Press, 1996], 231 and 40.) Finally, Rawls's justificatory methodology of reflective equilibrium stresses the need for normative principles to be in line with our settled convictions, and our settled convictions will include settled ideas about the worth of specific political institutions (this latter point is made explicit in the response to Habermas: Rawls, *Political Liberalism*, 381). As citizens of the United States, then, it would appear that the normative principles of the theory of political liberalism are methodologically required to come into line with at least the major features of our parochial political institutions.

[21] Rawls, *Political Liberalism*, 214.

The account of "public reason" as the special language of democratic consociation – a language denuded of references to particular
comprehensive doctrines and relying only on the special argot of the
overlapping consensus – combined with the claim that the Supreme
Court is the only institution that always properly speaks in the
democratic argot then obviates objections to judicial review from
democracy. "In a constitutional regime with judicial review, public
reason is the reason of its supreme court.... The supreme court is the
branch of government that serves as the exemplar of public reason....
It is the only branch of government that is visibly on its face the
creature of that reason and that reason alone."[22] This deflationary
strategy involves showing how the other branches of national government – the electorally accountable branches – do not properly limit
themselves to the democratic argot and so are not really democratic,
despite appearances. In a few short pages we are taken then from the
idealization of democracy as a special kind of mutual consociation
amongst citizens, to the claim that, institutionally realized, democracy
is a conversation carried out by linguistic experts – especially judges
and lawyers addressing them – and located in that political institution
most insulated from the input of citizens.

Are the representative branches of government really representative
of the people? Answering this question in the negative has furnished the
starting point for innumerable attempts to counter Bickel's countermajoritarian objections to judicial review. After all, if it were to turn out
that the Court were more representative of the people themselves than
the legislative and executive branches, the countermajoritarian objection
fails. One of the most fully developed and fascinating uses of this
strategy is Ackerman's in-depth normative and historical account of the
development of American constitutional law over two hundred years.[23]
Without doing full justice to this account, I think it is not wrong to boil
down its answer to the democratic objection. First, real and authentic
democratic politics is defined as those moments when the American
people constitute themselves as a people – as a group of fellow citizens
in a strong sense, "mobilized and capable of sober deliberation"[24] – and
take on the fundamental tasks of constitution writing, constitution
changing, and constitution elaborating. Understanding such higher
forms of lawmaking as the paradigm of democracy, Ackerman's two-
track model distinguishes it from ordinary lawmaking: those political

[22] Ibid., 231 and 35.
[23] Bruce Ackerman, *We the People: Foundations* (Cambridge, MA: Harvard University Press,
1991), Bruce Ackerman, *We the People: Transformations* (Cambridge, MA: Harvard
University Press, 1998).
[24] Ackerman, *We the People: Foundations*, 194.

process carried out by the legislative and executive branches that are supposed to be constrained by the constitutional structures elaborated by the people.

The deflationary aspect then kicks in by painting ordinary lawmaking by the government as, in general, a gradual erosion over time of the achievements by the people themselves in their higher lawmaking mode. Although Ackerman acknowledges that elected officials can sometimes act out of principled concerns for constitutional values and the public good, most of the time "elected politicians find it expedient to exploit the apathy, ignorance, and selfishness of normal politics in ways that endanger fundamental traditions."[25] Unfortunately, between those rare moments in a nation's history when the people take up the powers of constitutional lawmaking into their own hands, there is actually no people at all, no collective group of citizens deliberating together about their fundamental law, only a diverse collection of self-interested individuals attending to their private business. It seems we need, therefore, an institution specifically designed to maintain the people's intermittent constitutional achievements against self-serving and exploitative governmental officials: "How to preserve the considered judgments of the mobilized People from illegitimate erosion by the statutory decisions of normal government?"[26] Judicial review to the rescue. Since democracy is idealized as popular self-government through constitutional lawmaking, but this only occurs in rare times of crisis – in American history, only once every sixty or one hundred years or so – the Court represents the absent/ slumbering people under everyday conditions of ordinary lawmaking. "If the Court is right in finding that these politician/statesmen have moved beyond their mandate, it is furthering Democracy, not frustrating it, in revealing our representatives as mere 'stand-ins' for the People, whose word is not to be confused with the collective judgment of *the People themselves*."[27] So judicial review is not antidemocratic: during the interregnums of mass mobilization and popular constitutional deliberation, democracy is actually carried out by unelected judges and against the merely apparent democratic will of contemporary citizens and elected officials. Unless one happens to have the good fortune of living during those rare and propitious moments of higher lawmaking, democracy means submitting to the rule of judicial guardians. Having satisfied the first two argumentative constraints by giving a democratic justification for institutional panglossianism, the final remarkable move is the claim that even the higher lawmaking of people can be carried mainly through doctrinal changes by the Supreme Court. Taking the demise of *Lochner* era doctrine as paradigmatic, Ackerman's theory of dualist democracy

---

[25] Ibid., 307.   [26] Ibid., 7.   [27] Ibid., 262.

also fulfills the third argumentative constraint by explaining and justifying both firmament and favorite Court cases.

This short tour – which could surely be extended – through some jurisprudential justifications for judicial review in the United States was intended to lend support to my speculative hypothesis that the three argumentative constraints do not function symmetrically. Because institutional panglossianism and the differences between firmament and favorite Supreme Court precedents are relatively peremptory for legal scholarship, the normative ideals of constitutional democracy are functionalized to those two argumentative constraints. Having shown some of the distortions induced in the conceptions of democracy by instrumentalizing those to a fixed parochial context, I turn now to contortions in the conceptions of constitutionalism.

3. Contorting Constitutionalism

If there has been a fair amount of reflectivity about the meaning and import of ideals of democracy, even as conceptions of democracy are tailored to saving institutional panglossianism, the same cannot be said about the concept of "constitutionalism." For with respect to the latter, much jurisprudence simply assumes an equivalence between constitutionalism and judicial review as carried out in the United States system. But this unthinking equivalence, I will argue, creates two significantly contorting preemptory foreshortenings of the concept. On the one hand, it entails the denial that many national political systems are what they in fact appear to be: namely, functioning constitutional democracies. On the other, by reducing the practice of constitutionalism to that which is strictly speaking justiciable, it conceptually erases much of the actual text and, more importantly, the actual institutional structures and practices of constitutional government.

Let me first present some evidence that the synecdochical reduction of constitutionalism to the actual structure of judicial review as carried out by the Supreme Court of the United States is widespread. I start with judges' own statements, beginning with Chief Justice Warren's insistence on the Court's supremacy with respect to determining the meaning and import of the Constitution for all other governmental actors from 1958:

Marbury v. Madison ... declared the basic principle that the federal judiciary is supreme in the exposition of the law of the Constitution, and that principle has ever since been respected by this Court and the Country as a permanent and indispensable feature of our constitutional system. It follows that the interpretation of the Fourteenth Amendment enunciated by this Court in the *Brown* case is the supreme law of the land.... Every state legislator and executive and judicial officer is solemnly committed by oath taken pursuant to Article VI, clause 3, 'to support this Constitution.' ... No state legislator or executive or judicial officer can war against the Constitution without violating his undertaking to support it.[28]

This claim, strong as it is, does yet not equate American constitutionalism *tout court* with the practice and work product of the Supreme Court. Rather, it insists that, where the Court has spoken, its interpretation of the Constitution is supreme and controlling for all governmental officials. But similar sounding dicta from Justices O'Connor, Kennedy, and Souter in 1992 comes quite a bit closer to equating the Court's work product with constitutionalism *simpliciter*:

Like the character of an individual, the legitimacy of the Court must be earned over time. So, indeed, must be the character of a Nation of people who aspire to live according to the rule of law. Their belief in themselves as such a people is not readily separable from their understanding of the Court invested with the authority to decide their constitutional cases and speak before all others for their constitutional ideals. If the Court's legitimacy should be undermined, then, so would the country be in its very ability to see itself through its constitutional ideals. The Court's concern with legitimacy is not for the sake of the Court, but for the sake of the Nation to which it is responsible.[29]

Note the claim with respect to constitutionalism: United States citizens could not understand themselves as citizens under a constitutional system of government unless the Supreme Court is the only institutional representative of constitutional ideals. Finally, in a 2003 radio broadcast of a interview about her semiautobiographical book, Justice O'Connor makes explicit the reduction of constitutionalism in general to the practices of the Supreme Court in exercising judicial review.

[Interviewer]: Some of the Court's decisions in divisive cases remain controversial, ... and yet, public confidence in the Supreme Court remains strong. Why is that?
[O'Connor]: That's hard to say. You know, we've had a lot of years of experience now. Our Constitution has been in effect longer than any other constitution around the world, and I think the American people have grown to accept the role of the Court in deciding Constitutional issues and have tended to accept the notion of constitutionalism, if you will, and that we have a Court that has assumed this role, and a notion that its going to be accepted. Its so remarkable how the other branches of government have accepted the role of the Court as well.[30]

---

[28] *Cooper v. Aaron*, 358 U.S. 1, 18 (1958).
[29] *Planned Parenthood v. Casey*, 505 U.S. 833, 868 (1992).
[30] Sandra Day O'Connor and Pete Williams, "The Majesty of the Law: An Interview with Justice Sandra Day O'Connor," in *University of Louisville Kentucky Author Forum* (Louisville, KY: WFPL, 2003).

Of course, judges have a particular interest in identifying their own role and work product with constitutionalism: constitutionalism is a powerful idea in the United States, and such a self-identification at least avoids a facial confrontation with antidemocratic objections to judicial review. But the reduction of constitutionalism to parochial judicial practices is not restricted to judges. Theorists of various stripes also make similar moves. Rawls claims, for instance, that "the constitution is not what the Court says it is. Rather, it is what the people acting constitutionally through the other branches eventually allow the Court to say it is."[31]

A small step can be made away from such provincialism by identifying constitutionalism generally with the institutions and practices of judicial review – but it is a small step. We have already seen one attempt that defines constitutionalism (albeit "democratic" constitutionalism) as simply the judicial enforcement of individual liberty rights.[32] Dworkin makes the claim explicit: "By 'constitutionalism' I mean a system that establishes individual legal rights that the dominant legislature does not have the power to override or compromise."[33] He then proceeds to argue that, since we are talking about legal rights, we ought to "assign adjudicative responsibility [for constitutional interpretation of those rights] to judges, whose decision is final, barring a constitutional amendment, until it is changed by a later judicial decision."[34] In short, no judicial review, no constitutionalism. An excellent political science textbook collecting diverse theoretical and empirical writings on democracy similarly reduces issues of constitutionalism in general to specific debates surrounding practices of strong judicial review of legislative actions in the name of individual rights.[35] More examples could surely be given of this tendency aptly summed up (and decried) by Bellamy: "Rights, upheld by judicial review, are said to compromise the prime component of constitutionalism, providing a normative legal framework within which politics operates.... Constitutionalism has come to mean nothing more than a system of legally entrenched rights that can override, where necessary, the ordinary political process."[36]

---

[31] Rawls, *Political Liberalism*, 237–38.

[32] See text supra accompanying footnote 11.

[33] Ronald Dworkin, "Constitutionalism and Democracy," *European Journal of Philosophy* 3, no. 1 (1995): 2.

[34] Ibid.: 10.

[35] Robert A. Dahl, Ian Shapiro, and José Antonio Cheibub, eds., *The Democracy Sourcebook* (Cambridge, MA: The MIT Press, 2003). After a series of selections from *The Federalist Papers* mostly centered on the judiciary and judicial review, five of the six remaining selections in the "Democracy and Constitutionalism" chapter of the textbook are entirely focused on judicial review.

[36] Richard Bellamy, "The Political Form of the Constitution: The Separation of Powers, Rights and Representative Government," *Political Studies* XLIV (1996): 436.

What then is pathological about such reductions of constitutionalism to American-style practices of securing individual rights through an independent judiciary? To begin with, such a view conceptually entails rejecting any number of contemporary political systems as constitutional systems. Clearly the United Kingdom and several commonwealth countries are, on this understanding, simply not constitutional systems because they have no written constitutions to be interpreted by judges. But there would also be no "constitutionalism" in nation-states that do in fact have written constitutions, but no U.S.-style judicial review: for instance, Belgium, Finland, France, Israel, Luxembourg, the Netherlands, and Switzerland. Borderline cases would then be presented by political systems that have forms of judicial review which, unlike the diffuse system in the United States, are concentrated in special constitutional courts: for instance, many of the other European democracies, including most of the new Eastern European democracies. Perhaps judicial review of legislation is enough to warrant the label "constitutional"; perhaps not, if individuals cannot directly access that constitutional court for decisions in their own concrete cases and controversies, and so vindicate their individual legal rights in every situation.[37] Perhaps other borderline cases include countries that have judicial review but where it is nevertheless subject to various forms of authoritative constraint by the political branches, such as in Canada. The point, however, is that we shouldn't need to engage in such contortions to "save" the phenomena of all of these various political systems that look, for all intents and purposes, like *constitutional* democracies. Our conceptual resources shouldn't be so constrained by institutional panglossianism in the first place: countries without United States–style judicial review are not for that very reason un- or non-constitutional.

The second major reason we should reject this contorted notion of constitutionalism is that it equates constitutionalism with only that class of public issues that are *justiciable*. Because this view focuses almost exclusively on the actions of courts, all other aspects of actual constitutional texts, constitutional structures, or constitutional practices become mere residues, relegated to a different domain of concern. Even from a purely provincial perspective, however, this is inadequate. For the basic political structures and powers, which the Constitution of the United States is largely dedicated to establishing, would simply disappear from view. Article I, for instance, looks like constitutional law – "All legislative Powers herein granted shall be vested in a Congress of the United States, which shall consists of a Senate and House of Representatives ... " – but very little of that long Article is justiciable. Does this mean that, in fact, it is not

---

[37] I take up at length the differences between concentrated and diffuse systems of constitutional review, and between abstract and concrete review modalities in Chapter 8.

part of what we want to consider under the rubric of constitutionalism? One of the great documents of American constitutional theory, *The Federalist Papers*, dedicates only six of its eighty-five papers to the judicial branch – is the rest really about something else than constitutionalism? Koopmans captures the problem nicely:

> In the United States, the concept of 'constitutional law' is used in a narrower sense than in Great Britain: it covers only the areas of law concerning the constitution which have given rise to judicial decisions. The relationship between the President and Congress has not been the subject of any important body of case law, and the result is that it is chiefly examined in American books on "government" or "political science" rather than in those on constitutional law. I see no reason to adopt such a limited view of constitutional problems in this book.[38]

The fact that much of the constitutional provisions that establish, structure, and specify the various organs of government, their duties, and their interrelations are nonjusticiable provisions, furthermore, does not thereby invalidate their force, cogency, or effectiveness as binding *constitutional law*. Perhaps most important, we should not adopt a concept of constitutionalism that *a priori* blinds analysis to the tremendous amount and import of extrajudicial constitutional politics. Constitutional conflicts and resultant constitutional politics erupt not only over provisions ensuring to citizens their judicially enforceable individual liberty rights, but also over the fundamental procedures and structures of government themselves. An adequate theory of constitutional democracy should not take such issues off the table by a conceptual legerdemain. An exclusivistic focus on constitutionalism as judicially enforceable law then threatens to simply erase much of what constitutionalism – as a political ideal and a distinct set of political practices – is about.

C. FUNCTIONS AND INSTITUTIONS

We need then a fresh start, one that can avoid the argumentative pathologies of *ad hoc* provincialism, in particular one that is not subject to the constraint of institutional panglossianism. Let me be clear. I am not recommending that we start from a view from nowhere, from a pure normative perspective wholly disconnected from the realities of politics and its institutional structures as we have historically and currently known them. Although I cannot argue for the methodological claim here, my starting assumption is that normative political ideals and actual political arrangements are separable, at most, only analytically. In the domain of

---

[38] Tim Koopmans, *Courts and Political Institutions: A Comparative View* (Cambridge: Cambridge University Press, 2003), 3.

political theory, the ideal and the real, norm and fact, are dialectically intertwined, each shaping and delimiting the other. Just as our actual institutional structures have developed over time in response to and (hopefully) in accord with our preferred normative ideals of democracy, constitutionalism, and constitutional democracy, those ideals themselves are shaped by and adapted to the actual practices and structures of political institutions we have experience with or reasonably believe achievable in practice. The conception of deliberative democratic constitutionalism I defend in this book then is a normative theory – it articulates and defends certain specific conceptions of our political ideals that are used to evaluate the worth of particular political arrangements – but it is not an ideal theory – developed and justified independently of historical and empirical considerations and, in a second step, applied to the fallen world of only partially compliant institutional realities. It is, rather, a conception developed to evaluate institutional possibilities and proposals, one simultaneously developed out of and responding to the world of political institutions as we know them.

This methodological point about the reciprocity between normative ideals and institutional possibilities at the general level, however, should not obscure the basic inferential priority of normative ideals over extant institutional considerations. We cannot evaluate the worth of institutional structures and results except in the light of justified normative ideals. By contrast, accepting extant institutions as the measure of normative ideals will only lead to pathologies of ad hocery like those just canvassed, fundamentally distorting those ideals beyond usefulness and recognition, leaving them mere rhetorical honorifics.

1.   Judicial Review as One of Many Supreme Judicial Functions

Like other exercises in normative theory, this book will assume certain simplifications of the workings of actual constitutional democracies in order to focus on underlying ideals of constitutional democracy and their competing conceptualizations. One of the most important of these simplifications is to focus the arguments around the question of only one of the functions captured in the phrase "judicial review." In the U.S. judicial system, for example, the Supreme Court has many different roles and carries out many different functions. At least five can be analytically distinguished. Most of these functions, of course, are carried out not only by the Supreme Court but also by other national and subnational regional courts: for each of the functions, the Supreme Court has final but not exclusive jurisdiction.

First, as the supreme appellate court for the nation, the Court has the role of ensuring the internal coherence of individual case decisions and related doctrinal developments across the different normal and appellate federal courts below it in the hierarchy. To the extent possible and reasonable, the Court should attempt to make decisions in specific cases and controversies throughout the nation consistent, applying the same criteria for decisions where those criteria are based in coherent doctrinal rules and principles. Second, the Court has a significant role in ensuring the internal coherence of a system of ordinary national laws: different national statutes, regulations, common law rules, and so on should not conflict with one another and, when they do, the Court has final responsibility for resolving conflicts with a view to the coherence of national law. Third, the Court has the power to review the actions of officials of the national government to ensure that they are consistent with the corpus of controlling ordinary law. Thus, the Court has final jurisdiction over determinations of, for instance, whether relevant officials have faithfully carried out their duties as spelled out in statutes or administrative regulations or whether they have abused the discretion or misused the specific powers delegated to them by ordinary law. Fourth, the Court has the final responsibility for ensuring that subnational regional laws and the actions of subnational regional officials are in line with the demands of the national Constitution. While individual states, for instance, have their own constitutions, systems of ordinary law, and judicial systems, the laws and actions of states must suitably conform to the demands of national constitutional law. Often in practice this means that the Court is involved in settling jurisdictional disputes between national and state governments. Much the same goes for other subnational political authorities, even as special problems of federalism are raised most acutely with respect to the relations between the federal government and the individual states. Finally, fifth, the Supreme Court has the authority to review national ordinary law and the actions of national officials for their consistency with the Constitution of the United States and the doctrinal interpretations of its provisions as elaborated in controlling precedent. Here the Court has the power to "strike down" both statutes passed through the national legislative process and administrative regulations issued by various national agencies, as well as to review the actions of officials and governmental organs, when it finds that these ordinary laws and actions violate the higher law represented by the Constitution.

It is true that constitutional issues may well arise in the course of carrying out all five of these functions. Nevertheless, when I refer throughout this book to "judicial review," I am referring most centrally only to the fifth category of functions carried out by United States courts. For it is in carrying out this fifth function that the tensions between judicial review and democracy are felt to arise most acutely. Because democracy is strongly allied with the selection and control of governmental officials through periodic elections, and an independent judiciary is, by definition, not directly accountable through periodic elections, the judicial review of the work product of the electoral branches of government is thought to give rise to both the counter-majoritarian and paternalist objections. Of course, there is a great deal of disagreement about whether we should so strongly ally democracy with electoral accountability – as we will see in working through the various arguments in Chapters 2 through 7. But it will help to focus the discussion if we attend only to the function of national constitutional review when considering the objections to judicial review. In part, this should help ward off rhetorically undifferentiated fusillades about "government by judiciary" or the "despotism of black robes," for many of the targets of particular attacks on the judiciary are, in fact, straightforward legal consequences of the work product of electorally accountable branches of government: ordinary statutes, regulations, and official actions directed by them.[39] More important, however, focusing only on judicial review in this narrow sense will enable sustained attention to controversies over the ideals of constitutionalism and democracy underlying much of the debates about judicial review and, in particular, to the tensions thought to arise from the combination "constitutional democracy."

One other lamentable simplification should be mentioned: I assume throughout that the frame of reference is the delimited context of a single nation-state's political system.[40] Although some of the most fascinating and complex questions concerning judicial review and democracy are

---

[39] It is important to stress here how relatively rare judicial review, in the narrow sense used here, is in the United States. For the fifty-three-year period from 1803 to 1856, only two congressional statutes were declared unconstitutional by the Supreme Court: in the case that inaugurated judicial review in America (*Marbury*) and in solidifying the slave power by striking down the Missouri compromise (*Dred Scott*). This yields a judicial review rate of .0377 per year. In the thirty years after the Civil War, the nullification rate increased to around .67 per year (counting twenty nullifications over that period: Robert Lowry Clinton, "How the Court Became Supreme," *First Things* 89 [1998]). Over the thirty-five-year period (1953–1989) of the Warren and Berger courts – courts thought to be especially activist – the rate was around 4.63 nullifications of Congressional statutes per year (162 cases of judicial nullification out of 9,976 dispositions: Harold J. Spaeth, *United States Supreme Court Judicial Database, 1953–1997 Terms* [Computer File] (Michigan State University, Dept. of Political Science, 1998 [cited January 10 2005]); available from http://webapp.icpsr.umich.edu/cocoon/ICPSR-STUDY/09422.xml). In the thirteen years from 1990 through 2002, the rate was around 2.62 per year (thirty-four federal statutes were held unconstitutional: Lawrence Baum, *The Supreme Court*, eighth ed. [Washington, DC: CQ Press, 2004], 170). Discussion of other ways of measuring instances of judicial review, with figures including constitutional nullification of state laws and local ordinances, can be found at footnote 55 of Chapter 8. One method yields a measure of the yearly rate of all statutory nullifications as a percentage of the number of cases decided with full, signed opinions. The contemporary percentage here is just above 10 percent of Supreme Court cases per year.

[40] As is evident by my omission, in the previous list of five functions, of the United States Supreme Court's powers concerning international and transnational law and issues.

being raised at the transnational level – for instance with respect to the growing legal integration occurring across the nations of the European Union, and the increasing import and effectiveness of international judicial tribunals concerning criminal law, human rights, commercial law, and so on – I avoid consideration of such issues here. In part this is because an adequate consideration of these questions would already require a high degree of normative clarity about the proper conception of constitutional democracy. But this avoidance is also simply because the manifold of difficult issues raised would burst the bounds of manageability within a single book.

2. Function vs. Institution: Constitutional vs. Judicial Review

With this focus specified, the second major structural move of the argument is already apparent. I propose that we ought to understand and justify the function of *constitutional review* before we can adequately answer the design question of whether that function should be realized through the institutions of *judicial review*. To begin, this will go a long way toward avoiding the pathologies induced by institutional panglossianism. I will argue that constitutional review is an essential function of legitimate government according to the ideals of deliberative democratic constitutionalism. But this does not immediately entail that that function should be carried out by courts, much less that it should be fulfilled in a judicial system in the exact same way that it is in the United States. Distinguishing between function and institution can clarify the different kinds of issues at play, apart from the argumentative constraints of provincial jurisprudence. Furthermore, it can help to show how democratic objections to judicial review may be, on the one hand, objections to particular institutional ways in which the function of constitutional review is structured or, on the other, to the function of constitutional review itself. Without distinguishing institution and function, however, we can not discern the character of the objection, nor properly assess its argumentative support, as both the burdens of argument and the relevant types of reasons and evidence that are probative are quite different in each case. Roughly speaking, understanding and justifying the function of constitutional review will refer to and rely on normative political philosophy to a greater degree than considerations concerning how to institutionally structure that function if justified, since the latter requires a robust sense of the comparative possibilities and performance of various institutional designs, in different constitutional democracies, as we know them.

The basic inferential pattern followed then is first to articulate cogent and compelling normative accounts of the ideals of democracy, of constitutionalism, and of their interrelations in constitutional democracy. An adequate account of these ideals should be able to answer questions such as the following: what is democracy, how and why are democratic decisions legitimate, what is constitutionalism, why should we want political structures and procedures to be constitutionally structured, what is the nature of the relationship between democracy and constitutionalism? The normative ideals tailored to answering such questions – spelled out in terms of the specific conception of deliberative democratic constitutionalism – then provide the grounds for the claim that the function of constitutional review is justified as an important element of legitimate government. Only with this justification in hand can the institutional design questions be taken up. I claim that, in the light of what we know about the workings of various forms of political procedures, legal structures, and governmental institutions, a number of specific institutional proposals best comport with the ideals of deliberative democratic constitutionalism: proceduralist judicial review located in an independent constitutional court in a concentrated system of review, constitutional self-review panels in the legislative and executive branches, mechanisms for dispersing decisional authority concerning constitutional elaboration across the branches of national government, easing overly obdurate amendability requirements, and civic constitutional fora for both democratic deliberation about constitutional matters and as alternative mechanisms for constitutional amendment.

Although the direction of inference is from normative ideals to justification of the function of review to institutional recommendations, it is not the order in which the arguments are presented. Rather, I develop the normative ideals out of critical evaluations of various promising arguments for and against a judicial review, paying special attention not only to the underlying normative ideals they are based on but also to their insights into the peculiar relationships between constitutional law, political institutions, the democratic public sphere, and courts. The hope is to develop a normative theory that can productively incorporate essential insights while avoiding various deficiencies, a normative theory that is well suited, moreover, to the manifold complexities presented by institutional design.

2

Majoritarian Democracy and Minoritarian Constitutionalism

Before turning to the accounts of judicial review that ensue from deliberative democratic conceptions of constitutional democracy in later chapters, it will help to get clear about the various moves made in debates about judicial review under the terms of an older model of constitutional democracy, a model I will characterize in terms of the uncomfortable amalgamation of a majoritarian conception of democracy and a minoritarian conception of constitutionalism. The main point of this overview is to motivate the move beyond the standard amalgam conception of constitutional democracy by indicating some of the normative and conceptual deficiencies it evinces when considering judicial review. However, this overview will also indicate two of the main fault lines between different justifications of judicial review, fault lines that continue to be important in debates amongst deliberative democrats over judicial review and will reappear throughout the later chapters. One the one hand, there is a fundamental cleavage amongst theorists concerning how to understand the legitimacy of constitutional democracy; between, as I will explain, substantialist and proceduralist conceptions of legitimacy. On the other hand, there are differences over how properly to conceive of democratic decision-making processes: as aggregating prepolitical interests, or as sifting and evaluating competing reasons and opinions. Thus, although the deliberative democratic arguments for and against judicial review considered later reject, to varying degrees, the central elements of the majoritarian democracy–minoritarian constitutionalism conception, they can still be usefully characterized in terms of how they approach the questions of political legitimacy and political process.

A. JUDICIAL REVIEW AS SUBSTANTIALLY LEGITIMATE PROTECTION OF MINORITY RIGHTS

1. Judicial Review as the Protector of Values: Bickel

As indicated in the opening section of Chapter 1, Alexander Bickel's justification for judicial review is one purposely designed to counterweigh objections to the institution and its powers from the point of view of democracy – to address its "counter-majoritarian difficulty."[1] Although his theory is widely known and has been extremely influential (as both theoretical inspiration and argumentative foil), it is worth considering it briefly from the angle of political philosophy, that is, with special attention to normative ideals of democracy and constitutionalism it presupposes. At the core of Bickel's countermajoritarian concerns is a specific ideal of democracy: the current majority of citizens participating in elections should hold fundamental power over the policy decisions of representative government. Put another way, one perhaps more central to Bickel's thinking, there should be electoral majority power to control the policy decisions of governmental officials, a power the ultimate criterion of which is the effective ability to reverse those decisions should they fail to accord with present majority will.

Hence, the countermajoritarian difficulty arises with judicial review: assuming that the United States system aims at realizing a democratic form of government, ultimately there is no power, held by either a legislative majority or the electoral majority to which that legislative majority is beholden, to reverse the policy decisions of the Supreme Court when it strikes down an act of representative government as unconstitutional. To this countermajoritarian objection, Bickel also adds two other democratic worries about judicial review. First, quoting Learned Hand, he claims it undermines the consent of the citizenry to the current form of government that arises from the moral sense of being engaged in a collective process of self-governing. This is a slightly different reading of Hand's concerns than I gave in Chapter 1, but it is basically a different way of putting the same antipaternalist objection to judicial review. Second, Bickel approvingly quotes James Bradley Thayer's worries about the manifold ways in which the exercise of judicial review may weaken the democratic process over time, as both citizens and representatives become less and less concerned with high-quality legislative processes, offload difficult decisions onto the Court, and so gradually diminish their collective political capacities for self-government.

Of course, as Bickel takes pains to explain, there are indeed complexities that render majoritarian democracy in the United States

[1] Bickel, *The Least Dangerous Branch*, 16.

something much different than direct democracy, that is, than simple majority-rule votes by the entire electorate on single policy proposals, held continuously. Rather, electoral control by the majority of the citizens is held over representatives (both legislators and the president) who hold office for a period of time and are again subject to election; these representatives themselves decide through majority rule; representatives appoint others (like administrators and generals) to do a fair amount of work, even if such appointees only contribute to policy making in an interstitial or technical manner; the value of legal stability means that not every policy decision is up for grabs all the time; various processes of representing the will of the people are imperfect because of political inequality, institutional constraints, and bare inertia; elections do not themselves establish or set policy preferences but only control officials who do; and, representative majorities must be cobbled together through coalitions of minorities or "factions." Nevertheless, all of these complexities do not undermine Bickel's fundamental criterion for democracy: electoral majorities have the ultimate power to control governmental policy through the threat of reversal of unpopular decisions.

Once we combine this view of majoritarian control with Bickel's account of the specific capacities of representative institutions in their policy-determining functions, it should be clear that he endorses an account largely along the lines of market-models of democracy, such as Joseph Schumpeter's theory of competitive elitism or Robert Dahl's theory of pluralism.[2] According to such theories, democratic processes can be modeled as analogous to market processes of aggregating information about individual consumer desires – in this case the politically relevant desires of the electorate – and generating distributions – in this case of government-provided goods and services – that most effectively satisfy the largest possible number of the pre-process desires of individuals. Evidence that Bickel believes that the "objects" of political aggregation are the prepolitical desires of citizens and that what government should deliver are satisfactions, comes in his discussion of the comparative competences of legislatures and courts. According to Bickel, the separation of powers makes legislatures unique locations "for the *desires* of various groups and *interests concerning immediate results* to be heard clearly and unrestrainedly."[3] And he clearly believes that democratic

---

[2] Jon Elster, "The Market and the Forum: Three Varieties of Political Theory," in *Deliberative Democracy: Essays on Reason and Politics*, ed. James Bohman and William Rehg (Cambridge, MA: The MIT Press, 1997) supplies an excellent, concise, and general overview of market models of democracy. See further discussion of aggregative models of democracy in contrast to deliberative ones in Chapter 3.

[3] Bickel, *The Least Dangerous Branch*, 25, emphasis added.

government ought to effectively satisfy a large majority of those desires, as long as it does not infringe on our moral principles: "government should serve ... what we conceive from time to time to be our *immediate material needs*."[4] He also apparently endorses the pluralist version of the market models of democracy. In considering and rejecting James Madison's worries about the influence of factions, Bickel contends that such factions (understood as minority groups) must ultimately form coalitions with others in order get the majoritarian electoral support necessary to influence a majority of legislators: "The *price* of what [such minority groups] *sell* or *buy* in the legislature is determined in the biennial or quadrennial *electoral marketplace*."[5]

In contrast with this well-developed theory of democracy, including both normative ideals and models of practices and institutions, Bickel has surprisingly little to say about the import or practices of constitutionalism. I don't mean to say here that he ignores issues of constitutionality, that is, issues concerning what the meaning, scope, and import of specific clauses of the U.S. Constitution are, and concerning how the Supreme Court has ruled and should rule on various issues pertaining to those clauses. Indeed these constitute a large part of the focus of his work as an American constitutional law scholar. Rather, he has surprisingly little to say about the ideals or purposes served by having a written constitution in the first place, or what kinds of practices and political arrangements such a constitution would imply. Even though the U.S. Constitution places significant constraints on the political realizations of the immediate desires and interests of the electoral majority or the representative majority that they ultimately control, Bickel evidently takes the ideals and arrangement of the United States practice of constitutionalism largely for granted. Speculatively, then, it might be possible to espy a rather traditional American view of constitutionalism in his work: constitutionalism as the setting of principled side-constraints on the outcomes of majoritarian practices. The idea here is simply that there are some outcomes that we see as always undesirable or unjustifiable, and so we erect a constitution to specify certain substantive results of the democratic process as morally unacceptable and thereby legally estopped. Bickel clearly takes the U.S. Constitution to concern matters of principle that put limits on policy.[6] And he seems, for the most part, to think of "matters of principle" in two ways, both opposed to "matters of policy." On the one hand, principled considerations are opposed to considerations of immediate practical effects, canvassing rather the long-term effects of a decision. On the other

---

[4] Ibid., 24, emphasis added.   [5] Ibid., 18, emphasis added.

[6] At points Bickel simply defines constitutional acceptability as principled acceptability: "consideration of [a measure's] constitutionality (that is to say, of its acceptability on principle)," ibid., 22.

hand, the important long-term effects are those specifically upon our "more general and permanent interest," in securing "certain enduring values."[7] These substantive shared values then serve as the constitutional framework within which immediate satisfaction of desires and interests can be pursued.[8]

Since then, government should both enact policy satisfying citizen's immediate desires and interests and maintain our long-term principled values, and if processes of democratic representation are only good at the first task, Bickel recommends an institutional division of labor between a legislative forum of policy and a judicial forum of principle. On the one hand, the institutional structure of legislatures means that there will be insistent pressures to act on expediency rather than principle, and this pressure will in turn make it very difficult to develop a coherent body of principles over time that is adequate to new situations. "Not merely respect for the rule of established principles but the creative establishment and renewal of a coherent body of principled rules – that is what our legislatures have proven themselves ill equipped to give us."[9] On the other, the lack of electoral pressures on federal courts and the professional training of judges makes them better suited to such a careful specification, elaboration, and creative development of a coherent system of principle. "Courts have certain capacities for dealing with matters of principle that legislatures and executives do not possess. Judges have, or should have, the leisure, the training, and the insulation to follow the ways of the scholar in pursuing the ends of government."[10] Furthermore, courts can better see whether policies carried by general statutory and regulatory language in fact violate our enduring values, as "courts are concerned with the flesh and blood of an actual case."[11] Their insulation from immediate electoral pressures, finally, gives courts an exemplary position as an educative institution that, by giving a reasoned second-thought to a policy decision, may be able to call forth the better moral natures of citizens and so help them to temper their own demands on legislatures. Thus, in essence, courts are justified in exercising judicial review of governmental actions because they stand outside of the hustle and bustle of highly emotional majoritarian legislative processes, and are able to take the long view by protecting and developing

---

[7] Ibid., 24.

[8] Bickel sometimes also seems to suggest that principled values are served by law, whereas immediate desires are served by democracy – "Democratic government under law – the slogan pulls in two opposed directions," ibid., 27 – but this must be rhetorical excess, since democratic legislators presumably enact statutory *law*, and law may serve the *democratic* aims of satisfying the populace's desires and interests.

[9] Ibid., 25.   [10] Ibid., 25–26.   [11] Ibid., 26.

a system of principle designed to put value-based side-constraints on the realization of democratic desires. Judicial review is indeed countermajoritarian and so undemocratic, but it is justified in the service of protecting the substance of our long-term values.

2.   Judicial Review as the Protector of Minority Rights: Choper

Although Bickel's account is never very clear about where the vaunted values are to be found that judges are to use in considering matters of principle – a problem compounded by the need for relatively sharp specifications of such values in order to do any real work in adjudicating cases and delineating the precise limits of majoritarianism[12] – Jesse Choper's work can be seen as a step in that direction as he sharpens Bickel's justification for judicial review in the U.S. context, and provides support for its empirical premises. To begin with, Choper's account of democratic processes is along the same majoritarian lines as Bickel's, emphasizing the control of electoral majorities over government actors who develop and implement public policy. Majority rule is conceived of as "the keystone of a democratic political system in both theory and practice,"[13] and the majoritarian character of various institutions and agencies is to be assessed comparatively in terms of their responsiveness and accountability to current popular will. Notwithstanding a fair amount of complexity and careful statement, the upshot of Choper's investigation into political scientific comparisons of the three branches of the U.S. federal government is that the power of judicial review is countermajoritarian and so antidemocratic.[14]

Like Bickel, however, Choper believes that the political marketplace's satisfaction of majoritarian desires does not exhaust what is worthwhile in U.S. government. He asserts that a worthy democracy needs to be libertarian at the same time: it must recognize the normative value "of certain inalienable minimums of personal freedom (beyond the political rights of the ballot and free expression) that guard the dignity and integrity of the

---

[12] See discussion of "The Odyssey of Alexander Bickel" throughout chapter 3 of John Hart Ely, *Democracy and Distrust: A Theory of Judicial Review* (Cambridge, MA: Harvard University Press, 1980), 43–72. See further the discussion of Ely's critique of substantialist justifications for judicial review in Section B, and the discussion of the conditions of value pluralism in Section D.

[13] Jesse H. Choper, *Judicial Review and the National Political Process* (Chicago: University of Chicago Press, 1980), 4.

[14] "Given a realistic and balanced view of the operation of the political branches ... the Supreme Court is not as democratic as the Congress and President, and the institution of judicial review is not as majoritarian as the lawmaking process. The sundry controls of the people and their elected representatives may succeed in some instances and pose perilous threats in others. But these political checks do not democratize the Court or its power of judicial review," ibid., 58–59.

individual."[15] At this juncture, Choper is much more explicit in his conception of constitutionalism than Bickel, for he conceives of it essentially as both the establishment of the legitimate powers of government and the specification of clear limits to that power. Individual liberty rights enshrined in a constitution should then be understood to effect moral side-constraints on the powers of the majority over individuals.[16] So whereas Bickel's account is somewhat unclear about what constitutes the set of values judicial review protects, Choper's sharpens the focus of Bickel's matters of principle to questions of individual liberty rights.[17] Furthermore, for Choper, the point – the primary purpose – of the constitutional protection of individual rights is in fact to protect the interests of those minorities "who could not be expected to prevail through the orthodox democratic procedures."[18]

As in Bickel's account, judicial review plays a protective role in securing certain moral ideals from the expediency of majoritarianism: it is a justifiable mechanism for guaranteeing the individual rights enshrined in the Constitution that are intended to protect the interests of politically vulnerable minority groups *against* the will of the majority and the vicissitudes of the legislative process. As Choper puts it: "the overriding virtue of and justification for vesting the Court with this awesome power is to guard against governmental infringement of individual liberties secured by the constitution."[19] In answer to the question why a

---

[15] Ibid., 7.

[16] His account is somewhat more complex than this implies, as he analyzes the elements of the United States Constitution into four groups: (1) "housecleaning" provisions (e.g., the minimum age of officials), (2) separation of powers among the three federal branches, (3) federalist allocation of powers between the national government and those of the individual states, and (4) personal liberty rights. The central aim of Choper's book is to support a recommendation for judicial deference on the constitutional issues raised by the provisions in groups 1, 2, and 3, and active judicial review of personal liberties. Nevertheless, the provisions in groups 1, 2, and 3 can also be seen as constitutional constraints on governmental power; they are simply not substantive constraints on the specific policy decisions and outcomes of national political processes.

[17] It should be emphasized that this is only a comparative sharpening of focus, as, after a long review of the various types of individual liberty rights the U.S. Constitution might be thought to protect, and the manifold debates about how judges should detect and specify their exact content (pages 70–79), Choper demurs from taking any sides on the issues: "Although the Individual Rights Proposal plainly urges that judicial review should be exercised in behalf of personal constitutional liberties, this book in no way undertakes to say how this superintendence should be carried out," Choper, *Judicial Review and the National Political Process*, 79.

[18] Ibid., 64–65.

[19] Ibid., 64. The defense of constitutionalism as a counterweight to majoritarianism protecting minorities reaches back, in the American context, to the defense of the newly proposed U.S. Constitution in Alexander Hamilton, James Madison, and John Jay, *The Federalist with Letters Of "Brutus," Cambridge Texts in the History of Political Thought* (New York: Cambridge University Press, 2003). See especially Madison's *Federalist* papers 10

countermajoritarian government organ should carry out this function, Choper argues that the Supreme Court is the proper institutional body for this countermajoritarian power precisely *because* it

is insulated from political responsibility and unbeholden to self-absorbed and excited majoritarianism. The Court's aloofness from the political system and the Justices' lack of dependence for maintenance in office on the popularity of a particular ruling promise an objectivity that elected representatives are not – and should not be – as capable of achieving. And the more deliberative, contemplative quality of the judicial process further lends itself to dispassionate decisionmaking.[20]

Thus we have a functional justification for judicial review developed largely along the same lines as Bickel's: given the varying institutional incentives structured by varying electoral pressures, and the desire to protect some substantive values from the maw of majoritarianism, a democratically unresponsive institution is well-suited to carrying out the countermajoritarian function necessitated by constitutionalism. For Bickel and Choper, then, constitutionalism and democracy are antithetical political principles: the former sets certain substantive moral constraints on political outcomes while the latter licenses a political procedure, akin to a market, by which the largest number of desires and interests of the majority can be effectively identified and effectively satisfied through political policy.[21]

---

and 51. Also to be found there is Hamilton's insistence upon the independence of the judiciary from the legislative and executive branches: see especially *Federalist* 78. Of course the controlling justification for giving the *judiciary* the supreme power to interpret and enforce the U.S. Constitution was put forward by Chief Justice John Marshall in *Marbury v. Madison*: as the only legitimate interpreters of the law, the judiciary is the only governmental power in a position to decide *what* the law is. But, if the Constitution is the supreme law of the land, and if a legislatively enacted statute is in conflict with the Constitution, then a supreme judiciary must make the law internally consistent by striking down the statute. This argument from the requirements of legal consistency – an argument prefigured in Hamilton's *Federalist* 78 – should be distinguished from Choper's argument from the importance of minority rights. A third argument for judicial review is also (at least) implicit in *Federalist* 78: the judiciary plays a crucial role in the checks and balances established by the institutional separation of governmental powers, and judicial review is one of the judiciary's more powerful weapons.

[20] Choper, *Judicial Review and the National Political Process*, 68. Here Choper (and Ronald Dworkin and Christopher Eisgruber, as I will explain in Chapters 4 and 6, respectively) follows Bickel's contention that only the judiciary has the relevant capabilities to be a forum of principle.

[21] Starting from Rawlsian principles of justice, Samuel Freeman also understands constitutionalism as a way of securing legitimacy ensuring side constraints on majoritarian decision making: Samuel Freeman, "Constitutional Democracy and the Legitimacy of Judicial Review," *Law and Philosophy* 9 (1990–1991). The significant difference, as I explain in Chapter 5, is that Freeman conceives of constitutional

B. JUDICIAL REVIEW AS PROCEDURALLY LEGITIMATE PROTECTION OF DEMOCRACY

Bickel and Choper then offer two versions of the classic substantialist defense of the institution of judicial review within a constitutional democracy: although majoritarian democracy is important as a way of effectively directing governmental policy toward the satisfaction of the largest number of citizen's prepolitical desires and interests, electorally accountable institutions are not as good as independent courts at securing the right outcomes for political processes when issues of principle or individual rights are at stake. Judicial review then is justified as the best institutional means for ensuring that the substantive moral side-constraints on the outcomes of democratic aggregation are ensured.

Even if one shared its underlying normative conception of constitutional democracy, skepticism about the cogency of such a substantialist defense of judicial review might be raised in at least three ways. First, one might wonder whether in fact the central empirical claim is true: namely, that an independent constitutional court is better at securing principled values or individual rights than electorally accountable institutions. Maybe in fact majoritarian legislatures are just as good or better at securing fundamental values, guaranteeing individual rights, or protecting minorities.[22]

---

precommitments as themselves the results of exercises in popular sovereignty, exercises intended to ensure the continued existence of the necessary conditions for the exercise of democracy. Thus, in contrast to Bickel's and Choper's thesis of an antithesis between democracy and constitutionalism, for Freeman constitutionalism is itself an exercise of democracy, an originary and higher form of democracy that establishes the necessary conditions for the ordinary functioning of majoritarian democracy.

[22] In his classic essay Robert A. Dahl, "Decision-Making in a Democracy: The Supreme Court as a National Policy-Maker," in *The Democracy Sourcebook*, ed. Robert A. Dahl, Ian Shapiro, and José Antonio Cheibub (Cambridge, MA: The MIT Press, 2003 [1957]), Dahl did much to spur empirical work on such issues in the United States context by showing that in fact the Supreme Court had not historically lived up to the "standard view" of it as a bulwark against majoritarian tyranny by protecting the right of majorities. In fact, according to Dahl, as one policy initiating institution among others in the government, and where its justices are members of the political elite and the currently empowered national governing coalition, the Supreme Court has been largely irrelevant to whether or not legislative majorities have enacted policy: "lawmaking majorities generally have had their way," 248. At most, the Court has occasionally been able to delay legislative policy choices for a number of years. Worse for the "standard view," according to Dahl, is that in terms of the substantive protection of, say, oppressed minorities against majority tyranny, the actual results have been largely the opposite of the view's noble hope. On the whole in Supreme Court cases, "the victors were chiefly slaveholders at the expense of slaves, whites at the expense of nonwhites, and property owners at the expense of wage earners and other groups," Robert A. Dahl, *Democracy and Its Critics* (New Haven, CT: Yale University Press, 1989), 190. Many scholars have continued in a similar skeptical vein, challenging the notion that even the celebrated desegregation cases of the 1950s

Second, one might be concerned that the specific interpretations and extensions of the substantive values secured by a constitution – which are, after all, mostly instantiated in highly general and abstract language – are open to serious but reasonable disagreement in a pluralist society in which citizens hold to a variety of different hierarchies and schemas of fundamental values. Said another way, given both reasonable value pluralism among the citizenry and the generality of constitutional rights provisions, it seems unlikely that particular applications and extensions of the moral principles of those provisions can be taken as objectively correct by all or most citizens, and so be the object of a social consensus. Given reasonable disagreement, then, how can judges claim to have special insight into the morally correct interpretation and extension of abstractly worded constitutional side-constraints?

This worry about disagreement might then lead to the third source of skepticism. For ordinarily in those situations in which we collectively need a decision on some issue as a polity even though there are substantial disagreements among citizens, the ideal of democracy recommends that we use legitimate political procedures to determine the course of collective or governmental action. So understood, democratic procedures are taken to be a method of making decisions under conditions of substantive disagreement, a method that is legitimate because it treats each citizen as the political equal of all others. When we don't have unfailing access to the right answers on contested issues of substance, the fairness and equality realized in democratic processes of decision making can appear then

---

and 1960s in fact had much substantive impact on interracial justice: the literature starts with the classic empirically centered polemic, Gerald N. Rosenberg, *The Hollow Hope: Can Courts Bring about Social Change?* (Chicago: University of Chicago Press, 1991) (Rosenberg generates similar conclusions concerning women's rights and the rights of criminal defendants) and extends to the recent exhaustive legal history, Michael J. Klarman, *From Jim Crow to Civil Rights: The Supreme Court and the Struggle for Racial Equality* (New York: Oxford University Press, 2003). Spurred by Arend Lijphart, *Patterns of Democracy: Government Forms and Performance in Thirty-Six Countries* (New Haven, CT: Yale University Press, 1999), the important comparative study of the variety of political structures and processes in stable constitutional democracies, Dahl has further supported his empirical skepticism about the impact of judicial review on rights and minority protections by turning from intra-national historical evidence to international comparative evidence: "No one has shown that countries like the Netherlands and New Zealand, which lack judicial review, or Norway and Sweden, where it is exercised rarely and in highly restrained fashion, or Switzerland, where it can be applied only to cantonal legislation, are less democratic than the United States, nor, I think, could one reasonably do so.... It has not been shown either that fundamental rights and interests are better protected in polyarchies with judicial quasi guardianship than in polyarchies without it," Dahl, *Democracy and Its Critics*, 189. Further skeptical evidence from international comparative constitutionalism can be found in Ran Hirschl, *Towards Juristocracy: The Origins and Consequences of the New Constitutionalism* (Cambridge, MA: Harvard University Press, 2004).

legitimately preeminent over the realization of specific substantive values. But if this is the case, then to the degree that judicial review is anti-democratic, it is illegitimate. Said another way, because the value of political equality recommends a legitimate, democratically inclusive decision procedure when there is no reasonable expectation of consensus or near-consensus on contested matters of substance, judicial review is an illegitimate violation of political equality where the justices rely on or even positively develop substantive content in order to make controversial decisions about the specific application of abstract constitutionally entrenched side-constraints on majoritarianism.[23]

I look now to two theorists – John Hart Ely and Robert A. Dahl – who share these three skeptical worries about substantialist defenses of judicial review, but nevertheless articulate justifications for a limited role for electorally unaccountable courts in ensuring that the rules and structures necessary to healthy majoritarian democracy are followed. Both share the general normative conception assumed by Bickel and Choper – namely, majoritarian democracy and minoritarian constitutionalism – but nevertheless articulate proceduralist justifications for judicial review. On this view, electorally unaccountable courts exercising the power of constitutional review are not necessarily undemocratic, so long as they are only concerned with ensuring the necessary procedural conditions for the healthy functioning of democratic processes themselves, as opposed to ensuring substantively correct outcomes of those processes.

1.   Procedural Referees of the Political Marketplace: Ely

John Hart Ely has put forward one of the most influential theories of the proper role of judicial review in a constitutional democracy.[24] Ely's theory appeared in monograph form in 1980, in the midst of heated (and still ongoing) political debates in the United States about the role of the Supreme Court concerning, for instance, the proper level of judicial "activism" with respect to other branches of government, the proper

---

[23] These three sources of skeptical worry form the backbone of Jeremy Waldron's arguments against any and all justifications for judicial review. See the discussions in Chapter 4, Section C, and Chapter 5, Section B.

[24] Strictly speaking, Ely's treatment of judicial review is limited to the United States context, and is put forward in order to support a particular theory for the interpretation of certain provisions of the United States Constitution. It has, nevertheless, been influential beyond its limited context of genesis. See, for instance, the broad endorsement of Ely's conception in Jürgen Habermas, *Between Facts and Norms: Contributions to a Discourse Theory of Law and Democracy*, trans. William Rehg (Cambridge, MA: MIT Press, 1996), and see further Chapter 7. Ely himself recommended in 1986 that his theory of constitutional interpretation be applied to the new (1982) Canadian Charter of Rights and Freedoms; see John Hart Ely, *On Constitutional Ground* (Princeton: Princeton University Press, 1996), 18–24.

methods of interpreting statutes and constitutional provisions, and the acceptability of particular Supreme Court decisions made by the Warren and Burger courts concerning, for example, school segregation, the right to privacy, rights of criminal suspects, and abortion rights.[25] Jurisprudential theory, meanwhile, had been and continues to be preoccupied with methodological debates concerning what Ely calls "interpretivism" and "noninterpretivism." The issue here is whether judges should restrict themselves to a "strict construction" of the constitution in terms of the written text or the original intent of the framers, or whether they should go beyond such argumentative resources and adjudicate hard cases on the basis of values and norms that cannot be fairly discovered within the "four corners" of the relevant constitutional provision, the constitution as a whole, and perhaps also its history.[26] Ely's book aimed to show that, as framed, this debate relies on a false dichotomy, as neither approach to constitutional interpretation by an independent judiciary could be made consistent with both the actual text and structure of the U.S. Constitution, and, "the underlying democratic assumptions of our system."[27] His theory thus begins from an intellectual and political context that intensified the three skeptical worries I identified above concerning the traditional Bickel-Choper style defense of judicial review: (1) many participants evidently felt that the Supreme Court had not in fact

---

[25] See respectively, *Brown*, *Griswold v. Connecticut*, 381 U.S. 479 (1965), *Miranda v. Arizona*, 384 U.S. 436 (1966), and *Roe v. Wade*, 410 U.S. 113 (1973).

[26] Ely points out that judicial "'activism' and 'self-restraint' are categories that cut across interpretivism and noninterpretivism, virtually at right angles," Ely, *Democracy and Distrust*, 1. In principle, a strict interpretivist court may be quite active in rejecting the statutes of an assertive legislature, and a non-interpretivist court may adopt a passive role toward statues expanding the scope of constitutional provisions. In other words, the possible combinations of adjudicative methodologies and comparative judicial role will depend on the contingent history of legislative actions and past judicial decisions. From a quite different perspective Michael J. Perry, *The Constitution in the Courts: Law or Politics?* (New York: Oxford University Press, 1994), has argued that an interpretivist approach to adjudication that attends closely to original intent entails neither judicial passivism nor activism (which he calls "minimalism" and "nonminimalism"). Contrary to other originalist theorists such as Robert Bork – who argued in 1971 that an originalist or noninterpretivist approach to adjudication led to a commendable form of judicial passivism – Perry in fact argues for an *activist* (i.e., nonminimalist) originalism. Randy E. Barnett, *Restoring the Lost Constitution: The Presumption of Liberty* (Princeton, NJ: Princeton University Press, 2004) argues for a quite activist form of originalism that would overturn much of the twentieth century's constitutional doctrine in order to restore what Barnett takes to be the original meaning of the U.S. Constitution: the establishment of a minimally powerful national government substantively constrained by a broad and expanding set of libertarian natural rights focused especially on rights to property and freedom of contract. Not surprisingly, the attention that Barnett gives to democracy is little more than a dismissal of it as self-interested majoritarianism threatening a factional tyranny that runs rough-shod over individual liberties: see pages 32–39.

[27] Ely, *Democracy and Distrust*, vii.

done a good job of identifying and enforcing the "right" substantive values, which in turn (2) highlighted the value pluralism and apparently intractable but reasonable disagreement about fundamental matters extant in American society, which led many commentators, to (3) an increasingly shrill denunciation of Court exercise of the power of constitutional review as an antidemocratic, and so illegitimate, "usurpation" of the legislative power of the people.

Although the central aim of Ely's book is to provide a democratically respectable theory of constitutional interpretation for U.S. federal courts, he recognizes that such an interpretive theory ultimately depends on a particular conception of and justification for the judicial institutionalization of the function of constitutional review. It is the latter, proceduralist, theory of judicial review that I am primarily interested in here. Ely begins with the traditional objection to judicial review as the overturning of majority will by a body that is electorally unaccountable. "A body that is not elected or otherwise politically responsible in any significant way is telling the people's elected representatives that they cannot govern as they'd like."[28] This gives rise to an objection to any actual judicial decisions that overturn enacted laws on the basis of values and ideals that cannot be reasonably discovered within the "four corners" of the Constitution. Such an imposition of values external to constitutional provisions would then seem to be a kind of judicial paternalism.

The most immediate response to the specter of judicial paternalism is to insist that judges overturn statutes only on the basis of a strict "clause-bound interpretivism,"[29] and, if the text cannot support a decision, courts should simply adopt a passive stance. The attraction of strict interpretivism, combined with a plea for judicial passivism, is that it seems consistent with both the common understanding of adjudication as merely the application of positively enacted laws and, the democratic ideal that the legislature is the proper forum for the articulation and justification of the fundamental values that get transformed into legal norms. However, as Ely argues, there are a number of crucial constitutional provisions (such as the equal protection clause of the Fourteenth Amendment) that are open-textured and need to be filled in.[30]

---

[28] Ibid., 4–5.

[29] Ibid., 11. Prominent representatives of such an approach include original intent jurisprudence and textualist formalism. See Bork, "Neutral Principles and Some First Amendment Problems" and Antonin Scalia, "Common-Law Courts in a Civil-Law System: The Role of United States Federal Courts in Interpreting the Constitution and the Laws," in *A Matter of Interpretation: Federal Courts and the Law*, ed. Amy Gutmann (Princeton, NJ: Princeton University Press, 1997), respectively.

[30] Following Ludwig Wittgenstein's later reflections on language and rule-following, H. L. A. Hart argues that the open texture of legal rules – their characteristic incapacity to fully specify all correct applications of their provisions to particular cases – is entailed by the

Furthermore, the very content of such provisions invites a construction that reaches beyond their manifest textual content. If so, then the strict clause-bound interpretivist must admit that reliance on the manifest content of the relevant provision would force judges to adopt a non-interpretivist method. "The constitutional document itself, the inter-pretivist's Bible, contains several provisions whose invitation to look beyond their four corners – whose invitation, if you will, to become at least to that extent a noninterpretivist – cannot be construed away."[31]

According to Ely, a dilemma now arises. Although strict interpretivism fails by its own standards, none of the proposed noninterpretivist stra-tegies for filling in constitutional provisions are able to escape the charge of a paternalistic imposition of values by an electorally unaccountable body. All of the candidates for discovering extratextual fundamental values that might guide adjudication result, in the end, in judges applying substantive criteria to the outcomes of legislative processes, processes that are themselves supposed to be the well-spring of the substantive values embedded in legal norms. Whether these fundamental values are found in the judges' own values, in natural law, in neutral principles, in moral philosophy, in tradition, in current socially shared values, or in predic-tions about the future progress of the constitutional project, all of these substantivist approaches violate the democratic ideal of legislative self-government: they in effect involve the substitution of extralegislatively determined values for legislative value decisions.[32]

Rather than advert to the Supreme Court's role as a protector of substantively guaranteed individual liberty rights, however, Ely proposes a purely proceduralist theory of constitutional adjudication. He accepts

---

law's use of general terms. From this essential, inexpungeable characteristic of language and our incapacity to foresee all possible changes in social conditions, Hart argues that when judges apply legal rules to specific cases, they will inevitably have wide discretion in choosing how to interpret statutes in new situations within the penumbra of the statute's meaning. See Chapter 7, "Formalism and Rule-Scepticism," in H. L. A. Hart, *The Concept of Law*, second ed. (Oxford: Clarendon Press, 1994) (first ed., 1961). An early and influential attack on Hart's doctrine of judicial discretion is found in Ronald Dworkin, "The Model of Rules," *University of Chicago Law Review* 35 (1967).

[31] Ely, *Democracy and Distrust*, 13. Ely analyzes a number of such open-textured provisions in the United States Constitution: the First Amendment's protection of speech, the prohibition on cruel and unusual punishments in the Eighth, the Ninth Amendment's provision that "the enumeration in the Constitution, of certain rights, shall not be construed to deny or disparage others retained by the people," and, the due process, privileges or immunities, and equal protection clauses of the Fourteenth Amendment.

[32] Ibid., 43–72. Ely notes, in a brief section entitled "The Odyssey of Alexander Bickel" (71–72), that throughout his career, Bickel attempted many of these different solutions to the problem of the judicial identification of the fundamental values that could underwrite a counter-majoritarian constitutional jurisprudence of principle, but never found a satisfying solution. The moral according to Ely (ironically quoting from Bickel): "No answer is what the wrong question begets," 43.

that the open-textured nature of central constitutional provisions requires review processes to fill in those provisions. And he accepts that the legitimacy of legally enforced values can only be secured through the legislative process of representative self-government. Judicial review should therefore secure precisely those procedural conditions necessary to ensure that the legislative process, which gives rise to substantive decisions, is fair and open to all actors in the political marketplace. Courts would then act as referees for the processes of the democratic genesis of law, and, in seeking to concretize constitutional provisions, they should adopt a "participation-oriented, representation-reinforcing approach to judicial review."[33] According to Ely, this means that the Supreme Court should especially aim to correct two types of distortions in the political process. First, they should ensure that the legislative process is open to all on something close to an equal basis. Thus, especially high scrutiny should be given to legislation that enables electoral winners to block the channels of political change by denying access to positions and power to those who are currently not in power. Second, the Supreme Court should be particularly attentive to legislative processes that systematically disadvantage society's traditional unequals by providing goods only to citizens in the mainstream. "Insofar as political officials had chosen to provide or protect X for some people (generally people like themselves), they had better make sure that everyone was being similarly accommodated or be prepared to explain pretty convincingly why not."[34] Rather than restoring these imbalances on the grounds that the good in question is tied to some fundamental value that all citizens should have, the court should rather ensure that minorities traditionally discriminated against were equally represented in the political process.

The contrast here with Choper's account is instructive. Where Choper takes the point of substantive individual liberty rights largely to consist in the protection of minorities, Ely agrees that the protection of "discrete and insular minorities"[35] is an important goal of the U.S. Constitutional schema but argues that this can be more legitimately achieved by a judicial supervision of the democratic process, rather than an imposition of certain constitutionally unspecified side-constraints on the

---

[33] Ibid., 87.   [34] Ibid., 74.

[35] The phrase is from the famous footnote 4 to Justice Stone's opinion in *United States v. Carolene Products Co.*, 304 U.S. 144 (1938), and is meant to pick out those persistently disadvantaged minority groups consideration of whose interests are systematically and consistently disregarded by political majorities, in contrast to the electoral minorities that might be transitorily grouped around specific issues or policy concerns, but whose members can reasonably expect to be in the voting majority on other issues, and so have their interests treated fairly, on balance, by the majoritarian political processes.

outcomes of those processes. As Ely put it in an address to Canadian jurisprudes:

"Protecting fundamental interests and powerless minorities," the assigned topic. Those are two very different tasks, and my punch line, succinctly put, is that the protection of minorities, specifically under Section 15.1 of the Charter, is a job the judiciary can do in a principled manner, but that the former task, protecting fundamental interests or fundamental justice under Section 7, at least if you give it a substantive reading, is one you can't do in a principled way. Consequently, you should consider strategies for escaping the apparent instruction of the latter provision.[36]

The court should adjudicate, in sum then, on the basis of the participational goals of broadened access to political processes and equal, nondiscriminatory access to the bounty of representative government.

Ely's justification for having an unelected body as the referee of legislative processes can now be seen as arising from two commitments: to a conception of purely procedural *democratic legitimacy*, and to a conception of the *democratic process* as a marketplace of competing interests aiming to enact the aggregative will of all. Since the legitimacy of positive law is based not on the substantive content of its directives but on the procedural conditions of its genesis – in particular, the democratic character of those processes – it becomes especially important to ensure that those conditions are fairly structured and as open as possible to all citizens. Ely's commitment to a proceduralist conception of legitimacy is supported by rejecting a reading of the U.S. Constitution as a statement of fundamental values or moral commitments, whether static or evolving. Rather, according to Ely, a proper reading of the Constitution and the underlying premises of the American system of representative government

will reveal ... that in fact the selection and accommodation of substantive values is left almost entirely to the political process and instead the document is overwhelmingly concerned, on the one hand, with procedural fairness in the resolution of individual disputes (process writ small), and on the other, ... with ensuring broad participation in the processes and distributions of government.[37]

---

[36] Ely, *On Constitutional Ground*, 18. The references to "a principled manner" of judicial methodology should not be confused with Bickel's notion of the judiciary as a forum of substantive principle. As is evident in the rest of Ely's remarks, which can be considered largely a précis of *Democracy and Distrust*, and its application to the Canadian constitutional Charter, he is using the phrase "principled manner" as shorthand for the methods of judicial interpretation that are both possible and democratically legitimate.

[37] Ely, *Democracy and Distrust*, 87.

Because legitimacy hangs on fair political procedures, some institutional oversight is needed. But because Ely conceives of the political process as a marketplace of competing, self-interested parties, fairness can only be ensured on the supposition of an impartial, disinterested third party empowered to adjudicate disputes. Thus the oversight of the procedural conditions of the political process cannot be entrusted to one of the sides to the dispute – namely, the legislature. Rather, an independent, unelected judiciary is *institutionally* well situated to play the required referee role in a dispute between citizens and their representatives. Ely's conception of political democracy as either competition or negotiation amongst strategically acting individuals and groups, simply trying to maximize their prepolitical interests, thus plays a central role in his theory of judicial review.

The approach to constitutional adjudication recommended here is akin to what might be called an "antitrust" as opposed to a "regulatory" orientation to economic affairs – rather than dictate substantive results it intervenes only when the "market," in our case the political market, is systematically malfunctioning. (A referee analogy is also not far off: the referee is to intervene only when one team is gaining unfair advantage, not because the "wrong" team has scored.)[38]

Judicial review of legislation is thus justified, not because of a belief in the special competence of judges to be able to discern, and paternalistically enforce, the moral truth, but precisely because they are unelected, and so institutionally situated as disinterested parties in procedural disputes between the electors and the elected.[39]

How exactly *constitutionalism*, as an ideal and a set of practices, fits into Ely's picture of democracy is not entirely clear, however. Although, like Bickel, Ely intends to provide a theory that tests for constitutionality within the U.S. political system, and like Choper he has a brief account of the broad functional distinctions between various provisions in the U.S. Constitution,[40] he never articulates a justification for specific features of constitutionalism such as establishing the rule of law, entrenching certain legal provisions through a higher law/ordinary law distinction, structuring the institutions, processes, and practices of political decision making, or ensuring rights.[41] Nor does he provide an account of the relation between such features and the justification and forms of democracy.

---

[38] Ibid., 102–03.

[39] Ely extends this same reasoning in order to justify judicial review of relations between executive administrations, the legislature, and the people. See, for example, ibid., 131–34 and 36–70.

[40] See the quote from Ely, supra footnote 37.

[41] See Chapter 3, Section B, for a further explication of these four basic elements of constitutionalism.

Nevertheless, it seems plausible to read his work as largely in the same vein as Bickel and Choper here: majoritarian democracy is best when it is structured and limited by minoritarian constitutionalism. Recall that he takes the U.S. Constitution to be largely concerned with procedure: on the one hand, provisions structuring the political institutions and processes necessary for realizing inclusive and participatory democracy,[42] and on the other, provisions ensuring fair procedures for the resolution of disputes between private individuals and groups. As a secondary, but central task, the Constitution is also concerned with correcting the predictable defects of normal democratic political procedures, epitomized by the protection of discrete and insular minorities from unfair treatment by dominant majorities. This purpose is largely served by the post–Civil War Amendments (the Thirteenth, the Fourteenth, especially its equal protection clause, and the Fifteenth), which ought to be enforced through a stringent judicial scrutiny of the procedural legitimacy of legislation that distributes the bounty of government unequally based on suspect, prima facie discriminatory classifications.

Interestingly, in defense of his theory, Ely does at one point clearly endorse the legitimacy of substantive individual liberties that are not in any way connected with the rights essential to or supportive of political democracy, and he also seems to think that judicial review to ensure such rights is acceptable as long as the substantive individual right in question is clearly and unambiguously protected by the text of the Constitution.[43] Combined with his insistence that the U.S. Constitution was unique at the time of ratification for being effectively submitted to "the people themselves" and a history of constitutional development that has "substantially strengthened the original commitment to control by a majority of the governed,"[44] Ely's endorsement of explicit substantive liberty rights can be interpreted, I believe, as a conception of constitutionalism as the legitimate binding, by the current demos, of future democratic actors to certain well-specified constraints. As long as the endorsement of these constitutional constraints is popularly secured, they are legitimate checks on the actions of present majorities. It seems correct to say then that, in broad strokes, Ely's conception of the ideals of democracy and constitutionalism,

---

[42] I take it that the constitutional sections ensuring this "process writ large" are largely equivalent to what Choper would include in his first three functional categories of constitutional provisions. See footnote 16.

[43] "Some nonpolitical rights undoubtedly should be protected. They should, as an initial matter, be protected by the political process.... But I agree that that probably won't be enough.... Nothing I have said would suggest (and indeed most of my career has been devoted to the contrary proposition) that there is anything at all improper in vigorous judicial protection of those various rights that are marked for shelter in the constitutional document," Ely, *On Constitutional Ground*, 15.

[44] Ely, *Democracy and Distrust*, 7.

and their interrelationship, is largely the same as that of Bickel and Choper: majoritarian democracy constrained by minoritarian constitutionalism. The significant difference would then be that, for Ely, the interests of vulnerable minorities are to be protected by externally enforced procedural constraints on democratic decision processes, rather than substantive side-constraints on the outcomes of such processes.

Given his commitment to a procedural ideal of legitimacy and his commitment to a conception of democratic politics as the aggregation of private interests, it is not surprising that Ely's theory has been attacked both by those who reject a proceduralist account of legitimacy as insufficient for explaining the moral content of politically enacted rights, and by those who reject the aggregative conception of representative democracy as insufficient for explaining the deliberative, intersubjective character of political decision making.

First, there are criticisms of Ely's theory for its insufficient attention to *other* individual rights besides those that can be plausibly defended in terms of their direct relevance to the political process.[45] If the role of noninterpretivist constitutional review is confined solely to refereeing the political process, then it seems that the Supreme Court will no longer have much claim as a defender of a broad range of non-political individual civil and social rights. Ely's political proceduralism seems to leave no room for a claim that the legitimacy of any democratically enacted statute is called into question if it infringes on certain inalienable moral rights of individuals; rights that should be guaranteed by a countermajoritarian judiciary employing substantivist criteria as checks on the rightness of any given outcome. Ely himself considers this objection, and rejects it on the grounds that individual liberties are sufficiently secured by the underlying American theory of government:

I went through a period of worrying that the orientation here recommended might mean less protection for civil liberties. . . . Reflection has convinced me that just the opposite is true, that freedoms are more secure to the extent that they find foundation in the theory that supports our entire government, rather than gaining protection because the judge deciding the case thinks they're important.[46]

But Ely owes us something more here about what that theory of government is if his response is to remain more than mere hand-waving. For one might think, like Rousseau, that true self-government is

---

[45] See, for instance, Lawrence H. Tribe, "The Puzzling Persistence of Process-Based Constitutional Theories," *Yale Law Journal* 89, no. 6 (1980) and Ronald Dworkin, *A Matter of Principle* (Cambridge, MA: Harvard University Press, 1985), 59–69.

[46] Ely, *Democracy and Distrust*, 102, footnote *.

impossible unless all citizens alienate *all* of their rights before having some of them bestowed back upon them by a benevolent sovereign power.[47] In fact, one of the few indications of Ely's underlying theory of democracy – proffered in an endnote – should give pause to those who are looking for a strong defense of individual liberties. "I have suggested that the appeal of democracy can be best understood in terms of its connections with the philosophical tradition of utilitarianism.... Since nothing in the ensuing analysis depends on this claim, it is omitted here."[48] I think, to the contrary, that a fair amount does in fact so depend. An Achilles' heel of both republicanism and utilitarianism is their difficulty in giving sufficiently deontological justifications for individual liberties.[49] As Ely is unwilling to go into any detail concerning his account of democratic legitimacy, a quick dismissal of a hyperbolically constructed thought experiment at the end of his book will do little to assuage traditional liberal worries here.[50]

---

[47] See especially Book I, Chapter 6 of Jean-Jacques Rousseau, *"Of the Social Contract,"* in *The Social Contract and Other Later Political Writings,* ed. Victor Gourevitch, *Cambridge Texts in the History of Political Thought* (New York: Cambridge University Press, 1997).

[48] Ely, *Democracy and Distrust,* 187, endnote 14.

[49] For an attack on utilitarianism for its inadequacies concerning the priority of individual liberties, see especially Part 1 of John Rawls, *A Theory of Justice,* revised ed. (Cambridge, MA: Harvard University Press, 1999). On republicanism and individual rights in the United States, see the interesting historical claims in Akhil Reed Amar, *The Bill of Rights: Creation and Reconstruction* (New Haven, CT: Yale University Press, 1998). Amar argues that although we now regard those rights guaranteed in the Bill of Rights as substantive restraints on governmental action that protect individual liberty interests, this is anachronistic if attributed to the founding generation. At the time of the ratification of the Bill, the rights guaranteed were understood much more as sureties for certain forms of local action and intervention by citizens in order to ward off the agency costs of a centralized government that might become tyrannical. Thus speech rights were originally intended as sureties against federal government tyranny, not as individual civil liberties, and the right to trial by jury was not seen as an individual liberty owed to criminal defendants but, rather, as a republican mechanism to ensure citizen oversight (by the jury) of overreaching or self-dealing government agents such as federal prosecutors and judges. According to Amar's history, the guarantees of the Bill of Rights changed from largely structural guarantees assuring a republican form of government into individual civil liberties held by and protecting individuals largely due to the adoption of the Reconstruction-era Thirteenth, Fourteenth, and Fifteenth Amendments, and subsequent doctrinal developments. This conceptual transformation was, further, largely due to the perceived inadequacies of mere republican rights in protecting slaves, former slaves, and abolitionists from subordination and oppression. In short, according to Amar, U.S. history can be seen as a learning process yielding insights into the inadequacy of a republican conception of rights to be employed by active citizens, and using these insights to reconstruct the conception of rights in terms of individual liberties owed to persons *qua* persons.

[50] Ely, *Democracy and Distrust,* especially 181–3. Ely's thought experiment asks us to consider how unlikely it would be for the U.S. Congress to pass "a statute making it a crime for any person to remove another person's gall bladder except to save that person's life"

Another way to see how important Ely's underlying assumptions about democracy are to his theory of judicial review is to consider his conception of representative processes themselves. Recall that he models collective decision making as a kind of political marketplace, whereby individual members register their *de facto* preferences concerning the likely impact a decision will have on their private interests. On this account, voting – whether by citizens in elections or representatives in legislating – is an expression simply of an individual's belief concerning the best way to secure his or her own good in the light of his or her contingently given preferences.[51] In contrast, a deliberative conception of democracy insists that the common good of the citizenry cannot be determined through a simple aggregation of the largest sum of sufficiently identical private preferences. Rather, the common good can only be determined by collectively testing hypothetical proposals to find those based on reasons all citizens could reasonably accept. According to deliberative democrats, then, at least on the most fundamental issues, political decision processes should be oriented toward shaping collective

---

(ibid., 182, quoting Harry Wellington), even if Ely's theory would be forced to accept such a statute as constitutional. This hyperbolic example is then analogized to any individual right to private autonomy, and is intended thereby to show the implausibility of legislative infringements on the fundamental interests of individuals. See also Ely's rather undeveloped response to the objection that utilitarian theories of democracy are indifferent to individual rights: Ely, *On Constitutional Ground*, 15–18 and 306–11. Here, as in *Democracy and Distrust*, Ely takes advantage of the ambiguities of a theory that operates at both the level of abstract political theory and of constitutional theory within a pre-given context of settled rights in a specific country. Thus he can simultaneously insist – without really noting the tension – that "Some nonpolitical rights undoubtedly should be protected" even though such protection will not be sufficiently secured through majoritarian political processes (*On Constitutional Ground*, 15), and, that courts should only be concerned to "enforce for minorities those rights that the majority has seen fit to guarantee for itself" (ibid., 16). Apparently the "should" in the first quote has merely the force of an admonition to the majority. Of course, if one is the fortunate heir of a constitutional assembly where the majority did *in fact* see fit to enforce an extensive schedule of individual liberal rights, then it will not seem particularly problematic to endorse a political theory that can only understand the justification of individual rights in terms of benevolent majoritarian preferences.

[51] Note that this type of preference-satisfaction voting will easily lead to interest groups and blocs in conflict with one another, as individuals recognize the effectiveness of grouping together with others who have sufficiently similar preferences and preference rankings. This may well lead to the kind of factional power-politics the writers of *The Federalist Papers* were keenly worried about. As Dahl points out, however, as long as such factions or blocs do not constitute either permanent, systematically disadvantaged minorities who have no hopes of equal consideration in ordinary political processes, or entrenched powerful minorities who can almost always secure their exclusive interests through the ordinary political processes, *Federalist Papers*–style worries about representative factionalism will prove to be exaggerated. See Robert A. Dahl, *A Preface to Democratic Theory* (Chicago: University of Chicago Press, 1956).

arrangements that will be in accord – to use Rousseau's terminology – with the deliberative general will, not merely the aggregative will of all. Here voting is understood as a way of individuals' expressing their current convictions on which proposed governmental action will be the best way to secure that which is in the equal interest of all, or at least that which can be reasonably expected to realize a generalizable individual interest. On this account, the process of collectively deciding on how we are going to live our lives together under government requires debate and the giving of reasons – reasons that all could potentially accept for themselves. In this process of deliberation, citizens themselves may in fact *alter* their prepolitical preferences to bring them into line with the requirements for living with others. In this sense, voting is not a mere registration of preferences but instead is a specific mechanism adopted by mutually deliberating actors in order to reach some decision under time, knowledge, and coordination constraints. Voting is a way of temporarily calling a halt to deliberations under pressing needs for action.

Even if this description seems overly idealistic for a great number of routine political decisions, it still seems that the ideal of democracy includes the notion that citizens can only understand the laws as products of their own free will if those decisions have been reached on the basis of mutually acceptable reasons arising from thoughtful deliberation and opinion formation. If this notion of a "republic of reasons"[52] is a crucial part of the democratic ideal, then the duties of Ely's judicial procedural referees will extend further than merely ensuring against "antitrust violations" of the political marketplace.

Ely's procedural justification of judicial review is attractive precisely because it does not rely on the superior insight of judges into matters of moral principle or truth.[53] It is thus not subject to the skepticism concerning superior judicial moral competence which, combined with an

---

[52] The phrase is from Cass R. Sunstein, *The Partial Constitution* (Cambridge, MA: Harvard University Press, 1993). See especially Chapter 1 for an interesting discussion of how the notion of deliberative democracy involves a commitment to a ban on governmental action based on "naked preferences."

[53] Skepticism toward the presupposition of special judicial insight into moral principles is nicely captured in Nino's phrase "epistemic elitism": "The common view that judges are better situated than parliaments and other elected officials for solving questions dealing with rights seems to arise from an epistemic elitism. It assumes that in order to arrive at correct moral conclusions, intellectual dexterity is more important than the capacity to represent vividly and to balance impartially the interests of all those affected by a decision. It is understandable that scholars who celebrate the marvels of judicial review should identify themselves more closely with judges than politicians and, thus, are inclined to think, as Michael Walzer remarks, that what they deem to be right solutions – their own – would be more readily obtained by judges than politicians," Carlos Santiago Nino, *The Constitution of Deliberative Democracy* (New Haven: Yale University Press, 1996), 189.

insistence on the democratic principle of popular sovereignty, often leads to worries about judicial paternalism in the first place. However, without some fuller account of democratic legitimacy, Ely's reliance on majoritarian procedural legitimacy provokes liberal concerns about the security of nonpolitical, individual civil and social rights. In addition, Ely's market-modeled account of democratic processes in terms of prepolitical preference aggregation ignores the intersubjective deliberation about ends and responsiveness to public reasons that are ideally a part of democratic self-rule.[54]

2.   Judicial Review as Quasi Guardianship: Dahl

Up to this point in this chapter, the theories and claims examined have arisen in a somewhat parochial manner: raised by U.S. jurisprudes concerned ultimately to defend certain views about both the proper role of

---

[54] And not just ideally; while the deliberative democratic conception of democratic processes is an element of normative theory, it is more than a mere utopian demand ensuing from empirically untethered idealistic political theory: see, for instance, the empirical research surveyed in Michael X. Delli Carpini, Fay Lomax Cook, and Lawrence R. Jacobs, "Public Deliberation, Discursive Participation, and Citizen Engagement: A Review of the Empirical Literature," *Annual Review of Political Science* 7, no. 1 (2004). The history presented in Amar, *The Bill of Rights* is also instructive here, for it shows how the shift in the dominant conception of the meaning, incidence, and practical effects of the Bill of Rights was both widely dispersed throughout the populace and responsive, over the long term, to the force of reasons, not only or even largely, to the aggregate of private interests. The historical contexts relevant to the writing, ratification, and subsequent enforcement of, for instance, the Fourteenth Amendment show that high constitutional politics in the United States is not only the outcome of representative government enforcing the majority's prepolitical private interests. For how can such an aggregative conception of democratic processes account for the import and weight of abolitionist arguments made on behalf of constitutionally *unenfranchised* subjects, arguments, furthermore, that lead to policies undercutting the abolitionists' own private interests? Furthermore, the aggregative focus on the formal organs of government as the only important place for democratic politics simply ignores the rich interactions between those formal organs and the informal public spheres constituted by civic associations, the print media, the literary public, churches, lawyers, and affinity groups, interactions that allow for information, opinions and arguments to substantially influence the outcome of constitutional debates. Amar's history thus shows in rich detail the empirical appropriateness of the deliberative model of democratic politics, in contrast to the inadequacy of Ely's aggregative model. Similar considerations follow from Ackerman, *We the People: Transformations*, 99–254, where, even though the ratification of the Reconstruction Amendments is portrayed as more of a bare-knuckles political struggle, it is seen as a political struggle involving sustained public attention and debate concerning the transformation of fundamental constitutional law. According to Ackerman, in fact, the adoption of the amendments was legitimate only because it had the hallmarks of an authentic exercise of the deliberation and decision of "we the people," even though it was technically illegal according to the amendment procedures specified in Article V of the U.S. Constitution.

the Supreme Court in American political life, and the proper way to interpret and enforce the U.S. Constitution in light of that role. Although Bickel, Choper, and Ely provide explicit justifications for the institutionalization of the function of constitutional review in an electorally independent judiciary – justifications, moreover, specifically attuned to objections from the point of view of democracy – each theory has suffered from complementary normative and empirical deficits arising from that parochial starting place. On the one hand, relying on background conceptions of the meaning and justification of democracy and constitutionalism assumed to be shared by all Americans, each of the accounts of judicial review is subject to concerns precisely at those difficult junctures where implicit tensions are masked by theoretical inarticulateness about basic normative conceptions. On the other hand, significant empirical assumptions – about, for instance, the character of representative processes, or the relative powers and capacities of the various branches of government – have underwritten conclusions that are not obviously generalizable outside of the context of the United States's history, institutional structures, and political processes. I would like to turn then, briefly, to a consideration of Robert Dahl's theory of judicial review, for it promises both greater clarity on basic normative issues and more political scientific sensitivity to the complexities of political processes. Above all, it promises to raise the issue of the democratic legitimacy of judicial review at a general level, beyond the peculiarities of one nation-state's political system.

Consider first the similarities between Ely's and Dahl's conceptions of both the *prima facie* democratic objection to judicial review from anti-paternalism premises, and their limited justification for an electorally independent judiciary's oversight of the procedural conditions of the democratic process. Dahl's consistent theoretical foil to the political theory of democracy is the theory of "guardianship," which claims that "ordinary people ... are clearly not qualified to govern themselves ... rulership should be entrusted to a minority of persons who are specifically qualified to govern by reason of their superior knowledge and virtue."[55] Thus, Dahl links guardianship to political paternalism, and opposes democracy to both as the fundamental political principle. If, then, the electoral accountability of policy makers is a central defining feature of democratic systems,[56] and electorally unaccountable judges make

---

[55] Dahl, *Democracy and Its Critics*, 52.

[56] Of the six institutions Dahl claims large-scale democracy (what he calls "polyarchy") requires, the first two are elected policy-making officials and free, fair, and frequent elections: Robert A. Dahl, *On Democracy* (New Haven, CT: Yale University Press, 1998), 83–99. The list presented in Dahl, *Democracy and Its Critics*, 220–24 contains seven institutions, but in *On Democracy* universal suffrage and offices open to all are combined into one category called "inclusive citizenship."

significant policy decisions, then their policy decisions are not subject to democratic control. Furthermore, if these policy decisions are allowed to override contrary decisions of elected officials – as is the case with constitutional review by national courts of national legislation and administrative action – then these decisions have the facial appearance of paternalistic guardianship.[57] However, Dahl uses the term "quasi guardianship" to capture two features of judicial review on the American model. First, because federal judges – including Supreme Court justices – are appointed through a political process, are themselves members of the political elite, and depend heavily on the public's acceptance of the legitimacy of their decisions (having direct control over coercive means), the policy preferences of federal judges are not in fact likely to stray far from those of the current ruling coalition, and quite unlikely to be in opposition to the latter for any significant stretch of time.[58] Second, according to Dahl, and more important to my purposes here, there is in fact a legitimate democratic role for quasi guardianship: namely, to maintain exactly those rights that are either essential to or necessary for the healthy democratic functioning of political decision-making processes.[59] Thus for Dahl, as for Ely, the *prima facie* objection to judicial review from antipaternalism is inapplicable in exactly those cases in which such review maintains and reinforces the procedures of majoritarian democracy.

Unlike Ely's underdeveloped mentions of utilitarianism, however, Dahl has a much clearer and more convincing defense of the legitimacy of democracy on the aggregative conception, one not dependent on parochial appeals to a particular political system or a specific historical tradition of constitutional development. In particular, Dahl gives an explicit defense of the *preeminence* of democratic processes over other values.[60]

---

[57] Dahl is refreshingly consistent in distinguishing the hard problem of strong judicial review concerning the capacity of a court to rule on the constitutionality of the actions of coordinate branches, from the quite different problem posed in a federalist system whereby a high national court may be authorized to control the actions of state officials.

[58] Dahl has consistently made this point since Robert A. Dahl, "Decision-Making in a Democracy: The Supreme Court as a National Policy-Maker," *Journal of Public Law* 6 (1957).

[59] Dahl, *Democracy and Its Critics*, 176–92. As he puts the point in Robert A. Dahl, *How Democratic Is the American Constitution?* (New Haven, CT: Yale University Press, 2001), 153–4: "A supreme court should ... have the authority to overturn federal laws and administrative decrees that seriously impinge on any of the fundamental rights that are necessary to the existence of a democratic political system: rights to express one's views freely, to assemble, to vote, to form and to participate in political organizations, and so on. ... But the more [the court] moves outside this realm – a vast realm in itself – the more dubious its authority becomes. For then it becomes an unelected legislative body."

[60] Joshua Cohen, *Dahl on Democracy and Equal Consideration* [Draft manuscript] (1998 [cited March 31, 2005]); available from http://web.mit.edu/polisci/research/cohen/dahl_on_democracy.pdf gives a clear reconstruction of Dahl's argument that I have found very helpful.

His starting political axiom, as it were, is the "idea of intrinsic equality," an idea widely shared by disparate theorists: "at least on matters requiring collective decisions 'all Men' (or all persons?) are, or ought to be considered equal in some important sense."[61] Dahl then defends a conception of the "equal consideration of interests" as the best interpretation of the basic concept of intrinsic equality: "intrinsic equality means that the good or interests of each person must be given equal consideration" in collective decision-making processes.[62] Finally, as equal consideration of interests could be provided by, say, a benevolent dictator or a fabulously powerful utility calculator – in other words, because certain forms of guardianship also could give equal consideration to the interests of each – Dahl adds what he calls the presumption of personal autonomy in order to yield a defense of the legitimacy of democracy: "in the absence of a compelling showing to the contrary everyone should be assumed to be the best judge of his or her own good or interests."[63] Finally, Dahl defends aggregative democracy on two main grounds.[64] On the one hand, majority rule is the decision procedure most likely to maximize the satisfaction of individuals' prepolitical desires, preferences, and interests, and so to maximize overall social utility. On the other, majoritarian democracy is the political process that maximizes individual chances for living under laws of one's own choosing, that is, for achieving moral autonomy even under a set of collectively binding laws.

Although Dahl acknowledges that there may be other values that we might want political arrangements to serve beyond those strictly realized by the democratic process itself (such as political equality), he argues that given both reasonable disagreement about what the specific requirements of those other values are and the simultaneous need for

---

[61] Dahl, *Democracy and Its Critics*, 85.   [62] Ibid.

[63] Ibid., 100. Its unclear whether Dahl intends the presumption of personal autonomy as an empirical claim about first-person epistemic authority with respect to one's own interests, or as a moral postulate. Although he claims that it is a defeasible prudential principle mixing elements of empirical judgments about persons with some moral elements, his repeated reference to self-determination as an important democratic value, and his insistence that collective political processes should be organized to maximize chances for self-determination seem to lend more weight to the moral interpretation of the presumption.

[64] This is a significant simplification of a complex set of arguments presented over several chapters. In particular, Dahl catalogs and runs through a variety of justifications for democracy, and a number of arguments for majoritarianism, along with objections to majoritarianism, and the comparative strengths and weaknesses of alternatives to it. I refer to the two main lines of utility maximization and moral autonomy maximization largely because Dahl returns to these two themes repeatedly, and appears to endorse them in comparison with the other pro-democracy and pro-majoritarian arguments and considerations he canvasses.

collectively binding decisions, the selection and accommodation of those values in legal and political arrangements must be made through democratic procedures.[65] Said another way, the values of democracy have a political preeminence over other potential values political arrangements might instantiate or promote. If other values are to be politically enacted, the decision to do so must be made democratically, and the demos must have some fair chance for altering that choice in the future should it no longer be endorsed by the majority of citizens. "For my part, I believe that the legitimacy of the constitution ought to derive solely from its utility as an instrument of democratic government – nothing more, nothing less."[66]

Given Dahl's more stringent defense of the preeminence of democracy, it is not surprising that he is more skeptical than Ely of the judicial specification of individual nonpolitical rights. Although Ely seems to think that judicial review is perfectly acceptable here as long as a constitution sufficiently clearly enumerates the relevant rights, Dahl rejects nondemocratic determinations of the sphere of inviolable rights, beyond those rights that are either integral to or necessary for the exercise of democratic choice. "What interests, then, can be justifiably claimed to be inviolable by the democratic process or, for that matter, any other process for making collective decisions? It seems to me highly reasonable to argue that *no* interests should be inviolable beyond those integral or essential to the democratic process."[67] And it is precisely the inviolability of those interests integral or essential to democracy that renders their defense by nondemocratic quasi guardians acceptable.

Here however, we run up against a similar set of puzzles to those that beset Ely's theory where it had no clear account of constitutionalism, as Dahl, rather surprisingly, also has little to say about the concept or its import in political regimes. His basic idea seems to be along Diceyean lines, namely that a country's "constitution" is simply a name given to the

---

[65] The need for binding decisions and reasonable disagreement are essentially the same two conditions that Waldron, *Law and Disagreement* identifies as "the circumstances of politics," and then uses to also defend the political preeminence of majoritarian democratic decision processes. Waldron's argument is different, relying on a deliberative, not an aggregative, conception of the democratic process, and depending on individual rights to fairness, rather than utility maximization, as the central normative ideal that democracy realizes. See further discussion in Chapter 5, section B.

[66] Dahl, *How Democratic Is the American Constitution?*, 39. Libertarian worries about the safety of individual rights, deontologically conceived, may arise here, in much the same way they did with respect to Ely's theory. But at least Dahl has produced independent moral arguments in support of his claim to the political preeminence of democracy, arguments which, in order to adjudicate the debate, would need to be addressed in a much more fulsome way than I can here.

[67] Dahl, *Democracy and Its Critics*, 182.

ensemble of regnant political arrangements and practices,[68] and that in democratic countries the constitution centrally involves procedures of representative polyarchal rule. Hence, from a theoretical perspective entirely oriented to the realization of democracy, thinking about constitutions is a comparative affair: one of looking at the institutions, practices, and habits various political regimes might embody, and determining whether they are conducive to, harmful to, or have no effect upon the processes of democracy.[69] There is then, almost no attention to issues of the rule of law,[70] nor, more important, to the relationship between the legitimacy of ordinary law and the legitimacy of higher, constitutional law. This latter lacuna, furthermore, leads to puzzles about individual rights: can a democratic people legitimately, according to Dahl's criteria, constitutionally bind themselves now – say, through supermajority amendment rules, or even more strongly, through irrevocable entrenchment – to respecting certain substantive, nonpolitical rights in the future? If so, shouldn't these be legally binding requirements and so, at least if quite clearly specified, enforceable by courts even against officials of coordinate branches who might violate them? If not, are all democratic decisions always open to renegotiation and subject to change merely at the behest of what may be a merely transitory or poorly informed bare majority of voters or their representatives?

However, its hard to see what Dahl's answers might be here. On the one hand, it seems that he would reject the constitutionalizing possibilities, as it would imply that there were certain interests not directly connected to the democratic process, yet nevertheless inviolable by means of that process. Perhaps worse, electorally unaccountable officials would have authority to determine the scope and incidence of those fundamental interests, and so the preeminence of democracy for collective decision making would be violated. On the other hand, Dahl clearly endorses as consistent with democracy a variety of decision rules: not only strict majority rule, but also supermajority rules, forms of consensus-oriented decision rules, limits on national majorities such as federalist

---

[68] See generally A. V. Dicey, *An Introduction to the Study of the Law of the Constitution*, tenth ed. (New York: St. Martin's Press, 1965 [1908])., and the discussion in Chapter 3, sections B.1. and B.2.

[69] See, for instance, his scattered use of the term "constitution" simply to pick out the different political structures evinced by different regimes and political theories in Dahl, *Democracy and Its Critics*. The chapter on constitutions in Dahl, *On Democracy*, 119–29, is dedicated to looking at the variety of political arrangements established in modern constitutional democracies, and comparing them with respect to their effects on the health of the democratic process.

[70] Dahl does mention the idea that no official is above the positive law of the land as a requirement of the principle of fairness at Dahl, *Democracy and Its Critics*, 108, but says little else beyond that.

divisions of power, disproportionate representation for some sectional minorities, various mechanisms for slowing and delaying the decisions of present majorities, and so on. "Under different conditions, the democratic process may be properly carried out under different rules for making collective decisions."[71] But if, for instance, supermajority rules are appropriate under certain conditions where we reasonably expect majoritarianism to yield suboptimal results, and constitutional amendment rules are set up as supermajoritarian rules, then it would seem that changeable constitutional provisions protecting, say, private autonomy rights may not be antidemocratic but, rather, consistent with democratic values and processes. Without a clear account of constitutionalism and its relation to democracy, we seem to be vacillating between rejection and acceptance of the legitimacy of democratically enacted constitutional protections of substantive rights.

Although, then, Dahl provides much of the nonparochial normative defense of democracy and of the limited proceduralist role for judicial review in sustaining democratic processes lacking in Ely's account, because his theory provides no coordinated normative accounts of constitutionalism and democracy it leads to similar uncertainties as evinced in Ely's theory about exactly where and how substantive nonpolitical rights might fit in. By contrast, it seems to me that Dahl provides more convincing support for the confidence merely stipulated by Ely that, in the actual historical course of well-functioning democracies, extensive protections of individual rights and interests are in fact well established and maintained by ordinary democratic processes. Here Dahl's international comparative perspective is extremely helpful, for the question can be rather easily operationalized by comparing various well-established democracies with different regimes of constitutional review: from the American model of a supreme federal appellate court with judicial review powers, to the European model of specialized constitutional courts, to nations with no electorally independent bodies

---

[71] Ibid., 162. For the full discussion, see Chapters 11 and 12, 135–62. Even this acceptance is not so straightforward, however, for Dahl weakens the very notion of supermajoritarianism by allowing it to be overridden by simple majorities. Consider this strange passage: "A solution might be to try to combine the advantages of majority rule with the possibilities of supermajorities by using majority rule as *a first and last resort*. The members could decide in advance, by majority rule, that in certain cases a supermajority would be required," Dahl, *Democracy and Its Critics*, 154, emphasis added. It would seem, however, that majority rule could only be a "last resort" if a simple majority in the future could decide to ignore the supermajority decision rule laid down in advance, effectively nullifying supermajoritarianism and whatever advantages are taken to accrue to it. A similar puzzling passage concerning democratically enacted slow-down rules for legislating can be found in the last full paragraph of 185.

responsible for constitutional review.[72] The question becomes simply: is it true or false that those with judicial review protect the civil rights of citizens better than, and with a more extensive catalogue of rights than, those without comparative institutions? Here Dahl's judgment of the facts is unambiguous: "it has not been shown ... that fundamental rights and interests are better protected in polyarchies with judicial quasi guardianship than in polyarchies without it."[73]

In addition, as Dahl repeatedly points out, the issue here is not rights versus democracy *simpliciter* (or as he sometimes puts it, substance vs. process), as a substantial catalogue of citizens' rights needs to be specified, effectively available, and actually enforced for democracy itself to function: rights to participate in politics, to free expression, to vote, to have one's vote count equally, to be informed about alternative policies, to influence the agenda, to form political parties and associations, to have one's interests equally considered, to a free and independent press, and so on. Once we make the distinction between these rights related to democracy and other rights, however, it becomes clear that many potential counterexamples to Dahl's judgment about the relative inefficaciousness of judicial protection of rights lose their force. This is because what appear at first glance to be examples of grievous violations of individual or minority rights by a tyrannical majority, are not properly blamed on the workings of democracy. Rather, the rights violations either are themselves a direct diminution of democratic rights or are the results of a failure of adequate and legitimate democratic processes.

For example, one might object to Dahl's sanguine account of democratic processes and democratic rights by pointing to U.S. history, in particular the history of constitutional transformations from the Founding to the Reconstruction eras and on into the twentieth century. On one reading, this history indicates how U.S. citizens realized, over time, that political rights in combination with the institutional structures of republican self-government were alone insufficient for protecting the fundamental interests and rights of individuals and minorities, especially African Americans.[74] The example would seem to performatively show a people realizing, over time, the insufficiency of democracy to secure rights. But here Dahl could plausibly point out that the grievous

---

[72] Dahl apparently relies heavily on the remarkable comparative study, Lijphart, *Patterns of Democracy: Government Forms and Performance in Thirty-Six Countries* for his summaries of comparative political structures in well-established constitutional democracies, but Dahl cites no direct evidence for this specific judgment about the inefficaciousness of judicial review (a judgment, incidentally, repeated throughout his work).

[73] Dahl, *Democracy and Its Critics*, 189.

[74] The transformation of the rights specified in the Bill of Rights from guarantees of republican self-government into individual civil and liberty rights is, in fact, exactly the story told in Amar, *The Bill of Rights*.

violations of fundamental rights and interests perpetrated under the original constitutional scheme – and little could be more grievous than race-based chattel slavery – were precisely the result of what is perhaps the most significant type of democratic failure: namely, the exclusion of a group of adults from having any direct say in, or even indirect influence over, the political decisions that directly impact their own interests. Political disenfranchisement, in other words, was not simply one of the rights violations visited on both slaves and free blacks, but it also plausibly explains the other rights violations and exclusions continually suffered by them and their descendents. After all, the corrections that came at the end of this learning process were all tailored to ensuring the conditions for democratic political equality: they removed the exclusions from legal personhood and the coordinate ability to even be a rights bearer that slavery involved (the Thirteenth Amendment); ensured that all members of the community were equal citizens, afforded each all of "the privileges or immunities of citizens" previously enjoyed only by white adults, and required that all be guaranteed "due process of law" and "the equal protection of the laws" (the Fourteenth Amendment); and finally ensured against any race-based exclusions from the franchise (the Fifteenth Amendment).[75] In other words, the lesson learned before and after the Civil War in the United States was not that well-functioning democratic process cannot be counted on to protect rights, but that the democratic process itself was defective in not ensuring its own rights preconditions. The injustices perpetrated selectively on African Americans did not then show the impossibility of democracy to secure substantive justice, but rather that democratic defects of exclusion can lead to the selective deprivation of rights, since they make it impossible for those excluded to have their interests represented either directly or indirectly in the processes of representative democracy.[76]

Finally, in support of Ely's and Dahl's shared confidence in the provision of rights through democratic processes without quasi-guardianship interventions, Dahl points to abundant empirical evidence that, over time,

---

[75] It is surely worth noting here, as Dahl would, that both the Thirteenth and Fourteenth Amendments were needed to overturn extant Supreme Court doctrines, announced in *Dred Scott*, holding not only that slaves were property, but also that despite any citizenship they might have in their home states, they could have no U.S. citizenship and so no legal personality from the point of view of federal law. Furthermore, one also should note that the Court went out of its way to exercise its power of judicial review of national legislation – even though it could easily have avoided it – by striking down the Missouri Compromise as unconstitutional. So much the worse for the idealization of judicial review tending to protect powerless individuals and minorities from majority tyranny!

[76] It took another fifty years, however, before the same lessons of inclusion were constitutionally extended to women.

stable democracies tend to expand their protections for rights, expanding both in terms of greater inclusion of previously excluded groups of people and in terms of increasing numbers of types of rights protected.[77] This development is neither immediate, linearly progressive, nor the result of polite discussion among political elites alone, but rather occurs in fits and starts over long periods of time, and only through social contestation and struggles, where rival claims are made about the apparent moral necessity or arbitrariness of various categories and distinctions that may form the basis of legal forms of discrimination and unequal treatment. Nevertheless, as Dahl argues, there is an inner dynamic to the development of democratic political culture in the direction of inclusion, precisely because the kernel normative ideas of democracy are the ideals of intrinsic equality and personal autonomy.[78] In this sense, we can speak of a learning process that occurs in societies with well-established and stable democratic political institutions, as the same cultural formations and complexes of ideas support both those democratic institutions and the protection of individuals' fundamental interests and rights.

In acknowledging and celebrating such cultural learning processes – in particular, their efficacy in the democratic elaboration of constitutional law over time – Dahl should also, however, accede to some of the points emphasized by deliberative democrats with respect to democratic processes. For if in fact those processes, over time and through social struggle, are responsive to the force of good reasons – for instance by eliminating performative contradictions such as that contained in the simultaneous claims for the intrinsic equality of persons and the legitimacy of chattel slavery – then a purely aggregative model of politics is insufficient to characterize democracy. Attention must be paid not only to the satisfaction of individual interests – achieved either through markets of electoral "purchases" of representatives in return for government dispensed "wares" or through the pluralistic bargaining of major social actors representing group-shared interests and pressuring political officials for constituent-satisfying policies – but also to reasons-responsive forms of policy making whereby the cognitive content of politically shared normative principles are taken seriously as constraining the kinds of preference-satisfactions legitimately allowed. For the expanding protection of rights and fundamental interests witnessed in stable polyarchal

---

[77] The classic touchstone analysis here, which Dahl also refers to, is T. H. Marshall, *Citizenship and Social Class* (London: Cambridge University Press, 1950).

[78] Dahl, *Democracy and Its Critics*, 186–87, though he also points to the increasing scale and resulting anonymity of the modern nation-state as causal factors in the expansion of rights at 219–20. See also his account of the role of beliefs about the legitimacy and proper character of democracy as causal factors in the comparative receptivity and sustainability of polyarchal democracy in different countries and at different times at 260–64.

democracies appears best explained as the responsiveness of government policy making to reasons acceptable to all citizens treated as equals, rather than as interest- and pressure-group responsiveness of policy-making officials seeking to satisfy group-shared private desires.[79] Put simply, if Dahl is right about the directional cultural dynamic of democratic learning processes – and I think he is – and if, when interests and ideals come into political conflict, ideals many times eventually trump interests, then the aggregative model of democracy cannot be the whole story concerning the democratic processes.

C. MOVING BEYOND AGGREGATIVE MAJORITARIANISM AND MINORITARIAN CONSTITUTIONALISM

This chapter has canvassed the two main strategies for justifying the institutionalization of the function of constitutional review in an electorally unaccountable judiciary under the assumptions of one standard normative model of constitutional democracy. This model understands democracy paradigmatically as the making of collective political decisions through majoritarian decision procedures intended to aggregate and efficiently satisfy the individual interests and desires of citizens. It further conceives that, in order to secure certain values, there may be legitimate minoritarian side-constraints placed on majoritarian decisions: these side-constraints can be conceived of, so to speak, as the constitutional container of aggregative democracy.

Although they share this underlying model of constitutional democracy, the two strategies for justifying judicial review differ. The substantialist argument, represented by Bickel and Choper, acknowledges democracy as an important value, but is suspicious of the capacity for majoritarianism to fully satisfy the demands of justice or other politically important values. It then argues that certain institutional incentives give independent courts a better chance of securing these other values: judicial review with respect to such issues is justified as more likely than ordinary democratic processes to yield the right answers. The proceduralist argument, represented by Ely and Dahl, acknowledges that other substantive values beyond those connected to democracy may be worthy of political support and even constitutional enactment; but they deny that independent courts have

---

[79] Perhaps the simplest example of such reasons-responsive, rather than interest-responsive, policy making is the extension of voting rights to women. Women were not allowed to exert electoral pressure on democratically accountable officials in order to gain this right, and the men who voted for it arguably stood to lose many of the privileges of male supremacy. Surely forms of indirect political pressure were brought to bear, but at the end of the day what counted (literally) were the votes of enfranchised adult men who had been convinced that treating women as constitutional political unequals was unacceptable in the light of principles of political equality they already endorsed.

either the capability or the normative legitimacy to make such substantive decisions. Under conditions of reasonable disagreement about substantive values, their relative priority, and their specific incidence amongst the polity at large, and given the normative axiom of the political equality of citizens, proceduralists insist that only the democratic process can fairly bind a political community to a particular set of substantive decisions. The institutional incentives specific to courts do, however, render them better defenders of the rules of the democratic game than the interested players themselves. Judicial review of the procedures of democracy is legitimate; beyond that lies the realm of judicial paternalism.

Throughout the chapter, I have repeatedly stressed two kinds of worries about this standard model of constitutional democracy – one kind about democratic legitimacy and the other about democratic processes – worries that theories of deliberative democratic constitutionalism promise to address. Consider first worries raised concerning political legitimacy. If constitutionalism sets normative side-constraints on democratic decisions (whether procedural or substantive), how can we determine and specify those side-constraints once a society no longer shares (if it ever did) a homogeneous sense of a distinct set of metaphysically-grounded, objectively discernable moral truths?[80] Rawls expresses this condition with his well-known phrase "the fact of reasonable pluralism":

The diversity of reasonable comprehensive religious, philosophical, and moral doctrines found in democratic societies is not a mere historical condition that may soon pass away; it is a permanent feature of the public culture of democracy. Under the political and social conditions secured by the basic rights and liberties of free institutions, a diversity of conflicting and irreconcilable – and what's more, reasonable – comprehensive doctrines will come about and persist if such diversity does not already obtain.[81]

If we are faced with the fact of apparently ineliminable but not unreasonable disagreement over principles, value hierarchies, and the correct application of norms, and yet we still want to do justice to the notion of intrinsic equality of persons, and, finally, we have pressing needs for collective decisions, then democratic procedures apparently recommend themselves as fair dispute resolution mechanisms. But this would mean that any forms of quasi-guardianship, whereby nondemocratic means are used to settle some controversial matters of principle, are suspected of

---

[80] As Dahl colorfully puts the point, "In an earlier day it was perhaps easier to believe that certain rights are so natural and self-evident that their fundamental validity is as much a matter of definite knowledge, at least to all reasonable creatures, as the color of a ripe apple....This view is unlikely to find many articulate defenders today," Dahl, "The Supreme Court as a National Policy-Maker," 248.

[81] Rawls, *Political Liberalism*, 36.

illegitimate paternalism. We could put this in terms of a less well-known phrase from Rawls, "the fact of oppression":

> A continuing shared understanding on one comprehensive religious, philosophical, or moral doctrine can be maintained only by the oppressive use of state power. If we think of a political society as a community united in affirming one and the same comprehensive doctrine, then the oppressive use of state power is necessary for political community.[82]

This worry is more evident with respect to the substantialist justifications of judicial review, since they recommend that judges impose – that is, use the coercive power of the state to enforce as legally binding for all – the right answer on a democratic people that evidently believes it is not the right answer. But it is also detectable in the proceduralist defenses, precisely where they are unclear about whether a democratic people might entrench against future democratic process certain nonpolitical substantive values, and whether they might legitimately look to countermajoritarian institutions to protect these constitutional commitments.

The other kind of worry concerns the standard model's picture of democratic processes as largely majoritarian forms of interest aggregation. In its stark and unadorned form as a simple decision procedure, majority rule is not very attractive, even if it seems to be demanded by the coordinate facts of reasonable pluralism and oppression, and the political need for collectively binding law. On the one hand, pure majoritarian decisions seem to provide insufficiently compelling reasons for citizens to trust the worth of their outcome and so give their reasoned consent to their results. Why should the fact that my interests are shared by less than half of the population put me under an obligation to serve the interests of the majority? On the other hand, as rational choice and social choice theories have well-established, majoritarian decisions procedures are notoriously arbitrary. That is, rather than accurately aggregating the prepolitical, independent preferences of individuals, their outcomes can be swayed by situational features of the decision process, features that are nevertheless irrelevant to reaching the correct solution.[83] Bickel's and

---

[82] Ibid., 37.

[83] Kenneth J. Arrow, *Social Choice and Individual Values*, second ed. (New Haven: Yale University Press, 1963) showed that under certain conditions of preference diversity amongst the voting population, and given more than two alternative policy choices, majority voting would produce arbitrary cycling between different ranked sets of collective preferences. The problem is worsened by the fact that outcomes can be effectively shaped by setting the agenda order of the votes, even though the agenda setting is out of the hands of the full pool of voters: William H. Riker, *Liberalism against Populism: A Confrontation between the Theory of Democracy and the Theory of Social Choice* (Prospect Heights, IL: Waveland Press, 1982).

Choper's substantialist defenses play off of these unattractive features, and invite us to have wise judges make up for the normative paucity of majoritarian political processes by imposing moral side-constraints on the results of democratic aggregation, never really explaining, however, why we should accept democratic decision procedures in the first place. The two proceduralist strategies differ on addressing this point. While Ely surreptitiously smuggles in the substantive moral side-constraints by relying on the parochialism of a fortunate constitutional heritage, Dahl provides a set of theoretical and empirical arguments in support of his confidence that, in fact, democracies do rather well over time in legally securing desired principle and values, including extensive individual rights protections. But as I tried to show, in making these arguments, Dahl also had to concede the limitations of his central pluralist model of democratic processes as the efficient satisfaction of private interests. Thus, at this crucial point, where it needs to explain the reasons for the surprisingly rich normative results of stable, working democracies, Dahl's theory begins to push beyond the boundaries of a model of majoritarian aggregation, and towards the kind of deliberative model of democratic processes already envisioned by John Dewey:

Majority rule, just as majority rule, is as foolish as its critics charge it with being. But it is never *merely* majority rule. As a practical politician, Samuel J. Tilden, said a long time ago: 'The means by which a majority comes to be a majority is the more important thing': antecedent debates, modification of views to meet the opinions of minorities, the relative satisfaction given to the latter by the fact that it has had a chance and that next time it may be successful in becoming a majority....The essential need, in other words, is the improvement of the methods and conditions of debate, discussion and persuasion. That is *the* problem of the public.[84]

As I indicated earlier, deliberative theories of democracy promise to address both kinds of worries. On the one hand, they promise a richer, more convincing account of the legitimacy of constitutional democracy, one intent on fully coming to terms with the fact of reasonable pluralism by focusing on the role of publicly acceptable reasons in political decisions. On the other hand, they also promise a model of democratic processes that is both more attractive than mere majoritarian aggregation and more true to the actual deliberative character evinced by at least some forms of modern political interaction and decision. Theories of deliberative democratic constitutionalism are not, however, unified or in agreement upon how to understand the concepts of democracy,

---

[84] John Dewey, *The Public and Its Problems*, ed. Jo Ann Boydston, vol. 2: 1925–1927, *The Later Works of John Dewey, 1925–1953* (Carbondale: Southern Illinois University Press, 1984), 365.

constitutionalism, and their interrelations. The next several chapters will explore this variety by looking at various arguments for and against judicial review. For I am convinced that teasing these concepts out of the various theories can not only help to answer one of the old chestnuts of democratic institutional design – is judicial review democratic? – but also can help to get a clearer sense of the most convincing theoretical directions to take in normative theories of constitutional democracy.

3

From Majoritarian to Deliberative Theories of Constitutional Democracy

Before turning to the deliberative democratic arguments for and against the judicial institutionalization of constitutional review in subsequent chapters, it will help to have some rough sense of the basic theoretical distinctions and issues that will repeatedly reappear. My contention in those chapters is that the most important differences between the various arguments can be captured by attending to the underlying conceptions of "democracy," "constitutionalism," and their interrelationships in "constitutional democracy" that the various theories employ. And, as I hope to be able to show, the most convincing accounts of how the function of constitutional review should be institutionalized depend not only on empirical and prudential considerations arising from realistic appraisals of the performance of extant political institutions but also on normative considerations about the acceptable shape of political decision-making processes. Thus, it will help to get at least a clearer articulation of the central analytic and normative concepts applied.

A. DELIBERATIVE DEMOCRACY: FOUR AXES OF ANALYSIS

Major transformations have occurred in the last fifteen to twenty years of normative democratic theory, that is, in those theories that attempt to justify principles of political morality that should govern the structures of social and political institutions in contemporary democratic societies. This section focuses mainly on those changes initiated by one major subgroup of theorists: those who can plausibly be considered deliberative democrats.[1] The various issues and problems ranged under this banner

---

[1] Although far from an exhaustive list, prominent examples include Benjamin J. Barber, *Strong Democracy: Participatory Politics for a New Age* (Berkeley: University of California Press, 1984); James Bohman, *Public Deliberation: Pluralism, Complexity, and Democracy* (Cambridge, MA: MIT Press, 1996); Joshua Cohen, "An Epistemic Conception of Democracy," *Ethics* 97 (1986); Joshua Cohen, "Procedure and Substance in Deliberative

68

are wide and diverse. Some deliberative theories are concerned with expanding participation in the political marketplace of ideas or in formal political processes; some with how to encourage the civic capacities and virtues necessary for citizenship in a particular nation-state; some with how to encourage a public culture of openness, tolerance and public spiritedness; some with how to develop an intermediate civil society between private subjects and the state that would be based in diverse, active, and widely diffused public spheres; some with how to ground a just liberal order in the face of irreducible cultural and religious pluralism; some with how to design political procedures so that their outcomes can be understood by all as the result of the best reasons and most relevant information available; and so on.

I do not wish to prejudge internecine debates about the proper con-ception of deliberative democracy here, only to indicate how, as a general political concept, it differs from the political conceptions encountered in Chapter 2, conceptions that endorsed the package I called there major-itarian democracy constrained by minoritarian constitutionalism. From the name itself, one might reasonably infer that "deliberative democracy" focuses mainly on discussion and debate as central features of democ-racies, as opposed to voting and other forms of citizen pressure on gov-ernment officials. Although it is certainly true that the relevant literature has done much to expand notions of the character and import of civic talk of various forms and in diverse forums, mere discussion and debate alone cannot account for the distinctive character of deliberative democratic theory. This is because any minimally acceptable and accurate conception of democracy – not just the deliberative one – will need to acknowledge the inexpugnable role of information exchange and collection among citizens and between the citizenry and governmental officials, at the very least in order to promote some modicum of fit between the desires of the citizens and the policies adopted to fulfill those. Such fit – that is, appropriately adapted and efficiently executed policies – would be highly unlikely in the absence of ways for public opinion to influence state

---

Democracy," in *Democracy and Difference: Contesting the Boundaries of the Political*, ed. Seyla Benhabib (Princeton, NJ: Princeton University Press, 1996); John S. Dryzek, *Discursive Democracy: Politics, Policy and Political Science* (New York: Cambridge University Press, 1990), James S. Fishkin, *Democracy and Deliberation: New Directions for Democratic Reform* (New Haven, CT: Yale University Press, 1992); Amy Gutmann and Dennis Thompson, *Democracy and Disagreement* (Cambridge, MA: Harvard University Press, 1996); Habermas, *Between Facts and Norms*; Bernard Manin, "On Legitimacy and Political Deliberation," *Political Theory* 15, no. 3 (1987); Jane Mansbridge, *Beyond Adversary Democracy* (Chicago: University of Chicago Press, 1983); Nino, *The Constitution of Deliberative Democracy*. To this list should be added the theorists discussed in the rest of this chapter, as well as those in Chapters 4 through 7.

action.[2] One need only think here of traditional arguments for the democratic requirements of a free press and an open "marketplace of ideas," or of the centrality of public opinion polls to the actual workings of modern democratic governance. Furthermore, as many unsympathetic critics of deliberative democracy have repeatedly insisted, actual politics seems poorly modeled in terms of the kinds of discussion witnessed in university seminar classrooms – politics is not a polite "philosopher's café" where the truth can be sought independently of pressures for decisional agreement and action.

If deliberative democratic theory is to be, then, both distinguishable from traditional aggregative conceptions and yet appropriately applicable to the actual conditions of modern political governance, it must be about more than the good faith of exchange of reasons. I suggest that we place the notion of "reasons-responsiveness" at the core of deliberative conceptions. As a preliminary sketch, the desideratum of reasons-responsiveness can be understood to require that state action be responsive to good reasons; more concretely, public reasoning practices among citizens and officials should have some direct or indirect influence over the formulation of, decision upon, and execution of governmental action. Thus, deliberative democracy does not just stress reasoned civic discussion – it stresses *politically relevant and effective* reasoned discussion. How this is to be accomplished institutionally and practically, what the scope of such responsiveness must be, what the character of appropriate or sufficient reasons should be, who is to engage in reason-giving, when and with respect to what issues, and so on – all of these and more are live controversies in the literature.[3] Nevertheless, all deliberative democrats stress the need for a constitutive link between public exchanges of reasons and arguments concerning political matters, and the actual political adoption of policies and their execution through the use of governmental power.[4]

---

[2] For a clear explication of this point and its role in distinguishing aggregative and deliberative conceptions, see Cohen, *Dahl on Democracy and Equal Consideration.*

[3] Rainer Forst, "The Rule of Reasons: Three Models of Deliberative Democracy," *Ratio Juris* 14, no. 4 (2001) clarifies debates between liberal, communitarian, and what might be called "reflexive reasoning" conceptions of deliberative democracy by examining their respective takes on seven different sets of issues. The notion of reasons-responsiveness I employ is indebted to his conception of "the *rule of reasons* ... [as] the essence of the notion of deliberative democracy," 346.

[4] This is true even for those deliberative democrats that are more concerned with understanding and improving the thought processes that go on *within* (rather than between) individuals. See, for instance, the claim that many of the deficits in organizing deliberation in large, mass-scale complex democracies can be addressed through focusing on the imaginative and projective capacities of individuals when they deliberate for themselves: Robert E. Goodin, "Democratic Deliberation Within," in *Debating Deliberative Democracy*, ed. James S. Fishkin and Peter Laslett (Malden, MA: Blackwell, 2003). My claim

If we then ask why this notion of reasons-responsiveness is a democratic notion, the simplest answer seems to be that it is one way of interpreting the requirement of political equality that is at the core of all normative democratic theories. Rather than the equal impact of private interests on governmental actions, as majoritarian models stress, however, the idea in deliberative democratic theory is usually that reason-responsive government realizes an ideal of the equal justifiability, to each citizen, of the use of their collective political power. This idea can be put in terms of Rousseau's criterion for legitimate collective autonomy: I, as a citizen, can only understand myself as autonomous (as a self-ruling agent) while living under a set of collectively-binding and coercive laws, to the extent that I can understand those laws as, in some sense, self-authored and thus self-imposed.[5] I must be able to understand myself simultaneously as an author and a subject of collectively binding laws. Deliberative democrats then claim that it is precisely the fact that government action can be understood as the result of good reasons – reasons arrived at only after extensive deliberative collecting, sifting, and evaluating of relevant considerations, in a good-faith collective effort to realize political goals, while treating fellow citizens as free and equal – that allows individual citizens to understand laws as self-authored. Citizens can then be presumed to give their reasonable consent to such collectively self-authored laws, thus rendering (ideally) the incidence of the state's use of its monopoly on coercive force legitimate. When government is reasons-responsive, subjects can understand its actions as the product of the self-government of free and equal citizens.

Returning now to the two worries raised concerning majoritarian theories at the end of Chapter 2 – the apparent unattractiveness and sociological incompleteness of modeling the democratic process purely in terms of majoritarian procedures, and, the problem of legitimacy given the fact of reasonable pluralism in modern societies – newer theories promise to address both worries with the same answer: deliberation.

---

that deliberative democratic theory requires a constitutive link between public talk and political decision then rules out a theory such as Robert W. Bennett, *Talking It Through: Puzzles of American Democracy* (Ithaca, NY: Cornell University Press, 2003). Although Bennett rejects the notion that democracy in the United States is aggregative and majoritarian in favor of the claim that American constitutional democracy essentially structures wide and variegated conversations between officials and diverse publics, he argues – with merely descriptive and not normative intent – that all of this varied conversation serves mostly to buy the obedience of citizens to laws they do not like substantively, by giving them a satisfied sense of involvement after the determination of policies by governing elites. So although Bennett focuses on many of the same deliberative features of constitutional democracy as normative theorists, his theory attends to them only insofar as they contribute empirically to the stability of a particular governmental system, not because they ought to or do have any connection to actual political decision making.

[5] See Chapter 6 of Book I of Rousseau, "*Of the Social Contract.*"

On the one hand, richer models of public debate and discussion, models that do not deny the democratic role of majoritarian procedures but insist they do not exhaust the democratic process, are supposed to be more attractive and accurate. On the other hand, the character of good political reasons identified by the theory – and there are many different accounts here – is supposed to save democratic legitimacy even under conditions of modern diversity.

Although some might think that the dual demands of deliberative democracy for intensive, high-quality, and substantive debate and discussion on public issues and for the reasons-responsiveness of government actions are impossibly unrealistic from the get-go, much of the work on deliberative democracy has been devoted to showing the practical relevance of both demands.[6] Of course, even if actual democratic practices do not always live up to the standards articulated by deliberative democratic theories, this does not undercut the normative claims made by those theories. Finally, as the research area has matured, concerns have moved from articulating and justifying basic concepts at a theoretical level to diverse concerns with modeling, testing, and institutionalizing those concepts in actual constitutional democracies.[7]

With this preliminary sketch, I now turn to four cross-cutting axes of analysis that might account for the diversity and specificity of theoretical claims made by deliberative democrats. The four axes can be seen as answers to a set of questions, with each axis having two analytically distinguishable poles. First, what is the basic character of the democratic process, aggregation or deliberation? Second, why are democratic political decisions legitimate, because of the substance of their outcomes or the worth of their procedures? Third, is the democratic worth of specific political institutions, say legislatures or courts, merely instrumental to other noninstitutional values, or do they embody some intrinsic, and so

[6] Although this charge is well beyond the scope of this book, numerous theorists have argued that such conceptions are not, at least, wildly idealistic. See especially the books cited in footnote 1 *supra* by Barber, Habermas, Mansbridge, and Nino.

[7] For good overviews of the variety of issues and approaches in what might be called "applied" deliberative democracy, see James Bohman, "Survey Article: The Coming of Age of Deliberative Democracy," *The Journal of Political Philosophy* 6, no. 4 (1998) and Simone Chambers, "Deliberative Democratic Theory," *Annual Review of Political Science* 6, no. 1 (2003). An excellent survey of recent empirical research concerning the positive and negative effects of various deliberative processes and *fora* on democracy in the United States can be found in Delli Carpini, Cook, and Jacobs, "Public Deliberation, Discursive Participation, and Citizen Engagement." See also the literature reviewed in Archon Fung, "Recipes for Public Spheres: Eight Institutional Design Choices and Their Consequences," *The Journal of Political Philosophy* 11, no. 3 (2003) and David M. Ryfe, "Does Deliberative Democracy Work?," *Annual Review of Political Science* 8, no. 1 (2005). James Fishkin has done extensive experimentation and testing of various methods for bringing deliberation into public opinion polling. For a start, see Fishkin, *Democracy and Deliberation*.

nonfungible, values? Fourth, should the decisive power over collective political decisions be organized along more populist or expertocratic lines, that is, dispersed throughout the citizen population or more concentrated in the hands of relevant experts and political elites?

1. Democratic Process: Aggregation vs. Deliberation

At the very least, all normative democratic theories, of whatever stripe, are committed to an egalitarian ideal: in a democratic form of government all citizens ought to have some significantly equal opportunities to influence governmental actions. But beyond this, specifically deliberative theories share a rejection of traditional majoritarian models of the democratic process, with their focus on periodic mass elections for various office holders who are then entrusted with plenary power and expected to represent the interests of their constituents as they carry out the business of government. Although they do not deny that elections and the representation of interests are important functions for democratic governments, deliberative democrats tend to focus instead on the manifold sites and processes of discussion, debate, and reason-giving that, they claim, should accompany governmental actions at all stages of policy formulation, decision, and execution. One way of stylizing this difference is to use Rousseau's distinction between how to determine the will of all versus the general will. According to the will of all – that which aggregative democracy aims at – the common good of the citizenry can be determined by finding the largest sum of sufficiently identical individual interests. According to the general will – that which deliberative democracy aims at – the common good can only be determined by collectively testing hypothetical proposals to find those based upon reasons all citizens could reasonably accept (or at least not reasonably reject).[8]

---

[8] Jeremy Waldron, "Rights and Majorities: Rousseau Revisited," in *Liberal Rights: Collected Papers 1981–1991* (New York: Cambridge University Press, 1993) characterizes this distinction as one between Bentham's and Rousseau's notions of democratic decision making: see especially 394–400. Rousseau's work however, as Waldron recognizes, is filled with many different ideals of democratic decision making, and these different ideals are often conflated. For instance, Rousseau also seems to think that citizens' assemblies should focus on articulating their already existing underlying solidarity, a solidarity ultimately based upon a certain kind of consensus of feeling arising out of the similarity of their mores, education, socialization, and collective history. I make no claim here to accurately represent all of Rousseau's actual positions on deliberative democratic processes, as worked out in Book I, Chapters 7–8; Book II, Chapter 3; Book III, Chapters 1–5, 12–15, and 18; Book IV, Chapters 1–3 of Rousseau, "*Of the Social Contract.*" Rather, here and throughout the book I will consider the notion of deliberation through the exchange of reasons and opinions among citizens who seek to come to a collective decision – rather than authentic collective self-reflection on preexisting feelings of solidarity – to be the "Rousseauian" model of deliberative democratic processes.

A more contemporary rendition of the distinction asserts that, while traditional models conceive of democracy as a marketlike process of aggregating the preferences and interests of various constituencies, deliberative models see democracy as structured more by the logic of the forum. Whereas a market seeks to satisfy any and all prepolitical preferences as efficiently as possible, a deliberative forum looks to satisfy only those preferences which are compatible with the public good or are morally acceptable, to do so fairly to each citizen, and to ensure fairness by solving collective action problems on the basis of publicly articulable reasons.[9] The process of democracy is thus seen as essentially discovering, sorting, and evaluating reasoned opinions in order to make collectively binding decisions in accord with the common good, rather than aggregating desires efficiently in order to choose policies that maximize the realization of private individual preferences.[10]

It is worth noting that the single contrast between aggregative and deliberative processes actually contains two contrasts. On the one hand, in answer to the question concerning *what* gets processed in democratic procedures, aggregative models typically claim that individual's personal desires, interests, satisfactions, or utiles do, while deliberative models typically focus on individual's opinions, reasons, principles, or arguments on matters of public interest. On the other hand, there is the question concerning *how* the process actually goes about taking these inputs and rendering a decision: either by a more-or-less mechanical method of counting according to bare procedural rules, or through more qualitative and judgment-infused methods of sifting, comparing, critiquing, and evaluating reasons and arguments according to epistemic and normative standards, all oriented toward arriving (ideally) at a reasoned consensus. Normally the first pair in each contrast is associated with aggregative models (e.g., utiles are summed) and the second pair with deliberative models (e.g., reasons are evaluated). But strictly speaking they need not

[9] An early and influential example of this distinction in the deliberative democracy literature can be found in Elster, "The Market and the Forum: Three Varieties of Political Theory" (originally published 1986). Apparently coincidently, Manin makes the same market/forum distinction in an article published first in French in 1985: see Manin, "On Legitimacy and Political Deliberation," 355–57.

[10] Recall that, apart from the normatively unattractive features of pure majoritarianism, there are also apparently insurmountable collective choice problems in achieving what it sets out to achieve: an accurate reflection of the collectively aggregated prepolitical individual preferences. John Ferejohn, "Instituting Deliberative Democracy," in *Designing Democratic Institutions*, ed. Ian Shapiro and Stephen Macedo, *Nomos Xlii* (New York: New York University Press, 2000), 82, puts it nicely: "As is well known, with sufficient preference diversity, the aggregative model will generally produce arbitrary collective choices – choices that appear impossible to justify on any reasonable account of what the public good requires because they depend completely on substantively irrelevant features of the aggregation procedure."

be so associated: it is certainly possible to see, for example, democratic voting as aggregating over reasoned opinions to find the preponderance of the public will on an issue.[11]

Finally, as a methodological caveat, it is important to note that the basic distinction between aggregative and deliberative models of the democratic process, as well as the three other distinctions addressed below, are not all-or-nothing dichotomies, where instances can be properly categorized as falling exclusively under either one description or the other. Rather, examined instances should often be characterized as falling along a continuum between the two poles. For this reason, I prefer to think of the four axes as delineating analytic distinctions between ideal types, keeping in mind that actual examples of both the claims of democratic theories and extant political practices and institutions may contain admixtures of both contraries. I do claim, however, that the distinctions can be analytically useful in seeing the contours of the debates, in particular, by helping to highlight the commitments and entitlements of the various positions. Beyond the inherent imprecision of the distinctions, we also need to keep in mind that the complex theoretical requirements of any political and legal theory – including those of deliberative democracy and constitutional review – will further undermine a futile search for theoretical positions that are entirely contained within rigid, dichotomous understandings of the distinctions. Thus, for example, a democratic decision process that looks to rationally aggregate already given individual preferences will require at least some communication between participants, if only for individuals' private information-eliciting and strategic purposes.[12] And in some cases, rational deliberators may consider the simple aggregative weight of

---

[11] This, for instance, seems to be the position attributed to Rousseau in Waldron, "Rights and Majorities: Rousseau Revisited" and defended in the discussion of legislative deliberation and voting in Part I of Waldron, *Law and Disagreement*, 21–146. Although Waldron seeks to distance himself from deliberative theories of democracy (see pages 69–70 and 91–93), primarily on the grounds that such theories overidealize politics on the philosophy-seminar model, his essentially deliberative account of legislative politics and the inherent "dignity of legislation," as well as his consistent focus on the practical and theoretical problems of accounting for persistent, good-faith disagreement among citizens both, seem to me, to fit well within the deliberative democratic paradigm. Chapter 5, Section B takes up what I call Waldron's "deliberative majoritarianism."

[12] Beyond the mere information gathering needed for purposive-rational strategic action vis-à-vis other strategic actors, some aggregative theories of democracy also have noticed that public processes of interaction, information-exchange and debate can themselves change the preprocessed preferences of individuals, and in a salutary way, in the direction of the common good. In this sense, many aggregative theories already incorporate some of the insights usually countenanced as definitive features of deliberative theories. See, for instance, the discussion of "enlightened understanding" as a desideratum of a healthy democratic process, and its relation to the common good in Dahl, *Democracy and Its Critics*, 111–12 and 306–08.

majority preferences as probative, even if not dispositive, to the inherent inferential strength of reasons justifying a proposal.[13]

2. Legitimacy of Political Outcomes: Substantialism vs. Proceduralism

Before explaining the distinction between substantialist and proceduralist accounts of legitimacy, it may be worth clarifying the often overworked word "legitimacy." I use the term "legitimacy" (and its cognates) here in its normative, not its descriptive, sense. In general a legitimate political institution, rule, decision, arrangement, practice, and so on will, either directly or indirectly, lead to state actions that are normatively permissible, are defensible on the basis of good reasons, and give citizens, *prima facie*, good moral reasons for obeying the institution, rule, decision, and so on. Thus, I am not here directly concerned with factual matters often captured by the term "legitimacy" – those concerning, for instance, the actual extent of social obedience to the state, the degree to which a state is perceived by its members or others to have a monopoly on the coercive use of force within its territory, the extent of motivations for conformity versus disruption, and so on.[14]

---

[13] As will become apparent in considering the constitutional review theorists' respective accounts of democratic decision-making processes in Chapters 4 through 7, the two-part distinction between aggregation and deliberation is insufficiently differentiated to both accurately characterize the extant diversity of public reasoning and theoretically articulate the various kinds of reason-responsiveness different institutional actors ought to demonstrate. In particular, following Habermas, I will suggest that a theory of constitutional review needs to account for at least four kinds of democratic processes: preference aggregation, fair bargaining, ethical-political self-clarification, and deliberative consensus.

[14] Richard H. Fallon, Jr., "Legitimacy and the Constitution," *Harvard Law Review* 118, no. 6 (2005) distinguishes three senses of legitimacy encountered in American constitutional and jurisprudential discourses: the moral, the legal, and the sociological senses. I will substitute the broader term "normative" for "moral" as the latter connotes (to my philosophical ear) the relatively narrow category of individuals' obligations to distinct others, whereas "normative" has a broader reach, connoting issues for which we think there are justifiable intersubjective standards (norms, values, ideals, principles, goals, etc.); standards that make claims on our behavior, practices, institutions, or social arrangements, and which our behavior, practices, and so on can, in some sense, get right or wrong, fulfill or violate, and so on. Thus, "normative" in my usage includes not only individual moral matters (not to mention ethically valued ways of living individually and collectively) but also concerns social and political norms, rules, values, principles, and so on. The legal sense of legitimacy can be distinguished from the normative sense by using "legality," "legal validity," and other cognates: this is the central subject of various general philosophies of law. Legal positivism in general claims that legality can be established independently of normative legitimacy (see Hart, *The Concept of Law*; Hans Kelsen, *Introduction to the Problems of Legal Theory*, trans. Bonnie Litschewski Paulson and Stanley L. Paulson [New York: Clarendon Press, 1992]); natural law theories deny this

Turning then to the second axis of analysis, it concerns how we should think of the legitimacy of democratic decisions: as arising from their permissibility within some antecedently given normative limits, or as arising simply from the fact that they are the outcome of certain decisions mechanisms that enjoy the presumption of rationality. Whereas substantialist philosophers, such as Locke, argue that governmental decisions are only legitimate if they are not in conflict with the substantive normative constraints of a natural law that is binding even in the absence of an established state or legal system, proceduralist philosophers, such as Rousseau, argue that the decisions of a sovereign legislative assembly are legitimate simply because the deliberations have been procedurally structured in such a way that all members can understand themselves as subject only to those laws they have given to themselves. In short, this distinction is between substantive and procedural conceptions of democratic legitimacy.[15]

Another way to put this distinction is to say that a procedural account of legitimacy sees the outcomes of a decision process as justified simply because the specified conditions of the procedure have been met; a substantive account of legitimacy sees the outcome of a decision process as justified only if that outcome accords with some determinate ideals that are logically independent of the decision procedures employed.[16]

(see John Finnis, *Natural Law and Natural Rights* [London: Oxford University Press, 1980], Lon L. Fuller, *The Morality of Law*, rev. ed. [New Haven, CT: Yale University Press, 1969]). The controversy cannot even be posed clearly, however, unless we keep the normative and legal senses of legitimacy distinct. The distinction between the normative and the sociological senses is equally important, and for the same reasons: the interesting questions cannot even be asked without doing so. In German, there is a clearer semantic separation between *Geltung* (factual acceptance) and *Gültigkeit* (ideal validity, or justifiability). Throughout this book, I will reserve "legitimacy" and its cognates for the normative sense of the term, "legality" and its cognates for the legal sense, and employ phrases such as "citizen's beliefs in the legitimacy of …" to indicate the sociological or empirical sense of legitimacy.

[15] Establishing that my contestable interpretations of the conception and importance of this distinction to Locke and Rousseau are correct goes beyond the ambit of this book. Interested readers might refer to the following passages. For Locke's account of the substantive legitimacy constraints on legislation *via* the natural law, see §§134–42 of *The Second Treatise of Government* in John Locke, *Two Treatises of Government*, ed. Peter Laslett (New York: Cambridge University Press, 1988). For Rousseau's account of the procedural legitimacy of collective political autonomy, see Book I, Chapters 5–8; Book II, Chapters 1–2, 4, and 6; Book III, Chapter 1 of *The Social Contract* in Jean-Jacques Rousseau, *Discourse on Political Economy and the Social Contract*, trans. Christopher Betts (New York: Oxford University Press, 1994).

[16] This way of putting the distinction roughly corresponds to the distinction made in David M. Estlund, "Beyond Fairness and Deliberation: The Epistemic Dimension of Democratic Authority," in *Deliberative Democracy: Essays on Reason and Politics*, ed. James Bohman and William Rehg (Cambridge, MA: MIT Press, 1997), between a "procedural" theory of legitimacy and a "correctness" theory of legitimacy.

Thus, although Rawls's theory of justice argues for a substantive set of principles of justice that can be used to gauge the legitimacy of any agreements reached amongst citizens, Habermas's discourse theory argues only for certain procedural conditions that must be met in order for citizens' own agreements on substantive principles of justice to be legitimate. As Moon points out, it is precisely the difference between substantialism and proceduralism that explains, for example, the significant disparity between the ways Rawls and Habermas understand public reason – the centerpiece concept of democratic interaction for both thinkers. "For Rawls, public reason is a set of substantive principles to be used to answer fundamental questions. . . . Habermas, on the other hand endorses the public use of reason, which provides criteria determining the universal validity of moral norms, though it does not itself ground substantive norms."[17]

The methodological point concerning the merely analytic character of the distinction is perhaps even more important here than in the discussion of democratic processes. For with respect to legitimacy, we might find substantialism and proceduralism playing different roles at different levels of one and the same political theory. Thus, to take Rawls's well-known theory as an example, one might well say that it employs a proceduralist model of justification at the most abstract level of political philosophy, in order to generate an account of substantive principles of political justice, adherence to the latter of which then confers legitimacy on democracy at the level of constitutional choice. Thus, whereas Rawls's two principles of justice supply the substantive principles that the theory uses to test the legitimacy of the basic political arrangements of any society, including constitutional democracy, those two principles are themselves justified only because they are the outcomes of a certain (idealized) procedure for choosing political principles among free and equal persons.[18] Although the complexity of the relation between substantialism and proceduralism is even deeper than this for Rawls, this

---

[17] J. Donald Moon, "Rawls and Habermas on Public Reason: Human Rights and Global Justice," *Annual Review of Political Science* 6, no. 1 (2003): 257.

[18] Rawls preferred form of philosophical justification – what he calls "political constructivism" – is a form of proceduralism: "Political constructivism is a view about the structure and content of a political conception. It says that once, if ever, reflective equilibrium is attained, the principles of political justice (content) may be represented as the outcome of a certain procedure of construction (structure). In this procedure, as modeled by the original position . . . rational agents, as representatives of citizens and subject to reasonable conditions, select the public principles of justice to regulate the basic structure of society," Rawls, *Political Liberalism*, 89–90. This form of proceduralism then yields substantive principles applicable to democracy, principles, that is, that explain the legitimacy of democratic political institutions.

illustration should be sufficient to warn against overly simplistic and dichotomous uses of the distinction.

As another example, consider the relationship between the justification of constitutional rights, and their actual constitutional provision. It is perfectly consistent here to justify a particular provision in proceduralist terms while simultaneously recommending that it be constitutionally operationalized in a substantive test. One might think, for instance, of the religious neutrality of the state as a requirement of procedural fairness to both believers and nonbelievers, but ensure that neutrality through a substantive ban on any forms of state endorsement of religion or of requirements for particular sectarian professions of faith by citizens.[19] Alternatively, one could constitutionally operationalize certain procedural tests intended to secure a set of substantive values. Here, for instance, one might think that the value of individual privacy is ultimately grounded in a substantive understanding of the preeminence of individual worth and the freedom of the individual, but secure such values through a set of procedural requirements for any state interference in the private sphere.[20]

The methodological point can be generalized. For it would seem that even the most severe adherent to a procedural account of legitimacy must admit that the recommended procedures are recommended because they model or incorporate at least some substantive value, good, norm, or ideal. After all, this substantive component forms the reason for adopting the decision procedure in the first place.[21] Conversely, even the most ambitious attempts to specify a full and complete panoply of substantive principles and values as legitimacy requirements for political decisions

---

[19] The First Amendment to the U.S. Constitution has such a substantive provision, one arguably intended to ensure procedural fairness to all citizens: "Congress shall make no law respecting an establishment of religion."

[20] I take it that this is one prevalent understanding of provisions in the U.S. Constitution such as that in the Fourth Amendment: "The right of the people to be secure in their persons, houses, papers, and effects, against unreasonable searches and seizures, shall not be violated, and no Warrants shall issue, but upon probable cause, supported by Oath or affirmation, and particularly describing the place to be searched, and the persons or things to be seized." The manifold and continuing controversies concerning the judicial doctrine of "substantive due process" in the United States are largely centered around the complexities involved in this interplay between different types of justification for and operationalization of constitutional provisions.

[21] Consider Rawls's example of a system of fair gambling as an exemplar of pure procedural justice, in which "there is no independent criterion for the right result: instead there is a correct or fair procedure such that the outcome is likewise correct or fair, whatever it is, provided that the procedure has been properly followed," Rawls, *A Theory of Justice*, 75. Here we seem to have an example of unalloyed procedural legitimacy – but notice that the legitimacy of the outcome results not only from following the procedure but also from the supposition that the procedure will satisfy or operationalize a substantive ideal: namely, fairness or correctness or justice.

will recognize an inexpugnable role for merely procedurally legitimate decision processes in unforeseen or indeterminate cases. Admitting the possibility that one's preferred substantive theory of legitimacy can't be used to decide all issues, one must concomitantly admit that some decisions are legitimate simply as the result of recommended procedures.[22]

The need to avoid exclusivistic, dichotomous uses of the distinction is especially evident in acceptable theories of democracy. No sensible theory will claim that the legitimacy of any and every state decision or action hangs entirely or exclusively on a matter of either substance or procedure. Substantialists will usually claim that, even though many democratic decisions are justifiable simply because they result from a recommended procedure correctly followed, some determinate substantive content – defined independently of any procedures actually followed – sets constraints on the range of acceptable outcomes of any democratic processes. (What I called in the last chapter the substantialist restriction of majoritarian democracy by minoritarian constitutionalism seems to fit just this pattern.) And if a procedural account of legitimacy is to be more than an arbitrary and unjustifiable stipulation of pointless rules, it must explain the legitimacy conferring power of its recommended procedures in terms of some principles or ideals the procedures are purported to serve: increasing rationality, ensuring equality, allowing for autonomy, ensuring fairness, and so on. (The proceduralist theories of judicial review from the last chapter seem to adhere to this dictum.)

3. Democratic Worth of Political Institutions: Instrumental vs. Intrinsic

In addition to this difference over the correct model of democratic legitimacy, deliberative and aggregative theories of democracy also tend to differ over how to conceive of and explain of the *legitimacy* of democratic institutions. On traditional views, institutions such as elections, representative bodies, and party competition are justified as useful mechanisms for collecting preference information, aggregating these preferences, and efficiently choosing between various policy options.

---

[22] Consider one of the most comprehensive and ambitious theories of substantive legitimacy: Aquinas's natural law theory. It clearly recognizes, on the one hand, the perfection and immutability of substantive natural law principles and, on the other, the indeterminacy and mutability of applications of those principles to human reality. Hence, it recommends certain decision procedures, adherence to which confers legitimacy on the outcomes: for example, legal "dispensations" (deviations) from the letter of the law by authorized rulers, and, in general the claim that one of the three roots of legal justice is to be found in the criterion of establishment by a just authority. See specially Questions 94–97 of Saint Thomas Aquinas, *Summa Theologiae*, 60 vols., vol. 43 (New York: McGraw-Hill, 1964).

Whether the aggregative model is along the lines of Schumpeter's theory of competitive elitism in which expert politicians are seen as competing for support and then efficiently exchanging satisfying policies for the "money" of electoral votes,[23] or follows Dahl's corporative pluralism in which major social actors in the form of interest and pressure groups bargain through politicians and political parties for power over government policy making intended to satisfy their constituents,[24] market models see democratic institutions as instrumentally legitimate. Insofar as they achieve an efficient and more or less fair distribution of the benefits of government to all, they are to be recommended. When they don't work, so much the worse for democratic institutions.[25]

In contrast, deliberative theories tend to see central democratic institutions as intrinsically worthy, or at least as realizing some fundamental and thus nonnegotiable ideals, ideals that can only be realized through democratic institutions. So, for instance, the universality of the franchise is seen not merely as a more or less reliable means for information-gathering concerning preferences, but rather is conceived of as a requirement of treating each person as an equal and independent member of a consociation of citizens seeking to collectively rule their lives together. Likewise, bodies such as parliaments wouldn't be justified in terms of their functionality in determining the distribution and intensity of certain interests throughout the electorate but, rather, should be seen as places where essentially coercive policies can be justified – even to those who vote against them – precisely because those policies are based on the best publicly articulated and publicly acceptable reasons available after debate and discussion. Because deliberative conceptions of democracy treat all citizens as moral agents in terms of their reasoning capacities, such conceptions stress a unique legitimacy criterion: political decisions ought to, in some sense, arise out of and follow from the reasoned deliberations of free and equal citizens interested in solving collectively shared problems. Political institutions that serve this legitimacy criterion of reasons-responsiveness are then justified not merely instrumentally, but in terms of the fundamental ideals of political equality and autonomy that underwrite the legitimacy criterion. Such institutions are

---

[23] Joseph A. Schumpeter, *Capitalism, Socialism, and Democracy* (London: George Allen & Unwin, 1943).

[24] Dahl, *Democracy and Its Critics*.

[25] The instrumentalist orientation to the efficient distribution of the benefits of government holds true even for a minimalist defense of electoral democracy simply as a way of bloodlessly resolving conflicts, since this benefit of violence avoidance is to extend to all members of the body politic, except for that violent coercion by the state that is fairly authorized by voting: Adam Przeworski, "Minimalist Conception of Democracy: A Defense," in *Democracy's Value*, ed. Ian Shapiro and Hacker-Cordón Casiano (New York: Cambridge University Press, 1999).

not merely more or less fungible instrumental means to efficiency and functionality.

4. Accountability of Power: Populist vs. Expertocratic

Democratic theories of all stripes have tended to fall along a continuum with respect, finally, to who should have the decisive *power* to make collective decisions. Stylizing somewhat, we can say that at one extreme, populist theories of democracy insist that the greatest number of ordinary members of a society should have decisive power over most or all collective political decisions, usually on the theory that such expansive representation and participation is the best surety for policies and outcomes that treat all members fairly. At another extreme, expertocratic theories of democracy insist that only a handful of specially trained and prepared elites should have decisive power over most if not all collective political decisions, usually on the theory that only such limited access to power can ensure policies and outcomes that are the most rational and efficient even in the light of complexity and uncertainty.[26] Of course, most theories fall somewhere in between these two extreme types, attempting to combine both broad participation and high-quality decisions by experts. For instance, modern aggregative theories, recognizing both demands for universal suffrage and the scale and complexity of the modern nation state, tend to occupy a limited range between Dahl's more populist 'polyarchal' distribution of authority among various governmental organs and associational groups, and Schumpeter's more expertocratic concentration of basically plenary power in the elite winners of periodic elections.[27]

Deliberative theories also have mostly occupied a rather indistinct middle ground, though one often shading recognizably towards the expertocratic pole. In the famous section of the *Politics* in which the first

---

[26] My use of the terms "populist" and "expertocratic" throughout this book can thus be taken as shorthand for indicating two poles on a continuum measuring the responsiveness of governmental institutions and governmental actors, in their day-to-day decisions, to the inputs of citizens. In particular, my use of "populist" should not be confused with the ideological position labeled "populism" nor with a conception of direct, nonrepresentative democracy. Analogously, despite its pejorative ring, I intend "expertocratic" simply to denote one pole of the responsiveness continuum.

[27] For a frankly elitist defense of Schumpeter's expertocratic theory, yoked to a polemic against any forms of "idealism" in democratic theory – especially the idealizations contained in deliberative theories – see Richard A. Posner, *Law, Pragmatism, and Democracy* (Cambridge, MA: Harvard University Press, 2003), 130–212. For a defense of populist democracy as best realizable in the form of direct democracy through referenda, where democracy itself is justified as the best way to aggregate and most effectively fulfill the desires of the people under the principled constraint of political equality, see Michael Saward, *The Terms of Democracy* (Malden, MA: Blackwell, 1998), 1–120.

defense of democracy in terms of its deliberative advantages is found, Aristotle recommends an institutional division of labor that combines populism and aristocratic elitism: "Those with low property assessments and of whatever age participate in the assembly, and in deliberation and decision, whereas those with high property assessment are the treasurers and generals and hold the most important offices."[28] Contemporary theories of deliberative democracy likewise attempt to combine a focus on the quality of decision-making processes characteristic of expertocratic models with a focus on popular input and participation characteristic of populist models, without, however, succumbing to the potentially anti-egalitarian elitism of the former or the potentially ungrounded decisionism of the latter. It has remained, however, somewhat unclear in the literature exactly what kinds of institutional arrangements could actually approximately fulfill the twin legitimacy conditions of reasoned deliberation and popular participation.[29] Throughout, one can find more or less piecemeal recommendations for various institutional reforms that might promote wider and higher quality deliberation, recommendations, for instance, for strengthening the informal associations and organizations of civil society, for public ownership of mass media, for the diversification and dissemination of public spheres for exchanging opinions and knowledge, for citizen review boards with oversight powers on regulatory agencies, for deliberative polls and national deliberation day holidays, and so on.

At the level of normative theory as well, deliberative democracy has tended to follow the split between more populist and more expertocratic

---

[28] Aristotle, *Politics*, trans. Benjamin Jowett (New York: Random House, 1943), Book III, Chapter 12, 1282a27–32. It should be recalled that right after Aristotle canvases the argument for the epistemic advantages of deliberation by the many, even over deliberation by a few who are much greater in intellect and virtue (1288a40–1281b15), he puts forward a separate argument for democracy as a stability-enhancing inclusion of the otherwise disgruntled demos: "There is still a danger in allowing them to share the great offices of state, for their folly will lead them into error, and their dishonesty into crime. But there is a danger also in not letting them share, for a state in which many poor men are excluded from office will necessarily be full of enemies. The only way of escape is to assign them some deliberative and judicial functions," but no direct role in the great offices (1281b24–38).

[29] This is a judgment becoming more untrue over time because, as Simone Chambers puts it, "deliberative democratic theory has moved beyond the 'theoretical statement' stage and into the 'working theory' stage," Chambers, "Deliberative Democratic Theory," 307. Some of the theoretical issues that institutional design should attend to are addressed in Ferejohn, "Instituting Deliberative Democracy." Some significant institutional reform proposals include Joshua Cohen and Joel Rogers, *Associations and Democracy* (London: Verso, 1995); Fishkin, *Democracy and Deliberation*; Bruce Ackerman and James S. Fishkin, *Deliberation Day* (New Haven, CT: Yale University Press, 2004); and Ethan J. Leib, "Towards a Practice of Deliberative Democracy: A Proposal for a Popular Branch," *Rutgers Law Journal* 33 (2002).

tendencies found among aggregative theorists. Thus tendencies toward populism are often found in those theories influenced by more radical traditions focused on the critique of existing social relations.[30] Tendencies toward expertocracy are often evinced in theories influenced by sociological considerations of modern social and economic complexity and skepticism about society-wide capacities for public reasoning given distortions in the public sphere effected by state and corporate actors, general cognitive deficiencies in risk assessment, deep disagreements caused by cultural pluralism and ethnic and class-based heterogeneity, and so on.[31] Nevertheless, significant ambiguities persist concerning how to combine the egalitarian moral ideals fueling populism with the apparent sociological realism and the desire for high-quality political decisions that fuel expert elitism.

B.   CONSTITUTIONALISM: FOUR CENTRAL ELEMENTS

With this rough and provisional analysis of deliberative democracy in hand, I turn now to explicating four central elements that are part of the practices and institutions of "constitutionalism": the rule of law, a distinction between higher (entrenched) law and ordinary law, the establishment and arrangement of the institutions of government, and, the provision of individual rights. It should be stressed here that I am not proposing these four elements as a full account of the necessary and sufficient conditions of any conception of constitutionalism. Nor is this list intended to articulate the full panoply of arrangements, institutions, and legal relations that all actual constitutions may establish or strive to support. Some conceptions of constitutionalism will insist that certain essential elements are missing, or that one or more of the elements explicated here is not really part of constitutionalism. Rather, the point of the following is simply to point out four analytically distinct elements of the practice of constitutionalism that form important theoretical touchstones for the varying accounts of democratic constitutionalism supporting the theories of judicial review encountered in this book.[32]

---

[30] Barber, *Strong Democracy: Participatory Politics for a New Age*; John S. Dryzek, *Deliberative Democracy and Beyond: Liberals, Critics, Contestations* (New York: Oxford University Press, 2000); and Mansbridge, *Beyond Adversary Democracy*.

[31] Ackerman, *We the People: Foundations*; Bohman, *Public Deliberation: Pluralism, Complexity, and Democracy*; and Cass R. Sunstein, *One Case at a Time: Judicial Minimalism on the Supreme Court* (Cambridge, MA: Harvard University Press, 1999).

[32] My four basic elements may be usefully compared to the list of seven necessary and sufficient features of a constitution proposed by Joseph Raz, "On the Authority and Interpretation of Constitutions: Some Preliminaries," in *Constitutionalism: Philosophical Foundations*, ed. Larry Alexander (New York: Cambridge University Press, 1998). Although there is much overlap between the four elements I identify and Raz's list,

Of course, this is not merely a descriptive matter of "simply pointing out," for which elements of constitutionalism a theory emphasizes is closely tied to underlying normative conceptions of the legitimacy of state power and the legitimacy of law.[33] Thus, for instance, libertarians and liberals will often focus on constitutionalism as almost exclusively concerned with the assurance of individual rights against any political processes, and so they will, secondarily, also tend to tie the security of these rights to the higher law character of constitutions as deeply entrenching inviolable norms or values. Republicans and communitarians, by contrast, will typically focus on the ways in which constitutionalism should be grasped as structuring the common political power in a state apparatus for the purpose of realizing collective goods and common ends. In short, these elements of constitutionalism are neither merely analytic categories nor unalloyed descriptions but are, rather, part and parcel of the normative theories that support (or oppose) constitutionalism.

1. Rule of Law

The concept of the rule of law is perhaps best conceived of as composed not of one idea but of, rather, a complex of ideas, arising from a long history of various legal practices and experiences. Although there is, therefore, a fair amount of controversy about the specific import and role of the rule of law in political systems and in the structures of society, and especially about whether or how the rule of law is taken to be applicable in particular cases, there is nevertheless a fair amount of agreement on

---

there are three important differences. First, I do not insist, as Raz does, that constitutionalism need refer to a few canonical written documents: this unnecessarily excludes some evident constitutional democracies and overemphasizes how much work texts do, thereby slighting other institutions, practices, and understandings that are requisite to functioning constitutionalism. On this point, see David A. Strauss, "Constitutions, Written and Otherwise," *Law and Philosophy* 19, no. 4 (2000). Second, Raz's list does not explicitly contain requirements for the rule of law and the provision of rights, although both are strongly implied by several of the features he specifies. Third, Raz includes judicial review as one of the seven necessary features of any constitutional practice. Doing the same here would, in a strong sense, beg the question at issue in this book, not to mention rendering, by conceptual fiat, the evident constitutional democratic practices and structures of many current nation-states no longer "constitutional."

[33] Thus, I don't see how it would be possible to achieve what is claimed in Thomas C. Grey, "Constitutionalism: An Analytic Framework," in *Constitutionalism*, ed. J. Roland Pennock and John W. Chapman, *Nomos XX* (New York: New York University Press, 1979): the provision of "an analytic scheme – a vocabulary for the classification and comparison of different kinds of constitutions and constitutional practices. It is a pure exercise in formalism, not purporting to deal with substantive and normative problems" (190). A dubious methodological self-understanding aside, Grey's analytic scheme provides important and interesting insights into constitutionalism.

the basic contours of the concept.[34] To begin with, the rule of law is a normative concept, both setting standards for behavior and employable in the critical evaluation of particular performances. It requires, in some form or another, that state actions be controlled by legal rules, or at least rulelike legal norms and standards, rather than by the indiscriminate and unpredictable decisions of state officials operating in the absence of control by any preexisting legal standards.[35] This is, at any rate, one way of spelling out the classical notion of rule according to laws rather than according to persons: it prohibits arbitrary official action.

Traditionally the values tightly associated with the rule of law include stability, predictability, and systematic consistency: a good legal system, *qua* legal system, is to provide a reliable framework within which individuals and groups can plan, make decisions, and know their various legal obligations. But perhaps the most significant value of the rule of law comes when we remember that law is the medium through which the incidence of the state's use of its monopoly on coercive force is both implemented and controlled. This suggests that one of the central values of the rule of law is protection from arbitrary state rule.[36] This focus on

---

[34] I take it that my judgment here is largely congruent with the more complex and interesting meta-philosophical points made in Jeremy Waldron, "Is the Rule of Law an Essentially Contested Concept (in Florida)?," *Law and Philosophy* 21 (2002). I am, however, less convinced than he is that the concept of the rule of law is essentially contested at the *theoretical* level. In fact, what's remarkable is the relative lack of contestation at the theoretical level, especially for such an abstract, yet practical concept; see the discussion of the elements of the rule of law below. Perhaps there is an essential element of contestability when the abstractions are applied in the heat of political contests to particular concerns, but this seems not a special or distinctive feature of the concept of the rule of law but, rather, a general phenomenon to be witnessed when abstract practical concepts are operationalized in everyday social and political life. As Hobbes memorably puts the point, "I doubt not, but if it had been a thing contrary to any mans [sic] right of dominion, or to the interest of men that have dominion, *That the three Angles of a Triangle, should be equall to two Angles of a Square*; that doctrine should have been, if not disputed, yet by the burning of all books of Geometry, suppressed, as farre as he whom it concerned was able," Thomas Hobbes, *Leviathan*, ed. Richard Tuck, *Cambridge Texts in the History of Political Thought* (New York: Cambridge University Press, 1991), Chapter 11, 74.

[35] This notion of official action not subject to the rule of law might well be spelled out in terms of what Dworkin terms the strong sense of discretion, Dworkin, "The Model of Rules."

[36] In talking about the values that the rule of law is taken to serve, I hope not to take sides in the debates between natural law theorists such as Fuller and legal positivists such as Raz concerning whether the rule of law itself is ineluctably normative in a strong sense of embodying specific substantive moral values, or whether the worth of the rule of law is merely functional and so parasitic on whatever legally exogenous values or principles the law is employed to serve. For a clear discussion of this debate framed around a detailed discussion of the potential values served by Fuller's eight elements of the rule of law, see Andrei Marmor, "The Rule of Law and Its Limits," *Law and Philosophy* 23, no. 1 (2004). Marmor argues that the positivistic separation thesis between law and morality

protection from capricious state action would also go a far distance to explaining the way in which the rule of law realizes the other standard values associated with it. It is important for the law to be relatively stable so that individual subjects can have a fair inkling of what to expect by the way of sanction from the state with respect to their behavior and choices. And the same can be said for predictability: it is important not only because law provides a background structure to our life plans, contacts with others, and business strategies but also because it would be unfair to be liable to the state's power on the basis of unpredictable commands or the whim of various officials. Finally, the realization of the basic fairness required by legal stability and predictability would be impossible to achieve in the face of significant and numerous internal contradictions between the assortment of legal rules, norms, and standards.

The various elements and practices characteristic of the rule of law, like the values it is taken to support, are spelled out relatively consistently at a theoretical level. Lon Fuller provides a canonical formulation of what he calls the "internal morality of law": laws should be (1) rulelike, (2) publicly promulgated, (3) prospective rather than retroactive, (4) comprehensible, (5) systematically noncontradictory, (6) capable of being obeyed, (7) stable over a relatively long term, and (8) congruent in fact with the actual behavior of officials.[37] Aside from the clear summary of the conditions themselves, one of Fuller's crucial insights is that, because the eight

---

"is consistent with Fuller's basic insight that the rule of law, properly understood, promotes certain goods which we have reasons to value regardless of their purely functional merit" (43). A clear defense of Fuller's moralized conception of the rule of law against Raz's objections can be found in Coleen Murphy, "Lon Fuller and the Moral Value of the Rule of Law," *Law and Philosophy* 24, no. 3 (2005). Particularly intriguing is Murphy's argument that the rule of law requires a certain kind of reciprocity between individual subjects and government officials, and that it is precisely this reciprocity that entails certain forms of public accountability and thus forces unjust government action to be publicly owned as such: "The requirements of the rule of law set up conditions that ensure open and clear governance. When they respect the rule of law, then, government officials are forced to publicly endorse and implement unjust actions and immoral policies," 257. Thus, although the rule of law does not itself stop unjust government action, it forces it out in the open where it is less likely to be tolerated.

[37] Fuller, *The Morality of Law*, 33–94. Another remarkably similar list of the constitutive elements of the rule of law is presented in Joseph Raz, "The Rule of Law and Its Virtue," in *The Authority of Law: Essays on Law and Morality* (Oxford: Clarendon Press, 1979). More abstract summaries of the rule of law claim that one needs only two or three principles to characterize the rule of law. "First, there must be rules; second, those rules must be capable of being followed," Jane Radin, "Reconsidering the Rule of Law," *Boston University Law Review* 69 (1989): 785. "We may say that a legal system satisfies the requirements of the rule of law if its commands are general, knowable, and performable," William N. Eskridge, Jr. and John Ferejohn, "Politics, Interpretation, and the Rule of Law," in *The Rule of Law: Nomos XXXVI*, ed. Ian Shapiro (New York: New York University Press, 1994), 265.

elements may come into conflict with one another when we try collectively to realize them in actual practice, the extent to which an extant legal system achieves both the individual elements of the rule of law and the overall concept of legality in general is a matter of degree. In this sense, the rule of law is a regulative ideal: setting an internally complex standard for a legal system that is never fully realizable in actual practice.[38] Of course, the rule of law also may come into conflict with other values or principles we might want a political system to serve. Thus, considerations of commutative justice might be only realizable by sacrificing the bans on retroactive laws and laws unknowable to the citizenry,[39] or the desire for legislative popular sovereignty might lead to a sacrifice of the temporal stability and internal consistency of the legal code.[40]

What then is the relationship between the rule of law and constitutionalism? It seems clear that the rule of law is not simply equivalent to constitutionalism – it would certainly be possible to observe the rule of law in a society we would not want to consider constitutional in any modern sense. Nevertheless, the former concept is often doing the real work behind negative criticisms of certain laws, official actions, and legal decisions as "unconstitutional." And insofar as constitutions are considered binding law, they will need to live up to the "internal morality" of legality. It is important analytically, then, not to build too much normative content into the notion of the rule of law, for instance by inflating it into the defense of individual private autonomy rights or, more fulsomely yet, into the whole of the criteria governing the legitimacy of a democratic constitutional state.[41] Even if a constitution is conceived of exclusively on the model of the fundamental *law* of society, and so should instantiate certain formal demands for legality, the demands of the rule of law should not be confused with demands for the legal realization of various other political ideals and principles.[42]

---

[38] "The utopia of legality cannot be viewed as a situation in which each desideratum of the law's special morality is realized to perfection," Fuller, *The Morality of Law*, 45.

[39] The problem is memorably illustrated in Fuller's parable of the jurisprudential problem of the grudge informer: Ibid., 245–53.

[40] These and like scenarios seem to be behind the frequent stylizations of an ineliminable antithesis between democracy and constitutionalism. I return to this problem in Section C.

[41] Rosenfeld, for instance, after distinguishing thin and thick senses of the rule of law, argues that the rule of law alone – even in its various thick senses as embodied in American, British, French, and German traditions and practices of legality – is insufficient for legitimating constitutional democracies under modern conditions of social complexity and value pluralism: Michel Rosenfeld, "The Rule of Law and the Legitimacy of Constitutional Democracy," *Southern California Law Review* 74, no. 5 (2001).

[42] Castiglione claims that, on the liberal or libertarian conceptions of constitutionalism, "the real constitution of a society is considered to be neither the complex of its institutions nor the document establishing the form of the state and the structure of governance, but the

2. Higher vs. Ordinary Law, Entrenchment

Even if we were to focus exclusively on the legal character of a constitution, the rule of law alone would be insufficient to capture another central feature of constitutionalism. For there is a crucial sense in which, according to the constitutional conception, certain legal structures, procedures, and institutions need to be more entrenched – more protected from easy change – than others within the legal system. In this sense, a constitution is (to use two antithetical metaphors) fundamental or higher law with respect to ordinary law. This notion descends intellectually from the natural law tradition, where religiously revealed and theologically grounded law is understood as controlling the legitimacy of any laws declared or made by humans.[43] But, as a few centuries of constitutional experience have now made clear, the distinction between fundamental constitutional law and ordinary law is easily detachable from its historical roots. This is simply to say that a system of positive law can easily employ a distinction between fundamental and ordinary laws, whereby the former are constitutive of procedures for the valid enactment of the latter, without at the same time relying on an extralegal and extramundane source of normative standards or principles controlling the positive fundamental law. Whether this is a good thing, of course, is an entirely different question.

As I've already indicated, the notion of entrenchment is crucial to the higher/ordinary law distinction, and to the effective functioning of a constitutional system. There are any number of questions entrenchment raises, none of which I can answer here. First: how entrenched must provisions be in order to count as constitutional? Possible answers range from just barely more difficult to change than ordinary law, to impossible to change within the extant legal framework.[44] The actual degree of

---

legal system itself, whose central substantive concerns are the defence of traditional civil rights," Dario Castiglione, "The Political Theory of the Constitution," *Political Studies* XLIV (1996): 433.

[43] For an influential intellectual history of the natural law antecedents to the constitutional thought regnant at the time of the drafting and ratification of the United States Constitution, see Edward S. Corwin, *The "Higher Law" Background of American Constitutional Law* (Binghamton, NY: Cornell University Press, 1955 [1928]).

[44] In general I will employ the term "entrenchment" to refer to constitutional provisions that fall somewhere on this scale. Sometimes the word entrenchment is reserved for provisions that are impossible to change within the current constitutional regime – I prefer to reserve words such as "unchangeable" for the latter provisions. Examples are found in many constitutions. For example, the German Basic Law prohibits amendment with respect to the federalist division into Länder, the principles of legislative participation, and the principles underwriting the fundamental individual rights guaranteed in Articles 1 through 20 (see Article 79, Section 3). Less often noticed in debates about entrenchment in the United States is the fact that two provisions of the American constitution are explicitly excluded from control by the elaborate, supermajoritarian amendment procedures

entrenchment can often be detected by looking, in formal written constitutions at least, at any specified amendment procedures (though this
may not be a sufficient guide even with written constitutions). Judgments
concerning the proper degree of entrenchment obviously depend not
only on the various normative views one has of constitutionalism and its
relation to other political principles and practices but also on a host of
contextual specificities.[45]

Second: how is entrenchment to be secured? Answers to this question
open up a set of crucial questions concerning the different conceptions of
constitutionalism invoked. On one end of the continuum are theories
such as Dicey's account of the British constitution as the sedimented
results of particularistic judicial decisions and political practices. The idea
here is that the "constitution" of a country is largely a nonformalized
assemblage of legal and political habits and customs, composed of various
conventional legal and juridical practices, accepted and long-established
manners of structuring political institutions, diverse ordinary laws
establishing procedural rules for the enactment and incidence of other
laws, and so forth.[46] At the other end of the continuum are theories that

---

contained in Article V, subject rather to a unanimous consent standard. These two
provisions are thus virtually unchangeable: the allocation of exactly two Senators to each
state (Article V: "No State, without its Consent, shall be deprived of its equal suffrage in the
Senate"), and, the Constitution's protection of the slave trade for twenty years after
original ratification.

[45] For some of the issues relevant in the United States context, see the essays collected in
Sanford Levinson, ed., *Responding to Imperfection: The Theory and Practice of Constitutional
Amendment* (Princeton, NJ: Princeton University Press, 1995). Against skepticism about
the possibility of theoretical generalizations in this area, see Donald S. Lutz, "Toward a
Theory of Constitutional Amendment," in *Responding to Imperfection: The Theory and
Practice of Constitutional Amendment*, ed. Sanford Levinson (Princeton, NJ: Princeton
University Press, 1995). Lutz provides a fascinating attempt to systematically formulate
and test a set of empirical propositions about constitutional obduracy and amendment by
working up available American and cross-national comparative data.

[46] At points, Dicey overemphasizes judge-made common law as the sole source of the British
constitution: "such principles, moreover, as you can discover in the English constitution
are, like all maxims established by judicial legislation, mere generalizations drawn either
from the decisions or dicta of judges, or from statutes which, being passed to meet special
grievances, bear a close resemblance to judicial decisions, and are in effect judgments
pronounced by the High Court of Parliament." Dicey, *An Introduction to the Study of the
Law of the Constitution*, 197. But perhaps these are moments of rhetorical excess in the
service of his deeper argument that the British constitution is not the source of ordinary
law, but rather the consequence of the long-term use – by many political actors and
organs – of ordinary law. And even if Dicey's common-law view of constitutional rights was
accurate at one point in time, it is no longer adequate for grasping the structure of rights
in the United Kingdom today, given the various human rights statutes and treaties
enacted and endorsed by Parliament that have a higher-law status with respect to
ordinary statutory law. For an overview, see Vernon Bogdanor, "Constitutional Reform in
Britain: The Quiet Revolution," *Annual Review of Political Science* 8, no. 1 (2005).

focus exclusively on, and require, the canonical legal formulations found in a constitution written and enacted in order to function as fundamental law. Fundamental law in such a conception of constitutionalism can only be changed through the formal amendment procedures specified in the canonical constitutional text. Here, then, the entrenchment of higher law is secured only through those purely legal means provided in the constitutional code.[47]

Stylizing, we might call the first model of entrenchment the common law model and the second the civil code model. This stylization should not obscure the fact, however, that much of the actual effectiveness of constitutional entrenchment – on both models – depends not on strictly legal provisions and juridical pronouncements, but on the well-established practices and institutions that structure the state and the use of political power generally. The U.S. constitutional regime, for example, might be thought of as a mix of the civil-law and common-law models of entrenchment, as it contains both formal amendment procedures that have been periodically exercised, and methods of judicial amendment exercised through the power of reviewing legislative and executive actions for constitutionality.[48] Nevertheless, these two modes of "amendment" should not cause us to overlook the fact that significant features of the political structure are deeply entrenched, yet not the result of either "amendment" modality. For example, the two-party political system, the way in which electoral college electors are bound to candidates, various features of the split between military and civilian governance, the legislative initiative power of the president, and the fact that every individual state has "a republican form of government" are all entrenched features of the United States constitutional regime, yet they are not the result of strictly legal modes of entrenchment, that is, of either

---

[47] Although this idealized model of higher law entrenchment through pure legality is probably impossible to realize in practice – at the very least because laws only have their incidence through their use by officials – Dicey's richer model is at least descriptively much more accurate. There is then a real asymmetry between the empirical relevance of two poles of the continuum with respect to actual constitutional regimes.

[48] The hybridity of the U.S. constitutional regime is captured nicely by Strauss, "Constitutions, Written and Otherwise," 458: a dominant American "conception of constitutionalism ... [as] a practice based on a document that provides widely accepted resolutions of otherwise controversial issues – can now be seen as only part of the story, and probably not the most significant part. In practice, constitutionalism involves resort to principles that are only tenuously connected to the written document, that are the product of an evolutionary process rather than a discrete decision, and that do not provide widely accepted resolutions but simply provide a way to decide for now an issue that will remain controversial." It's worth noting, however, that Straus's conception is still quite judge-centered, ignoring nonjuridical sources of constitutionally entrenched arrangements.

the amendment process or of judicial review.[49] As political scientists employing the methods of "new historical institutionalism" repeatedly point out, "ultimately, neither the text nor judicial logic determines the social meaning of the fundamental law. Instead, it is institutional practice and its interpretation by people who matter."[50]

Third, who has the power to entrench constitutional arrangements? In the context of a democratic constitution, the legitimate authority for the original enactment of a constitution and its subsequent amendment is thought to be found in the power of the people as a whole. Thus, entrenchment can be thought of here as a way for the *constituent* legislative power of the people to control the *ordinary* legislative power that the people delegate to governmental officials.[51] According to this democratic version of constitutionalism, the higher law of the constitution is conceived of as the product of free and equal citizens structuring their legal and political interrelations in such a way that they do not need to continuously exercise their collective authority for self-legislation but can delegate such ordinary legislative processes to their representatives. The representatives are then controlled both by the constitutional

---

[49] The first three features are pointed out in Grey, "Constitutionalism: An Analytic Framework," 192; Grey, however, conflates the source of constitutional arrangements with the degree to which they are entrenched, claiming that the "extralegal norms" informing the constitutional regime in this case are more subject to change simply because they are extralegal; Dicey's more political scientific acuity would have helped here. The legislative initiative powers of the American president, and many other entrenched features are discussed in Dahl, *How Democratic Is the American Constitution?* Robert F. Nagel, "Interpretation and Importance in Constitutional Law: A Re-Assessment of Judicial Restraint," in *Liberal Democracy*, ed. J. Roland Pennock and John W. Chapman, *Nomos XXV* (New York: New York University Press, 1983), discusses insightfully the way that the constitutional requirement for a republican governmental form is a binding practice, but nevertheless not binding in the way in which those formal legal rules that lawyers and judges prefer are binding.

[50] John Brigham, "The Constitution of the Supreme Court," in *The Supreme Court in American Politics: New Institutionalist Interpretations*, ed. Howard Gillman and Cornell Clayton (Lawrence: University Press of Kansas, 1999), 26. For such "new institutionalist" approaches to the relationships between courts and politics in the United States context, see the papers in the former volume, as well as its companion: Cornell Clayton and Howard Gillman, eds., *Supreme Court Decision-Making: New Institutionalist Approaches* (Chicago: University of Chicago Press, 1999).

[51] The distinction between the constituent and ordinary legislative powers goes back at least to Locke: "The *Legislative cannot transfer the Power of Making Laws* to any other hands. For it being but a delegated Power from the People, they who have it, cannot pass it over to others. The People alone can appoint the Form of the Commonwealth, which is by Constituting the Legislative, and appointing in whose hands that shall be," John Locke, "The Second Treatise of Government," in *Two Treatises of Government*, ed. Peter Laslett (New York: Cambridge University Press, 1988), section 141, page 362. It has been influentially articulated and defended under the label of the "dualist" theory of democracy in Ackerman, *We the People: Foundations*.

provisions established by the people in the use of their constituent power, and by various formal and informal mechanisms (e.g., elections, public opinion, degrees of obedience, etc.) that maintain control over the ordinary legislative power exercised by their representatives.[52] Of course, this official and idealized account of the people as the agents of entrenchment fails to take account of the complexity of mechanisms available for constitutional development, prominent among which may be the initiative of a supreme judiciary that is not directly accountable through election. One of the central problems of this book may then be restated not as an institutional design issue – what are the proper powers of the various organs of a deliberative constitutional democracy? – but, rather, as a question of entrenchment – who has the legitimate authority in such a political regime to entrench constitutional provisions?

The most telling question with respect to the higher law/ordinary law distinction for the purposes of a normative theory of constitutionalism is: why should any type of law be entrenched in comparison with other types;

---

[52] The distinction between constituent and ordinary legislative powers should not be taken to imply a strictly dichotomous dualism of constitutional law and ordinary law. For there is no necessity for having only two hierarchically arranged levels of law, and in fact more levels are usually present in contemporary legal systems. Particularly important here – as emphasized in Martin Shapiro and Alec Stone Sweet, *On Law, Politics, and Judicialization* (New York: Oxford University Press, 2002), 136–42 – are sources of individual legal rights that function as higher law with respect to ordinary statutes but are not, strictly speaking, part of constitutional law. That is, they are neither explicit provisions of a written constitution nor adjudicative elaborations of such that operate effectively as constitutional law. In Europe, but also in the United States, such sources include statutes passed through normal legislative channels that nevertheless have controlling force over other ordinary statutes. For example, civil rights acts and administrative procedures acts may function as quasi-higher law in being a ground for judicial review of government actions. The European Convention of Human Rights is also an important source of rights with a higher-law status: although not invokable by individual citizens (because it is an international treaty between states), it nevertheless obliges nation-states to conform their statutes with its provisions. In the United Kingdom, courts have taken on a relatively active role in the "principled construction" of parliamentary statutes, and this traditional common-law source of statute-controlling rights has recently been supplemented by a parliamentary act ensuring human rights. As Shapiro and Sweet emphasize, attention to these intermediary forms of higher law is absolutely essential for comparative political scientists who wish to study the so-called constitutionalization of politics. Looking only at the work-product of European constitutional courts is insufficient if regular appellate and administrative courts are also involved in the application and interpretation of intermediary higher law. In the United States, by contrast, where the same federal appellate courts have authority to interpret both the constitution and ordinary statues, there is not as great a danger of loosing sight of such quasi-constitutional law. Some of the questions raised by the differences between the American and European modes of institutionalizing constitutional review are addressed in Chapter 8.

why have higher law at all?[53] I can only list some of the possible answers here. Theories that stress rule of law values such as stability, predictability, and consistency will see entrenchment mainly as a way of bringing a measure of hierarchical order to the complex system of individual laws and legal norms.[54] Also oriented to the functional values associated with legality are those conceptions that stress the so-called settlement function of constitutional law. Given both a polity's desire to solve certain social coordination problems and the fact that the members of the polity will often disagree about the proper nature and requirements of proposed solutions, a constitution plays the role of settling certain fundamental features of government. The benefits of such settlement are taken to be superior to an anarchic lack of settlement, even though the content of the agreed-on settlement may be suboptimal from the point of view of the distinct political moralities of the members.[55] Theories more attuned to the natural and rational law traditions will stress those substantive values they believe can be secured against the winds of political change only by deeply entrenching their guarantees in a body of controlling fundamental law.[56] Libertarians worried about the excesses of any exercise of state

---

[53] This normative question should be distinguished from the empirical question: what in fact explains why entrenched constitutions have been enacted or rejected? This latter question is the focus of political-scientific studies of constitutionalism; the usual claim here is that constitutions can be modeled as the outcome of bargaining and influence jockeying among a society's political elites and major interest groups, each looking to secure their own interests while hedging against future uncertainty promised by the vagaries of ordinary political processes: Tom Ginsburg, *Judicial Review in New Democracies: Constitutional Courts in Asian Cases* (New York: Cambridge University Press, 2003); Hirschl, *Towards Juristocracy*. Of course, the results of such empirical research can be used as the basis of normative critique: for instance of the inherent elitism of constitutional discourse, and the way in which focus on its technical problems distracts the populace from truly important political questions such as fundamental justice, equality, and a fair distribution of resources.

[54] See, for instance §§ 27–31 of Kelsen, *Introduction to the Problems of Legal Theory*, 55–75. Kelsen explicitly ties together a number of features in his conception of a constitution: the hierarchy of legal norms (a systematic set of higher law/lower law distinctions), the overall unity of a legal system, explicit entrenchment of higher law (at least minimally more difficult to change than lower law), and a definition of the constitution as the constitutive higher law for all lower law in the system. Even though for Kelsen, then, a constitution brings a measure of certainty to a legal system, there are inevitable indeterminacies in any system of law (see §§ 32–42, pages 77–89), implying that no legal system – as a system of general norms – is fully determinative and decisive in its concrete applications.

[55] Larry Alexander, "Introduction," in *Constitutionalism: Philosophical Foundations*, ed. Larry Alexander (New York: Cambridge University Press, 1998), and Larry Alexander, "The Constitution as Law," *Constitutional Commentary* 6 (1989).

[56] Bickel's and Choper's theories clearly subscribe to such a view. Dworkin's theory, discussed in Chapter 4, is a prominent representative: Dworkin, "Constitutionalism and Democracy."

power – as threatening both individual liberty and the economic benefits taken to follow ineluctably from such liberty – might look to entrenchment as one way of limiting the power of the state.[57] Those oriented to democratic values may see entrenchment as a way of protecting against well-known defects of direct democracy and forms of majoritarian aggregation in the formulation of ordinary law.[58] Along similar lines, some democrats might see constitutional entrenchment as a way for the people to collectively precommit themselves to certain decisions even in the face of future irrationality when deciding upon ordinary laws: "A constitution is Peter sober while the electorate is Peter drunk."[59] Finally, some committed to democracy might see constitutional entrenchment as a way of securing the necessary conditions for legitimate democratic decisions concerning both ordinary law and higher law itself.[60]

3. Political Structuration

Although the rule of law may be understood as a requirement of legal constitutions, and entrenchment might be considered the feature that distinguishes constitutional from other legal systems, focus on the specifically legal character of constitutionalism should not become one-sided. For this would obscure a third central element: a constitution is also the organization of state institutions, and the structuring of the ways in which they can and cannot use the various forms of power available to them.[61]

---

[57] Canonical here is the polemical Friedrich A. Hayek, *The Constitution of Liberty* (Chicago: University of Chicago Press, 1960). A balanced, historically based view of constitutionalism as a practice of limiting government power – specifically through the establishment of multiple centers of countervailing political power – is presented in Scott Gordon, *Controlling the State: Constitutionalism from Ancient Athens to Today* (Cambridge, MA: Harvard University Press, 1999).

[58] This is essentially Dahl's view.

[59] Stephen Holmes, *Passions and Constraint: On the Theory of Liberal Democracy* (Chicago: University of Chicago Press, 1995), 135. See also the discussion of Samuel Freeman's theory in Chapter 5.

[60] As I explain in Chapter 7, this is essentially Habermas's conception, and the one I endorse as "deliberative democratic constitutionalism." Nino, *The Constitution of Deliberative Democracy* seems to fit this basic pattern, as he sees actual adherence to a set of entrenched constitutional practices as a prerequisite for deliberative democracy. A significant difference is that, rather than conceiving of political equality and democratic deliberation as procedural requirements for the justification of only politically binding norms as Habermas does, for Nino democracy is essentially instrumentally justified as the only way of achieving objective knowledge about the correct formulation of political *and* moral norms.

[61] In many research domains, and from many different scholarly traditions, there is now a minor flood of work insisting that legalistic conceptions of constitutionalism are overly narrow and one-sided. As a quite partial list, the following is merely indicative: Andrew Arato, *Civil Society, Constitution, and Legitimacy* (Lanham, MD: Rowman & Littlefield, 2000);

This element of constitutionalism draws on the classical descriptive sense of constitution first clearly articulated in Aristotle's *Politics*,[62] and artfully updated in Dicey's account of the unwritten constitution of the United Kingdom:[63] that is, the "constitution" of a society refers to the basic arrangement of institutions for the formation and use of political power, and may also, more expansively refer to the arrangement of other major social institutions (economy, family, religion, etc.) and their interrelations with the political system.

Consider a conception that is now developing in political science and political theory, at least where constitutions are not dismissed out of hand "as idealistic and, as a consequence, insignificant ... as formal legal frameworks bearing little or no relation to the real workings of the political system."[64] Taking seriously "the political significance of constitutions," such newer research stresses both "how politics requires certain normative and social preconditions that constitutions strive, with varying degrees of success, to embody," and "how constitutions in their turn employ the resources of politics both to establish and sustain themselves."[65] The central analytic lens used here is a focus on constitutions as achieving

---

Sotirios A. Barber and Robert P. George, eds., *Constitutional Politics: Essays on Constitution Making, Maintenance, and Change* (Princeton, NJ: Princeton University Press, 2001); Bellamy, "The Political Form of the Constitution: The Separation of Powers, Rights and Representative Government", Castiglione, "The Political Theory of the Constitution", Simone Chambers, "Democracy, Popular Sovereignty, and Constitutional Legitimacy," *Constellations* 11, no. 2 (2004); John Ferejohn, Jack N. Rakove, and Jonathan Riley, "Editors' Introduction," in *Constitutional Culture and Democratic Rule*, ed. John Ferejohn, Jack N. Rakove, and Jonathan Riley (New York: Cambridge University Press, 2001); John E. Finn, "The Civic Constitution: Some Preliminaries," in *Constitutional Politics: Essays on Constitution Making, Maintenance, and Change*, ed. Sotirios A. Barber and Robert P. George (Princeton, NJ: Princeton University Press, 2001); Stephen M. Griffin, *American Constitutionalism: From Theory to Politics* (Princeton, NJ: Princeton University Press, 1996), Kramer, *The People Themselves*; Rosenfeld, "The Rule of Law and the Legitimacy of Constitutional Democracy", George Thomas, "Recovering the Political Constitution: The Madisonian Vision," *The Review of Politics* 66, no. 2 (2004); Tushnet, *Taking the Constitution Away from the Courts*, Neil Walker, "The Idea of Constitutional Pluralism," *The Modern Law Review* 65, no. 3 (2002); Keith E. Whittington, *Constitutional Construction: Divided Powers and Constitutional Meaning* (Cambridge, MA: Harvard University Press, 1999).

[62] "A constitution is the arrangement of magistracies in a city-state, especially of the highest of all. The government is everywhere sovereign in the city-state, and the constitution is in fact the government," Aristotle, *Politics*, III.6, 1278b10.

[63] "Constitutional law, as the term is used in England, appears to include all rules which directly or indirectly affect the distribution or the exercise of the sovereign power in the state," Dicey, *An Introduction to the Study of the Law of the Constitution*, 23.

[64] Richard Bellamy and Dario Castiglione, "Introduction: Constitutions and Politics," *Political Studies* XLIV (1996): 413.

[65] Ibid.: 413–14.

various forms of political structuration. Castiglione clearly formulates this political and institutional understanding of constitutionalism:

> In very broad terms, a constitution *constitutes* a political entity, establishes its fundamental *structure*, and defines the *limits* within which power can be exercised politically.... Constituting a polity is the act of giving origin to a political entity and sanctioning its nature and primary ends.... A constitution ... gives *form* to the institutions and procedures of governance ... of a political community.[66]

Of course, at least in modern practices of formalized constitutionalism, this structuring of political power is deliberately achieved through *legal* means. So the issue is not whether we must pay attention either to law or to political structures; rather, we must attend to both simultaneously, and in ways that can illuminate their intertwining. Thus, although constitutional law constitutes and thereby structures the exercise of political power, political processes at the same time are often responsible for major transformations in constitutional structure, import, and application.[67]

Aside from insisting on the element of political structuration for reasons of descriptive adequacy, this element is the centerpiece of normative theories of politics. After all, we are concerned to support, enact, and promote *good* constitutions, and in the mainstream of political theory this has meant some significant attention both to criteria of political legitimacy or value, and to institutional design proposals informed by such criteria. The evaluative question "why constitutionally structure power?" is relatively easy to answer at a general level. Given that a collectivity looks to solve certain collective action problems through political power, the basic values of good government are the effective realization of collectively shared political goals, and the efficient use of collective resources to that end. Any decent governmental form also will need to secure a more or less minimal series of prerequisites in order to achieve that: requisite levels of internal social peace, freedom from external force, governmental stability, the rule of law, and so on. But the constitutionalization of political power is aimed particularly at resisting pathologies of governance structures well known from historical experience that arise from the state's access to coercive means. Constitutionalism, in explicitly allocating various types of political authority to different offices and diversely organized formal and informal political institutions, seeks to prevent predictable abuses of power: for instance, tyranny, oppression, official self-dealing, other forms of corruption, abuse of the powerless, regressive or discriminatory distributions of the benefits of government, and so on.

---

[66] Castiglione, "The Political Theory of the Constitution," 421–22.
[67] Particularly good on this interconnection is Whittington, *Constitutional Construction: Divided Powers and Constitutional Meaning*.

Beyond these kinds of values that might be applicable to all government forms, and for which constitutionalism may promise a solution,
particular constitutions also may seek to incorporate other substantive
ideals and principles specific to one or other political concepts: liberty,
equality, fraternity, justice, rights, democracy, economic growth, and so
on. In other words, the explanation for the value of political structuration
will then depend on the particular conception of political morality
employed in the theory. The difficult questions here, then, are what are
the proper principles of political legitimacy or value, and, how can
institutional arrangements be designed to fulfill or foster those principles? Without these specific commitments, it is difficult to say further why
practices of constitutionalism, and particular institutional designs, should
or should not be recommended.

I would like to add one note here, however. Many analyses take the
political structuration element of constitutionalism to be essentially about
limits placed on government power, effected either through substantive
restrictions on the scope and content of laws and official actions, or,
through the separation or devolution of government powers.[68] Surely
both kinds of techniques are prominent features of many actual constitutions. But neither the mechanisms employed for limiting power nor
the notion of limits itself should be mistaken for constitutional political
structuration. This is simply because a constitution first and foremost
constitutes political power – and not just in an etymological sense. It may
be constituted in a certain way such that there are in fact structural, legal,
political, and other informal limits to that power, but the power is first
constituted as political power through a constitution itself. A government
is empowered by a constitution; without the positive constitution of
political power, and its allocation in and authorization of various institutions and offices in the first place, there would be no power to constrain.[69] In addition to this conceptual point, a focus on limits alone

---

[68] "Briefly, I take 'constitutionalism' to denote that the coercive power of the state is
constrained," Gordon, *Controlling the State: Constitutionalism from Ancient Athens to Today*, 5.

[69] The priority of constituting to limiting I am indicating here is conceptual. Obviously, it is
not true diachronically. In fact, most constitutions were forged and imposed on more or
less recalcitrant extant governments, often specifically with the aim of limiting previously
witnessed abuses. Those unconvinced by my conceptual considerations might be more
convinced by empirical and mathematical work that seems to point the same way. "We
think it important to stress that a constitution serves as much to create and empower
governmental institutions as to place limits on the actions of governmental officials.
Indeed, modern work in game theory and economics suggests that by placing limits on
official action, a constitution can actually increase, not diminish the capacities and powers
of governmental agencies. By restricting the ability of officials to renege on agreements, a
constitution may permit government to make credible commitments to repay its debts, to
maintain a stable money supply, and to make credible threats of retaliation," Ferejohn,
Rakove, and Riley, "Editors' Introduction," 24–5.

seems to me to overload the concept of political structuration with a specific normative account of governance and with an inchoate but nevertheless overly particular set of prudential judgments about the tendencies of government. To put it simply, talk of constitutions as essentially limiting usually relies surreptitiously on a context-specific pessimism about political power and a quasi-anarchist suspicion of the legitimacy of government *tout court*.

3. Rights: Private vs. Public Autonomy

The fourth central element of constitutionalism is the entrenched guarantee of fundamental rights. I say fundamental here to distinguish the rights important to constitutionalists from the garden-variety rights that are attendant on any and all cognizable legal claims where duties are imposed on certain parties. In contrast, fundamental rights are guaranteed to all citizens (and often to all subjects) of a political regime, independently of any particular legal relationship entered into by the rights-bearer, and function, in general, as pre-eminent legal entitlements with respect to other types of legal rights.[70] Thus, simply by virtue of membership in a politically defined group (as citizens, subjects, etc.), persons are entitled to have their fundamental rights protected against infringements both by other persons (including fictive legal persons like associations and corporations) and by the state itself. These rights are then preeminent with respect to other legal claims, and with respect to other social and political goals whose means of achievement might violate those rights.[71]

I've no ambition to survey the variety of theories of rights here; they are both well known and too diverse. It will help in the discussion of theories of judicial review, however, to recall two different sets of contrasts with respect to rights: the first concerning their justification and status, the second concerning the different kinds of rights. There are at least two quite divergent ways of conceiving of how those rights that are to be constitutionally secured should be justified, and so what their status is: the

---

[70] Whether and what kinds of priority relations obtain when two different fundamental rights come into conflict is a complex question addressed diversely by different theoretical accounts of fundamental rights.

[71] I mean with this notion of preeminence to indicate, in a theoretically noncommittal way, the Kantian idea that fundamental rights claims have a categorical normative force that, in cases of conflict, is superior to the mere hypothetical normative force of claims for the realization of values, goods, and benefits. This notion is captured in Dworkin's phrase "rights as trumps," Ronald Dworkin, *Taking Rights Seriously* (Cambridge, MA: Harvard University Press, 1978). What I am here calling preeminence should not, however, be confused with the notion that a right is absolute, according to which no other claims or reasons of any kind could ever outweigh or otherwise supersede the absolute right.

moral-objectivist versus the political-conventionalist conceptions. On the moral conception, rights are owed to persons simply as persons (or as members of an even broader class of rational willers, purposive agents, sentient creatures, etc.). Justified rights claims are then thought of as independent of the existence or effectiveness of any positive legal or political system. Hence this conception of rights might be called objectivistic: rights "exist" or "are true" independent of any artificially constructed form of social order and any extant legal or political system. They are justified in terms of pure moral reasons concerning what persons owe to each other, and so are objectively valid in the sense that they do not logically require any political or legal recognition.[72]

The political-constructivist conception of rights is often motivated by a suspicion about the strong metaphysical assumptions underpinning moral-objectivist accounts. Taking the legal model of garden-variety rights as paradigmatic, this conception assumes that there can be no fundamental rights outside of their positive recognition by some legal-political system, just as there can be no ordinary rights in the absence of an established regime of law that could both cognize and give them actual effect. Rights, of whatever sort, are then conventions specific to extant legal and political systems. Starting from a skeptical ontological argument then, such conceptions usually seek the justification of fundamental rights in terms of the normative requirements of political and legal consociation.[73] Constitutional rights then secure the necessary conditions for legitimate forms of legal society and political cooperation.[74]

---

[72] The modern natural law tradition furnishes the paradigm here, one made vivid by the thought experiment of the state of nature: if moral rights are justifiable in the state of nature, that is, in the absence of any overarching political authority with coercive power, then such prepolitical rights can said to be objectively valid and binding. An obvious example is the account of the state of nature in Chapter 2 of Locke, "The Second Treatise of Government."

[73] The modern social contract tradition again provides a clear exemplar in Hobbes's accounts of the state of nature and the status and justification of rights in Chapters 13 and 14 of Hobbes, *Leviathan*.

[74] Although the moral-objectivist conception is often associated with substantialist defenses of judicial review underwriting recommendations for its strong use to secure fundamental rights, and the political-constructivist conception is often associated with proceduralist accounts of judicial review underwriting recommendations for its limited use to secure the preconditions of politics, the automatic association should be resisted. The distinctions do appear to work well with respect to Bickel's and Choper's accounts in contrast to Ely's and Dahl's. Nevertheless, contemporary justifications for fundamental rights have become increasingly dubious of relying on moral realist presuppositions and so have adopted increasingly constructivist argumentative strategies. They need not thereby surrender the strong cognitivism of their justificatory claims, nor the claims that constitutionally-secured rights are ultimately grounded in prepolitical, prelegal moral rights. Congruently, substantialist defenses of judicial review need not conceive of rights objectivistically.

If we turn now to the different types of rights that might be guaranteed by a constitution, there are at least two main classes whose distinction has already played a role in the discussions of Chapter 2: individual rights that secure a domain of self-directed action free from the interference of others (including the government), versus individual rights that secure the equal opportunity to exercise the powers of citizenship through political participation. Whether stylized as the liberties of the moderns versus those of the ancients,[75] or as rights to private autonomy versus those to public autonomy,[76] the distinction is crucial with respect to theories of judicial review that are attuned to the values of democracy. For it seems relatively clear that, as Ely and Dahl argue, the apparent conflict between democratic accountability and strong judicial review of legislation is at least lessened (if not fully resolved) in those cases in which the rights enforced by an unaccountable judiciary are those procedurally required for accurate and legitimate processes of legislation in the first place, as opposed to cases in which the rights enforced are private liberty guarantees whose justification and conception is taken as exogenous to democratic political processes.

On either of the justificatory conceptions of rights, and including both private and public autonomy rights, it is relatively easy to answer the question "why constitutionalize rights?" Here the crucial notion is that insofar as fundamental rights are unqualifiedly owed to a polity's subjects – either qua moral rights bearers or qua members of the political community – they are well suited to be higher law, that is, to being entrenched for the relatively long-term, difficult-to-change through ordinary legislative processes, and so more or less secure against temporary coalitions and pluralities. Fundamental rights properly belong to fundamental law.

It is important at this point not to overemphasize the element of rights to the exclusion of the other elements of constitutionalism, especially of political structuration. There is a temptation in much liberal scholarship to conceive of constitutionalism only in terms of the protection of fundamental rights, effectively foreclosing access to the role of constitutions in structuring political institutions and, in democratic constitutions, to the structuring of the organs of representative government. As Bellamy points out, "Constitutionalism has come to mean nothing more than a system of

---

[75] Benjamin Constant, "The Liberty of the Ancients Compared with That of the Moderns," in *The Political Writings of Benjamin Constant*, ed. Biancamaria Fontana (New York: Cambridge University Press, 1988).

[76] This terminology, adopted by Habermas, is meant to clarify the distinction between rights necessary to individual self-rule (private autonomy) and collective self-rule (public autonomy) without conflating it with the classical continental distinction between subjective rights and objective law: Habermas, *Between Facts and Norms*, 84–104. For a simpler, more historically informed presentation, see also Appendix I: 463–90.

legally entrenched rights than can override, where necessary, the ordinary political process."[77] Ronald Dworkin's account is an admirably clear formulation of this kind of reduction of constitutionalism to the legal assurance of substantive individual rights – "By 'constitutionalism' I mean a system that establishes individual legal rights that the dominant legislature does not have the power to override or compromise" – and, as I will show in Chapter 4, leads to an argument for a strong form of judicial review of legislation to insure individuals' fundamental rights.[78]

It is also worth noting that not all defenders of fundamental rights believe that their preeminence automatically translates into an institutional design whereby the protection of rights is removed from the hands of legislatures. In fact, one will look in vain in Locke, one of the founders of modern fundamental rights theory who argued for the objective existence and preeminent moral justification of rights, to find an argument for the *constitutionalization* of such rights against legislative authority. What one finds, by contrast, is a claim that legislators ought to be bound by the demands of individual rights claims grounded in natural law, and an argument that the ultimate and only authority for enforcing such rights against legislative encroachments is, simply, the sovereign people exercising their justified right to dissolve the present government.[79]

---

[77] Bellamy, "The Political Form of the Constitution: The Separation of Powers, Rights and Representative Government," 436. Incidentally, this overwhelming focus on rights, and their judicial enforcement, can go a long way toward explaining the polemical context of scholarship going against that grain. Whether it is Dahl repeating again and again how many (political) rights guarantees are secured by democracies simply as democracies, or Amar's revisionist history of the U.S. Bill of Rights in terms of the structures needed for a republican form of government rather than for the security of prepolitical moral rights, or Whittington's study of important forms of constitutional development not performed by courts – Americans, at least, seem to need constant reminders against an overly narrow conception of constitutionalism in terms merely of the juridical guarantee of basic rights.

[78] Dworkin, "Constitutionalism and Democracy," 2. Not only does Dworkin reduce "constitutionalism" to the regime of individual legal rights that can be juridically enforced, he also at various points performs the same feat for the concepts of "democracy" and "the rule of law." I discuss his redefinition of democracy in the next chapter. With respect to the rule of law, see Dworkin, *A Matter of Principle*, 11–12.: The "rights conception of the rule of law … assumes that citizens have moral rights and duties with respect to one another, and political rights against the state as a whole. It insists that these moral and political rights be recognized in positive law, so that they may be enforced *upon the demand of individual citizens* through courts or other judicial institutions of the familiar type, as far as this is practicable. The rule of law on this conception is the ideal of rule by an accurate public conception of individual rights."

[79] See Locke, "The Second Treatise of Government," Chapter 11, for the rights-based limits on the legislative power and Chapters 18 and 19 for the justified right to rebellion. Jeremy Waldron is one of the few contemporary theorists who accepts both a strong fundamental rights-based criterion of political legitimacy and yet rejects their constitutionalization, defending instead a form of pure parliamentary sovereignty for the specification of fundamental rights. See Section B of Chapter 5 for further discussion.

In addition to the desire to entrench rights against encroachment given their importance, the other main reason to constitutionalize rights might be to have their incidence controlled outside of governmental organs directly controlled by electoral mechanisms; it may help to have rights enforced by panels independent of normal politics. And here, given the continuity of ordinary legal rights and fundamental rights as *legal* claims, it might be thought that an independent judiciary has the requisite technical competences for best handling fundamental rights claims as well. As we have seen already in Ely's argument, however, the situation is not so simple, as judicial review, at least as practiced in the United States, not only secures individual litigants from infringements of their fundamental rights against statutory and regulatory encroachments but also effectively nullifies the legal effect of the offending law (or its offending portion) for all future cases as well. In addition, American style judicial review goes further with respect to constitutional provisions, because specifying and concretizing the contours of quite abstract constitutional provisions becomes the functional equivalent of elaborating new fundamental rights provisions. In both ways, then, judicial review on the American model is not merely a practice of guaranteeing single litigants their constitutionally provided rights but also operates effectively as a practice of constitutional legislation. Legal competence alone seems then an insufficiently thin reed to defend such practices against democratic objections.

C.   CONSTITUTIONAL DEMOCRACY?

Democracy and constitutionalism represent two internally complex ideas, with various normative theories further deepening the conceptual density by prioritizing different conceptions and practices within each broad idea. When they are brought together into a concept of constitutional democracy, it seems that the combinatorial possibilities are virtually endless. I hope to be able to bring some order to this complexity in the following chapters by using the question concerning the institutionalization of constitutional review to elucidate the various competing conceptions of deliberative democracy, constitutionalism, and their interrelationships. Primarily, these chapters are intended to get straight about what the best positions and supporting arguments are with respect to debates over constitutional review. But there is a secondary aim as well: to refract some of the clarity back onto more abstract and theoretical debates about deliberative democracy and its connection to constitutionalism and, in so doing, provide further support for the deliberative democratic paradigm by showing its usefulness in analyzing concrete problems of political design.

Even within the conceptual territory mapped in this chapter, there are too many ways in which one might analyze the relation between the various axes of deliberative democratic theory and the elements of constitutionalism. So let me end on a simple note. There are basically three theoretical options for conceiving of the relationship between constitutionalism and democracy: they can be equivalent, antithetical, or mutually presuppositional. First, they can be seen as more or less synonymous, so that use of one of the terms necessarily implies all of the various principles, ideals, institutions, and practices involved with the other as well. Although this is often observed rhetorically, its not very helpful for theoretical clarification, and would be pretty hard to pull off if the map of the territory presented in this chapter is even remotely accurate.

Second, they can be seen as basically antithetical: constitutional concerns pull one way, democratic concerns pull the other. One might point here to the way in which democracy seems to require the in-principle political contestability of any policy decisions, while the rule of law seems to require, in contrast, a fair amount of legal stability over time. Constitutional concerns with the inviolability of individual rights might come into conflict with democratic concerns for the people as the ultimate legislative power. And so on, and on, with possibilities both obvious and subtle. Within the antithetical conception of the relationship, there are two options for normative political theory: one can prioritize either constitutionalism or democracy. In effect, all of the defenses of judicial review encountered in Chapter 2 employ this antithetical model, either seeing democracy as properly limited by the antithetical constraints of constitutionalism (Bickel, Choper, and, at points, Ely), or, setting democracy as the keystone value with constitutionalism merely a set of unfortunate institutional necessities for its best realization (Dahl, and Ely, most of the time). Among the theories of judicial review I analyze in Chapters 4 through 7, those put forward by Dworkin, Eisgruber, Perry, Rawls, and Waldron also employ this basically antithetic conception of the relationship. Partisans of constitutionalism prioritized over democracy will often have fewer worries about the antidemocratic character of a judicial institutionalization of constitutional review (Dworkin, Eisgruber, Perry, and Rawls), whereas partisans of democracy over constitutionalism will tend to be more skeptical about judicial review (Waldron and, at some points, Michelman).[80]

Third, the relationship can be conceived of as mutually presuppositional: according to this view, democracy in some important sense cannot

[80] In some ways, this can be seen as a continuation of long-running debates between political liberals and civic republicans concerning the priority of private and public autonomy. I hope, however, to bring a different set of concerns to the fore in the following, focusing not just on the priority of different sets of values but also on the relationships between conceptions of democratic legitimacy, democratic process, constitutional entrenchment, and so on.

be realized independently of constitutionalism, and constitutionalism likewise inevitably requires forms of popular participation in government. Here the idea is not that constitutionalism and democracy are, ultimately, the same thing, but rather that, in order for either of them to realize their internal political principles, the institutions and practices associated with each separately might be both jointly required and mutually reinforcing.[81] I take it that the accounts of judicial review put forward by Freeman and Habermas subscribe to such a view.[82] As will be seen however, their differing accounts depend on diverse understandings of the presuppositional relationship, and lead to quite different theories of judicial review.[83] Enough scene-setting, then; on with the arguments themselves.

---

[81] It's unclear whether the kind of analysis put forward, for example, by Preuß is of the synonymous or presuppositional variety: "Constitutionalism in the modern sense of the terms embodies the philosophical and juridical response to man's quest for political freedom. It encompasses the values, principles, reasoning, institutional devices and procedures which shape the idea of an institutional framework by which political freedom is secured," Ulrich K. Preuß, "Constitutionalism," in *Routledge Encyclopedia of Philosophy*, ed. Edward Craig (New York: Routledge, 1998), 618.

[82] The relationship of mutual presuppositions has also been stressed in Holmes, *Passions and Constraint: On the Theory of Liberal Democracy*, Nino, *The Constitution of Deliberative Democracy*, and Cass R. Sunstein, *Designing Democracy: What Constitutions Do* (New York: Oxford University Press, 2001).

[83] One more important theoretical option should be mentioned here. One might agree, as Michelman does, that constitutionalism and democracy presuppose one another, but argue that the combination of the two is inherently paradoxical because it leads to an infinite regress: the practice of democratic self-rule can only be legitimate if it is established through constitutional legal structures, but those constitutional structures themselves (in the absence of metaphysical moral foundationalism and in the face of reasonable, persistent disagreement) can only be legitimated through actual democratic means, but those latter democratic considerations of the constitutional structures would themselves have to be legitimately legally constituted, and so on. Frank I. Michelman, "Constitutional Authorship," in *Constitutionalism: Philosophical Foundations*, ed. Larry Alexander (New York: Cambridge University Press, 1998). Agreeing with the notion that democracy and constitutionalism are mutually presuppositional, Habermas responds to the infinite regress by claiming that constitutional democracy, as a practice unfolding over time, evinces the character of a self-reflexive learning process, where changes over time are understood to be (in the long run) developmentally directional. See his response to Michelman: Jürgen Habermas, "Constitutional Democracy: A Paradoxical Union of Contradictory Principles?," *Political Theory* 29, no. 6 (2001).

4

Deliberative Democracy and Substantive Constitutionalism

The procedural justifications for judicial review examined in Chapter 2 are attractive precisely because they do not rely on the superior insight of judges into matters of moral principle or truth.[1] They are thus not subject to the skepticism concerning judicial moral competence which, combined with an insistence on the democratic principle of popular sovereignty, led to worries about judicial paternalism in the first place. However, without some fuller account of democratic legitimacy, both Dahl's inattention to private autonomy rights and Ely's reliance on antitrust-style procedural legitimacy lead to liberal concerns about the security of nonpolitical, individual civil and social rights. In addition, Ely's purely Lockean account of democratic processes in terms of prepolitical preference aggregation and Dahl's more sophisticated account of majoritarian aggregation through pluralistic interest-group bargaining both ignore the inter-subjective deliberation about ends and responsiveness to public reasons that are ideally – and often actually – an effective part of democratic self-rule. In other words, from the perspective of deliberative democracy sketched in Chapter 3, the bare or pure procedural accounts of judicial review examined in Chapter 2 rely on insufficiently differentiated accounts of both democratic legitimacy and democratic processes.

---

[1] Skepticism toward the presupposition of special judicial insight into moral principles is nicely captured in Nino's phrase "epistemic elitism": "The common view that judges are better situated than parliaments and other elected officials for solving questions dealing with rights seems to arise from an epistemic elitism. It assumes that in order to arrive at correct moral conclusions, intellectual dexterity is more important than the capacity to represent vividly and to balance impartially the interests of all those affected by a decision. It is understandable that scholars who celebrate the marvels of judicial review should identify themselves more closely with judges than politicians and, thus, are inclined to think, as Michael Walzer remarks, that what they deem to be right solutions – their own – would be more readily obtained by judges than politicians," Nino, *The Constitution of Deliberative Democracy*, 189.

This chapter turns to two theories of judicial review that promise to remedy these lacunae by providing richer accounts of democratic deliberation and of the legitimacy conditions required for morally acceptable political outcomes. Although their respective insights begin to point the way to a satisfactory theory, I argue that because each is grounded in a substantive conception of legitimacy, they are each equally subject to Hand's objection to judicial review as unacceptably paternalistic, at least under conditions of irreducible pluralism.

A. KEEPERS OF THE SUBSTANTIVE FLAME OF AMERICAN
    EXCEPTIONALISM

1. Perry's Theory of Judicial Review

Like Ely and most jurisprudential theorists after him, Michael J. Perry starts his theory of judicial review with a recognition of the indeterminacy of constitutional provisions. But from there, Perry develops a defense of judicial review that is committed to the Rousseauian notion of deliberative forms of decision making and the Lockean notion of substantive moral constraints on the legitimacy of outcomes. Perry starts from the notion that political discourse is an attempt to come to a collective, ethical self-understanding about our moral and religious aspirations. In this process of becoming clear about who we are as Americans, the U.S. Constitution takes on the dual roles of a founding cornerstone of our identity, and of the guiding beacon that can lead us to a realization of deep moral truths. However, since the provisions of this identity-constitutive document are indeterminate with respect to their application to specific situations and with respect to the precise contours of their moral content, they need to be specified more completely.

Who should carry out such specifications? Perry's answer is unequivocal: a politically unaccountable judiciary. The members of the legislature are ill suited to carrying out the subtle discussions needed to discern the objective hierarchy of values in a truly dialogic manner, as their capacities for judgment are impaired by the ever-pressing task of getting reelected. "A [legislative] regime in which incumbency is (inevitably?) a fundamental value seems often ill suited, in a politically heterogeneous society like the United States, to a truly deliberative, dialogic specification of the indeterminate constitutional norms."[2] Since "specifications of indeterminate constitutional directives are a species of political-moral judgment [and] ... a dialogic capacity is an important element of the capacity for good judgment,"[3] we need a coterie of guardians of the moral truths of our society who can engage in subtle dialogical

---

[2] Perry, *The Constitution in the Courts: Law or Politics?*, 107.   [3] Ibid., 111.

interchanges with other judges. It is of paramount importance that they have been entrusted with these duties on the basis of their special capacities for good judgment, and that they be able to discuss, among themselves (through their written opinions) the reasons for their decisions.[4]

Thus, for example, Perry justifies judicial review in human rights cases on the basis of those objective values discovered in the history of the American process of moral self-development. Because legislators are beholden to conventional convictions and dogma through the electoral process, they "are not well suited to deal with such issues in a way that is faithful to the notion of moral evolution or, therefore, to our religious understanding of ourselves. Those institutions, when they finally confront such issues at all tend simply to rely on established moral conventions and to refuse to see in such issues occasions for moral reevaluation and possible moral growth."[5] In contrast, noninterpretive judicial review, particularly on such important issues as human rights, enables us "as a people, to keep faith with ... our religious understanding of ourselves as a people committed to struggle incessantly to see beyond, and then to live beyond, the imperfections of whatever happens at the moment to be the established moral convictions."[6] If there can be right answers to some moral questions, especially those concerning fundamental human rights – and there can be if we accept Perry's natural law theory of morality[7] – then "the politically insulated federal judiciary is more likely, when the human rights issue is a deeply controversial one, to move us in the direction of a right answer ... than is the political process left to its own devices, which tends to resolve such issues by reflexive, mechanical reference to

---

[4] As should be clear, Perry's account of judicial deliberation and decision is heavily indebted to Aristotle's account of the capacity of *phronesis*, even to the extent that both claim natural endowment inequalities amongst humans based on their comparative capacities for insight into the proper relation between moral universals and particulars. See the *Nicomachean Ethics* in Aristotle, *The Complete Works of Aristotle*, trans. Jonathan Barnes, 2 vols., *Bollingen Series* (Princeton, NJ: Princeton University Press, 1984), especially Book VI.

[5] Michael J. Perry, *The Constitution, the Courts, and Human Rights: An Inquiry into the Legitimacy of Constitutional Policymaking by the Judiciary* (New Haven, CT: Yale University Press, 1982), 100.

[6] Ibid., 101.

[7] These arguments are most clearly articulated in Michael J. Perry, *The Idea of Human Rights: Four Inquiries* (New York: Oxford University Press, 1998). In this short book, Perry argues that human rights can only be understood in religious terms, that, so understood, human rights are universally binding and context transcendent, and that human rights are grounded in "the very order of the world – the *normative* order of the world," 38. But note that all Perry needs to make the argument referred to here – the argument from the claim that there are right answers to fundamental value questions, to the justification of judicial review – is the claim to strong moral cognitivism, not any specific version of moral realism. In other words, his argument needs only the premise that, on fundamental questions of individual rights, there are right and wrong answers: Perry, *The Constitution, the Courts, and Human Rights*, especially 96–114.

established moral conventions."[8] The basic purpose and justification for the institution of *constitutional* review is then to serve as a beacon and indicator of the exceptional moral truths that were discovered at the start of our collective religious-political learning process; *judicial* review is further justified because of the superior capacities for moral discernment and dialogue that we can only expect to find in judges insulated from electoral pressures.

2. A Constricted Account of Public Reason

Although a number of criticisms might be raised against this justification for judicial review, I want to focus on two that arise from Perry's institutionally and ethically constricted account of the public use of practical reason. The first concerns his theory of political processes relevant to judicial review and the second his substantivist account of political legitimacy in Aristotelian terms. As should be clear, Perry's theory of judicially instituted constitutional review, in insisting that there are certain moral truths that any legitimate governmental directive has to respect, has been driven to recommending precisely the kind of judicial paternalism that Hand and Ely were both worried about. From his account of the legitimacy conditions of a constitution and his argument about the superior dialogical and moral capacities of the judiciary, Perry argues that noninterpretive review – review, that is, that depends on the discernment and specification of extraconstitutional moral content – should be entrusted to an unelected body of guardians who will enforce our own best moral interests even over our own objections as expressed through the legislature. However, the point of endorsing either an extremely restrained approach to adjudication, as Judge Hand recommends, or a proceduralist account of the role of the judiciary as a referee in the political marketplace as Ely does, is precisely to capture the ideal of popular sovereignty and its rejection of forms of political paternalism. If citizens are to be able to understand themselves as both free and equal under law, they must be able to understand the state's laws as laws they have given to themselves – not as laws that have been imposed on them by a wise council of tutors in moral truth.[9]

---

[8] Perry, *The Constitution, the Courts, and Human Rights*, 102.
[9] It is interesting to note that Perry's argument here shares with Rousseau the same combination of a neoclassical distrust in the original reflective capacities of the masses with a conception of political deliberation as reflection on a homogeneous, collectively practiced form of ethical life. In Rousseau, this theoretical combination results in those puzzling passages where he argues – contrary to his explicit principle of political legitimacy – that the polis will require some singular, original genius of a lawmaker in order to give the people the laws at first that they are later supposed to give to themselves. See Book II, Chapter 7, "Of the Lawgiver," Rousseau, "*Of the Social Contract*," 76–79.

The first objection to Perry's specific argument for noninterpretive judicial review is that it is driven in part by a false dichotomy concerning the location of political judgment: it must either be found in the legislature or the judiciary. But this overlooks those broader, uncentered public spheres and associational fora in which citizens discuss and debate, and form the opinions that are then (or ought to be then) fed into the formally organized channels of political organizations. The false dichotomy ignores, in other words, precisely those sites of political dialogue and judgment that theories of deliberative democracy have focused on. Even if we accept a substantive account of political legitimacy (although I think we should not), there are at least two potential further locales where there might be that kind of political judgment Perry believes is required for constitutional specification: namely, the executive branch and the broader nongovernmental public sphere. With regard to the executive, it is at least more accountable to the electorate than the judiciary, and so concerns about paternalistic review might favor some forms of executive review, although Perry doesn't consider such alternatives to the status quo. He also ignores the broader public as a potential source of contributions to constitutional dialogue and judgment.

I should note that Perry does explicitly recognize the paternalistic objection to the institutionalization of constitutional review in a politically unaccountable judiciary, and he specifically recommends two institutional reforms to the U.S. arrangements that would make judicial review "more responsive to 'We the people' now living, who, after all, unlike our dead political ancestors, are supposed to be politically sovereign": term rather than life appointments for federal judges,[10] and adoption of a mechanism akin to the Canadian 'notwithstanding clause' of Section 33 of the Canadian Charter of Rights and Freedoms.[11] The first would make the judiciary, especially the Supreme Court, more accountable to the

---

Perry's argument simply substitutes a paternalistic collective body – the judiciary – for a single father of the laws. One significant difference, of course, is that Rousseau believes that the masses will eventually develop the requisite reflective capacities through their enculturation within a free society, whereas Perry seems to have *a priori* reservations about the very possibility of an egalitarian distribution of moral capacities.

[10] Term appointments of members of constitutional tribunals, and appointment by legislatures rather than the executive, are common arrangements in European constitutional democracies. See Chapter 8, Section B1 for further discussion.

[11] See the arguments at Perry, *The Constitution in the Courts: Law or Politics?*, 196–201. The relevant clause of the Canadian Charter allows the legislative branch to pass a statute that would be in conflict with specific judicial decisions concerning the requirements of fundamental freedoms, legal rights, and equality rights (although not democratic rights and mobility rights). Such an exceptional act by the legislature in passing a law 'notwithstanding' judicial specifications of rights becomes inoperative after five years unless restated.

electorate through more frequent judicial appointments and their attendant confirmation hearings; the second would facilitate increased political and moral dialogue between the courts and other branches of government and would increase the power of nonjudicial branches concerning issues of constitutional fundamentals. "Were it adopted, the Canadian innovation would present the people – or the people's political representatives in the Congress and the White House – with more rather than fewer opportunities to exercise their constitutional and moral responsibility."[12] Perry argues that such an arrangement becomes compelling precisely when the crucial premise of superior judicial competence loses its cogency; that is when "we are skeptical *both* about the capacity of ordinary politics to specify constitutional indeterminacy *and* about the capacity of many of our judges and justices to do so."[13]

Yet, again, the comparative evaluation of capacities for moral discernment that Perry makes does not grapple with the possibility of citizens themselves exercising these powers in nongovernmental public fora, precisely the kind of fora one might look to when one centers an account of democracy on a Rousseauian account of procedures of public deliberation aiming to ensure true popular sovereignty. His rejection of the possibility of extragovernmental sources of moral judgment forces a false dichotomy in identifying the proper location of paternalistic guidance: the choice for Perry seems only between locating it in the legislature or the judiciary. For all of his insistence on the importance of dialogue and discussion on fundamental constitutional issues, this debate is to be institutionally restricted to those who can be expected to have the requisite ethical capacities of judgment: judges, law professors, and lawyers. Noting that the specific capacity for contextually sensitive moral and political judgment is possessed, for Perry, only by those who have a virtuous character,[14] one wonders what could be the empirical support for the claim he needs to vindicate that the judiciary houses such persons to a greater degree than the public at large? Once we expand the purview of those we might want to compare for their discernment capacities, the institutional argument that legislative debate is subject to distorting

---

[12] Ibid., 201.

[13] Ibid., 197. I return to this institutional proposal in Chapter 9, Section B; although I endorse the proposal, I do so not based on considerations of respective capacities for moral judgment as Perry does.

[14] See for instance his discussion of judgment and moral indeterminacy in Chapter 5 of ibid., especially 72–76. The virtue requirement for phronetic capacities is made clear in Perry's approving quotation on page 111 of A. Kronman: "'To possess good judgment ... is not merely to possess great learning or intelligence, but to be a person of a certain sort, to have a certain character, as well'" (citing A. Kronman, "Living in the Law," 54 University of Chicago Law Review 835, 837 [1987]).

pressures is alone insufficient to justify confidence in the judiciary's empirical claim to superior virtue and moral reasoning capacities.

This is related to the second problem with Perry's account: his account of dialogic, practical reasoning is ethically constricted, specifically to ethical-political explorations concerning the proper contours of the good life for *us*, given who we are in the light of our particular, constitutive moral and religious traditions. Like other neo-Aristotelian theories of practical reason, Perry's has tendencies towards a partialistic and potentially exclusionary perfectionism that does not sit well with the manifest ethical pluralism of contemporary societies. Since Hobbes, political theory has struggled to come to terms with the wars of religion and the increasing ethical pluralism of heterogeneous populations in modern nation-states and internationally. The prospect for justifying basic political institutions and decisions in terms of a substantive ethos specific to one or more systems of revealed religion is quite limited in contemporary pluralistic contexts. Whether one simply starts with the fact of a plurality of incompatible and warring comprehensive doctrines as Hobbes does,[15] or tries to explain the origins of pluralism as the outcome of the burdens of judgment facing reasonable and rational persons attempting to come to an understanding about how to live together in a free and open society as Rawls does,[16] hopes for agreement on some notion of a religiously based American exceptionalism seem quixotic at best. In fact, Perry's protestations that both the American political community at large and the judiciary *are* and *should be* pluralistic are reminiscent of the "religious tolerance" Rousseau calls for at the end of *The Social Contract*. As long as we all accept the "civil profession of faith" – after all, we shall be banished if we do not accept it, or killed if we renege on an earlier acceptance – then we should be "tolerant" of the different particular dogmas that interpret and specify that commonly accepted faith.[17] Perry's specific brand of constitutional originalism indicates that this communal faith need not be – and is not for Americans – a faith in one revealed religion and with a specific doctrinaire interpretation. Rather, it is a civil profession of faith in the original constitutional framers' insights into moral truth as refracted

---

[15] See especially chapters 11 ("Of the difference of Manners") and 12 ("Of Religion") of Hobbes, *Leviathan*.

[16] See Rawls, *Political Liberalism.*, especially xxiii–xxx, 36–38, and 54–58.

[17] See Book IV, Chapter 8 of Rousseau, *"Of the Social Contract,"* especially 149–51. Recall that the distinctly nonneutral dogmas of this civil profession should, for Rousseau, include: "the existence of the powerful, intelligent, beneficent, prescient, and provident Divinity, the life to come, the happiness of the just, the punishment of the wicked, the sanctity of the social Contract and the Laws; these are the positive dogmas. As for the negative dogmas, I restrict them to a single one; namely intolerance: it is a feature of the cult we have rejected," 150–51.

through the lens of various Protestant doctrines. Nevertheless, insofar as all citizens do not share this perfectionist vision of ethical-religious truth, any unaccountable body that decides substantive issues in accordance with that vision of truth will be even more disconnected from the practices of inclusive self-government precisely for relying upon it in justifying their decisions. Perry's ideal of the practical reasoning involved in constitutional review thus exacerbates, rather than solves, the democratic deficit of judicial review.[18]

In sum, the account of practical reason underlying Perry's justification of judicial review locates its exercise solely in those officials populating formal governmental bodies and presupposes a dedifferentiated picture of moral reason as a perfectionistic process of ethical-religious self-clarification. Although he is sensitive to the normative claims of popular sovereignty and deliberative politics, his theory of judicial review exacerbates its paternalist taint by combining a substantive account of political legitimacy with an account of political processes focused exclusively on formal governmental bodies and the elites that populate them.

B.   GUARDIANS OF THE MORAL LAW IN THE FORUM OF PRINCIPLE

1.   Dworkin's Theory of Judicial Review

Like Ely and Perry, Dworkin develops his theory of adjudication in response to the indeterminacy of constitutional provisions and the inadequacy of strict interpretivist responses to the problem. According to Dworkin, without some theoretical guidance, the crucial judicial decision concerning what level of generality to adopt in reading abstract, open-textured provisions that clearly contain moral content is left without an anchor. Of course judges must attend to the specific language of the provision, but, in addition, they must decide particular cases consistently with precedent and must uniformly apply a principle invoked in one case to other cases involving similar issues. Even so, these three counter-weights to arbitrary specification – that is, of text, precedent, and consistency – are jointly insufficient. In addition, a judge constrained by what

---

[18] Habermas makes much the same argument concerning Perry's ethically constricted notion of practical reason and its problems for a democratic understanding of judicial review: "Perry sees the constitutional judge in the role of a prophetic teacher, whose interpretations of the divine word of the Founding Fathers secures the continuity of a tradition that is constitutive of the community's life. … By assuming it should strive to realize substantive values pregiven in constitutional law, the constitutional court is transformed into an authoritarian agency," Habermas, *Between Facts and Norms*, 258.

Dworkin calls "integrity" must also be guided by moral principles.[19] In a sense, the "moral reading" of the United States Constitution that Dworkin favors follows from the very constraint of the text itself: the abstract clauses of, for instance, the Bill of Rights, "must be understood in the way that their language most naturally suggests: they refer to abstract moral principles and incorporate these by reference, as limits on government's power."[20] Part of a consistent moral reading of the Constitution, according to Dworkin, involves a distinction between principles protecting individual rights, understood as deontic trumps, and governmental policies intended to further the realization of particular goods or values. In contrast to Perry's theory, the constitution does not simply enshrine a particular constellation of ethical-religious values that must be weighed against each other and transitively ordered in each case by judges. Rather, individual rights have lexical priority in political arguments: they express principled considerations that cannot be simply weighed on the same level as various competing values, goods, policy goals, and the like.[21]

Even if we accept that the Constitution must be read morally, at least in part, and that this involves understanding rights deontologically, this does not yet guide the judge in deciding how to formulate these abstract moral principles and rights. At this point, Dworkin puts forward his preferred conception of democracy. This conception combines a hybrid theory of democratic processes drawing on both aggregation and deliberation, with a substantivist account of democratic legitimacy.

He begins by distinguishing two kinds of collective action: statistical and communal. "Collective action is statistical when what the group does is only a matter of some function, rough or specific, of what the individual members of the group do on their own, that is, with no sense of doing

---

[19] Ronald Dworkin, *Law's Empire* (Cambridge, MA: Harvard University Press, 1986) is dedicated to spelling out the adjudicative constraints involved in the comprehensive notion of legal integrity. Especially noteworthy here is the suggestion that judges think of their decisions as part of a chain novel written by many different authors, where each "chapter" (i.e., each decision backed by opinion) aims to make the best sense of the story (i.e., the developing legal system of a particular nation-state) as a whole. See especially Chapter 7, "Integrity in Law," in which he claims that a judicial decision must not only "fit" the ongoing practice of the law (and so be constrained by text, precedent, and consistency) but also must "justify" that practice as the best that it can be (and so be constrained by the best interpretation of relevant moral-political principles instantiated in that practice).

[20] Dworkin, *Freedom's Law*, 7.

[21] Dworkin, *Taking Rights Seriously*, develops the distinction between principles, policies, and legal rules (see Chapters 2 and 3, especially pages 22–31 and 71–79), and defends the conception of rights as deontic requirements of principle that trump considerations of policy (see especially Chapters 4 and 6).

something *as* a group."[22] "Collective action is communal, however, when it cannot be reduced just to some statistical function of individual action, when it presupposes a special, distinct, collective *agency*. It is a matter of individuals acting together in a way that merges their separate actions into a further, unified, act that is together *theirs*."[23] These action types clearly correspond to the distinction between the will of all and the general will: Lockean democracy through aggregation aims at statistical collective actions that satisfy the prepolitical preferences of individuals taken as individuals, whereas Rousseauian democracy through deliberation aims at communal collective actions that satisfy the requirements of the people acting together as citizens.[24]

Dworkin then argues that, if the communal conception of collective self-determination is the right characterization of democracy, then any adequate democratic regime must meet certain conditions. These conditions will then furnish substantive checks on the legitimacy of the outcomes of collective decisions. In particular, in order to treat each member of the collectivity as an equal moral member, each member must be afforded "a *part* in any collective decision, a *stake* in it, and *independence* from it."[25] Having a *part* in collective decisions means that each citizen must have an opportunity to influence those decisions in a way in that does not systematically discriminate against him or her on the basis of morally arbitrary qualities. This condition forms the justification for political procedures concerning voting and representation, and for the expressive and associational liberties required to actualize them. Having a *stake* in collective decisions means that the "community must express some bona fide conception of equal concern for the interests of all members, which means that political decisions that affect the distribution of wealth, benefits, and burdens must be consistent with equal concern for all."[26] This condition prohibits the community from disregarding, in their decisions, the differential impact that a proposed policy might have for the needs and interests of all of its members. It does not require that distributions be strictly egalitarian; rather it insists that the interests of all be fairly considered in setting up distributive arrangements.[27] Finally, the

---

[22] Dworkin, *Freedom's Law*, 19.   [23] Ibid., 20.
[24] Dworkin himself makes this connection explicit: "Rousseau's idea of government by general will is an example of a communal rather than a statistical conception of democracy. The statistical reading of government by the people is much more familiar in American political theory," ibid. I assume that this more familiar American political theory is an aggregative theory of democracy inspired by Locke.
[25] Ibid., 24.   [26] Ibid., 25.
[27] For Dworkin's preferred conception of distributive equality see his Ronald Dworkin, *Sovereign Virtue: The Theory and Practice of Equality* (Cambridge, MA: Harvard University Press, 2000). Note, however, that he believes that the specific *conception* of equality put forward in this book – one requiring a rather extensive redistribution of wealth from the

condition of *independence* sets limits upon the scope of collective powers over individuals' lives, commonly through individual liberties against state infringement on how citizens choose to realize their individual conceptions of the good life.

Dworkin's next move is to argue that democracy should be properly understood as a form of communal, not statistical, collective action. His basic idea is that all of the arguments for a purely statistical notion of democratic action presuppose the communal conception of collective action, and so presuppose that the conditions of moral membership in a collective venture have been satisfied.[28] Thus, the core of democratic self-government cannot be thought of as simply rule by a majority, as this is a statistical notion of collective action. Rather, majority rule must be structured so that it meets the principled conditions of communal collective action, and this is precisely the function of constitutional structures that set limits on how members of a political community may be treated. Dworkin's theory thus:

> *denies* that it is a defining goal of democracy that collective decisions always or normally be those that a majority or plurality of citizens would favor if fully informed and rational. It takes the defining aim of democracy to be a different one: that collective decisions be made by political institutions whose structure, composition, and practices treat all members of the community, as individuals, with equal concern and respect.[29]

In this way, Dworkin attempts to redefine the concept of democracy by splitting the notion of democratic political processes into two kinds along the lines of Locke and Rousseau – namely, statistical and communal – and insisting on a substantive account of constitutional legitimacy along Lockean, natural law lines.[30] His specific moral reading of

---

rich to the poor – is not a requirement of the United States Constitution, and so should not form the basis for American judicial review: Dworkin, *Freedom's Law*, 36. His point here about the requirement of "stake" is thus intended to express a more abstract requirement of the *concept* of equality in any adequate understanding of democracy.

[28] Dworkin considers, and rejects, three main types of arguments given to support a merely statistical conception of democratic processes: arguments from the values of collective political liberty, of political equality, and of community: Dworkin, *Freedom's Law*, 21–33.

[29] Ibid., 17, emphasis added.

[30] I use the adjective "Lockean" to modify natural law here to indicate that Dworkin's theory does not descend from Aristotle and Aquinas but, rather, insists, with Locke, that certain substantive moral tenets are binding on any and all actions, independently of any collective processes of deliberation or decision, and that these take the shape of rights held by individuals as trumps over collective actions. As he puts this point, "if the political principles embedded in the constitution are law ... in spite of the fact that they are not the product of deliberate social or political decision, then the fact that law can be, *in that sense, natural* argues for the constraint on majority power that a constitution imposes," Dworkin, *Taking Rights Seriously*, viii, emphasis added.

the constitution and his conception of democracy draws from the Rousseauian notion of collective action certain substantive conditions that can be applied to the outcomes of *any* political procedure in order to test for their legitimacy.

> Democracy means government subject to conditions – we might call these the "democratic" conditions – of equal status for all citizens. When majoritarian institutions provide and respect the democratic conditions, then the verdicts of these institutions should be accepted by everyone *for that reason*. But when they do not, or when their provision or respect is defective, there can be no objection, in the name of democracy, to procedures that protect and respect them better.[31]

For Dworkin, then, democracy properly understood is achieved whenever the substantive outcomes of a political process – *whatever* those processes happen to be and *however* they are institutionalized – are legitimate in light of the ideal of equal status for citizens. Another way to put this point is to say that Dworkin holds a purely instrumentalist conception of the worth of those institutions traditionally considered democratic: for instance, regular popular elections for representatives open to all citizens, legislative assemblies, various forms of direct and indirect accountability for administrative agencies, and so on all only earn a regime the title of "democratic" to the extent that they lead to the right results. Accordingly, there is no intrinsic *democratic* worth or value to such institutions: any democratic worth they might have is entirely derived from the moral worth of their substantive results.[32]

Given this singular redefinition of democracy, the question remains concerning its relation to the judicial review of legislation. Dworkin's answer is predictable: there should be a division of labor between those governmental bodies concerned with issues that are appropriate to statistical collective action and those concerned with ensuring the legitimacy conditions of communal collective action. Because the legitimacy conditions concern individual rights and fundamental moral principles, they should be handled by an independent judiciary that has the requisite competences, and lacks the distorting pressures of power blocs and private interests. Like Perry, Dworkin believes that legislatures cannot fill this role, as their debates are rarely of high quality with respect to fundamental moral principles, their decisions are often substantially influenced by power blocs, and they usually aim at compromises that undermine the deontic quality of principles. The institutional solution is

---

[31] Dworkin, *Freedom's Law*, 17, emphasis added.
[32] Once, of course, the equal status of all citizens is secured by whatever means best do so, Dworkin might ascribe some residual democratic worth to what we ordinarily refer to as democratic institutions for deciding nonfundamental conflicts of interest; see further discussion at the end of Section B2.

to entrust guardianship of the "democratic" conditions to an insulated "forum of principle" within which judges can draw on their special legal competence for integrating all of the relevant considerations needed for legitimate decisions.[33] According to the persuasive redefinition of democracy as *whatever* institutional arrangements best fulfill the legitimacy conditions of natural-law-like fundamental axioms concerning the equal moral status of individuals, judicial review does not compromise democracy; to the contrary, it enhances democracy. "Individual citizens can in fact exercise the moral responsibilities of citizenship better when final decisions involving constitutional values are removed from ordinary politics and assigned to courts, whose decisions are meant to turn on principle, not on the weight of numbers or the balance of political influence."[34]

To this defense of judicial review based on a skeptical portrayal of "ordinary politics" and a claim to special judicial competence, Dworkin adds an interesting empirical argument. His claim here is that, when an issue becomes an adjudicated constitutional issue, an issue of fundamental political morality, rather than simply a policy claim to be decided through bargaining and compromise, the quality of the public debate on that issue increases. "When a constitutional issue has been decided by the Supreme Court, and is important enough so that it can be expected to be elaborated, expanded, contracted, or even reversed, by future decisions, a sustained national debate begins, in newspapers and other media, in law schools and classrooms, in public meetings and around dinner tables."[35] This debate will be of much better quality than what could be produced through the legislative process on its own, and will have the participatory benefits of involving a larger percentage of the citizens in public deliberations sensitive to the complexity of the considerations involved.[36]

---

[33] Dworkin inherits this distinction between the legislature as the forum of policy and the judiciary as the forum of principle from Bickel, *The Least Dangerous Branch*. Bickel, of course, was much less concerned to reconcile any tensions between constitutionalism and democracy given his libertarian conception of the former and his pluralist conception of the latter. Thus Bickel simply equates the countermajoritarian character of judicial review with its counterdemocratic character: see Chapter 2.

[34] Dworkin, *Freedom's Law*, 344. This argument from the necessary conditions of democracy to the justification of judicial review was first presented *in nuce* in Dworkin, "Constitutionalism and Democracy."

[35] Dworkin, *Freedom's Law*, 345.

[36] Dworkin cites the debate over abortion after the *Roe v. Wade* decision as an example: "the public discussion of [abortion] in America has involved many more people, and has been more successful at identifying the complex variety of moral and ethical issues involved, than in other countries where a political compromise was engineered. In France, for example ... ," ibid.

2. Institutional Design and Moral Competences

As a historical counterfactual, the claim that the quality of particular public debates were improved by the intervention of judicial review is difficult to evaluate. Jeremy Waldron suggests that the quality of debate over a controversial issue such as abortion has in fact been of equally high caliber in countries such as Britain and New Zealand where statutes are not reviewed by a judiciary for constitutionality. He then suggests why this might be so: "It is sometimes liberating to be able to discuss issues like abortion directly, on the principles that ought to be engaged, rather than having to scramble around constructing those principles out of the scraps of some sacred text, in a tendentious exercise of constitutional calligraphy."[37] But even if Dworkin's empirical claim were correct, it's not clear that the argument in fact supports *judicial* review. Rather, it would certainly lend weight to some institutionalized form of *constitutional* review, but this could take place in the legislature, in the executive, in an independent constitutional court, and so on. In other words, it leaves open the possibility that constitutional review could be carried out by a governmental body that was more accountable to citizens than the U.S. Supreme Court is.

In order to justify placing the function of constitutional review in a politically unaccountable judiciary, Dworkin needs the additional claim of a special judicial competence that outstrips that of ordinary citizens when it comes to constitutional issues. His books, such as *Taking Rights Seriously* and *Law's Empire*, can be read as sustained attempts to vindicate this claim. The portrayal of the tasks of adjudication as, literally, Herculean

---

[37] Waldron, *Law and Disagreement*, 290. Not only does the constitutionalization of a controversial issue sometimes constrain the terms and arguments that may be employed in broad public debates, but it also may lead to significantly degraded legislative debate on an issue. For instance, during a Kentucky congressional debate concerning possible enactment of a law prohibiting nude dancing, one legislator *opposed* to the measure actually voted *for* it, and was reported to have given this explanation for the vote: the legislator "said the bill is clearly unconstitutional, and ... voted for it only so it can be struck down in the courts if it becomes law," John Cheeves, "Committee OKs Ban on Nude Club Dancing," *Lexington Herald-Leader*, February 11, 2000. One further observation concerning abortion decisions in comparative contexts is worth noting: legislative resolution of hotly contested issues, as compared with judicial resolutions, may have the effect of stabilizing social acceptance once a decision is made, especially for those on the losing side. Broad discussions preceding legislative decision processes "may have a pacifying effect. Experience in France provides an illustration. After intense debates in both chambers, a statute authorizing abortion subject to certain conditions was promulgated in 1975. It carried liberalization less far than the American Supreme Court had done. However, the American decision produced irreducible and sometimes violent opposition (under the battle cry 'pro-life'), whereas, in France, passions seemed to simmer down after the statute had been adopted. This is striking in a country like France, with a Catholic past," Koopmans, *Courts and Political Institutions*, 92.

certainly lends credibility to the notion that only judges can carry out the complex tasks of ensuring sensitivity to the often technical language of statutes, the consistency of principle application across disparate cases, the coherence of various historical precedents, and so on. But all this is, I think, somewhat misleading, as the issue here concerns – according to Dworkin's argument from the improvement of public debate – only whether an independent judiciary has a special competency in basic moral-political reasoning, and not a special competency in specifically legal consistency and integrity. Is it really true that only judges have the requisite competence to detect and interpret the basic moral principles that underlie the conditions we set on our collective political arrangements, and that this competence should be grounds for allowing them to not only set the basic terms and limits of subsequent debate but also to decide the issue for a significant period of time?

In a sense, the problem here is that Dworkin has tried to split the difference between Locke and Rousseau on the character of democratic processes. On the one hand, he has assigned the deliberative argument over constitutional essentials – the debate over the proper legal structure of the general will – to the judiciary (under the tutelage of moral philosophers). On the other, he has assigned the self-interested bargaining – the struggle of individual actors and social powers to secure their own interests – to the legislature.[38] This division of labor is only warranted, however, on a rather pessimistic characterization of citizens' capacities to engage in arguments over principles. The veracity of this pessimism, and Dworkin's faith in judicial competence, are indeed empirical matters. But it is worth asking whether judges are any less inclined to attempt to hide their own biases, ideological preferences, and interests behind a screen of principle and legalese than ordinary citizens in ordinary political dialogue.[39]

A committed substantialist might at this point be tempted to throw out Dworkin's attempts to persuasively redefine democracy in order to return to what seemed his original insight from the 1960s through the 1980s: because of the special characteristics of common-law style adjudication, judicial bodies are much more likely to get the right answers than other political bodies, whether the question is what the law is or what the law ought to be. Lawrence Sager gives at least an outline of what one such

---

[38] Recall that Bickel argues from this distinction to a justification for judicial review as "a principle-defining process that stands aside from [and above] the marketplace of expediency," Bickel, *The Least Dangerous Branch*, 69.

[39] The biases and distortions in judicial opinions and decisions have come under withering empirical scrutiny by both legal realists and critical legal theorists. I return to the question of whether the special *legal* discourse employed in judicial decisions is an appropriate idiom for public reasoning concerning controversial moral-political principles and their applications in Chapter 6.

argument might look like. If the question is simply what sorts of admittedly fallible political institutions "are able to do better or worse in the enterprise of making judgments about what rights we should all have,"[40] Sager's unambiguous answer is: courts using a common law adjudicative protocol are better than other political organs or actors. Three reasons are sketched for this epistemic superiority. First, unlike electorally accountable officials, judges are impartial toward various litigants since they are not tied to anyone's particular interests through elections. At the same time, because of their orientation toward coherent doctrinal development, courts achieve impartiality through their heightened attention to principles that must be generalized across cases. Second, courts exercising judicial review of legislation are like specialized "quality control inspectors"[41] in an auto assembly plant who exercise their power only after the product has been built and are only concerned with ensuring substantive justice, as opposed to accountable officials who are like mere line-workers in the assembly plant attending simultaneously to many different concerns beyond quality such as cheap and fast production and the superficial appearances of their product. Third, because common-law adjudication is both a collaborative enterprise spread out across various courts and through time and slowly develops doctrinal precedents through the adjudication of concrete cases and controversies, courts can better achieve a reflective equilibrium between particular applications and abstract legal norms.[42]

Although no empirical evidence is given for these frankly comparative claims, and no considerations are given to think that other political organs can't or don't achieve equally good or better results on these three dimensions, Sager at least provides the outlines of what a Dworkin-style defense of his claims for the heightened moral capacities of courts might look like. The problem is that, even sharpened up in this way, the argument only adds up to the claim that courts are better at getting the right answer with respect to *justice in the application* of constitutional principles, not with respect to determining the *justice of those constitutional principles* in the first place. Even assuming that Sager's arguments are true, they establish only that courts are better at the impartial application of already justified principles of justice to specific cases, are better quality controllers of the justice of legislation and regulation in the light of already justified principles of justice, and are better at achieving the reflective equilibrium necessary to develop doctrinal principles intended

---

[40] Lawrence G. Sager, *Justice in Plainclothes: A Theory of Constitutional Practice* (New Haven, CT: Yale University Press, 2004), 198.

[41] Ibid., 200.

[42] Sager names these three reasons twice in the book, without further argument: ibid., 73–75 and 199–202.

to operationalize in concrete cases already justified principles of justice. The same problem befalls Dworkin's claims that the Herculean tasks of adjudication warrant a claim to heightened judicial competence sufficient to authorize courts to determine the basic content of the abstract principles in the first place. Whether we are concerned with principles of justice, as Sager is, or principles of democratic consociation, as Dworkin is, the claim that must be supported is not that courts are better at applying justified principles in a coherent system of legal rules but rather that they are better product designers, better at identifying and justifying the content of those principles in the first place. Even if the empirical claims are true that support a division of labor between aggregative line workers (elected officials) and deliberative quality controllers (judicial officials), there is little here to think that functionally specialized quality controllers are better at identifying and justifying the standards for their work in the first place. In fact, if Dworkin's and Sager's arguments do establish the claim that courts are better moral reasoners in all ways – in correctly identifying, justifying, and applying principles – than any electorally accountable officials or bodies, then it is difficult to understand how both could endorse any form of constitutional construction, ratification, and amendment by electoral mechanisms in the first place. Surely if politically insulated common-law courts are better at getting the right answers on all registers of substantive correctness, then we should emphatically not endorse "popular constitutional decision making through the ratification of constitutional text"[43] nor say that "There seems only one way in which a society that aspires to be a democracy should decide what abstract rights or principles to declare in its constitution. It should do so by popular referendum."[44]

Besides these empirical questions concerning the character of democratic processes, there is a deeper, normative problem to which Dworkin's defense of judicial review leads: once again, the specter of judicial paternalism. In opting for a substantivist account of legitimacy, Dworkin has severed the internal connection between legal legitimacy and the procedural conditions of a law's genesis that Rousseau, and Kant following him, argued for. If fundamental moral principles are to be detected and specified by an independent judiciary, with guidance from preferred moral philosophers, then the principle of popular sovereignty is severely compromised. For popular sovereignty entails that citizens are only free in a form of political association if they can somehow understand themselves as the authors of the laws that structure their interactions, as both sovereign citizens and legal subjects at the same time. Dworkin seems to be saying, in effect, that the people are allowed to be sovereign with respect to policy decisions, but when it comes to principles and rights,

---

[43] Ibid., 163.   [44] Dworkin, "Constitutionalism and Democracy," 10.

they must simply submit to the paternalistic imposition of the "conditions of democracy" by an unaccountable Hercules. Under this division of labor, the moral competence of citizens does not and cannot extend to collective decisions concerning the fundamental conditions under which they are going to regulate their lives together.[45]

Of course, Dworkin does not suggest that legitimacy is *always* disconnected from procedurally correct enactment. He does, after all, endorse some ordinary democratic procedures with respect to some (policy) issues. In other words, his theory of democratic legitimacy is mixed in that it allows for some procedurally secured legitimacy, but with *ex ante* substantive constraints on outcomes. Thus the internal link between legal legitimacy and actual procedural genesis is only severed with respect to constitutional essentials: "matters of principle" in Dworkin's language. I am not suggesting that Dworkin is entirely deaf to the notion of popular sovereignty; only with respect to those issues of moral controversy and fundamental principle best left to judicial guardians of the moral law. Even if Dworkin prefers to retain the label of "democracy" only for those regimes that substantively guarantee the natural rights of equal respect and concern for citizens, something important has been lost when popular sovereignty does not extend to decisions concerning the very conditions under which we collectively act as a political community.

Another way to put this same point is to focus on what showing equal respect to each individual citizen *as* a moral member of the community means. For if there are in fact disagreements among citizens not only about values and policies, but also about how to determine and specify the

---

[45] A way of seeing this same problem, not from the point of view of political autonomy but from that of the moral autonomy of individual legal subjects is presented in Neil MacCormick, "The Relative Heteronomy of Law," *European Journal of Philosophy* 3, no. 1 (1995). MacCormick argues that moral autonomy, as a matter of the self-determination of one's own will according to reasoned considerations, is necessarily compromised to some extent by common and binding legal norms in the absence of moral agreement on the content of those norms. Accordingly, to the extent that individual judges' decisions rely on controversial moral premises as Dworkin recommends, they increase rather than decrease the heteronomous character of legal norms because they foreclose possibilities for the moral self-determination of individual subjects. "So far as there is room for impartial and institutional legal expertise, we rely on judges to have it. But when it comes to moral justification, there is no room for a claim to institutional expertise. At this level, the judge's reasoning convinces or fails to convince by the authority of its reasons, not by reason of its authority.... This in fact supports a more, rather than less, legalistic approach to decision-making in the sphere of the state. The more we take legal decision-making within state law to be a public matter drawing on public sources, the less we force agents into the position of having to knuckle under the decisions of particular judges and other legal officials as though they enjoyed some general moral authority. They do not. They enjoy technical-legal authority, and the institutional authority required for deciding particular cases conclusively," 83–84.

fundamental moral principles that are to structure their political interactions, then it seems perverse to shut citizens out of the debate over
those constitutional essentials. This notion of respecting fellow citizens is
central to the critical thrust of Jeremy Waldron's rights-based argument
against any form of judicial review of democratic legislation examined in
the next section. Of course, Dworkin does not wholly deny citizen input
into constitutional debates: citizens justifiably have the political process of
amendment open to them, and there is indirect representative control
over court appointments. Nevertheless, on the much more frequent – and
usually more contested – questions of how to *specify* the constitutional
provisions and amendments, treating citizens as autonomous moral
agents seems to require an institutional openness to citizen participation
and the full spectrum of information, reasons, and arguments that they
might think relevant to that task of specification. Effectively shutting them
out of those debates requires the presumption that judges know better
than citizens do themselves how to live their lives as free and autonomous
citizens in a form of political association under law.

C.   ARE SUBSTANTIALIST DEFENSES OF JUDICIAL REVIEW SELF-DEFEATING?

Although I've only examined four theories of judicial review that rely on
the premises of substantialist constitutionalism (via Bickel, Choper, Perry,
and Dworkin), it should be clear by now that all seem to face one common
objection to their theories (among other noncommon objections). They
each invite charges of judicial paternalism precisely where they overlook
the conditions of modern pluralism. Rather than simply making an
inductive inference from four instructive negative examples, Chapter 5
will examine a formal argument put forward by Waldron from the persistence of good-faith moral disagreement in modern societies – that is,
from the fact of reasonable pluralism – to the conclusion that judicial
review *always* results in undemocratic paternalism. Before ending this
chapter, however, I would like to examine a different argument against
judicial review Waldron has repeatedly advanced.[46] For, if successful, this
interesting *rights-based* objection to the judicial review of legislation in the
name of *protecting* individual rights would present a significant internal
critique of the kinds of substantialist arguments put forward by Bickel,

---

[46] See Jeremy Waldron, "A Right-Based Critique of Constitutional Rights," *Oxford Journal of
Legal Studies* 13 (1993), all of which appears to be incorporated in various chapters of
Waldron, *Law and Disagreement*. Both Thomas Christiano, "Waldron on Law and
Disagreement," *Law and Philosophy* 19, no. 4 (2000), and Cécile Fabre, "A Philosophical
Argument for a Bill of Rights," *British Journal of Political Science* 30 (2000), helpfully and
clearly distinguish between these two different forms of argument in Waldron.

Choper, Dworkin, and Perry; a critique, namely, that they are essentially self-defeating.

1. Waldron's Rights-Based Argument against a Bill of Rights

Waldron's argument begins from a supposition about the combination of attitudes adopted by those who would argue for a constitutional entrenchment of individual rights intended to constrain the actions of a democratically accountable representative legislature. Such persons must believe that they have singularly accurate insight into what is a matter of fundamental right and what isn't, and have sufficient self-confidence that they can translate these insights concerning the nature of fundamental rights into the correct legal language that would adequately protect those rights. Of course, because they want those rights entrenched against future potential legislative majorities, and legislators are to be thought of as representing the views of citizens, this attitude of self-confidence in their own understanding of rights must also be combined with an attitude of distrust toward the like capacities for moral and legal insight on the part of their fellow current and future consociates.

The problem as Waldron sees it is that this combination of attitudes of self-confidence and mistrust of others is fundamentally incompatible with the other-regarding attitudes one would need to have in order to think that protecting the equal rights of others is worthwhile. If one really has a deep enough mistrust toward the malfeasance of other citizens, deep enough to motivate a desire for constitutionalization in order to protect those rights, then its difficult to understand why one would think other citizens worthy of rights in the first place. After all, "the attribution of rights to individuals is an act of faith in the agency and capacity for moral thinking of each of those individuals."[47] In addition, the self-confidence underlying one's own assessment that certain rights formulations should be constitutionally protected is incompatible with the *equal* attribution of such capacities for autonomous agency and moral thinking to one's fellow citizens. Finally, a rights-based theorist ought to believe not only that people have the capacity for the responsible exercise of their own rights but also that they have the primary claim to determining the correct limits to those rights, given their responsible reasoning powers. "Theorists of rights, then, are committed to the assumption that those to whom rights are assigned are *normally* those to whom decisions about the extent of rights can be entrusted."[48] Therefore, the attribution of moral rights to others is incompatible with the attitudes toward one's fellow citizens underlying the thought that such rights should be specially protected from democratic procedures.

---

[47] Waldron, *Law and Disagreement*, 222.   [48] Ibid., 223.

Waldron explicitly couches this argument at the level of attitudinal attributions, and so it might be seen as a sort of invalid *ad hominem* argument against defenders of the constitutional protection of rights. But it can, without significant loss, be couched in theoretical terms: a claim that the equal moral rights of each citizen ought to be legally protected against democratically enacted infringements presupposes both that individuals are sufficiently worthy of rights, and that individuals are not sufficiently worthy of rights.[49] If it is true that such claims are self-defeating, then it would strike at the heart of substantialist defenses of judicial review, for they almost always suggest that judicial review of legislation is justified by its superior results in protecting individual rights, and they take the protection of rights to be intrinsically justifiable, that is, as criterial in one way or another for political legitimacy.[50] In essence, Waldron's argument dares such theories to take their commitments to the equal moral autonomy of citizens seriously.

2. Limitations of Waldron's Argument

My sense, however, is that there is less to this argument than at first appears. To begin with, the claim that persons are sufficiently autonomous and responsible to merit the attribution of rights does not entail the claim that we should thereby fully trust their actual exercise and specification of those rights.[51] Or, if it does entail this, then we seem to have a pretty quick and easy moralistic argument in favor of political anarchism: the attribution of moral rights presupposes an attribution of autonomy to

[49] See, for instance, the clear outline of the argument at Christiano, "Waldron on Law and Disagreement," 534.

[50] What distinguishes the substantialist views can be seen as a question of how they attempt to justify the rights as fundamental. Traditional views of what I called in Chapter 2 'minoritarian constitutionalism' such as Bickel's or Choper's simply take individual rights to be justified independently – perhaps in natural law or in right reason or in religious revelation – of any concerns about political legitimacy or authority, and so of any concerns about democracy. The originality of Dworkin's view is that he attempts to show how democracy itself, properly understood, includes such rights as constitutive conditions. Additionally, substantialist theories of judicial review need not in principle be based in individual rights. One could, for instance, claim that judicial review was justified through its results in making citizens more virtuous or improving their own good (against their own democratically expressed wills ostensibly). But in that case, one seems to promote an explicitly and distinctly paternalistic theory of judicial review, one that would fully merit Dahl's label of a political theory of guardianship – without any pretense concerning the prefix "quasi-."

[51] I draw here on Fabre, "A Philosophical Argument for a Bill of Rights," 91 – "saying that people are worthy of respect, and therefore have rights, does not entail that they will always respect other people's rights" – but it should be insisted that the point is not just about individuals' actions vis-à-vis the rights of others, but about their legal specification of the scope and limits of others' rights as well.

persons, any attempt to legally coerce individuals to act against their will contradicts that attribution of autonomy, therefore any forms of coercion, and any state formation employing coercive means, in the name of protecting autonomy are self-defeating! Surely it is part of the "circumstances of politics"[52] – however envisioned or explained – that some forms of moderate diffidence towards the actions of our fellow citizens are warranted, at the least by empirical experience.[53] But this means, as Christiano nicely puts it, we "accept legal restrictions on what people do because we do not fully trust people to act out of respect for other's liberal rights. ... The fact is that a system of legal rights is grounded in a kind of balance between trust and distrust of the individual bearers of the rights."[54]

Equally important, the overly personalized approach to the issue of rights and limits on democracy Waldron pursues with this argument – asserting that complex questions of the proper institutional design and implementation of modern government can be helpfully reduced to a simple question about the consistency of moral attitudes we take to our fellow citizens on a more or less one-on-one basis – effaces any theoretical sensitivity to questions about the structural differences between citizens individually and citizens in groups, between citizen opinion and its collection and representation in polls, in the mass media, and in broad public arenas, between citizens and their elected legislative representatives, between various groups and bodies of legislators themselves, between legislatures and private interest groups, lobbyists, and various forms of associations, between other branches of government and the legislature, and so on and so on.

For example, Waldron's morally aprioristic argument seems to assume that majoritarian, multimember representative legislatures more or less directly translate into statute law the preponderance of their constituents' fully reflective, good-faith opinions concerning the nature and importance of various rights and their most effective and accurate legal

---

[52] Waldron, *Law and Disagreement*, 101–03 introduces the phrase to refer to the need for a common framework of action coordination, combined with the fact of persistent disagreement about what that framework should consist in.

[53] Recall, for instance, the strikingly allied characterizations given by Hume on the ineliminable fact of moderate diffidence between persons that makes justice useful, and Kant on the "unsociable sociability" that both threatens and makes possible political cooperation. See Hume's claim that humans exhibit towards others neither "perfect moderation and humanity" nor "perfect rapaciousness and malice," David Hume, "An Enquiry Concerning the Principles of Morals," in *Enquiries Concerning Human Understanding and Concerning the Principles of Human Morals*, ed. P.H. Nidditch (New York: Clarendon Press, 1975), Section I, Part I, 188, and the fourth proposition of Immanuel Kant, "Idea for a Universal History with a Cosmopolitan Purpose," in *Kant's Political Writings*, ed. Hans Reiss (New York: Cambridge University Press, 1980).

[54] Christiano, "Waldron on Law and Disagreement," 536.

realizations. Without this (rather unrealistic) assumption however, it would be quite hard to make the easy elision Waldron does between "those to whom rights are assigned" and "those to whom decisions about the extent of rights can be entrusted."[55] It may well be correct to say that "it simply will not do for theorists of rights to talk about us as upright and responsible autonomous individuals when they are characterizing our need for protection against majorities, while describing the members of the majorities against whose tyranny such protection is necessary as irresponsible Hobbesian predators."[56] But surely this kind of attitudinal explanation for the need to protect individual and/or minority rights is not the only kind of explanation one could plausibly put forward for rights-infringing legislation. To attend only to such personalistic and attitudinal explanations would be to presuppose no substantial structural differences between the legislative outputs of a small group of face-to-face moral co-reasoners concerning some difficult problem of self-legislation and the "self-government" instantiated in large, complex contemporary nation-states. Just to take an obvious alternative explanation, substantial differences in the effective capacity of differently situated social groups to have their voices heard and opinions understood in formal parliamentary or congressional processes often lead to statute law that cannot be fairly considered as the result of a collection of the preponderance of opinion amongst the full citizenry concerning the proper scope and limits of rights.[57] And the structure of electoral accountability in legislatures itself, as Ely emphasizes in his expansion on the famous footnote four of *Carolene Products*, can lead to legislative results that infringe on the very rights of democratic participation that are essential to the fully inclusive, good-faith discussion and disagreement on rights that Waldron idealizes as democratic politics.[58] What we "distrust" in these cases are neither the motivations of our fellow citizens, nor their deficient reasoning capacities but, rather, certain rather predictable and understandable problems in the political institutions and processes we must make use of in order to

---

[55] Waldron, *Law and Disagreement*, 223 quoted *supra* footnote 48.   [56] Ibid., 14.

[57] This distinction between formally equal rights to political participation and the effective equality of those ostensibly equal participatory rights forms one of the pillars of the defense of judicial review against Waldron's critiques advanced in Aileen Kavanagh, "Participation and Judicial Review: A Reply to Jeremy Waldron," *Law and Philosophy* 22, no. 5 (2003). According to Kavanagh, once one sees how the opinions and interests of marginalized groups are often effectively shut out of the considerations of majoritarian legislatures that are formally open to them, judicial review itself could be justified as a way of promoting effectively equal participation. Litigation aimed at overturning rights-infringing legislation can, according to this conception, give voice to the legitimate concerns of excluded groups, in particular, by forcing concerns about minority rights onto the political agenda of public political discussion that would otherwise be ignored in formal democratic processes.

[58] See Ely, *Democracy and Distrust*, especially 73–179, and the discussion of Ely in Chapter 2.

legitimately rule ourselves through law. These and other kinds of worries about how well our actual representative and political processes work – worries often cited in substantialist justifications for judicial review – need presuppose no particular "disreputable" attitudes or attributions on the part of a rights theorist's or rights theory's defense of the substantive legitimacy of judicial review.

Whereas Waldron's rights-based attack on rights-based defenses of judicial review as essentially self-defeating is not convincing, it can nevertheless help us to get clear about the moral risks involved in the protection and specification of rights by a democratically unaccountable constitutional court: we risk treating our fellow citizens as less than equal in their capacities to think about the nature of rights and to be co-participants in appropriately setting the scope and limits of the rights protected by the legal system. If nonlegislative organs of constitutional review can be defended from the point of view of democracy, or at least as not necessarily antidemocratic, such defenses will need to take seriously the basic premise of the equal moral worth of democratic citizens – an equal moral worth, moreover, that respects each citizen's capacity for good-faith reflection and deliberation about the nature, scope, and limits of their collective structures of self-government, including not only the legal rules constitutive of political processes but also the legal rules that limit what they can do to each other. Said another way, democratic theories, and deliberative democratic theories in particular, ought to be especially wary of arguments that rely on the supposition of the superior moral insight or general moral reasoning capacities of some select group of elites, unless of course they can supply very good reasons for expecting heightened powers of rationality from that group *and* from the institutional structures and roles they occupy. That is to say, they must be as attentive to the normative premise of the equal moral worth of the reasoning of citizens as to the political structures effected by the constitutionalization of deliberative forms of democratic governance. Perhaps an account that focuses on constitutionalism as an originary exercise of democratic popular sovereignty – as a form of democratic precommitment to the conditions of democracy – can fulfill these desiderata better.

5

Disagreement and the Constitution of Democracy

Perhaps we should change our focus from constitutionalized practices of democracy to democratized practices of constitutionalism. Dworkin and Perry both seek to respond to democratic objections to judicial review by relying on a theory of the legitimacy constraints of democracy. According to this view, on some matters, legitimate democracy requires getting the right moral answers. Thus, democratic processes must be constitutionalized to ensure such right outcomes on fundamental moral matters. To the extent that judges are better positioned to engage in principled moral reasoning, the arguments continue, we ought to entrust them with ensuring the constitutionalized legitimacy conditions of democracy. I argued that this latter institutional move, however, threatened to simply revive the paternalist worries forcefully articulated by Learned Hand. Waldron's rights-based objection to rights-based judicial review, although not dispositive, provided further warning of the moral costs of treating fellow citizens as incapable of reasoning together about the content and proper scope of the legal rights required for democracy.

An alternative strategy for justifying judicial review that this chapter investigates is to understand a constitution itself as a product of true democracy, of real popular sovereignty. It is then up to the people, exercising their constituent power at the level of a constitutional assembly, to decide what particular institutional arrangements will best carry forward their collective ideals and decisions. The specific character and structure of those arrangements – whether they are populist or elitist, deliberative or aggregative, sensitive or insulated, electorally accountable or politically independent, and so on – is then a secondary matter. What is central is that the constitutional arrangements the people decide on are, first and foremost, democratically legitimated by the fact that they are the result of authentic popular sovereignty. This second strategy, then, focuses not on the constitutional conditions of democracy but on the democratic character of constitutional enactment itself.[1]

A. DEMOCRATIC PRECOMMITMENT TO JUDICIAL REVIEW: FREEMAN

1. Precommitment as an Act of Popular Sovereignty

In a pathbreaking article, Samuel Freeman puts forth a philosophically sophisticated account of democratic constitutionalism, starting from Rawlsian premises, intended to show that judicial review need not be considered antithetical to democracy.[2] Structurally, his account shares several features of the deliberative democratic justifications for judicial review evinced in Perry's and Dworkin's theories. The advantage of attending to his conception, however, is that he more clearly recognizes a point I have been emphasizing throughout: "Ultimately, the case for or against judicial review comes down to the question of what is the most appropriate conception of constitutional democracy."[3] Not surprisingly, his account of the normative foundations of constitutional democracy is somewhat more convincing than theirs: less rococo and ad-hoc than Dworkin's, less subject to the perils of ethically particularistic perfectionism than Perry's. The disadvantages are almost the obverse, as I hope to suggest by the end of the chapter. In not attending to the legal role of constitutional provisions in ongoing democratic processes, Freeman's account misses the central difficulties of indeterminacy and democratic disagreement that arise from the conditions of modern politics that authoritative lawmaking is intended to solve.

First, like them, Freeman advances a critique of aggregative (what he calls "utilitarian") accounts of democracy for being insufficiently attractive from a normative point of view. The basic idea is that any purely procedural account of democracy in terms of majority rule and equal participatory rights can only secure the values of procedural fairness, but cannot guarantee morally acceptable outcomes. "There are moral limits to the extent of the exercise of equal political rights through majority legislative procedures, and there is no assurance that these limits always will be

---

[1] This strategy of appealing to the constitution itself as the highest expression of popular sovereignty, an expression then that all branches of constituted government must then abide by, is central to Hamilton's defense of judicial review in number 78 of Hamilton, Madison, and Jay, *The Federalist with Letters of "Brutus."*

[2] Freeman, "Constitutional Democracy and the Legitimacy of Judicial Review."

[3] Ibid.: 331. The point is put too strongly, however. As I show with respect to Freeman later, and will continue to emphasize throughout, the underlying normative ideals of constitutional democracy are central to the consideration of the institutions of constitutional review but not uniquely dispositive. See also Chapters 8 and 9.

respected by the workings of these procedures."[4] Second, he advances a thicker, more substantialist account of these moral limits, an account intended to highlight the importance not only of equal political rights for democracy but also of imprescriptible equal basic rights ensuring the freedom and independence of each. The claim then is that democracy worth the name and aspiration cannot be limited to rights securing fair political procedures but also must include such substantive rights as those to private property, freedom of conscience, rights to a fair legal process, and individual liberty rights securing a sphere of private decisional autonomy. Third, as is clear from this richer account of democratic legitimacy, Freeman's argument centrally contends that the justification for equal political participation rights – and the formal democratic processes of decision making they constitute – must be founded in a deeper notion of justice. The principles and values of this more fundamental notion of justice, then, explain not only the import of equal rights to political participation but also the worth of the equal civil rights necessary to securing the freedom and independence of each. Of course, the value of whatever institutional arrangements are decided upon to secure such political and civil rights is instrumental: only to the degree to which they secure these rights are such political institutions worthy of support. In other words, Freeman's defense of judicial review is, like Perry's and Dworkin's, founded on a substantialist notion of legitimacy, one whose fulfillment is independent of the results of any actual political actions or decisions of citizens expressed through the extant legal and governmental system. Fourth, Freeman's theory, given the critique of aggregative democracy, the substantialist redefinition of democracy and the instrumentalist theory of political institutions it gives rise to, is then able to explain how judicial review need not be considered undemocratic. As long as judicial review functions to ensure the legitimacy conditions of civil and political rights – that is, equal basic rights securing both the private and the public autonomy of each – then it is not inconsistent with democracy. It should rather be seen as one possible way in which actual democratic processes could guarantee democratic legitimacy.[5]

---

[4] Ibid.: 336–7.
[5] These broad features of a substantialist defense of judicial review as a central institution of democracy – or at the very least, as not undemocratic – are largely shared by many contemporary theorists. Besides Dworkin, Freeman, and Perry, a short list would also include the theories advanced by Christopher Eisgruber and John Rawls (I consider a subset of Eisgruber's and Rawls's claims, concerning judicial reasoning as a form of democratic deliberation, in Chapter 6). Similar strategies are employed in Fabre, "A Philosophical Argument for a Bill of Rights," Stephen Holmes, "Precommitment and the Paradox of Democracy," in *Constitutionalism and Democracy*, ed. Jon Elster and Rune Slagstad (New York: Cambridge University Press, 1988), and Kavanagh, "Participation and Judicial Review."

The interesting part of Freeman's theory is how he fills out the structure of this widely shared argument strategy. In particular, Freeman's innovation is to give a much more convincing account of the *democratic* character of a political regime that guarantees equal basic civil rights. The crucial move here is to follow social contractarians such as Locke, Rousseau, Kant, and Rawls in insisting on a distinction between the ordinary power of an extant government to make laws, and the originary constituent power of the sovereign people to establish government in the first place. This latter constituent power – the power of free and equal consociates looking to regulate their life in common by establishing a set of governmental institutions – is that power that should be considered *popular sovereignty* proper. The legislative power, as well as the other powers of an established state, themselves gain their authority only as powers delegated by the people themselves. Democratically legitimate political authority arises, then, not from any determinate form that governmental processes and institutions might take, such as electoral representation or the majoritarian character of the legislative process, but rather from the fact that the people, in their sovereign constituent capacities, have contracted among themselves to establish those governmental processes and institutions.

In exercising their popular sovereignty through their constituent constitution-creating power, the people might decide on various mechanisms for securing their original freedom and equality, once they have adopted institutions forming a state. The specifically democratic character of those institutions comes not from their particular structure or the character of their ongoing processes, but from the fact that they could have been unanimously agreed to in a constitution-making social contract. Therefore, the people could decide upon a constitution that gave the judiciary the power to review the constitutionality of legislation, and, as this would be an expression of their popular sovereignty, such a decision could not be labeled undemocratic. Seen in this light, judicial review:

> is not a limitation upon equal sovereignty, but upon ordinary legislative power in the interest of protecting the equal rights of democratic sovereignty. So conceived, judicial review is a kind of rational and shared precommitment among free and equal sovereign citizens at the level of constitutional choice.... By agreeing to judicial review, they in effect tie themselves into their unanimous agreement on the equal basic rights that specify their sovereignty. Judicial review is then one way to protect their status as equal citizens.[6]

Freeman thus understands constitutionalism in general – including the "traditional constitutional devices that limit legislative procedures ... [such

---

[6] Freeman, "Constitutional Democracy and the Legitimacy of Judicial Review," 353–4.

as] bicameralism, federalism, and other checks and balances ... [and] a bill of rights, with or without judicial review"[7] – as a kind of precommitment to legitimacy-ensuring side constraints on legislative decision making, in particular side constraints that guarantee such equal basic civil rights as access to a just legal system, private property, free religious conscience, a sphere of private autonomy, and so on. Such constitutional side-constraints, and whatever institutions might be reasonably thought necessary to secure them, can then be seen as democratic because they all could have been agreed on by free and equal consociates expressing their constituent powers of popular sovereignty at the level of constitutional choice.

2.   Institutionalization, Disagreement, and Ongoing Democracy

How strong a democratic argument for a judicial institutionalization of constitutional review is this? To begin with, as Freeman himself recognizes, the argument establishes at most the theoretical necessity of the function of the review of legislative outputs for consistency with the substantive values secured through individual constitutional rights guarantees.[8] It does not specifically endorse using a judicial body to fulfill that constitution-conserving function. Rather, according to Freeman, institutionalization is merely a strategic question depending on whether there are good grounds for thinking that "legislative procedures are incapable of correcting themselves"[9] and that courts would do a better job of ensuring the liberal conditions of democracy. In fact, Freeman argues that once one accepts the particular normative content of the constitutional precommitment to securing equal basic rights, the question about what institutions should be erected to secure the terms of that precommitment will turn entirely on context-specific matters of fact. Any actual arguments for a judicial institutionalization of constitutional review would need to be tailored to the specific "social and historical circumstances. It is a matter for *factual determination* whether the overall balance of democratic justice can be more effectively established in a democratic regime with or without judicial review."[10]

It seems unlikely, however, that such a determination could be a simple matter of fact, given that there are ongoing disagreements, at the very least at the level of the specification of abstract constitutional principles,

---

[7] Ibid.: 354.
[8] "Final authority to interpret the constitution is a *necessary* power of government that is distinct from the ordinary powers of the legislative, judicial, and executive functions.... The final authority of interpretation might be seen as an institutional expression of the constituent power of sovereign citizens," ibid.: 357, emphasis added.
[9] Ibid.: 361.   [10] Ibid.: 361–2, emphasis added.

about what "the overall balance of democratic justice" means over the long sweep of history and in any particular case. The "facts" which might establish the inference to a judicial institutionalization of constitutional review – facts such as that a particular judiciary in a particular country is more likely to hit on just solutions than other possible political actors or institutions – are themselves normatively suffused. Taking the "fact of reasonable pluralism" seriously, we cannot expect that the judgment of such facts will be a simple empirical matter of pointing to brute states of affairs and historical details. Such judgments will, rather, be inextricably bound up with differing conceptions of the principles of justice and associated weightings of various values, and so will be complex amalgams of normative and empirical assessment.[11]

The shortcomings of merely empirical judgments here point to the problem that Freeman's argument, as he himself recognizes, merely establishes the potential compatibility of judicial review with a system of democratic sovereignty. Nothing in the argument actually necessitates support of such an institutionalization of the function of securing the sovereign people's precommitments. From a perspective that seeks to secure reflective equilibrium between the theoretical conception of democratic justice and the everyday practices of constitutional democracy extant in the world, this agnosticism with respect to questions of institutionalization might be seen as an advantage. For it prevents the theory from being committed to the claim that a whole series of nation-states that appear to be, on balance, just as good as others at securing democratic justice without institutionalized judicial review are, nevertheless, normatively deficient precisely because of their lack of such an empowered court.

Even though he doesn't present positive arguments for judicial review, Freeman does at least outline what considerations he believes might lead a specific group of constitutional contractors to consider the option should certain facts obtain. I would now like to explore a potential dilemma that arises for his contractarian understanding of constitutional

[11] A rather simple way to see this point concretely is to consider the widely divergent conceptions of the same constitutional provision which are endorsed by jurisprudes who all adopt the ostensibly purely empirical method of constitutional interpretation called variously "originalism" or "textualism," a method designed specifically to forestall the need for normative judgments on the part of judges employing the method. Are these wide divergences really simply the result of factual disagreements, and, if so, why do the disagreements persist even after the relevant historical 'empirical evidence' has been presented? See, for example, the widely divergent conceptions of the expressive freedom protected by the First Amendment to the United States Constitution in originalist scholarship: Amar, *The Bill of Rights*, 20–26 and 231–46, in contrast with Bork, "Neutral Principles and Some First Amendment Problems," and in contrast with Scalia, "Common-Law Courts in a Civil-Law System: The Role of United States Federal Courts in Interpreting the Constitution and the Laws," 37–38, 45, and infra 140–8.

choice, a worry inspired by Waldron's emphasis on the persistence of reasonable disagreement on fundamental matters of justice among political consociates.[12] In considering the strategic question of institutionalization, Freeman argues that judicial review would only be recommended in those sociohistorical contexts where we could not trust ordinary legislative processes to maintain the conditions of democratic justice; where citizens, that is, had good reason for "protecting their sovereignty and independence from the unreasonable exercise of their political rights in legislative processes."[13] In the best case scenario, a sociohistoric situation "where there is widespread public recognition and acknowledgement of the equal rights of democratic sovereignty, and where it is publicly accepted that the purpose of legislation is to advance the good of each"[14] there would be no need for judicial review, as ordinary legislative processes could be trusted to maintain democratic justice. But, Freeman argues, *"in the absence of widespread public agreement on these fundamental requirements of democracy*, there is no assurance that majority rule will not be used, as it so often has, to subvert the public interest in justice and to deprive classes of individuals of the conditions of democratic equality. It is in these circumstances that there is a place for judicial review."[15]

The question now is, having admitted that in the world of ordinary legislative politics there will be disagreements among representatives concerning the legitimacy conditions of democracy properly and richly understood, how far up the levels of lawmaking is Freeman willing to let such dissensus ascend? If there is in fact widespread disagreement among representatives on the fundamental requirements of democracy at the level of ordinary statutory enactment, we can probably expect a like disagreement among citizens themselves. Furthermore, we should probably also expect the same to obtain at the level of the specification of those constitutional principles the people have already agreed to. After all, one of the contentious issues with respect to statutory enactments suspected of being constitutional violations is usually whether or not they fall afoul of one or another "properly" specified constitutional provisions. Why shouldn't we expect a quite similar level of dissensus about fundamental principles of democratic justice at the constitutional convention level? But if fundamental disagreement obtains here as well, then we can not expect either unanimous consent or anything approaching it when the people express their popular sovereignty through exercising their constituent

---

[12] See generally Waldron, *Law and Disagreement*. I have not found the specific argument I present here in Waldron's work, though it certainly has close affinities with much that he says. A fuller treatment of Waldron's arguments from the circumstances of disagreement to the conclusion that no form of judicial review is democratically acceptable is in Section B of this chapter.

[13] Freeman, "Constitutional Democracy and the Legitimacy of Judicial Review," 353.

[14] Ibid.: 355.   [15] Ibid., emphasis added.

constitution-making power. We should, rather, expect a quite similar range of disagreements about the meaning and import of the basic principles of justice as is evinced in the everyday legislative processes. But once the notion of consent (either unanimous or to whatever super-majoritarian degree) at the level of constituent power is gone, so is the democratic legitimacy that was supposed to accrue to whatever institutions and arrangements would have been agreed to in the original social contract. Disagreement at this level threatens the contractarian legitimacy of the agreement, and therewith the democratic pedigree of whatever institutions and constraints are agreed to there.

Alternatively, the contractarian argument might be able to save the strong notion of agreement on basic principles of democratic justice – and thereby retain the notion of constitutional constraints as "democratic" – by theoretically hypothesizing that, at the level of their constituent power at any rate, the people collectively would agree on just that substantive conception of democratic justice that the theorist insists upon. Thus, even though the actual people appear to evince widespread disagreement on the substantive requirements of democratic justice, to judge by their actually professed beliefs in legislative contexts, the theory can assure us that they would nevertheless agree in the hypothetical contracting situation. The dilemma seems then to be this: either realistically admit fundamental disagreement all the way up to the level of constitutional choice and thereby give up the notion that whatever is agreed to there – including mechanisms of judicial review – is an expression of free sovereign, self-binding precommitment, or, unrealistically restrict persistent disagreement to the lower level of ordinary lawmaking and thereby save the democratic defense of judicial review as the outcome of consent in constitutional choice. But this second option is unrealistic precisely because it relies on a kind of overly confident assumption on the part of liberal theory: namely, that the theory is able to correctly project the specifics of the substantive content of its theory of justice into the heads of hypothetical contractors, despite evidence that some significant proportion of actual democratic consociates do not agree with the theory's conclusions.

Perhaps, however, the fact that Freeman's argument doesn't positively justify judicial review – content rather to consider certain conditions under which its use would be legitimate and might be recommended – is not an advantage, but actually a symptom of a broader problem: namely, that if the general argument for precommitment as an act of popular sovereignty is sufficient to dispel democratic worries, then the argument could be used to establish much more than envisioned or desired. To see this problem, consider what else such an argument might be taken to establish as sufficiently democratic: any number of apparently undemocratic day-to-day ordinary lawmaking mechanisms such as legislation by an elected or aristocratic monarch, forms of legislative outsourcing from one nation to another's parliament, or perhaps even day-to-day rule by a few well-trained philosophers. We don't need outlandish examples however, for Freeman's argument appears fully consistent with a sympathetically democratic interpretation of Hobbes's contractarian arguments for monarchy[16] and Rousseau's for a temporary dictatorship.[17] Surely in all of these cases we can describe the original constitutional choice as democratic, but I think we should have real reservations about calling the ongoing workings of such political arrangements democratic. Waldron helpfully characterizes this difference as "the distinction between a democratic method of constitutional choice and the democratic character of the constitution that is chosen."[18] Of course, Freeman does contend that equal rights to political participation in ordinary lawmaking are an important part of the more capacious package of rights ensuring democratic justice, and so they cannot simply be dispensed with without good reason. He in fact reviews and apparently endorses four types of arguments for equal rights to political participation that are said to be based in the exact same ideals that underlie the originary endorsement of constitutional constraints on majoritarian actions.[19] Nevertheless, such equal participatory rights, according to the broader argument, can be "democratically" overridden in the design of ordinary political institutions whenever we have reasonable cause – for instance, under expectable conditions of legislative disagreement about the fundamentals of justice – to fear that the exercise of those rights would lead to a lesser degree of democratic justice as the outputs of those institutions.

The obverse, in Freeman's argument, of the celebration of constitutional constraints as specially democratic is the comparative belittlement of the workings of representative legislatures as democratic only in a derivative sense, as it were. Following Locke, he describes the process of statutory lawmaking as an ordinary power of government, on a par with all of the other powers in terms of its democratic value: legislative authority, like all governmental authority, is a merely fiduciary power

---

[16] See especially Chapter 19, 129–38 of Hobbes, *Leviathan*. I say "sympathetically democratic interpretation" of Hobbes's arguments for monarchy, as Freeman insists that the kind of social contract he endorses is not a compromise among individuals competing for scarce resources but, rather, a mutual endorsement of shared principles of association that the contractors intend to carry on for the indefinite future: Freeman, "Constitutional Democracy and the Legitimacy of Judicial Review," 356. Yet it doesn't seem outlandish to suppose that there might be sociohistorical facts – for instance, violent and persistent social unrest – that might make sovereign precommiters consider reducing their equal political participation rights effectively to nothing in order to secure other fundamental interests.

[17] See Book IV, Chapter 6, 138–40 of Rousseau, *"Of the Social Contract."*

[18] Waldron, *Law and Disagreement*, 256.

[19] Freeman, "Constitutional Democracy and the Legitimacy of Judicial Review," 340–1.

delegated by the sovereign people.[20] Although this is true as far as it goes – as far, that is, as we are considering the democratic character of the originary constitutional choice situation – left at that, the generalization about fiduciary powers cannot make any apparent distinctions with respect to democratic value between various institutions erected to carry out the constitutional design, distinctions that seem rather easy to make from the ordinary perspective of assessing various political arrangements for the degree to which they are democratic or not.[21]

The reason such distinctions between, for instance, populist and elitist lawmaking institutions, seem easy to make is that it is part of our democratic ideals to insist on a deep internal connection between the legitimacy of political institutions and the character of the procedures they use to generate decisions. Thus the worries I've just expressed about the overly broad institutional reach of Freeman's argument and its concomitant diminution of the democratic role of legislative processes can both be seen as applications of a general point I have been emphasizing throughout. Democratic legitimacy cannot be severed from the ongoing existence of robust democratic processes of opinion-formation and decision making.[22] For if we restrict responsive democracy only to the level of constitutional choice, it will be impossible to fulfill the Rousseauian condition for democratic autonomy: namely, that I am only free to the extent to which I can understand the laws binding me as, in some sense, self-given laws. And I can only understand myself as simultaneously the author and addressee of those laws to the extent to which, even when I disagree with the concrete proposal and vote against it, I can nevertheless understand those laws as the results of a legally constituted

---

[20] Ibid.: 348–50.

[21] The point about sovereign constituent power as the power of the people to authorize the various branches of government is also true to Locke's theory, but that theory is distorted by the construal given by Freeman. For not only did Locke think that legislative power was given on fiduciary trust by the sovereign people, he also claimed that once that legislative power was legitimately operating, it is the supreme power in the state, and should have *no* explicit constitutional constraints on its power – certainly no other ordinary organ of government could substantially limit its powers through something like a power for the substantive review of its handiwork. See Locke, "The Second Treatise of Government," especially Chapters 11, 12, 13, and 14. For a clear elucidation of this point in contrast to Freeman's reading of Locke, see Jeremy Waldron, "Freeman's Defense of Judicial Review," *Law and Philosophy* 13 (1994): 33, footnote 13.

[22] It's not the case that Freeman is wholly insensitive to the potential damage to the democratic character of political processes posed by judicial review: "Judicial review limits the extent of the exercise of equal rights of political participation through ordinary legislative procedures.... Since it invokes a non-legislative means to do this, it may well be a constitutional measure of last resort," Freeman, "Constitutional Democracy and the Legitimacy of Judicial Review," 353. Nevertheless, the logic of his argument severs the internal connection between democratic constitutional choice and on going democratic political processes.

political process of argument and reason-giving in which I had some prospect of actually participating in on equal terms with my fellow citizens. Finally, this legitimacy condition applies equally at the level of constitutional choice and ordinary statutory legislation. As Freeman emphasizes, it is surely true that constitutional choice must be understood as the most fundamental form of the exercise of popular sovereignty. This does not entail, however, that such democratic choice can simply end at that if a regime is to have democratic legitimacy.

Although Freeman employs the language of precommitment, I believe that this is not his central or most important idea.[23] Rather, Freeman's contribution is to have refocused the debate concerning judicial review, away from the jurisprudential terrain of the problem of legal interpretation of indeterminate clauses, and back to the fundamental normative questions of how to conceive of constitutional democracy. His central idea here is to envision constitutional constraints as potentially legitimate exercises of democratic sovereignty at the level of constitutional choice. In this basic point, I think he is correct. But I believe his next step of claiming that popular sovereignty at the level of constitutionalism is thereby sufficient to dispel worries about the democratic character of the ongoing workings of the processes established by that precommitment is false. Freeman is surely correct to emphasize the need to understand the establishment of a constitution and its ongoing refinement through amendment as the most basic acts of popular sovereignty of a people, and to emphasize this point against those who would see a constitution as a fundamentally antidemocratic instrument intended to ensure the protection of principles of natural law, principles correctly discerned by a few (Founders) of exceptionally good judgment: "For it is now our constitution; we now exercise constituent power and cannot be bound by our ancestors' commitments. Only our intentions, as free and equal sovereign citizens, are then relevant in assessing the constitution and assigning a role to the document that bears that name."[24] Nevertheless, the democratic nature of originating constitutional actions, even by our own generation, is not sufficient to establish the democratic character of the institutions, arrangements, and practices

---

[23] Waldron, both in his review of Freeman's argument in particular (Waldron, "Freeman's Defense of Judicial Review"), and in his broader consideration of "precommitment" arguments for judicial review (Chapter 12, 255–81 of Waldron, *Law and Disagreement*) pays a great deal of attention to the significant disanalogies between individual precommitment – where we think the idea of self-binding may be a paradigmatic form of autonomous action – and precommitment in the context of the constitutional choice of political institutions among common citizens. As I emphasize in the text, this seems somewhat to miss the general point that Freeman is focusing on: that of the democratic character of the choice of constitutional constraints in general.

[24] Freeman, "Constitutional Democracy and the Legitimacy of Judicial Review," 370.

that are agreed to in such originary actions. Our account of constitutionalism and democracy needs to comprehend the constitutive relationships not just between democratic popular sovereignty and constitutional enactment but also between established constitutional structures and the ongoing practices of democratic political practice they make possible. In other words, we need to understand the co-constitutive interconnections between constitutionalism and democracy.[25]

B. DELIBERATIVE MAJORITARIANISM AND THE PATERNALISM OF JUDICIAL REVIEW: WALDRON

Freeman meets the countermajoritarian objection to judicial review by redefining democracy as, most fundamentally, the exercise of popular sovereignty at the level of constitutional choice, and the subsequent choice of constitutional structures that would guarantee the substantive liberal legitimacy conditions of the equality, independence, and autonomy of each citizen. I have argued, however, that such a substantivist theory of constitutionalism still fails to meet the paternalist objection to judicial review, in large part because it failed to respect the expectable and deep disagreement of citizens under the conditions of modern pluralism.

Perhaps then, under conditions of modern pluralism, the practice of constitutionalism, and in particular the countermajoritarian features of constitutional constraints on majoritarian decisions are in fact fundamentally undemocratic and unsupportable. This at least is one of the central claims of Waldron's work, to which I now turn. Waldron promises a formal argument from the fact of such persistent disagreement to the illegitimacy of any form of constitutional constraint on majoritarianism. If his argument is successful, it would leave pure parliamentary sovereignty, unconstrained by any forms of constitutional review however institutionalized, as the sole legitimate form of democratic decision making in the circumstances of contemporary politics. I hope to show that such an argument is not successful, leaving the door open, rather, to a proceduralist defense of constitutional review that might be institutionalized in a number of ways.

1. Deliberative Majoritarianism and the Argument against Judicial Review

In order to understand the force of Waldron's formal argument against judicial review – whether justified and understood on substantialist or proceduralist grounds – it will help to first clearly reconstruct his theories

---

[25] See Section C of this chapter, and Chapter 7.

of democracy and constitutionalism. By using the analytic developed in Chapter 3 – considering first the aspects of democratic legitimacy, democratic process, institutional legitimacy and accountability, and then the four elements of constitutionalism – I hope to be able to show exactly why Waldron defends an anticonstitutionalist theory of pure parliamentary sovereignty.

Waldron's brief against judicial review – in fact, against any form of political institution or political decision procedure beyond the supremacy of multimember, representative legislative assemblies deciding exclusively through majority rule – begins from what he calls "the circumstances of politics." On the one hand, political consociation presents a coordination problem whereby each recognizes that certain goals and goods can only be realized by deciding upon and adapting a common framework for action. On the other hand, precisely such a decision on a common framework seems threatened by the persistent and deep disagreement on fundamental moral and political issues evinced in contemporary pluralistic societies. Insisting, however, that we should not pathologize such disagreement as the result of either intellectual failings or deviant motivations on the part of some consociates, Waldron points to what Rawls calls the "burdens of judgment" to explain the divergence of citizens' good faith beliefs about the correct framework for collective action: the issues to be decided on are complex, people's different experiences and social positions will give rise to reasonable differences in their perceptions and judgments, and the multiple values involved can be reasonably weighed and prioritized in different ways.[26] Thus the conditions of politics are twofold: the need for coordinating collective decisions, in the face of reasonable and expectably persistent disagreement on substantive values and their proper realization.[27]

Given the need for a decision combined with persistent, expectable disagreement as the circumstances of politics, Waldron argues for majoritarian aggregation of equally weighted votes as the most justifiable democratic process. He is concerned, however, to answer the traditional charge against majority rule that it is an arbitrary decision mechanism.[28]

---

[26] For explications of "the circumstances of politics," see Waldron, *Law and Disagreement*, 11–12, 55, 73–75, and 112–13.

[27] These two conditions are essentially the same two that Dahl, *Democracy and Its Critics*, references in defending the political preeminence of democracy over other values: see the discussion in Chapter 2, Section B.2.

[28] Recall that this is the charge forcefully put by Dewey that I referred to at the end of Chapter 2. Note also Waldron's nice point against those who would overstylize a contrast between the arbitrary decision methods of majority rule adopted in general elections and legislatures, and, the nonarbitrary reasoning-giving decision methods characteristic of courts. After all, multimember courts (such as constitutional courts) invariably adopt a majoritarian decision rule because of their own internal conditions of disagreement.

He does this, in part by emphasizing that *what* are counted in voting are not the prepolitical preferences or private interests of each voter but, rather, the good-faith opinions of each individual concerning what is the best course of collective action among the choices available. Thus, rather than a method for an utilitarian aggregation of private and independent utiles, majority rule counts the preponderance of public opinion on the issue. Thus, Waldron's conception of democratic process is an interesting combination of elements from the opposition I stylized in Chapter 3: like Locke, he believes that the uniquely appropriate democratic process is majoritarian aggregation, but like Rousseau, he also believes that what counts are opinions, not interests or satisfactions.[29] Hence his conception of democratic process might be called "deliberative majoritarianism": although essentially deliberative, it emphasizes ineliminable dissensus and insists on the theoretical distortions introduced by the idealization of consensus.[30]

A complete answer to the charge of the arbitrariness of majoritarianism can only come, however, with some normative defense of the legitimacy of majority rule. Here Waldron has recourse to his basic justificatory framework of respect for individual rights, and the ascriptions of equal autonomy to each that underlie that respect.[31] The idea is simply that majoritarianism is the only decision procedure that is fully respectful of the equal autonomy of each citizen. On the one hand, given that consensus on complex political issues is not to be expected, majority rule respects the worth of each as a thinking, intelligent co-citizen, endeavoring in good faith to give her or his considered opinion on the proposal under discussion. Under conditions of disagreement, majority rule does not try to turn away from the diversity of citizens' beliefs, but respects equally the opinions of each, even if not all opinions can become directive of the state's power. Majority rule then is fair to each in giving equal

---

Thus, if the disparager of legislative majority rule is right that "voting yields arbitrary decisions, then most of constitutional law is arbitrary." Waldron, *Law and Disagreement*, 91. I return to the contrast between legislative voting and judicial reasoning in Chapter 6.

[29] For a particularly lucid account of this distinction in terms of Bentham and Rousseau, see Waldron, "Rights and Majorities: Rousseau Revisited," 394–400.

[30] Waldron's brief and vague dismissal of "proponents of 'deliberative democracy'" apparently hinges on the twin contentions that they see consensus on political matters as the legitimacy criterion for democracy, and that anything less than consensus is to be explained away as a pathological failure of the deliberative process (for instance, due to the motivations of some of the participants), Waldron, *Law and Disagreement*, 90–93. Conceding that "the very best theories of deliberative democracy are characterized by their willingness to accept [persistent, reasonable disagreement] and incorporate it into their conception of deliberation," 93, Waldron nevertheless gives virtually no more attention to such theories.

[31] See the discussion of Waldron's rights-based critique of the argument for judicial review as the best way of protecting rights in Section C of Chapter 4.

respect to the good-faith opinions of each. On the other hand, major-itarianism respects the equal worth of each citizen, consistent with a like respect for all others, since its decision procedure weights all votes equally. Majority rule, then, is fair in another sense, in giving equal decisive power over collective decisions. So, perhaps surprisingly given the usual association of rights-based normative theories with counter-majoritarian side-constraints on majoritarianism, Waldron's rights-based theory endorses the principle of majority rule as the only way of taking the rights of each individual to fair and equal political participation seriously. Respect for individual rights in his hands leads, then, to a proceduralist rather than a substantialist account of democratic legitimacy as following only from majoritarian political decision processes.

Perhaps Waldron's most important contribution consists in elaborating a clear defense of the intrinsic worth of legislative assemblies, of rescuing the "dignity of legislation" from theoretical oversight in both jur-isprudence and political philosophy. The idea here is that there are good normative reasons for the fact that large, multimember representative assemblies oriented toward producing statute law exist "in almost every society in the world."[32] Given the complexity of coordination issues that law needs to resolve and given the inherent plurality and diversity of complex societies where we should expect persistent disagreement, leg-islatures are the form of lawmaking body best situated to deal with that complexity while simultaneously respecting the equal autonomy of citi-zens. First, the diversity and large number of representatives in an assembly reflect the spread of popular opinions extant within society on major issues. Second, the formal procedures and structural properties of assemblies are oriented toward organizing deliberation and decision making in such a way that authoritative decisions can be reached without univocity. Third, perhaps most important, majority rule is a nonarbitrary way of respecting the opinions of each.[33] In short, Waldron's detailed analysis of the features of legislatures and the process of legislation is intended to show that multimember representative assemblies are not just contingently useful political devices that could be discarded with should better ways be found of reaching desired political outcomes. In fact, given the argument from disagreement for majoritarian proceduralism, there could be no theoretical access to the correct procedure-independent

---

[32] Waldron, *Law and Disagreement*, 10.

[33] For Waldron's rich account of these features of parliamentary legislatures and their relation to a normative theory of parliamentary sovereignty, see especially Chapters 2–5 of ibid. He explores the same ideas about the appropriateness of legislatures through a resuscitation of underdeveloped themes concerning legislative lawmaking in the history of political philosophy, specifically in Aristotle, Kant, and Locke, in Jeremy Waldron, *The Dignity of Legislation* (New York: Cambridge University Press, 1999). I return to Waldron's discussion of legislation later in this chapter, and in Chapter 8.

political outcomes in the light of which we could judge legislatures as instrumentally worthwhile or not.

The upshot from these arguments should not be surprising for the last axis of democratic analysis: Waldron clearly favors a governmental structuring of power that is at the populist end of the accountability spectrum, and he is strongly suspicious of any more expertocratic allocation of power. In fact, he seems to regard most forms of extralegislative governmental power as regrettable reflections of an antiegalitarian and antidemocratic bias against ordinary citizens. Thus, for instance, any legal theory that attempts to analyze the increased efficacy of judicial decisions in some governmental areas or the heightened capacities of the judiciary is immediately suspected of harboring "one of 'the dirty little secrets of contemporary jurisprudence' … 'its discomfort with democracy'."[34] And whereas Waldron always focuses on the elitism of legal decision making by unelected judges (never apparently considering that many judges in many nation-states are subject to repeated electoral control), he has almost nothing to say about the executive branch and the substantial increase of administrative lawmaking powers.[35] The contrast is insistently between popularly accountable legislators and unaccountable judges.

What then does Waldron think of constitutionalism understood as a practice of intentionally structuring governmental processes and powers through law in order to realize the benefits of some or all of the four basic elements constitutions are often thought to secure?[36] To put it briefly, it's not at all clear what Waldron's position is here.

Given that Waldron's basic normative framework is that of the fundamentality of equal liberal rights, it would be hard to imagine him

---

[34] Waldron, *Law and Disagreement*, 8, quoting Roberto Unger *What Should Legal Analysis Become?* (London: Verso, 1996).

[35] At the one point in *Law and Disagreement* (pages 49–50) where Waldron gives any consideration to the executive branch of government, his bias toward a British model of pure parliamentary sovereignty leads to very strange, putatively universal, claims: "Almost everywhere, legislatures are assemblies rather than individuals, and assemblies of anything from fifty to almost three thousand members, not assemblies of cabinet size. No doubt we should qualify this by observing that subordinate legislation is often made by single individuals or by very small rule-making agencies. But this should not distract us: such individuals and agencies *always derive their authority from a sovereign legislature* that comprises hundreds of members," 49 (emphasis added). This passage simply ignores both the popular authorization of the executive branch through elections independent of legislative elections in presidential systems, and the popular authorization of all of the branches of government thought to be effected through constitutional ratification.

[36] Recall the distinction introduced in Chapter 3 between the descriptive sense of "constitution" – in which it refers to the particular configuration of governmental power extant in any political community – and the normative sense of "constitutionalism" – in which it refers to the intentional organizing of the organs of government according to a set of higher laws oriented toward structuring and limiting the exercise of state power. Obviously, my question in the text employs the second normative sense.

rejecting the baseline platitudes of the rule of law, such as that that like cases are to be treated alike. But beyond this and allied generalities (e.g., no *ex post facto* laws, no offense in the absence of an applicable law, rules must provide effective conduct guidance) – generalities that can't be expected to do much concrete work of sorting violations from fulfillments of the rule of law at that level of abstraction – Waldron would seem to suggest that the persistence of fundamental disagreement over the proper conception of the rule of law should put the lie to the idea that it could be furthered through the practice of constitutionalism. In fact, in an article in which he argues that the rule of law is an essentially contested concept, Waldron seems to claim that the idea of government bound by fundamental or higher law – that is, one of the elemental ideas of constitutionalism – is itself one of the contesting conceptions of the complex concept of the rule of law.[37] Given that the rule of law is itself subject to persistent disagreement leading to radically antithetical readings of its proper realization – "litigation or self-restraint, judicial supremacy or judicial deference, rules or standards, mechanical judgment or reasoned discretion"[38] – it seems unlikely that Waldron could, then, recommend constitutionalism in the name of furthering rule of law values.

On the allied questions of whether Waldron supports the practices of constitutionalism that revolve around the entrenchment of higher law on the one hand, and the structuration of political institutions on the other, the answers are again ambiguous, but this time because it's unclear how far Waldron takes his defense of majoritarian decision procedures to reach. For, arguing simply from the demands of fairness to each that Waldron takes the ideal of liberal rights to lead to, it would seem that any higher constitutional law would require unfair supermajorities to change, unfair because only bare majoritarianism doesn't bias the outcome in favor of or against the status quo. Furthermore, it seems that like considerations would apply to any constitutional organization of political organs that would require supermajoritarian procedures to change. Yet surely this cannot be the whole story, considering that, to begin with, Waldron appears in favor of some form of entrenchment of multimember representative legislative assemblies, and in favor of such bodies to the exclusion of other forms of institutionalizing legislative power. In addition, he also endorses (albeit intermittently) certain political procedures such as federalism and supermajoritarian requirements for some legislative proposals that can only be considered as antimajoritarian decision procedures. Its hard to see, however, exactly how either the entrenchment of legislatures or such constitutional "slowing-down devices" can be made consistent with

---

[37] Waldron, "Is the Rule of Law an Essentially Contested Concept (in Florida)?," 156–7.
[38] Ibid.: 144.

the overriding principle of majority rule that results from the combination of fairness to each as a rights-bearer with the circumstances of
politics. Therefore, it's difficult to say exactly what Waldron's overt
commitments to constitutionalism are with respect to the higher law/
lower law distinction and the issue of the entrenchment of determinate
forms of and organs for the organization of political power.[39]

Finally, it is surely clear that he endorses neither the constitutionalization of fundamental individual rights, say in a bill of rights,
nor the empowerment of an independent judiciary to ensure those
rights against legislative processes.[40] Waldron would prefer that moral
rights be protected, if they can and are to be legally protected at all,
through legislative means, in particular through the pervasive influence
of a spirit of rights in both legislatures and the electorate at large.[41]
Thus, in sum, Waldron decisively rejects one of the elements of constitutionalism, and appears at the very least, suspicious towards the
other three.

Here is one possible reconstruction of Waldron's formal argument
against any form of judicial review of legislation for its constitutionality,
whether understood and justified on substantialist or proceduralist
grounds:[42]

a. The commitment to democracy is centered on respecting the ideal
   of the equal autonomy of each citizen as a moral rights-bearer;
b. Disagreement over the identification, prioritization, and specific
   appropriate application of substantive political values, including
   rights, is persistent, expectable, and not pathological under
   conditions of societal complexity and value pluralism;
c. Collective decisions on a common framework of action are needed,
   despite disagreement, in order to secure some political goods;
d. The authority/legitimacy of political decisions within a polity must
   then be procedural, that is, independent of any of the particular
   substantive conceptions of political value that are subject to
   reasonable contestation;
e. Respecting each as an equal rights-bearer demands *fairness* in
   political decision procedures, and in two ways: (aspect 1) equal
   respect for the good-faith opinions of each concerning proposals for

---

[39] The question of Waldron's commitment to constitutionalism is discussed further in
subsection 3.
[40] See Section C of Chapter 4 and later in this chapter for a reconstruction of his arguments.
[41] I take it that this is the upshot of the discussion of Locke and Mill that ends the book:
Waldron, *Law and Disagreement*, 306–12.
[42] Other reconstructions emphasize different aspects: e.g., Christiano, "Waldron on Law
and Disagreement," 534, or Fabre, "A Philosophical Argument for a Bill of Rights," 94–5.
Newly introduced elements in this reconstruction will be clarified presently.

collective decisions, and (aspect 2) equal decisive power for each in the decision procedure;

f. Given both the pressure for collective decisions and the problems of political complexity and scale, fairness (aspect 1) is best achieved in elective, multimember representative legislatures whose members make decisions even as they represent the diversity of political opinions extant among the citizenry;

g. Fairness (aspect 1) is violated by judicial review, as the opinions listened to are not representative of the citizenry, but are those of a few unelected judges;

h. Majority rule is the single decision procedure that fulfills fairness (aspect 2), as only it gives a maximal decisional weight to the opinion of each consistent with an equal weighting of the opinions of others;

i. Any constitutional rules, structures, or procedures (including judicial review) that restrict the reach and decisiveness of majoritarian legislative power will violate fairness (aspect 2) as countermajoritarian; and

j. Therefore, judicial review is nonauthoritative/illegitimate and ought not be employed in a democracy.

It is important to note here that, although Waldron's argument is couched in the language of "majoritarianism," his objection to judicial review should not be understood as a reprise of Bickel's "counter-majoritarian" concerns, concerns which were rooted in the notion that majoritarianism is justified through its utilitarian aggregation of private interests. In contrast, Waldron's argument centers the justification of majority rule in the notion that it is the singular decision procedure consistent with respect for each as an autonomous agent. Said another way, derogations from majority rule are objectionable precisely because they are heteronomous substitutions of the will of some for the will of all, even against the fairly expressed wishes of all. Any infringement on democratic self-rule – such as allowing a small number of unaccountable judges to decide matters of basic rights – is, for Waldron, objectionable as a paternalistic infringement on the equal right of each to have his or her say with respect to matters needing collective political decision. The countermajoritarian character of judicial review is, for Waldron, objectionable because its paternalistic. It should also be noted, however, that because it is the countermajoritarian character that is objectionable about judicial review, due to the electoral unaccountability of constitutional court judges, if Waldron's formal argument is successful, it simply doesn't matter whether judicial review is understood and defended on sub-stantialist or on proceduralist grounds. In either case, it will embody a countermajoritarian decision procedure, one objectionable because countermajoritarian procedures are paternalistic, and so cannot be seen as democratically legitimate.[43]

2. Fairness, Majoritarianism, and Democratic Legitimacy

To begin to consider the strength of this argument, it will help first to focus on the issue of disagreement; specifically, concerning at what level and to what extent we should expect reasonable persistent disagreement between democratic consociates. Taken at a very deep level and understood to be quite wide-ranging, such disagreement in fact would seem to show Waldron's argument to be self-defeating.[44] For, if the disagreement arises concerning the quite general but foundational normative claim at step (a), then the very concept of democracy as aimed at respecting the equal autonomy of citizens cannot be used to support either the account of legitimate authority at step (d) or the account of fairness as realizing that respect at step (e). A foundational argument subject to uncertainty about the proper identification of its normative basis because of disagreement cannot then provide grounds for normative recommendations of certain political values or arrangements.[45] By contrast, if there's general agreement on the proposition that democracy is bound up with respecting the equal autonomy of citizens – a proposition that Waldron considers "basic" to rights-based theories of democracy – then the self-defeating objection disappears at

---

[43] Those who are perfectly content with the antidemocratic character of judicial review – perhaps on the grounds of a rights-based fundamentalism – of course won't be disturbed by this inference. But for them, Waldron also puts forward a rights-based critique of the institution; see Section C of Chapter 4.

[44] Several commentators point out the self-defeating character of Waldron's democratic argument against judicial review from the premises of disagreement. See Christiano, "Waldron on Law and Disagreement," 519–22, Fabre, "A Philosophical Argument for a Bill of Rights," 93, and Kavanagh, "Participation and Judicial Review," 467–8.

[45] It is important to note that I am not making a meta-ethical claim here about the self-refuting character of relativism, but rather a claim about the self-defeating character of the practical recommendations the formal argument is taken to support. For, the disagreement about normative content that drives Waldron's argument does *not* entail a relativistic rejection of the objectivity of values or the cognitive content of value claims. The point is, rather, one about the circumstances of politics: though each of us might be firmly committed to such objectivity or cognitivity, nevertheless, none of us has unimpeachable access to that by which we could identify our preferred value candidates as the indisputably correct ones. This is the general point of Chapter 8 of Waldron, *Law and Disagreement*, nicely entitled "The Irrelevance of Moral Objectivity." "The idea of objective values ... is an idea with little utility in politics. As long as objective values fail to disclose themselves to us, in our consciences or from the skies, in ways that leave no room for further disagreement about their character, all we have on earth are *opinions* or *beliefs* about objective value," ibid.: footnote 62, 111.

the most fundamental level.[46] However, it is only displaced to the next level up. For now we should wonder whether in fact Waldron's dual-aspect conception of fairness at step (e) is really the best or the only way to capture the democratic ideal of respecting the equal autonomy of each. Shouldn't we expect this abstract conception to also be the subject of reasonable disagreement, thereby debarring the use of it in a justification for the singular democratic appropriateness of legislative majoritarianism?

We might think that the worry is less pronounced than this, however, on the supposition that there is in fact much less disagreement at the most general levels about what democracy entails and what broad kinds of rights a democratic regime should respect.[47] We might be willing to agree, for instance, that democratic regimes generally evince significant degrees of popular accountability, legal regularity, and respect for private autonomy, features in fact secured through a relatively stable, universal set of rights categories: rights to equal individual liberties, membership rights, rights to legal actionability, political participation rights, and rights to a sufficiently equal opportunity for the exercise of rights.[48] Then our concerns about disagreement would probably be limited to those that originally motivated the jurisprudential debates about judicial review: given the indeterminacy of abstractly characterized categories of necessary rights, who or what organ within the polity should be empowered to specify and appropriately apply these general guarantees to more specific situations and controversies, and with respect to what kinds of methods and standards? If we have agreement at least on the general categories of democratic rights, however, there can be no democratic objection proceeding from the ineliminability of disagreement at that level, then, to the establishment of a bill of rights intended to entrench these categories of rights against infringement, contra the claim at step (i). The remaining objection is, at most then, to judicial supremacy in the final specification and application of those rights in controversial cases, as opposed to pure parliamentary

---

[46] For Waldron's methodological account of a rights-based theory and the justificatory role of basic judgments, see ibid., 214–17. It is crucial to his argument here that the foundational nature of rights in a normative theory does not necessarily imply the need for either legal or constitutional rights to protect them: "We cannot infer much about the practical recommendations of a normative theory from the character of its fundamental premises," 216–17. This is a way of uncoupling the easy inference from a rights-based normative theory to the endorsement of constitutional rights protected by judicial review.

[47] That is to say, general agreement among those committed to democracy in some form or another – after all, the objections to judicial review and constitutionalism in general being considered here are nonstarters for antidemocratic theories.

[48] The list follows the categorization of rights found in Habermas, *Between Facts and Norms*, 122–31. I discuss this further in Section B of Chapter 7.

sovereignty for interpreting the bill of rights *or* some other arrangement outside of the range of the court-parliament dichotomy.

Hopefully such considerations indicate that the depth and degree of expectable and persistent disagreement among those already committed to democracy cannot be judged by theoretical considerations alone. It is, rather, largely an empirical question, although not an easy one to settle for that, given the obvious inextricability of normative judgments from the criterial question of which regimes even count as democratic.[49] As one set of empirical indicators, we might think about the direction of constitution writing and the degree of democratic ratification over time. My sense of the history of the explicit practice of written democratic constitutionalism, barely over two hundred years long, is that constitutions have been increasingly subject to more scrupulous democratic ratification over time, as previously disenfranchised groups are increasingly recognized as deserving of equal participatory rights and included in both ordinary democratic and constitutional political processes. At the same time, remarkably, constitutional specificity has increased – just consider the increasing length of actual constitutions over time – indicating that there is more and more agreement on the core elements of the constitutional conditions of democracy.[50] The problem then arises just where the jurisprudes focused: namely, in the specification and application of broad constitutional generalities to particular problems and controversies. If this thumbnail historical judgment is accurate, then Waldron's argument from disagreement cannot be directed at the antidemocratic character of a constitution or a bill of rights but, rather, only at a placement of the more-or-less final power of constitutional specification in a judiciary insulated from popular accountability.

Presuming that Waldron could meet the self-defeating objection at the general level of the normative considerations of his argument, he might object to softening the anticonstitutionalism of his position by pointing to the notion of majoritarian fairness. Surely, he might say, constitutional

---

[49] Lijphart, *Patterns of Democracy: Government Forms and Performance in Thirty-Six Countries*, is a particularly ambitious but succinct study proposing several criteria for democratic regimes and applying them across a range of regimes.

[50] Cass Sunstein gives one very plausible reason why the more abstract principles enshrined in constitutional provisions are subject to much less disagreement and conflict than the more specific interpretations and applications of those principles: the former are often the result of incompletely theorized agreements, and so do not raise as many points of contention. See Cass R. Sunstein, *Legal Reasoning and Political Conflict* (New York: Oxford University Press, 1996), especially 35–61. Sunstein, *One Case at a Time: Judicial Minimalism on the Supreme Court*, 11, suggests that "constitution-making is often possible only because of the technique of producing agreement on abstractions amid disagreements about particulars," that is, of employing incompletely theorized agreements.

constraints that restrict the reach and finality of legislative majoritarianism violate the second aspect of democratic fairness: equal decisional weight for each. Of this I have no doubt, but I also doubt whether this aspect of the notion of fairness is one we should endorse in the first place, or whether even Waldron can really endorse it fully.

In Waldron's explicit defense of majority rule as fulfilling the criterion of fairness in terms of equal decisional weight (step [h]), he contrasts majority rule only with a random coin-toss decision procedure and a decision procedure ceding all power to one member of a group.[51] The argument here begins with the consideration that, in contrast to the coin-toss, an actual vote gives some minimal decisive weight to the actual opinions of the consociates, thereby respecting them as autonomous. Second, bare majority rule is better than the appointed decider method, as it gives decisive weight, and equal weight, to the opinions of all of the consociates rather than those of just one. That apparently is the end of the positive argument for majoritarianism as uniquely fulfilling the criterion of fairness (aspect 2)! In fact, he acknowledges that it only establishes the compatibility, but not the necessity, of simple majority rule with fairness as the realization of equal respect. But after a brief rejection of Mill's argument for plural voting for experts – after all, the identification of who are the experts at specifying rights will be subject to reasonable disagreement – Waldron merely reiterates his support for the unique fairness of simple majoritarianism: "I suspect (though I doubt that one can prove) that majority-decision is the *only* decision-procedure consistent with equal respect in this necessarily impoverished sense"[52] – impoverished because, of course, richer senses of equal respect are subject to political disagreement. He does not consider, however, any of the other decision rules beyond bare majority, such as unanimity or various levels of supermajoritarianism, the kinds of decision rules often associated with constitutionalism. Yet it seems clear that both unanimity and various stringencies of supermajority rules do in fact meet both of his stated criteria for decisional fairness. On the one hand, the actual opinions of the consociates have minimal decisional weight – they are actually counted – and, on the other, the opinions of each have an equal weight in the final tally – they count equally. What distinguishes bare majoritarianism from these latter rules is simply the degree to which the status-quo-ante is favored, and this is an issue quite distinct from that of fairness as equal decisional weight for each.[53]

---

[51] See Waldron, *Law and Disagreement*, 113–16.   [52] Ibid., 116, emphasis added.

[53] Apparently at one time, Waldron did think that any supermajority rules violated fairness in those cases where consociates voted their interests (not their good-faith opinions) and the status quo favored the interests of some. "On any issue where views align themselves with interests, people are not symmetrically situated in super-majoritarian

If central practices of constitutionalism – such as entrenchment in higher law, political structuration, and a bill of rights – can be understood precisely as favoring the status quo by requiring supermajoritarian procedures for amendment, then Waldron has failed to give an argument from fairness (aspect 2) to the rejection of constitutionalism: steps (h) and (i) are unsubstantiated. However, even if Waldron would be willing to say good riddance to supermajoritarian procedures on the grounds of decisional fairness, its unclear how he could endorse the political arrangements he apparently does. For instance, he seems to endorse forms of legislative representation that skew the direct numeric proportional equality between the number of assembly members and their constituents, such as bicameralism with one house representing the diversity of geography or other forms of federalism at the level of national legislatures.[54] In one of the only passages directly addressing issues of constitutional design, Waldron appears, in fact, to endorse supermajoritarian requirements:

There are a variety of ways in which a democratic constitution may mitigate this inconstancy [of rapid legislative reversals and re-reversals on rights]. The legislative process may be made more complex and laborious, and in various ways it may be made more difficult to revisit questions of principle for a certain time after they have been settled. (Such "slowing-down" devices may also be supported in the political community by values associated with the "rule of law.") None of this need be regarded as an affront to democracy; certainly a "slowing-down" device of this sort is not like the affront to democracy involved in removing issues from a

---

decision-procedures. The only decision-procedure that situates them symmetrically is the one that stipulates, in a binary dispute, that the status quo is to survive if and only if more than half of the voters support it and that the proposed alternative to the status quo is to be implemented if and only if more than half the voters support it," Waldron, "Freeman's Defense of Judicial Review," 40–41. I failed to find anything resembling this passage in *Law and Disagreement* which "embodies portions" (vii) of the article. I speculate that it is not surprising that the exclusivist defense of bare majoritarianism didn't survive because it embodies an image of interest-based voting, the rejection of which is central to the project of recovering the dignity of legislation.

54 This may be incorrect, but I take it that such legislative arrangements would naturally follow from the notion that legislative assemblies are recommended precisely because they mirror extant social complexity, and from the interesting discussion given to feudal forms of federalism at Waldron, *Law and Disagreement*, 56–68. "Though in the modern world we associate the legislature's character as an *assembly* with the idea of democratic representation, in an older understanding – an understanding which may *enrich* democratic jurisprudence rather than simply being an elaboration of it – law-making was associated with a process that related a legislative proposal to the complexity and multiplicity of persons, regions, relations, and circumstances, with which the proposed law would have to deal," ibid., 55.

vote altogether and assigning them to a separate non-representative forum like a court.[55]

But the problem of endorsing the preemptive character of major-itarianism would be deeper than this apparent contradiction of claims for Waldron, as it would in fact seem to lead to a rejection of repre-sentative assemblies in the first place, leaving directly democratic votes amongst the entire citizenry on statutes (and constitutional provisions) as the only democratically legitimate option. Recall that the argument for majoritarianism is motivated by the combination of the circum-stances of politics with the normative requirement for scrupulous fair-ness toward each *and* respect of the opinions of each thinking individual *qua* individual. However, any individual elected representative must represent significant numbers of electoral constituents – primarily in terms of their numerous and diverse opinions, rather than their inter-ests – but as a single voter in the representative assembly, he or she can't possibly do justice to the variety of opinions on the matter which their constituents are bound to have – even if they are all members of a single party or ideological faction. According to Waldron, ideally con-sidered, "the modern legislature is an assembly of the representatives of the main competing views in society, and it conducts its deliberations and makes its decisions in the midst of the competition and controversy among them."[56]

Perhaps Waldron could respond that multimember representative assemblies at least represent this diversity better than electorally unac-countable judges serving on a high constitutional court with very few other members – and solving their own internal court disputes by a bare majority rule to boot! Thus, the effects of the deindividualization and homogenization of the citizens' diverse opinions in a legislative assem-bly could then be seen as a pragmatic response to problems of scale and manageable complexity.[57] But, I think, this response misses the force of the original objection. The problem is that Waldron's formal argument relies, at least at steps (h) and (i), on a stringent and preemptive notion

[55] Ibid., 305–06. Note also the characteristics he builds into an ideal-typical model of legislative assembly: "members of the assembly represent not only different interests and regions, but come from completely different backgrounds, ethnic and cultural, as well as representing whatever political differences divide them," 73.

[56] Ibid., 23. This conception of the diversity of assemblies as mirroring the diversity of opinion and disagreement amongst the electorate is emphasized throughout the book, for instance at 10, 23–24, 27, 73–75, 99, 145, and 309. I return to this theme later.

[57] This is the approach Waldron seems to endorse in considering how to democratically conceptualize collective decision making among millions: ibid., 108–10.

of majoritarian fairness.[58] If that stringent notion is not sufficiently preemptive to delegitimate the apparent disrespect to individuals' claim to equal decisive power evinced by representation, then it cannot also retain its preemptive force as a democratic objection to the legitimacy of countermajoritarian decision procedures. Put alternatively, why should we accept only the stringent formulation of democratic equal respect in terms of majoritarian fairness, given the reasonable possibility of other conceptions of democratic equal respect?

4. Distortions in Democratic Processes of Representation

Up to now, I have been focusing on the issue of democratic legitimacy, in particular on Waldron's account of the relationship between the normative ideals of democracy, the conditions of political consociation, and the authoritative character of decisions made in the light of democratic procedures. But it is also worth exploring his account of democratic processes, for I believe that the force of the moves from (e) through (j) largely derive their force from an unconvincing account of how legislative assemblies carry out their representative functions. Thus I'd like to turn from internal tensions in Waldron's account of majoritarian legitimacy, to certain shortcomings in his account of democratic processes, shortcomings that should cause us to call into question the second main prong of his formal argument against judicial review from the notion of fairness (aspect 1).

First recall Waldron's ideal-typical account of why we have multimember legislative assemblies: "The point of a legislative assembly is to represent the main factions in the society, and to make laws in a way that takes their differences seriously rather than in a way that pretends that their differences are not serious or do not exist."[59] The problem with this account is simply that it assumes that the legislature is largely a transparent mirroring of the demos: the diversity of opinions and ideas, and their statistical distribution of support, evinced in the legislative chamber or chambers will, according to Waldron's assumption, largely mirror the diversity and statistical distribution of the same throughout the population of citizens.[60]

---

[58] Here I have found Christiano's discussion and criticism of Waldron's claim to the preemptive character of majoritarianism particularly helpful: Christiano, "Waldron on Law and Disagreement," 523–33.

[59] Waldron, *Law and Disagreement*, 27.

[60] F. R. Ankersmit, *Aesthetic Politics: Political Philosophy Beyond Fact and Value* (Stanford, CA: Stanford University Press, 1997) captures this problem in an interesting way by emphasizing the significant differences between a mimetic and an aesthetic conception of political representation. In a mimetic conception – a conception apparent in Waldron's assumptions – the goal of representation is a faithful mirroring of the citizenry, whether of their interests, opinions, or both. The aesthetic conception, by contrast, not only

This seems unrealistic at best and a potentially dangerous idealization at worst. It means that the theory will be largely blind to any structural mechanisms that impede – perhaps chronically impede – this easy correspondence between public and legislative opinion.

This is not, however, a mere lacuna in the quest for a complete political theory, as Waldron seems to imply when he recognizes the deficiency.[61] For, precisely this characteristic inattention to the structural difference between democratic governmental institutions and the citizenry also, it seems to me, plays the central role in vitiating his formal argument against Ely-style justifications for judicial review as a referee of representative processes. Let me explain by first noting a few peculiarities of how the issue is framed. At the beginning of the book, Waldron claims that the issue concerning the legitimacy of judicial review involves only three terms: "rights, courts, and legislation."[62] That is, the question is about the power of making laws in a democratic polity, including laws concerning individual rights, and what we face is a simple dichotomy concerning who is to choose and specify rights: either legislatures or courts. But this is a false dichotomy: legislatures and courts could share the task, an elected rights board could do it, an executive agency could do it, the public at large might do it, constitutional juries might do it, and so on.[63]

At the end of his book, Waldron emphasizes that taking rights seriously is largely a matter of the ideas that citizens and governmental officials have about individual rights, that is, largely a matter of political culture. In support, he cites as examples Locke's political theory, where a strong natural-law defense of individual rights is understood to be effectuated entirely through the self-understanding and self-restraint of legislators alone, and Mill's defense of individual liberty as oriented primarily to encouraging a set of moral convictions on the part of citizens that would promote a spirit of liberty.[64] As salutary as such inspiring appeals to individual moral attitudes may be, and as much as I would not like to deny

---

recognizes the persistent difference between the original (the citizenry) and its copy (in the legislature), but takes this difference as constitutive of the very kind of *political* representation involved. According to Ankersmit, the political theorist of democracy, like the aesthete, should not only think a faithful mimicking of the original is impossible to achieve, but undesirable as well. However helpful this contrast, I don't mean to endorse the rest of Ankersmit's aestheticization of politics.

[61] "Note for reviewers: one of the glaring defects of this book is that it does not include an adequate discussion of representation," Waldron, *Law and Disagreement*, footnote 60, 110.

[62] "If there is to be judicial review of legislation in the name of individual rights, then we should understand all three elements – rights, courts, and legislation – in a way that respects the conditions of disagreement that lie at the heart of our politics," ibid., 16 and again on 20.

[63] Recall that Perry's search for the best moral judgment and virtue moral rested on a like false dichotomy between only legislatures and courts: See Section B of Chapter 4.

[64] Waldron, *Law and Disagreement*. 307–11.

the important role political culture plays in the actual functioning of constitutional democracies, there appears to be something *institutionally* shortsighted about faith in such moral ideas alone as sure guides to a well-functioning set of political institutions.[65] Surely all those who have labored at constitutional conventions believe themselves to be doing something more than encouraging a spirit of liberty among their fellow citizens: they believe themselves to be tackling some well-known problems of political structuration by using well-adapted institutional designs. Another way to see this point more concretely is to focus on Waldron's persistent disregard of the manifold opportunities and possibilities open to ostensibly accountable governmental officials for self-dealing in such a way that they are more or less insulated from electoral pressures.[66] Of course, it is precisely these kinds of procedural manipulations that Ely's specific argument for judicial review is tailored to: namely, those that distort the transparent mirroring of electoral and official opinion.

It seems that the way to get smoothly from the specification of fairness as respect for the opinions of each at step (e) to step (f) endorsing representative legislatures and condemning judicial review at step (g) as a paternalistic substitution of the ideas of a few for the ideas of all is to simply gloss over the fact that legislatures can be said to effect the same paternalistic substitution under certain well-known conditions distorting representative processes. But it is only on condition of maintaining the idealizing mirroring assumption of legislative representation that Waldron can sustain the formal argument against all justifications for judicial review: those based both on the maintenance of substantive values, as well as those based upon the maintenance of legitimacy-conferring democratic processes. Consider, for instance, his confidence in the bulwark of well-established traditions of political culture in the United States and

---

[65] Thus, surprisingly for someone who takes seriously the actual institutional structures of some governmental institutions – namely, the internal structures of legislative assemblies – I detect in Waldron's arguments a short-sighted form of the moral *a-priorism* driving a distorting abstraction from institutional reality that I warned against at the end of Chapter 1. Said another way, I wish that Waldron's had more fully followed his own warnings about the dedifferentiating effects of "the pretensions of general jurisprudence" and paid more attention to institutional specificity. Ibid., 45–46.

[66] This disregard is also a bit puzzling for such an astute student of Rousseau's political theory, which, after all, hangs much on the fundamental distinction between the sovereign and the government, and then attends to the institutional distortions possible in translating sovereign will into governmental action: not only on tracing the three different wills potentially operative in officials' actions (the sovereign will of the people, the officials' own particular wills, and the corporate will of their governmental institution), but also on designing the structure and interrelations of different kinds of governmental bodies according to certain contextually-specific expectations about which of these wills might be favored or prominent at any time. See *On the Social Contract*, especially Book III, Chapters 2–8, and his worries about illegitimate assemblies in Book III, Chapter 13.

Great Britain as alone sufficient to secure the individual rights of minority dissent in the face of bare majoritarian legislation.[67]

Rather surprisingly, Waldron does not take direct issue with Ely's actual arguments for judicial review, preferring either to lump them with Dworkin's quite different kind of argument for the judicial securing of the substantive conditions of democracy,[68] or simply to impugn the supposed motivations of unnamed theorists who are attracted to Ely's view.[69] The closest he seems to come to confronting Ely's arguments is in considering the claim (unattributed to any theory or theorist) that judicial review is supported by the principle that no one ought to be a judge in her or his own case. After contending plausibly that this principle of *nemo iudex in sua causa* sweeps too broadly when we are considering the basic decision procedures of collective government – after all, everyone in the nation-state will be affected by the decision – Waldron claims that at least no one is excluded when procedural rights are determined collectively.

> It seems quite inappropriate to invoke this principle in a situation where the community as a whole is attempting to resolve some issue concerning the rights of *all* the members of the community and attempting to resolve it on a basis of equal participation. There, it seems not just unobjectionable but *right* that all those who are affected by an issue of rights should participate in the decision (and if we want a Latin tag to answer *nemo iudex*, we can say, 'Quod omnes tangit ab omnibus decidentur').[70]

To begin with, the argument from *nemo iudex* is structurally different than Ely's referee claim: whereas the former insists that a second, impartial party (courts) is needed where a first party (the majority) is trying to decide in its own case (concerning the powers of the majority), the latter insists that in a dispute between two parties (the people and their legislators), a third impartial party (courts) may be needed if one of the parties (the legislators) can easily manipulate the settled rules of interaction.

But if the principle of *quod omnes tangit* is supposed to be an answer to Ely's claim that we need an impartial referee to see both that the channels

---

[67] Waldron, *Law and Disagreement*, 280–1.   [68] Ibid., 285.

[69] Ibid., 295. In Waldron, "Rights and Majorities: Rousseau Revisited," there is a brief one-paragraph recapitulation and rebuttal of Ely's defense of judicial review, but the same conflation of the people and their legislative representatives is evident there as well, in that case driving a false dichotomy between judges on the one hand, and the people and their representatives on the other, as the only two parties to choose from when considering how to police the procedural preconditions of representative democracy: "It is true that the processes of democracy must be sustained and policed, but this is something with which citizens and their representatives should be concerned....A concern for the fairness and integrity of the process is something that Rousseau's citizen will exhibit along with everything else. He does not need a judge to do it for him" (418).

[70] Waldron, *Law and Disagreement*, 297–98, emphasis original.

of electoral change are kept open and that legislative processes are kept fully representative, then it rather astonishingly begs the central question. After all, the procedural rights being decided on here are *not* being decided on by "the community as a whole" or "*all* the members of the community" but by a very few *legislative representatives* of the community who may be able to change the procedures in such a way that they are no longer *representative* (if they ever were to begin with). When we are worried about self-dealing manipulations of the rules of the game by elected officials to the detriment of the democratic process which is supposed to ensure the authority/legitimacy of the laws made, it is simply beside the point to invoke *quod omnes tangit* and say that the people as a whole should be able to decide the political procedures that apply to the people as a whole. Well, of course – but this is irrelevant to the situation we face: the ineliminable structural difference between representative governmental institutions and the citizenry as a whole whose opinions they are supposed to represent.

Waldron's final consideration with respect to proceduralist justifications of judicial review revolves around the contention that respect for the equal autonomy of each citizen requires taking seriously their opinions not just about the shape and character of substantive rights that law should afford but also about the procedural rights that structure that lawmaking process. The idea here is that the same faith that underwrites confidence in the competence of democratic citizens to think seriously and debate in good faith about issues of substance also must underwrite confidence in their capacities to think about how to structure political procedures.

> Working in this [Enlightenment-inspired, rights-based] tradition of political thought, we will not get very far with any argument that limits the competence of popular self-government and stops it short at the threshold of political procedure, assigning questions about forms of government to a body [such as a court] of a different sort altogether. Democracy is in part *about* democracy: one of the first things on which people demand a voice about, and concerning which they claim competence, is the procedural character of their own political arrangements.[71]

Here I am inclined to entirely agree with Waldron, for it seems correct to say that, at the level of constitutional choice, the people express their ultimate sovereign authority, an authority that can be legitimately be used to structure and authorize both constitutional substance and procedure.[72]

---

[71] Ibid., 296.
[72] Recall also the discussion in Chapter 3, Section A, in which I argued that, in fact, at the level of constitutional design substantive rights can often have procedural justifications and that many apparently purely procedural guarantees in fact are intended to guarantee substantively justified principles.

So the question here is not about whether we can trust ordinary people to think procedurally, or whether we should rather trust a few wise lawyers and judges to think procedurally, as Waldron would have it. For on Ely's proceduralist understanding of judicial review, the point is not to write the constitutional procedures of democracy but, rather, to preserve the popular sovereignty expressed in the constitutional structuring of the rules of ordinary democratic politics against whatever advantages might be gained by representative institutions through distorting those rules in the first place. Said another way, the "distrust" motivating Ely's case for judicial review does not concern the capacity of citizens to think procedurally, but the realistic distrust of the ability of representative institutions to make themselves unrepresentative by altering the constitutional structures that are intended to ensure representation. The proceduralist defense of judicial review may well depend on a kind of distrust, but it is not distrust of the thinking capacities of fellow citizens but, rather, a distrust of certain predictable consequences of the structural features of representative democratic institutions.

To summarize a long discussion, recall that I laid out Waldron's account of democratic legitimacy and majoritarian democratic process in order to reconstruct his formal argument from democracy against any forms of judicial review. I then claimed that his account of democratic legitimacy might be self-defeating if good-faith disagreement among citizens is too deep and too sweeping. I also suggested, however, that there was some empirical evidence from the historical development of practices of democratic constitutionalism to ground the hope of more agreement on democratic institutions and the rights needed to ensure them, at least at a general level. I then argued that, since the case for the unique legitimacy and preemptive character of bare majoritarianism is both overdemanding in its requirements and inconsistent with Waldron's own preferred forms of democratic decision making, it could not be used (as in steps [h]) and [i])) to support pure parliamentary sovereignty and to delegitimize judicial review in the name of equal decisional weight for all citizens. I then developed concerns about the unrealistic picture of democratic processes that the other prong (steps [f]) and [g])) of Waldron's argument depends on, specifically whether we should think that elected legislative assemblies are always representative of the opinions of the citizenry in the way required for the argument. In considering what was left out of this picture – namely, the foreseeable structural deformations that might make a political process undemocratic and nonrepresentative – I argued that the formal argument did not then reach to or adequately refute the concerns motivating proceduralist defenses of constitutional review performed by an electorally independent body. I also raised concerns about the realism of hopes for a political culture of rights as sufficient to forestall democratic troubles, and about the misplacement of the antipaternalist complaint of disrespecting people's capacities for thinking procedurally when directed at Ely-style defenses of judicial review.

C. UPSHOT: WE NEED A THEORY OF DEMOCRATIC CONSTITUTIONALISM

Freeman's defense of judicial review as a possible choice open to a sovereign democratic people at the level of constitutional choice rightly emphasizes the originary nature of popular sovereignty at the level of constitutional choice. I argued, however, that it failed in overlooking the internal connection between the legitimacy of democratic constitutional choice and the ongoing democratic character of politics established by those choices. In a sense, Freeman offers a defense of judicial review that is content to maintain democratic legitimacy at the originary level of establishing a polity, while establishing substantive constitutional checks on the outcomes of ordinary democratic political processes. In doing so, he offered an account of constitutionalism that succumbed to paternalist worries motivated by the reasonableness of ineliminable disagreement among citizens about the particular shape, entailments, and specific applications of democratic rights. His account severs the internal connection between the democratic legitimacy of constitutional choice and the ongoing democratic specification and realization of the constitutional structures chosen.

In contrast, Waldron's convincing insights into the internal deliberative structure of modern legislative assemblies, and into the way in which the fact of reasonable disagreement forces political theory to proffer a results-independent account of democratic legitimacy, alerted us to the paternalistic perils of substantivist understandings of judicial review. However, his account of majoritarian fairness as the uniquely legitimate decision procedure led to an unconvincing repudiation of constitutionalism *tout court* in favor of pure parliamentary sovereignty. And his attack on proceduralist defenses of judicial review relied on an overly idealized account of legislative representation that appears institutionally insensitive to structural deformations in representative processes themselves. Waldron seems then, to have severed the internal connection between the ongoing democratic specification and realization of rights and the maintenance of the constitutional structures that ensure the legitimacy of such democratic processes.

In a sense, we seem to be vacillating between a democratic defense of constitutionalism and an anticonstitutionalist defense of democracy. But are the principles of constitutionalism and democracy as antithetical as Freeman's and Waldron's arguments seem to imply? It is time to get off the see-saw by trying to conceive of democracy and constitutionalism as co-constitutive, rather than antithetical, principles. I suggest that one way to do this – while retaining fealty to the insights both into the need for a structuring of democratic processes and the need for taking reasonable disagreement seriously – is to adopt Cass Sunstein's suggestion that we think of constitutionalism as a practice intended to structure and make use of disagreement as a creative resource, as far as possible, and to limit its destructive capacities when not.

In any democracy that respects freedom, the process of deliberation faces a pervasive problem: widespread and even enduring disagreement. A central goal of constitutional arrangements, and constitutional law, is to handle this problem, partly by turning disagreement into a creative force, partly by making it unnecessary for people to agree when agreement is not possible.[73]

The normative question then becomes not why should we have democracy or why should we have a constitution, but, rather, why should we have constitutional democracy? I argue that Habermas's account of deliberative democratic constitutionalism presents the most convincing normative account of the co-constitutive character of constitutionalism and democracy in Chapter 7. Following Habermas's and Sunstein's lead there, I take up some of the particular ways in which commonly accepted constitutional structures and democratic institutions can be seen as a result of such a co-constitutive view, before returning to the question of how to institutionalize the function of constitutional review.

Before turning to those issues, however, I take up in Chapter 6 one form of defense of judicial review that deliberative democrats in particular seem peculiarly attracted to. It can perhaps be thought of most easily as attacking the claim Waldron makes that the opinions considered by a constitutional court are not fully representative of the opinions of the citizenry, or at least not as representative as those considered by legislatures (see step [g]). The idea here, as will be seen, is that special characteristics of juridical discourse make it more fully representative of the people's principles than can be achieved in legislatures. I argue against such arguments, that attention to the actual work-product of courts can show how juridical discourse is in many ways strikingly inappropriate to the kinds of principled moral deliberation claimed for it by such arguments.

[73] Sunstein, *Designing Democracy: What Constitutions Do*, 8.

6

The Seducements of Juristic Discourse as Democratic Deliberation

The basic question at the heart of this chapter is whether we find in judicial opinions a language well-suited for principled moral and political argument in a democracy. At the most simple level, this chapter answers in the negative, based on the contention that juristic discourse is well tailored to arguments concerning legal rules, but not those concerning the principles, ideals, and values that underwrite and justify the laws we give to ourselves as democratic citizens. If this is right, then one prominent form of argument advanced by some deliberative theories of democracy justifying strong practices of judicial review in constitutional democracies should be abandoned. Recall that central to the antipaternalist attack on judicial review, whether as formulated by Hand, Dahl, Ely, or Waldron, is the notion that, because their members are electorally accountable, legislatures are representative institutions, whereas constitutional courts are not representative because their members are not electorally accountable. Perhaps, however, as deliberative democracy seeks to deemphasize voting as the paradigmatic democratic action, while celebrating deliberative reasons-responsive cooperation as the ideal of democratic citizenship, electoral accountability should no longer be thought central to the degree of representativeness of a political institution. On this idea, at least, the representativeness of an institution should be gauged in terms of its responsiveness to reasons, and in particular to certain kinds of reasons. The form of deliberative democratic defense of judicial review I examine and critique here builds on the deliberative conception of democratic processes and thereby attempts to explain why we should understand constitutional courts, despite their electoral unaccountability, as *representative* institutions. In particular, I attempt to undercut the claim shared by such defenses that, because of the special sensitivity of courts to principled moral reasoning in comparison with other governmental organs, we ought to have a division of labor between governmental institutions sensitive to reasons and those sensitive to majoritarian desires. Furthermore, this suggests that, if we want to promote principled democratic discussion and debate – and especially if we have the deliberative democratic aspiration to have at least some important political decisions turn on the most reasonable outcomes of such discussions and debates – then we as political theorists and political participants ought to turn our attention to alternative fora beyond constitutional and supreme courts.

The chapter begins by reconstructing the relevant arguments of three prominent theorists – John Rawls, Christopher Eisgruber, and Frank Michelman – who recommend or endorse an institutional division of deliberative labor on the basis of the unique abilities of constitutional courts to engage in principled moral and political reasoning (Section A). The section also includes a brief look at a wide variety of democratic justifications for judicial review which seem similarly seduced by juristic discourse. Section B is devoted to a critical examination of the shared claims about the character of judicial reasoning through a selective tour through some decisions of the Supreme Court of the United States concerning religious freedom, criminal punishment, individual rights to private autonomy, and electoral equality. The point of the examples is to highlight the significant disanalogies between juristic discourse and principled moral and political discourse, at least in the U.S. system. Section C argues that this disanalogy is not accidental, given a specific legal-institutional context where a constitutional court is also the apex of the appellate judiciary and employs common-law methods of adjudication. Deliberative democrats are right to stress the wide public debate and discussion necessary to make good on the promise of democratic legitimacy. The chapter's arguments recommend, however, that we should eschew the seductive claim that juridical discourse is a paradigmatic language for democratic deliberation, and thereby also avoid the conception of constitutional courts as a representative institution that can solve the problem of deliberative legitimacy. The section concludes with consequences of these arguments for institutional design, the relationship between legal and moral-political principles, and the diversity of practical reason.

A.   A DIVISION OF LABOR BETWEEN JURISTIC DELIBERATION AND POPULIST AGGREGATION?

Chapters 1 through 5 have been concerned with various arguments for and against a judicial institutionalization of constitutional review, arguments that have been concerned to claim the best conception of constitutional democracy as support. Throughout, I have been disentangling and highlighting the diverse conceptions of democracy, of constitutionalism, and particularly of the relations between democracy and constitutionalism as the crucial determinants of the overall shape and character of the arguments and of their concomitant limitations and problems. By contrast, the species of argument for judicial review that this chapter is concerned with – that which conceives of courts as the crucial location for democratic deliberation on matters of fundamental moral and political principle – might be thought to resolve a tension internal to the ideal of democracy alone, a tension acutely felt in deliberative conceptions of democracy. Recall that deliberative democrats, like all democratic theorists, are committed, on the one hand, to an egalitarian political ideal: in a democratic form of government all citizens ought to have some significantly equal opportunities to influence governmental actions. But deliberative democrats are also committed, on the other hand, to a specific interpretation of the egalitarian political ideal: political decisions ought to, in some sense, arise out of and follow from the reasoned deliberations of free and equal citizens concerned to solve collectively shared problems. Thus the theory endorses a legitimacy criterion that combines an ideal of the equal political influence of each with an ideal of the reasons-responsiveness of governmental institutions. Consider, for instance, the way in which Cass Sunstein's formulation pays fealty both to egalitarian influence and reasons-responsiveness: "I contend that a constitution should promote *deliberative democracy*, an idea that is meant to combine political accountability with a high degree of reflectiveness and a general commitment to reason-giving."[1]

These two ideals may, however, come into tension. To see how, consider the various positions that deliberative theories of democratic legitimacy may occupy on the fourth axis of analysis I introduced in Chapter 3: namely, the axis that concerns the accountability or answerability of power, ranged from the populist to the expertocratic extremes.[2] On the one hand, institutions that are highly responsive to and answerable to the opinions and interests of ordinary citizens – populist institutions – will be favored by those who set the egalitarian component of the legitimacy criterion at the forefront of their theories. On the other, those who take reasons-responsiveness to be preeminent, especially those who are impressed by the difficulties of ensuring high-quality decisions under modern conditions of uncertainty, cognitive deficiencies and distortions, social complexity, pluralism, and so on often will favor institutions intended to produce rational, efficient decisions by limiting decisional

[1] Ibid., 6–7.
[2] Recall also that I use these two labels as shorthand for indicating two poles on a continuum measuring the responsiveness of governmental institutions and governmental actors, in their day-to-day decisions, to the inputs of citizens, and that my use of "populist" should not be confused with either an ideological position or with a conception of direct, nonrepresentative democracy.

control to a handful of specially trained and prepared elites – that is, expertocratic institutions. The difficulty is then how to design democratic institutions able to approximately realize the twin ideals embedded in deliberative conceptions of democratic legitimacy. Not surprisingly, significant ambiguities persist in the literature concerning how to concretely realize the egalitarian moral ideals fueling populism while appropriately acknowledging the apparent sociological realism and the desire for high-quality political decisions that fuel expert elitism. The tension here might then be thought endemic to deliberative democracy, independently of any considerations about constitutionalism.

One solution often envisioned, even if only dimly, is a kind of division of labor between institutions that ensure popular input and institutions that ensure decisions according to reasoned deliberations. Although plausible candidates for the former include legislatures, citizen review boards, and even executive officers, theorists have idealized courts, especially judges, as the best candidates for the latter. The idea arises here from the thought that, because juridical decisions are legally binding decisions that are regularly accompanied by supporting reasons in the form of judicial opinions, they represent a paradigmatic type of deliberative decision. In contrast, the legally binding decisions of the more populist-sensitive institutions need not be supported by reasons, and so are seen as aggregative but nondeliberative. The egalitarian ideals of popular political influence are to be served by the traditional aggregating institutions of electoral, majoritarian democracy; the deliberative ideals of reasoned decision making are to be served by the traditional judicial institutions constituted by a legal elite trained in practical reasoning.

John Rawls, Christopher Eisgruber, and Frank Michelman are three theorists who, I believe, can plausibly be considered among the ranks of those deliberative democrats who supply explicit arguments to support a political division of labor between populist, majoritarian institutions and expert deliberative institutions, a division of labor that would then apparently satisfy the dualistic deliberative criterion for democratic legitimacy.[3]

---

[3] Some might contest my characterization of Rawls as a deliberative democrat. Sheldon S. Wolin, "The Liberal/Democratic Divide: On Rawls's *Political Liberalism*," *Political Theory* 24, no. 1 (1996), for instance, seems to see few if any traces of democracy in Rawls's work, either in its earlier form of a theory of justice, or its later emendation into a specifically political – as opposed to comprehensive moral – theory of liberalism. In his review, Wolin promises to raise "what is for Rawls a nonquestion of the status of democracy within his version of liberalism," 97. At the very least, Joshua Cohen, "For a Democratic Society," in *The Cambridge Companion to Rawls*, ed. Samuel Freeman (New York: Cambridge University Press, 2003), shows that democracy is not a nonquestion; at the most, he successfully demonstrates Rawls's democratic theory as fully deliberative. For an important treatment of Rawls as a deliberative democrat, in the context of an interesting overview and critique of the field, see Samuel Freeman, "Deliberative Democracy: A Sympathetic Critique," *Philosophy and Public Affairs* 29, no. 4 (2000).

In the following, I am not concerned with the theorists' general justifications for judicial review, only with their claims that courts – and especially supreme courts with the power to invalidate legislative and executive actions based on the court's interpretation of a constitution – provide a unique forum in which reasoned deliberation about matters of basic political principle can be not only aired but also become decisive for a nation-state as a whole.[4] If they are right that supreme constitutional courts provide an exemplary site for generating the high-quality political deliberations theorists desire, then they will have provided at least a strong *prima facie* case for shunting some important collective decisions into electorally independent courts, while restricting the scope of decisions open to the more populist-sensitive organs of democratic governments.

The three theories differ, however, in the specific manner in which they attempt to show constitutional court judgments and supporting opinions as democratically respectable. Rawls's conception of political liberalism supports the idea that juristic discourse is the paradigmatic idiom for public deliberation because it adheres to the neutral canons of "public reason," carefully eschewing reference to citizens' diverse comprehensive worldviews, while nevertheless rendering decisions based on fundamental political values shared by all reasonable citizens. Courts are democratic because they exemplify how to *speak in* the political language shared by citizens. Eisgruber, in contrast, argues that courts are the paradigmatic location for principled moral argument about public issues, whereas governmental institutions sensitive to popular input are capable only of bargains and compromises on matters of mere policy. Courts are democratic because they *speak for* the people on certain fundamental issues of principle. Michelman, finally, claims that judicial review of legislation could be seen as worthy of respect by free and equal democratic citizens, at least when such powers of review were exercised in a way that warranted the expectation that judicial interpretations of fundamental law resulted from deliberations that were as open as possible to the full breadth of public debate and disagreement on the relevant issues. Citizens could, under such conditions, understand judicial review as an institution simultaneously realizing the dualistic deliberative legitimacy condition of egalitarian reasons-responsiveness. Constitutional courts

---

[4] It is important to note as a caveat that Eisgruber, Michelman, and Rawls explicitly claim that they are not providing arguments to the effect that strong institutions of judicial review are *indispensable* to *any* constitutional democracy. They seek rather more modest goals: to show that judicial review is at least compatible with constitutional democracy, properly understood, and that in many cases it may actually enhance well-functioning deliberative democracy. Christopher L. Eisgruber, *Constitutional Self-Government* (Cambridge, MA: Harvard University Press, 2001), 108, Frank I. Michelman, *Brennan and Democracy* (Princeton, NJ: Princeton University Press, 1999), 59–60 and 135, Rawls, *Political Liberalism*, 240.

would then, on Michelman's theory, be democratic to the extent that they *speak with* the people. On all three theories, juristic discourse is the idealized language for public deliberations among citizens because judicial decisions are backed up by reasoned opinions and either, *à la* Rawls, rendered in the correct idiom of public reason or, *à la* Eisgruber, turning on issues of principle not policy or, *à la* Michelman, the results of broad public and expert processes of communication, debate, and discussion.

1. The Juridical Exemplification of Public Reason: Rawls

In order to understand why Rawls lionizes a supreme constitutional court as "the exemplar of public reason"[5] in a constitutional democracy, it's necessary to look at the problem he takes the conception of "political liberalism" to be solving. Although his 1971 *A Theory of Justice*[6] outlined a powerful set of arguments for a deontological justification of liberal principles of justice – what he called "justice as fairness" – Rawls came to believe that it was seriously deficient in its unrealistic assessment of the extent to which all citizens in actually existing constitutional democracies would or could unreservedly endorse the basic principles of justice as fairness. In particular, Rawls became much more sensitive to the apparently ineliminable plurality of irreconcilable moral worldviews in healthy democracies: "A modern democratic society is characterized not simply by a pluralism of comprehensive religious, philosophical, and moral doctrines but by a pluralism of incompatible yet reasonable comprehensive doctrines. No one of these doctrines is affirmed by citizens generally. Nor should one expect that in the foreseeable future one of them, or some other reasonable doctrine, will ever be affirmed by all, or nearly all, citizens."[7]

The theoretical problem raised by this situation – what Rawls calls the "fact of reasonable pluralism" – is that the *legitimacy* of a democratic government hangs on the acceptance, by its citizens, of the basic moral soundness of at least the fundamental principles that are to govern their consociation, the principles that a constitution is intended to instantiate and promote. But how can diverse citizens, with their different and incompatible moral worldviews, agree on the same set of moral principles? Rawls's solution is that citizens can agree on a set of specifically *political* principles – what he calls the "overlapping consensus" – which simultaneously are shared by all of the various reasonable comprehensive doctrines, are grounded in those more encompassing moral views, and yet are nevertheless neutral with respect to each of the comprehensive

---

5 Rawls, *Political Liberalism*, 231.   6 Rawls, *A Theory of Justice*.   7 Rawls, *Political Liberalism*, xviii.

worldviews. As long as citizens mutually agree to resolve their fundamental political disagreements on the basis of these neutral principles
that they all already agree to (although each for their own reasons), then
a democratic regime can gain the legitimacy and stability it requires.
Furthermore, it is crucial that citizens understand the overlapping
consensus to apply not to any and every political issue, nor to any and
every social issue, but only to the most basic of political arrangements
and underlying principles. "Political values alone are to settle such
fundamental questions as: who has the right to vote, or what religions
are to be tolerated, or who is to be assured fair equality of opportunity,
or to hold property."[8] The "gag rule" on citizens of restricting their
appeals only to the publicly shared principles, combined with the limitation of the applicability of those principles only to fundamental
matters of basic justice and constitutional essentials, are then intended
to ensure that citizens can treat one another as reasonable and moral
consociates in settling their disagreements, even when they hold irreconcilable moral worldviews.[9]

Finally, Rawls understands the content of "public reason" to be
comprised of the substantive political principles shared in the overlapping consensus, in addition to commonly shared standards of evidence, inference, and justification. So, on the one hand, public reason
contains substantive political principles: principles such as those
guaranteeing individual liberty of conscience, rights to due process of
law, equal voting rights, and so on, as well as those underlying the
structure of democratic government and political processes. On the
other hand, public reason also contains generally accepted methods of
inquiry and deliberation: "we are to appeal only to presently accepted
general beliefs and forms of reasoning found in common sense, and
the methods and conclusions of science when these are not controversial."[10] The proper use of public reason, then, is the key to the
legitimacy of democratic decisions, as it ensures that citizens can
accept the moral soundness of the basic structures and principles of
their government.

We are to apply public reason, and public reason alone, when we are
trying to decide on matters of basic justice and constitutional provisions
concerning governmental institutions and individual rights. As citizens,
then, we have a "duty of civility" toward fellow citizens who may not
share our own comprehensive doctrine to adopt the neutralized

[8] Ibid., 214.
[9] Here Rawls draws on Stephen Holmes, "Gag Rules or the Politics of Omission," in
Constitutionalism and Democracy, ed. Jon Elster and Rune Slagstad (New York: Cambridge
University Press, 1988).
[10] Rawls, *Political Liberalism*, 224.

principles and forms of reasoning of public reason when addressing matters of importance. This duty of civility applies when considering fairness toward individuals and other constitutional essentials, whether we are ordinary voters considering such matters, or legislators, or candidates for public office, or political party members, or officials discharging our appointed functions, or, most significantly here, judges interpreting the constitution and in so doing exercising the power to review the actions of other official actors and organs. The democratic *process* then, in order to be legitimate, requires that at least on the most fundamental matters, decisions should be made on the basis of the shared content and canons of public reason, rather than on the basis of compromise, bargaining, differential power and threat-potentials, or bare majority rule. In other words, aggregative processes are sufficient for nonfundamental, everyday matters, but deliberative processes, under the specific conditions imposed by the fact of pluralism and the restrictions of public reason, are required to decide basic issues of political morality.

For my purposes, the most striking claim that Rawls makes with respect to the way decisive *power* is distributed through political processes is that a constitutional court, one entrusted with the power of judicial review, not only should employ public reason, but that it is, for a society, "the exemplar of public reason."[11] He explicates this claim in terms of three theses. First, and most important, a supreme court is the exemplar of public reason insofar as it "is the only branch of government that is visibly on its face the creature of that [public] reason and of that reason alone."[12] Unlike other branches of government that may consider ordinary political matters, and so may invoke particular comprehensive doctrines, a supreme court has "no other reason and no other values than the political"[13] values comprising public reason. In other words, only a constitutional court consistently speaks and decides issues solely on the basis of the impartial language tailored to consociation across pluralistic diversity. Second, a supreme court is the exemplar of public reason insofar as it plays an educative role with respect to a society's publicly shared reason. Because such courts should interpret a nation-state's constitution and traditions in a way that justifies those as a whole, in the light of the publicly shared conception of justice, a court can show citizens the political values all can be expected to share and embrace. Third, a supreme court with the power of judicial review also educates the public by intervening decisively in constitutional controversies on the basis of shared political values, rather than on the basis of partisan struggles "for power and position."[14] In this way, a court "give[s] public reason

---

[11] Ibid., 231.   [12] Ibid., 235.   [13] Ibid.   [14] Ibid., 239.

vividness and vitality in the public forum; this it does by its authoritative judgments on fundamental political questions."[15]

What are we to make of these striking claims? To begin, it is important to note that Rawls merely stipulates that public reason is the reason of a supreme court, and that a supreme court can play an exemplary educative role with respect to the duties of civility. The closest he gets to an argument supporting such contentions is an invocation of Ackerman's dualist theory of United States democracy, followed by a supposition that in such a dualist regime, "the political values of public reason provide the Court's basis for interpretation."[16] Second, in Rawls's defense, it also must be noted that there is no evidence, empirical or otherwise, adduced precisely because he is putting forward the exemplarity claim as an illustration of what he means by the concept of public reason. He is not attempting to make claims about institutional design, or even about the comparative capacities or separate roles of various governmental organs.[17] In fact, he explicitly says that "while the Court is special in this respect, the other branches of government can certainly, if they would but do so, be forums of principle along with it in debating constitutional questions."[18] The point of the discussion of supreme courts in the context of Rawls's overall political theory is simply to demonstrate what he means by public reason by pointing to what he takes to be its clearest example.

A third point is that if Rawls is wrong to point to constitutional court decisions as exemplifying the sole use of public reason – as I will argue in Section B – then his subsidiary claims about the educative role of court decisions with respect to public reason will also fall. A supreme court could not educate ordinary citizens either about their duties of civility or about the contents and guidelines of public reason if its decisions were not solely or largely based in – and facially seen to be based in – that special argot of impartial, public political morality.[19]

The fourth point is that if, however, Rawls were right, then we would have some strong *prima facie* reasons to accord courts a preferred place with respect to democratic deliberations, especially with respect to highly

---

[15] Ibid., 237.   [16] Ibid., 234.

[17] For a political theorist, Rawls has surprisingly little to say about the design of governmental institutions.

[18] Rawls, *Political Liberalism*, 240.

[19] There are of course, other quite significant sociological barriers to the putative educative functions of constitutional court decisions: for example, whereas the outcomes of high-profile cases are occasionally reported in mass-media outlets, it is rare for the grounding reasons presented in the opinions to be fairly and comprehensively reported, and, it is perhaps even rarer that those opinions are read by citizens other than legal elites. I am grateful to Roger Hartley and Gerald Rosenberg for insisting on the importance of these empirical barriers. My point in this chapter is to show that, even if constitutional court opinions were well-reported front-page news, their juristic character would nevertheless render them ineffective as exemplars of public reason.

contested but fundamental issues of governmental structure, individual rights, and abstract constitutional provisions. It would appear that deliberative democratic theory ought to recommend deference to the legal elites of a supreme constitutional court as the paragon of public reason, while restricting the more populist branches of government to the messier issues of everyday ordinary politics, where we need not worry about the dirty-hands problems of bare struggles for influence, position, and raw power. We should then have a division of labor between expert deliberators trained in the moral argot of public reason and populist aggregators who respond directly to the amoral imperatives of interest groups and their threats. For Rawls, then, the fact (if it is a fact) that supreme court judges exemplify how to speak in the special language of democratic political consociation renders them exemplars of democratic discussion.

2. The Juridical Representation of the People's Moral Reason: Eisgruber

Although Rawls himself does not attempt to use this apparent deliberative advantage of courts to justify judicial review as legitimate and recommended, Eisgruber does. However, unlike Rawls who focuses on the restricted and denuded language of public reason that supreme courts are supposed to specialize in, Eisgruber focuses on the institutional incentives that make courts preferred fora for deliberations concerning matters of fundamental political morality, especially in comparison with the branches of government that are more sensitive to popular and electoral pressures.[20] Thus, both idealize courts as unique sites of principled deliberation, even though Rawls takes the language of judicial decisions to be crucial, whereas Eisgruber focuses on the unique institutional location of courts vis-à-vis electoral pressures.

Like other deliberative democrats who follow the lines of Alexander Bickel's distinction between kinds of public forums such as Dworkin,[21] Eisgruber conceives of electorally insulated courts as the paradigmatic location for principled moral argument about public issues, as, on his account, governmental institutions sensitive to popular input are capable only of bargains and compromises on matters of mere policy. The first major premise in his justification of judicial review is the distinction between matters of principle and policy. Principles reflect our fundamental values, and they should trump our interests. As citizens, we are happy to let ordinary laws and governmental actions be the result of partisan processes that aggregate across our divergent interests and

---

[20] Eisgruber, *Constitutional Self-Government*.
[21] Bickel, *The Least Dangerous Branch*, Dworkin, *Freedom's Law*. See, respectively, Chapters 2 and 4 for further discussions of Bickel's and Dworkin's theories of judicial review.

decide such issues of mere policy in a more or less majoritarian manner. We are happy, in Eisgruber's words, to let such decisions result from "an effort to pander to voters, campaign for higher office, engineer an interest-group deal, or honor a party platform."[22] However, we take some matters to reflect fundamental and nonnegotiable values, and we expect the decisions of a democratic government to respect this difference. As moral citizens, we should not allow such matters to be decided by crass partisan mechanisms. We want the decision, rather, to reflect our convictions about what is right, no matter what we as private subjects desire. As Bickel puts the point, such decisions should be the result of "a principle-defining process that stands aside from the marketplace of expediency."[23] On matters of principle, then, we insist on *deliberative* processes that can present, sift, and evaluate moral reasons, rather than mere aggregative processes that reflect the preponderance of private interests across the electorate.

If we then ask what governmental institutions could perform such sensitive moral deliberations while remaining true to the demands of principle even in the face of countervailing interests and pressures, a body disciplined by the use of reason and separated from the vicissitudes of majoritarian excitement recommends itself: a court at the apex of appellate jurisdiction, with members having life-tenure and so insulated from electoral accountability, and, finally, entrusted with the power to decide the most fundamental issues of political principle for the nation-state. In other words, the Supreme Court of the United States. Eisgruber supports his second main premise – that such a supreme court is better suited than any other governmental organs to make principled decisions – through a comparative analysis of institutional incentives in the United States constitutional scheme.[24] Because legislatures and chief executives are subject to insistent and cyclical electoral pressures, their incentives

---

[22] Eisgruber, *Constitutional Self-Government*, 4.

[23] Bickel, *The Least Dangerous Branch*, 69.

[24] This account of comparative institutional incentives is significantly the same as the one given by Bickel over forty years ago: "Courts have certain capacities for dealing with matters of principle that legislatures and executives do not possess. Judges have, or should have, the leisure, the training, and the insulation to follow the ways of the scholar in pursuing the ends of government," ibid., 25–26. A bit strangely, however, Eisgruber reads Bickel as running essentially a competence-based – rather than structural incentives-based – argument for judicial review: namely, that judges, trained as lawyers, are simply better principled reasoners than legislators and executive officials: Eisgruber, *Constitutional Self-Government*, 68. But if this were so, then Bickel's celebrated disdain for "self-excited majoritarianism" and his long discussion of the ways in which appellate and supreme courts are and are not insulated from popular sentiment would all be somewhat hard to explain. Bickel's account of institutional incentives is, then, largely the same as Eisgruber's.

will tend toward decisions that accurately reflect the base interests and desires of the populace, even as they have little or no incentives to defer to principled considerations when they would require overriding such interests and desires. In terms of power, then, Eisgruber recommends more populist-sensitive decision mechanisms for issues of policy, while reserving expertocratic mechanisms for sensitive matters of principle requiring deliberation.

The final major premise in Eisgruber's brief for judicial review is the claim that, although the practice may be *countermajoritarian*, it is not *antidemocratic*. Unlike traditional defenses of judicial review which celebrate it (especially as practiced in the United States) as a libertarian counterweight to majoritarian democracy,[25] Eisgruber aims to show that judicial review is not only democratically legitimate, but also democracy-promoting. His basic argument here is twofold. First, the Supreme Court of the United States is not radical with respect to the principles it uses to decide controversial constitutional issues. Because the justices have a "democratic pedigree" through the presidential nomination and senatorial confirmation process, their principles will more or less reflect the current social consensus of the electorate concerning fundamental moral and political values.[26] This claim, in essence, seeks to portray the members of the Supreme Court as less Olympian and detached than often portrayed, and more accountable to popular will than is apparent from their electoral status alone.

Second, and more important, he argues that democracy should not be understood in terms of majority rule or the general satisfaction of interests, as aggregative models suggest. Although he never clearly defines his preferred conception of democracy, in an aside at the end of a critique of originalist jurisprudence, he suggests that "sustained public argument about the meaning of equality and other ideals might plausibly be regarded as the essence of democracy."[27] Given this deliberative

---

[25] Bickel, *The Least Dangerous Branch*; Choper, *Judicial Review and the National Political Process*. See further Section A of Chapter 2.

[26] This point should be long familiar, given Dahl, "The Supreme Court as a National Policy-Maker." Dahl, however, is more careful than Eisgruber to avoid eliding the preferences of national political elites and those of the electorate: "It is unrealistic to suppose that a Court whose members are recruited in the fashion of the Supreme Court justices would long hold to norms of justice that are substantially at odds with the rest of the political elite," 291.

[27] Eisgruber, *Constitutional Self-Government*, 35. Here he also cites a few pages (287–90 and 297–98) from one of his earlier articles: Christopher L. Eisgruber, "Disagreeable People," *Stanford Law Review* 43 (1990). Not much more insight is forthcoming however, as the cited pages merely claim that "the animating principle of any democracy is the equality of the people" (289), and that Americans do in fact argue a great deal about justice and lawfulness.

model of democracy and the justices' democratic pedigree, then, the Supreme Court is not antidemocratic. It is, rather, "a kind of *representative* institution well-shaped to *speak on behalf of the people* about questions of moral and political principle."[28] Judicial review is one legitimate institution among others for democratic self-government, provided that we understand democracy along the lines of the legitimacy criterion stressed by deliberative democrats: fundamental decisions, at least, ought to be based on the best publicly articulated and publicly acceptable reasons available after debate and discussion. Supreme Court judges are uniquely positioned to be disinterested arbiters and representatives of "the people's convictions about what is right."[29] On these matter at least, according to Eisgruber, judges speak better for the people than any other governmental actors.

3. Juridical Communication with the People in Moral-Political Reason: Michelman

Unlike Eisgruber's contention that the Supreme Court is democratic because its insulation from the people allows it to *speak* best *for* the people's moral principles, or Rawls's contention that such a court *speaks* best *in* the people's public moral-political language, Frank Michelman's theory claims that the Court's decisions can be seen as democratically legitimate only when it publicly *speaks with* the people on fundamental moral-political issues.[30] Like Rawls, Michelman starts with a strong legitimacy criterion for true self-government: all citizens must be able to grasp the basic framework of political decision making as worthy of their respect, rather than as a mere brute coercive mechanism that should be obeyed only out of prudence. And like Rawls, Michelman also claims that

[28] Eisgruber, *Constitutional Self-Government*, 3, emphasis added.   [29] Ibid., 5.
[30] See, for instance, Frank I. Michelman, "The Supreme Court, 1985 Term – Forward: Traces of Self-Government," *Harvard Law Review* 100, no. 4 (1986), and Michelman, *Brennan and Democracy*, especially Chapter 1. Although the former – a seminal article articulating the historical sources of and supporting the political and legal theories behind the so-called republican revival in American jurisprudence – suggests at times an understanding of the Supreme Court along the lines of Eisgruber's representative function of speaking for the people on behalf of their reason, the article's substantive critiques of Bruce Ackerman's and Ronald Dworkin's theories of adjudication as insufficiently open to the full dialogue and debate of deliberative democracy already show Michelman to be moving toward the position he definitively outlines in his 1999 book. Thus, although he suggests early on that the Supreme Court might have the role "of representing to us the possibility of practical reason" (Michelman, "Traces of Self-Government," 24), it's clear that by the end of the article he is endorsing the pluralism of debate and discussion – here, however, only within the appellate system – as the key to understanding the democratic role of the Court (see especially Michelman, "Traces of Self-Government," 74–76).

reasonable pluralism – the ineliminability of disagreement over fundamental moral matters – is a fact of modern life that threatens the fulfillment of this legitimacy criterion.

Because his focus is limited, however, to an established nation-state, Michelman can suppose that this problem of disagreement is solved at an abstract level by citizens' consensual endorsement of the U.S. Constitution as respect-worthy. But the same structural problem reappears at the level of how best to interpret and concretely apply the political principles instantiated in the Constitution. Given their abstract formulation and the need for fixed and settled judgments about how those principles affect the lawmaking process in concrete situations, it seems that we must face the "fact or reasonable interpretive pluralism": namely, that persistent disagreement concerning the correct interpretation of constitutional law is ineliminable given what Rawls identifies as the "burdens of judgment."[31] This persistent interpretive disagreement then threatens the fulfillment of the legitimacy criterion for collective self-government, as specific interpretations will have to be institutionally fixed even though some citizens reasonably disagree with them. One way to manage this dilemma, Michelman suggests, would be to focus on the "the *democratic character* of a country's processes of basic-law interpretation."[32] If whatever institutional arrangements were responsible for fixing the interpretation of basic law in a nation were seen to be responsive to the best reasons and arguments available – and not, say, to pressures or bare preferences – then even citizens who substantively disagreed with an interpretation would be able to see it as the outcome of a process of democratic interpretive deliberation, and so as worthy of respect.

Rather than directly arguing that a judicial institutionalization of this interpretation function is either logically necessitated or the best possible solution, Michelman argues for the more modest thesis that, under certain conditions, a governmental division of labor whereby the judiciary is responsible for interpretations of fundamental principles would meet the

---

[31] Michelman, *Brennan and Democracy*, 54–55. As he points out, this fact of reasonable interpretive pluralism reacts back "up" the ladder of abstraction, calling into question agreement on the abstract principles themselves, as "the matters left to be resolved by interpretation of these abstract principles are often themselves such major political-moral issues that resolutions of them one way or the other cannot readily be held separate from determinations of what the principles – in effect, the basic laws – themselves actually *are*" (Michelman, *Brennan and Democracy*, 49). I leave this complication out of my presentation here, as it would take me too far afield into Michelman's critiques of Ronald Dworkin's substantive and Robert Post's proceduralist theories of democratic legitimacy. For a fuller presentation of the semantic reciprocity between an abstract norm and its interpretation, see Frank I. Michelman, "The Problem of Constitutional Interpretive Disagreement: Can 'Discourses of Application' Help?," in *Habermas and Pragmatism*, ed. Mitchell Aboulafia, Myra Bookman, and Catherine Kemp (New York: Routledge, 2002).

[32] Michelman, *Brennan and Democracy*, 57.

public reasoning legitimacy criterion. His argument starts from a thesis evident also in Rawls's and Eisgruber's theories: constitutional interpretation on fundamental matters of moral and political principle is a delicate and complex matter requiring philosophical acumen, sustained focus of judgment, and insulation from considerations of preference and policy.[33] Furthermore, we should not saddle either legislators or ordinary citizens with such tasks, given that they are already responsible for more prosaic policy matters that can often be decided on the basis of mere preference. Thus, "the judiciary, we may think, has some institutional advantages over other branches of government when it comes to deciding philosophical questions."[34] This is a comparison he believes supportable on the grounds of prudence and experience alone, not of logical necessity or the ineliminable structural features of political institutions in general. Nevertheless, we – as citizens who recognize the persistence of reasonable interpretive disagreement – could find the constitutional system respectworthy if we believe that, on the whole, the judiciary will do a better job of getting the moral-political content of the basic law right than other mechanisms would.

Michelman's distinctive premise completing his brief for the possible legitimacy of judicial review is that we could trust that this concretization process is in fact epistemically reliable only to the extent that justices are fully open to, and in conversation with, the widest diversity of opinions and arguments on these fundamental matters. In other words, we citizens would have reason to treat collectively binding basic-law interpretations as worthy of respect – even when we reasonably disagree with them – if we could see those interpretations as the result of a free and open deliberative process. The basic idea behind this premise is that moral claims are more likely to be right when they have survived systematic exposure to countervailing reasons and considerations brought forth by persons in diverse circumstances, in order to correct for such all-too-human defects of practical reasoning as insufficient knowledge, inferential mistakes, individual bias, partiality, conceptual narrowness, insufficient imagination, and so on.[35] Insofar as the justices of the Supreme Court of the United States, who are responsible for interpretations of basic law in the United States, are open to "the full blast of sundry opinions and

---

[33] See ibid., 22–23, endorsing Dworkin's arguments to this effect.
[34] Ibid., 57.
[35] Here Michelman's thought is deeply indebted to Habermas's "discourse theory of morality." A clear overview of this Habermas-style move from moral considerations of impartiality to the need for actual intersubjective discourse on moral claims in order to ensure epistemic reliability, to the justification of deliberative democracy as a nonideal approximation of the procedures of intersubjective moral discourse under time and knowledge constraints and decisional pressures can be found in Nino, *The Constitution of Deliberative Democracy*, especially 107–43.

interest-articulations in society, including on a fair basis everyone's opinions and articulations of interests,"[36] citizens can grasp the process of deliberative interpretation as respect-worthy, and so as part of a system of legitimate self-government. According to Michelman, as long as the justices consistently *speak with* the American people when they decide on fundamental but contested matters of moral-political philosophy, legitimate deliberative democracy can exist with a division of labor between populist policy-making institutions and an expertocratic moral-reasoning institutions.

Furthermore, should the Court actually exhibit this kind of communicative openness, it would additionally mitigate whatever lingering traces of paternalism might be felt to inhere in an unaccountable judiciary settling contested interpretations of basic law, for to the degree to which that Court is open to the influence of public opinion, citizens could believe that their opinions and interests were counted equally in the decisions made by the judiciary, not just in those of the electorally accountable branch. Terming these considerations "dignitary" as opposed to the prudential-epistemic considerations, Michelman explicitly connects them to the anti-paternalist worry about the respect deserved by each citizen as an equally autonomous consociate in the collective process of self-government. Such open communicative jurisprudence would then be seen as "official efforts that pay *us* the respect of striving to make themselves ever more effectively available to be influenced by public debates."[37]

4   The Wide Influence of the Seducements of Judicial Discourse

We have then three theories, united in viewing reasoned deliberation about fundamental moral-political matters as an essential component of legitimate democracy, and united in their support for an (American-style) institutional division of labor that assigns such deliberation to politically insulted courts, on the grounds of their heightened capacities for the abstract and complex discourse necessary for proper treatment of moral-political problems. To stylize somewhat, we might say that Rawls believes that the Supreme Court has a special claim to *exemplifying* the kind of moral-political discourse citizens should also engage in, Eisgruber believes that the Court has a special claim to *representing* the moral-political discourse of citizens within the governmental apparatus, and Michelman believes that the Court has a special responsibility for *communicating* with the citizens in a moral-political discourse when it settles matters of fundamental interpretation. Thus, each theory's support for

[36] Michelman, *Brennan and Democracy*, 60.   [37] Ibid., 59.

American-style judicial review hangs on the presupposition that such a court is particularly well suited to engage in the difficult but ineliminable deliberative moral-political discourse that fulfills one of the crucial legitimacy criteria for constitutional democracy: the reasons-responsiveness of governmental actions. Judicial review is democratically legitimate, then, precisely because Court decisions turn on deliberative reasons of moral-political principle.

At this point, a strong antipaternalist objection to judicial review might be thought sufficient to dispose of such theories, on the grounds that, if our democratic ideals force us to take seriously the equal autonomy of all democratic citizens, then it is simply impossible to square that commitment with an institution that claims to exemplify, represent, or communicate the reasons of the citizenry *against* the explicit statements of the citizenry's reasons as actually exemplified, represented, and communicated through actual democratic practices. After all, isn't this maneuver of celebrating the principled reasoning capacities of an elite set of judges akin to the classic paternalist claim that a few guardians know the true interests of their wards better than the wards themselves know them? The problem with this easy dismissal of the theories considered in this chapter is that it is overly normativistic and idealistic. For, as I was at pains to point out in response to Waldron's antipaternalist inspired rejections of judicial review in Chapters 4 and 5, normative arguments about the appropriate realization of democratic ideals cannot avoid dealing with the *comparative* characteristics, capacities, and limitations of various political institutions. The design and consideration of political institutions must recognize that they do *not* simply and directly translate or mirror the interests, opinions, or ideas of the *demos*. Said another way, the easy antipaternalistic objection seems to employ an overly stringent criterion of democratic legitimacy – a criterion that would apparently rule out any institutions mediating between the citizens and political decisions – while relying on an unacknowledged conflation of the opinions of the citizenry with the outputs of elective legislatures, but without any explicit consideration of why we should take this conflation as a given. By contrast, at least the three theories considered here have shouldered the requisite argumentative burden by giving some reasons why we should think that the products of one particular kind of political institution, *in comparison with* other political institutions, has certain characteristics that warrant the expectation that its products do in fact exemplify, represent, or communicate with the people's moral-political principles.

Another reason for not simply dismissing the theories is that the lure of juridical reasoning is quite seductive vis-à-vis the promise of high-quality political decisions. This is especially the case for deliberative theories of democracy which hang so much of the legitimacy of political decisions and institutions on the warranted expectation that fully democratic processes will produce better – more reasonable and rational – outcomes than nondemocratic processes. In fact, a surprising number of contemporary theorists, despite the wide variety of their justifications for and conceptualizations of judicial review, agree with the basic premise shared by the three theories examined here: that constitutional courts, and especially the United States one, have an institutionally unique relationship to moral-political discourse. Rawls's thesis that constitutional juridical discourse exemplifies public moral-political discourse, rather than a mere fight for power and position, is of course quite similar to the views of Bickel and Dworkin that courts are uniquely suited to be the governmental "forum of principle" in contrast to other governmental organs that are structured around reason-independent contests over policy fought out in the media of majoritarian preferences, power, and position.[38] Bickel and Dworkin in fact explicitly endorse the thesis – shared by Rawls and Eisgruber – that the moral-political discourse exemplified by a supreme constitutional court can educate the citizens in how to reason with one another on contested issues and so improve their deliberations.[39] Michelman's focus on the ways in which juridical discourse must communicate with the public when dealing with fundamental moral-political matters has strong resonances both in empirical studies of the flow of information, reasons, and influence between the judiciary, other

[38] See Bickel, *The Least Dangerous Branch*, especially 23–33, and Dworkin, *Taking Rights Seriously*, especially 22–31 and 71–79. For instance, Spector argues that judicial review is fully consistent with deliberative democracy by combining a derogatory account of legislative processes as inevitably faulty with an idealization of the impartiality of judicial reasoning. The link to deliberative democracy is then made via Rawls's hypothetical contracting situation: deliberative democrats (supposedly) want the outcomes of politics to be as close as possible to what original contractors would agree to at the stage of constitutional convention, and this is precisely what constitutional courts provide better than legislators: "Constitutional adjudication can correct the deliberative failings of actual legislative processes if the supreme court can reproduce the sort of impartial deliberation that characteristically occurs at the constitutional convention," Horacio Spector, "Judicial Review, Rights, and Democracy," *Law and Philosophy* 22, no. 3–4 (2003): 321. Notably, the comparison here is between *actual* legislative processes and judges' *hypothetical* idealizations about the kind of deliberation that *would* occur at those constitutional conventions where the veil of ignorance (at the correct level of opacity) *would* have been properly employed.
[39] Bickel, *The Least Dangerous Branch*, 26, and Dworkin, *Freedom's Law*, 345–46. The educative thesis is at least as old as – if not older than? – Eugene V. Rostow, "The Democratic Character of Judicial Review," *Harvard Law Review* 66 (1952): 208: "The Supreme Court is, among other things, an educational body, and the Justices are inevitably teachers in a vital national seminar." Strong reservations about the empirical sustainability of this educative thesis are raised from a transnational comparative perspective in Jeremy Waldron, "Judicial Review and the Conditions of Democracy," *The Journal of Political Philosophy* 6, no. 4 (1998).

governmental actors, and the public sphere,[40] and in normative accounts of the need for juridical reasoning process to become more communicative, accounts often influenced by Jürgen Habermas's theory of discourse ethics.[41]

By far the greatest resonance is found, however, in Eisgruber's thesis of juridical discourse as serving a representative function. The basic idea here, endorsed under many variations, is that when the Supreme Court exercises its power of constitutional review, it is representing the highest and truest interests of the American people – their interests in collective self-government structured by fundamental moral-political principles – against whatever other unsavory and partial interests may have been responsible for the discredited legislation, policy preference, or policy implementation. In this story, juridical discourse represents – speaks for – the true people and their deepest interests, and against those who – despite their apparent heightened accountability to the people – would falsely claim to speak in the people's name. Such theories have a provenance at least as far back as Hamilton's claim in *Federalist Paper Number 78* that judicial review of legislation merely represents the higher will of the people, the will enshrined in the constitution, against the necessarily subordinate will of the legislature.[42]

In contemporary jurisprudence, however, there is a veritable efflorescence of such theories, all aiming to reduce the manifest tensions between the normative ideals of democracy – deliberative and republican ideals in particular – and the institutions and practices of American-style judicial review. What's remarkable in this literature is how prevalent the general strategy clearly articulated by Eisgruber is: namely, to conceive of constitutional juridical discourse, in some way and with respect to some types of issues, as more representative of the deep, true, or important will and interests of the people than the discourses employed in other ostensibly more representative governmental organs. By such a conception, then, the Supreme Court of the United States, or its close relatives in other nations, is transformed from an antidemocratic anomaly into a, if

---

[40] A sample of contemporary work in this broad research domain: Klarman, *From Jim Crow to Civil Rights*, and Alec Stone Sweet, *Governing with Judges: Constitutional Politics in Europe* (New York: Oxford University Press, 2000).

[41] See, for instance, Habermas's endorsement of Dworkin's theory of constructive judicial interpretation, as long as constructive interpretation is reconceived in terms of a conversation among various relevant actors, rather than merely the solitary deliberations of judge Hercules in Habermas, *Between Facts and Norms*, especially Chapters 5 and 9.

[42] Hamilton, Madison, and Jay, *The Federalist with Letters of "Brutus,"* 377–83. "Nor does this conclusion [concerning the power of judicial review] by any means suppose a superiority of the judicial to the legislative power. It only supposes that the power of the people is superior to both; and that where the will of the legislature declared in its statutes, stands in opposition to that of the people declared in the constitution, the judges ought to be governed by the latter, rather than the former" (380).

not *the*, democratic paragon.[43] Thus, Ackerman argues that the Court
vigilantly represents the authentic will of We the People, as it was originally
determined and expressed during those episodic moments when we awoke
as a People and engaged in higher, constitutional politics, during those
sovereign interregnum eras when we no longer exist as a People but, rather,
only as a population of individual, privatistic liberal citizens. The Court then
represents and protects the authentic will of the People by using its special
reasoning powers to interpret the higher law the People have made, and to
enforce it against the inevitable imprecations of the citizen's everyday
nominal "representatives" as they chip away at those constitutional
achievements while We the People enjoy our privatistic slumbers.[44] Dworkin
argues that the Court speaks for the people considered as a collective self-
governing association by attending to the principled democratic conditions
necessary for legitimate political association.[45] Freeman argues not only that
judicial review represents the people's sovereign precommitment to maintaining the equal value of rights that they would have expressed in a foundational, legitimacy-conferring social contract, but also that the high court
exemplifies public reason when it does so.[46] Alon Harel claims that judicial
review of legislation in order to protect fundamental rights is a representative institution because, properly understood, rights reflect social
values. Properly exercised then, with suitable attention to those social values,
judicial review is but one among several mechanisms for representing the
moral convictions of the people.[47] Perry argues that the Supreme Court is

[43] The differences among such jurisprudential theories might be then correlated with a
third variable beyond the normative tenets of democracy and the celebration of American
institutions: namely, a desire to develop an *acceptable* theory of Constitutional
interpretation. As explained in Chapter 1, Section B, an acceptable theory must, on
the one hand, endorse the doctrinal mainstream by showing how to justify all of the major
firmaments in American Constitutional law (affirming *Brown* or *Roe* and rejecting *Plessy* or
Lochner), while, on the other hand, simultaneously developing a distinctive and original
theory of interpretation resulting in all and only those Court decisions beyond the
doctrinal mainstream that the theorist endorses (his or her favorites).

[44] See especially Part II (pages 165–265) of Ackerman, *We the People: Foundations*. "From this
point of view, the Supreme Court is hardly a conservative friend of the status quo, but an
ongoing representative of a mobilized People during the lengthy periods of apathy, ignorance,
and selfishness that mark the collective life of the private citizenry of a liberal republic,"
265, emphasis added.

[45] Dworkin, *Freedom's Law*, especially 1–38. See further Chapter 4, Section B.

[46] Freeman, "Constitutional Democracy and the Legitimacy of Judicial Review." Page 365
spells out the Rawlsian claim that, as the Court issues decisions backed by reasoned
opinions, it exemplifies the public use of reason. See further Chapter 5, Section A.

[47] Alon Harel, "Rights-Based Judicial Review: A Democratic Justification," *Law and
Philosophy* 22, no. 3–4 (2003). Perhaps Larry Alexander is correct here that, once the
concepts of democracy and democratic representation are stretched so far, it would be
better to give up "the impossible task of fitting the square peg of judicial review in the
round hole of democracy" Larry Alexander, "Is Judicial Review Democratic? A Comment

the best institution for representing our foundational American ideals of progress in the realization of unchanging moral and religious truths, as its superior powers of moral deliberation, discernment, and judgment allow it to best specify indeterminacies of application in those ideals and truths.[48] In a similar vein, Jed Rubenfeld claims that the Court, on account of its superior capacities for practical reasoning about moral commitments, represents the people's true, long-standing commitments that enable self-government, specifically by upholding the text of the Constitution against the pressures of the people's current but merely evanescent desires, as represented by the more popularly accountable branches of government.[49] Lawrence Sager suggests that as democracy requires both electoral and deliberative equality, the first is ensured through an equal right to vote for representatives and the second is ensured through unaccountable courts with the power of judicial review. Such courts ensure that each citizen gets an impartial and fair hearing on the basis of reasons (rather than differentials of wealth, power, or influence) concerning whether his or her rights have been violated by the institutions serving electoral equality.[50]

This list could easily be extended. In each case, one central premise of these representational arguments is that, in some manner, an institution such as the Supreme Court of the United States is uniquely qualified to represent the people's principles *because* of its specially heightened capacities for reasoned deliberation about fundamental moral-political matters. And, whether implicit or explicit, it appears that a central motivation for such a belief in the judiciary's heightened capacities for moral-political reasoning is the character of reasons-responsiveness evinced in judicial opinions: judicial decisions are backed by reasoned opinions. But, as I will now argue, equating the reasons used by judges

---

on Harel," *Law and Philosophy* 22, no. 3–4 (2003): 283. Notably, however, in his own drive to save the legitimacy of judicial review, Alexander wholly gives up the notion that democracy or democratic institutions have any intrinsic value. According to him, giving up the impossible task is a simple entailment of conceiving of democracy and democratic institutions as having merely derivative and instrumental worth in terms of their good or bad consequences in realizing other values, including the intrinsic values of individual rights. The supposed harm to democracy inflicted by judicial review that worries Harel is then not worrisome, since democracy has no value in and of itself. For Alexander, judicial review is just another consequentially justified governmental arrangement, assessable at the same level as any other, for whether it gets the right decisions in terms of other values. Guardianship, democracy, dictatorship, whatever – all are acceptable, as long as they preserve intrinsic values.

[48] Perry, *The Constitution in the Courts: Law or Politics?* See further Chapter 4, Section A.

[49] Jed Rubenfeld, *Freedom and Time: A Theory of Constitutional Self-Government* (New Haven, CT: Yale University Press, 2001).

[50] Sager, *Justice in Plainclothes*, 202–07 and 24–25. Sager makes his debt to Eisgruber for this democratic conception of judicial review clear at footnote 5, 238.

with the moral-political reasoning required by democratic deliberation is to be subject to the seducements of juristic discourse.

B.   ACTUAL JURISTIC DISCOURSE IN THE UNITED STATES SYSTEM OF CONSTITUTIONAL ADJUDICATION

To return to Rawls's, Eisgruber's, and Michelman's specific claims, juristic discourse is the idealized location for public deliberations amongst citizens because the reasoning employed in judicial decisions are either rendered in the correct language of public reason, turn on issues of principle not policy, or warrant the claim to heightened moral-political reasonability through being open to the full blast of wide public opinion and debate, respectively. Whether then a division of labor between expertocratic constitutional courts and other more populist governmental organs is supported because jurists *speak in* the people's legitimate language of public reason, or because they alone can *speak for* the people on matters of principle, or because they *speak with* the people in defining fundamental law on such difficult matters, all three arguments presuppose that juristic discourse is a language well suited to the tasks of democratic deliberation on fundamental matters.

However, what is most striking when one actually reads opinions of the U.S. Supreme and various Appeals Courts is that they are not, in the main, concentrated on the principled moral-political reasoning these theories idealize but, rather, on the *technicalia* of legal argument: jurisdiction, precedent, consistency, authorization, distinguishability, separation of doctrine from dicta, justiciability, canons of construction, and so on. I contend that this is no mere accident however, for juristic discourse, at least in the United States, is a language of reasons tailored to maintaining the rule of law in a complex court system with constitutional review performed throughout the regular appellate court hierarchy, not a language of reasons well suited to public political disagreements about which collective decisions should become binding for fellow citizens and the basic terms of our political consociation. This section is dedicated to an analysis of the ways in which juristic discourse is not an idiom well suited for carrying out the kind of public deliberation required to meet the legitimacy criterion of deliberative democratic theory, and of the ways in which juristic discourse may actually detract from the sought-for qualities of reasoned public deliberation. I begin with empirical examples of the predominance of juristic principles over moral-political principles in some recent U.S. Supreme Court cases in this section, before moving in Section C to a more theoretical consideration of the institutional characteristics and location of the Court that explain that predominance.

1. Framing the Inquiry

The point of the following case studies is to test whether Rawls's, Eisgruber's, and Michelman's distinctive claims for the legitimacy and potential benefits of judicial review in a deliberative democracy in terms of the special capacities of the judiciary for moral-political reasoning hold up, by looking at some of the actual work product of the Supreme Court of the United States as evidence. In addressing the central concern – does actual juristic discourse employ and reflect a discourse appropriate to collective public reasoning about difficult matters of fundamental moral-political principle? – it will help to keep three types of questions about the cases and the Court in mind. First is a threshold question of evidence: do the cases being considered deal *prima facie* with the kinds of fundamental moral-political issues that the three theories take as central to their democratic defense of judicial review, that is, can they rightly be considered evidential for the theoretical claims? If the answer is yes, then the second and most important question is simply: do the cases provide confirming or disconfirming evidence for the theories? Specifically, the question is: are the cases being considered instances where we can fairly say that the Court's decisions employ and crucially turn upon reasoning based in fundamental moral-political principles, so that the they confirm the theories' specific claims about how the Court exemplifies, represents, or communicates in moral-political reason, and thus uniquely fulfills a special role in deliberative democracy. Third, even if the answer to this second question is negative, we might still want to consider the extent to which the Court's interventions might play a salutary role in the wider public sphere by stimulating and improving public debate on fundamental moral-political issues and by educating the citizenry in the language, substance, and cannons of a shared culture of public reason, thereby lending support to Rawls's and Eisgruber's subsidiary claims for the democratic value of constitutional rulings for public political culture.

Obviously this inquiry presupposes that juristic discourse is usually more than a mere show or appearance of reasons cloaking the "real" non-rational "causes" that explain judicial decisions. Although I can't argue for it here, I am convinced that full-bore skepticism about the dispositive power of juristic reasons – the kind often associated not only with strong legal realism but also with the certain exaggerations of the results of empirical research focused on "judicial politics"[51] – is overblown and false. I don't want to claim that such (extralegal) factors as judges' personal ideologies and attitudes, strategic considerations, or interbranch rivalries *never* play a role in judicial decisions. The issue rather is whether

---

[51] For a good compact overview, see Lee Epstein, "Judicial Decision Making," in *Encyclopedia of Law & Society*, ed. David C. Clark (Thousand Oaks, CA: Sage, 2005).

such factors are fully determinative of, or merely influential in, those decisions. Although only the former claim would invalidate the inquiries of this chapter, the latter seems the more reasonable position empirically, and doesn't force us to construct elaborate error theories to explain away the manifest character of the actual practices and self-understandings of lawyers and judges. More important, the three theories under consideration here also do not rely on some kind of naïve idealization of legal reasoning as fully determinative of all judicial outcomes. In order for their claims to make sense, all they need is the weaker supposition that in many extraordinary cases of constitutional review by the nation's highest court, reasons have substantial weight in the final decisions, and those reasons are largely congruent with the ones expressed in the supporting judicial opinions.

With these preliminaries, I would now like to consider four examples of recent constitutional controversies in order to gauge the extent to which they bear out the claims of the three theorists: religious freedom and the Pledge of Allegiance; criminal punishment and California's "three strikes" sentencing rule; rights to individual liberty concerning physician-assisted suicide and homosexual sex; and, electoral equality in political districts and apportionment.[52] Almost all of these case examples show that the language of reasons employed by judges – the reasons that overwhelmingly have decisive weight – is a specifically legal language, not one of moral-political principles. Supreme Court judges are rightly engrossed with the *technicalia* of the rule of law, not with arguments about fundamental moral and political principles. By the same token, juristic discourse is not well-tailored to the kind of widely dispersed democratic deliberation and debate about the proper terms of mutual consociation that self-governing citizens can and ought to engage in *as* mutual citizens. The point of the following is, then, neither to impugn the Court's juridical forms of reasoning, nor to suggest that they decided the cases incorrectly or unjustly. It is, rather, to loosen the institutional seducements that reasons-responsive judicial review understandably presents to deliberative democrats. In fact, I consider the procedural correctness of judicial decisions – rather than the substantive rightness of the outcome – to be the key to their legitimacy in a constitutional democracy. Thus, in no way do I mean to demean the legalisms of juristic discourse; only to suggest how far actual jurisprudence is from the idealized picture of it

[52] By considering sets of both private and political autonomy cases, I also intend make my arguments equally convincing for theorists who favor substantialist defenses of judicial review and for those who prefer more proceduralist accounts. Both forms of deliberative democracy are susceptible to the seducements of juristic discourse, whether the argument is that the unique reasoning capacities of courts are likely to result in the correct outcomes, or that such reasoning capacities are required in order to ensure that the legitimacy-ensuring rules of the democratic process are maintained.

presupposed by the arguments put forward by Rawls, Eisgruber, and Michelman.

2. Four Examples

a. Freedom of Religion and the Pledge of Allegiance

Consider first a question the Supreme Court of the United States agreed to decide during its 2004 term: does a law directing the daily recitation in elementary school of the Pledge of Allegiance, which contains the words "one Nation under God," violate the moral-political principle of the separation of church and state? Note first that the Court agreed to hear the case, on appeal from the ruling of the Ninth Circuit Court of Appeals.[53] It could well have simply avoided hearing and deciding the case, without public comment or any supporting reason, as it does with thousands of other appeals every year. Instead, the Court apparently decided (or rather four members decided) that it raised a significant enough constitutional issue that made it worthy of including it among the approximately eighty or so cases it now decides a year.[54]

Turning to the first question framing our inquiry, it seems quite clear that the case raises exactly the kind of issue theorists of the special representative function of juristic discourse focus on. The relationship between the laws of the state and religion is clearly a matter of fundamental moral-political principle on each of the three theories: religious establishment is in fact the paradigm case of *nonpublic* reason according to Rawls's political liberalism; it is undoubtedly an issue on the principled, not the policy, side of Eisgruber's distinction; and in the U.S. constitutional context it is certainly a matter of basic law that is nevertheless subject to reasonable interpretive pluralism, *à la* Michelman. The correct moral-political considerations to bring to bear, however, are not self-evident or easily applied: the Pledge is not compulsory as students may legally refuse to say it; they are young elementary school students and so may be especially susceptible to conformist pressures; the Pledge does not mention any specific religious dogmas or apparently favor any sect of monotheism; the Pledge has contained the contested words only during

---

[53] *Elk Grove Unified School District et al. v. Newdow et al.*, 542 U.S. 1 (2004).

[54] It is also important to recall here that, of those cases the Court does hear, only a small percentage – around 10 percent per year – are instances of judicial review in the narrow sense I have used throughout the book, that is, of the judicial oversight of the constitutionality of legislative statutes and administrative regulations. See footnote 39, Chapter 1 and footnote 55, Chapter 8 for further statistical support. The vast majority of cases focus either on intrajudicial matters such as maintaining consistency in the application and elucidation of the doctrine of the federal judiciary and insuring sufficient legal regularity amongst the rulings of the various federal appellate courts, state and local courts, or on the interpretation and application of statutory and regulatory law.

the second half of its century-long existence; the parents of the child at the center of the case disagree about the acceptability of the Pledge; there is dispute about whether the federal constitutional prohibitions on governmental religious establishment and measures restricting the free exercise of religion actually apply to the individual states as well; and so on. The case then presents a clear opportunity for the Court to carry out its theorized special representative function by settling the matter through the deliberative use of practical reason.

When we turn to the second question of how well the Court fulfilled its theorized reasoning functions, however, the three theories are sure to be disappointed, for the Court's majority decision and supporting opinion turned exclusively on the specifically legal principle of standing: "We conclude that, having been deprived under California law of the right to sue as next friend, Newdow [the respondent father who brought the original suit] lacks prudential standing to bring this suit in federal court."[55] Thus, rather than deciding broad questions about the meaning and import of the principle of separation of church and state as effected through the Establishment and Free Exercise clauses of the First Amendment to the Constitution of the United States, or even deciding narrower questions of whether this specific California law establishing the daily school recitation of the Pledge violates the clauses, the Court invoked a specifically legal principle to simply avoid such questions.[56] Said according to the representative theories' claims, after agreeing to carry out its democratic tasks of exemplifying, representing, or communicating in the people's moral-political reason, the Court switched to its preferred legalistic language and found a way of shirking its civic duties. A decision that turns on accidents of the standing of one of the parties simply cannot be said to employ and crucially turn on reasoning based in fundamental moral-political principles in the way envisioned by Rawls, Eisgruber, or Michelman. Its hard to see how this performance can be said to be an exemplar of the use of that public reason citizens are to use as their terms of mutual consociation, or to represent the people's moral-political convictions against the pandering policies of electorally accountable government organs, or to be at least a respect-worthy intervention in self-government on the basis of its openness to the full blast of

---

[55] *Newdow*, 17–18.

[56] One can almost sense the sigh of relief in the majority opinion as it discusses how it discovered new evidence, after agreeing to hear the case, about the potential conflicts of opinion and interest between the estranged father and mother, and their relationship under California law that would now allow the Court to avoid ruling on the moral-political merits of the Constitutional claim, disposing of the case instead on the legal grounds of the father's lack of standing in federal court. Chief Justice Rehnquist, in the opening sentence of his concurring opinion argues that "the Court today erects a novel prudential standing principle in order to avoid reaching the merits of the constitutional claim," ibid.

public opinions and debates on matters of interpreting the substantive moral-political principles of basic law.

Perhaps, however, *Newdow* does better on the subsidiary question, showing how the intervention of the Court can serve to improve the overall reasonableness and deliberative character of widely dispersed and various public discussions and debates on the principles properly governing the separation of church and state. Here one might point beyond the back and forth between the majority opinion and Justice Rehnquist's dissent concerning the precedential pedigree and appropriate scope of various formulations of the legal doctrine of standing, looking rather to the substantive discussion of the Establishment clause and its relation to the Pledge in the smaller half of Rehnquist's opinion, and in the diverse positions on the merits of the case canvassed in the separate opinions penned by Justices O'Connor and Thomas. Surely, here at least, one could hypothesize some salutary impact on broad public processes of democratic deliberation about fundamental political principles. No doubt, but the claim must be sharper than this: namely, that American judicial review contributes in a unique and irreplaceable fashion to that debate. Here it is hard to see how the Court's actual work-product made such an irreplaceable contribution. Furthermore, given that the case was reported largely in terms of the Court using various legalisms to duck the potentially culturally explosive consequences of a direct ruling on the constitutionality of the Pledge, it seems a bit strong to see the Court's role in *Newdow* as a singular contribution to democratic debate, one where the Court's use of principled reason was unmatched by other governmental institutions.[57] So, although this case does not facially falsify the claims concerning the educative and rationalizing effects on Court's decisions on democratic discourse, it does little to support them either.

b. *Criminal Punishment: "Three Strikes" sentencing*

Consider next a different moral-political question that the recent case of *Lockyer v. Andrade* raises: Is a prison sentence of two consecutive twenty-five-years-to-life terms an appropriate punishment for the petty theft of approximately $150 worth of videotapes, where that theft resulted in a third lifetime felony conviction?[58] Is this a just punishment? Put in the

---

[57] Consider how the headlines in major newspapers reported the decision: "8 Justices Block Effort to Excise Phrase in Pledge" (*New York Times*, June 15, 2004, Section A, Page 1); "Justices Keep 'Under God' in Pledge; Atheist Father Lacked Standing to Sue on Behalf of Daughter, Court Rules" (*Washington Post*, June 15, 2004, Page A.01); "Justices Keep 'God' in Pledge of Allegiance; In tossing out a California atheist's challenge, the high court avoids the question of constitutionality; This leaves the door open to similar lawsuits" (*Los Angeles Times*, June 15, 2004, page A1)

[58] *Lockyer v. Andrade*, 538 U.S. 63 (2003).

terms of the United States Constitution, and as rendered to the Court by the defendant, the question is whether Andrade's punishment violated the Eight Amendment prohibition against inflicting "cruel and unusual punishments." As an issue of the judicial review of legislation, the case presents the question of whether California's controversial "three strikes and you're out" sentencing law violates the Constitutional prohibition on cruel and unusual punishments.[59] We are faced here with an issue that I think all three of our theories would have to acknowledge as a fundamental matter concerning the moral-political principles that structure our terms of mutual consociation – this is no matter of mere policy or ordinary law application.

If Rawls, Eisgruber, and Michelman are correct, we should expect something basically akin to ordinary practical reasoning when we turn to the *Lockyer* opinion. Because the decision is embedded in a particular national legal and constitutional context, we should not expect a discussion proceeding from pure moral first principles in terms of, say, fundamental retributivist or deterrence-based justifications for punishment and their particular application to the case or statutes at hand. Rather, the principles to be employed must somehow be drawn from U.S. public political morality, including legal codifications of principles and principles socially and traditionally a part of American life. Even if the moral-political principles involved are, however, specific to the legal and constitutional traditions of a particular nation, we should still be able to identify recognizable reasoning from principles – principles that can be clearly seen to be part of the overlapping consensus of public reason, or representative of the principled convictions of the people, or whose formulation and interpretation can be open to wide public debate and discussion. From Rawls's point of view, we should start with the principles instantiated in the U.S. Constitution, which legally represent our public reason. At the least, cruel and unusual punishment is barred, though a judge may need to account for disagreement about whether this is itself a fundamental constitutional principle, or an entailment from a more general public political principle. For Eisgruber, the search is a bit different: a judge should look to those principles that she sincerely finds, after consulting her own intuitions and checking them against historical and current evidence of popular opinion, to "represent the people's convictions about justice."[60] Here I suspect a judge would find a relatively heterogeneous amalgam of abstract retributivist and deterrent intuitions, combined with a list of distinctly prohibited specific penal techniques. It is harder to say exactly how Michelman conceives the process of principle

---

[59] California Penal Code, Sections 666–667.
[60] Eisgruber, *Constitutional Self-Government*, 110.

detection to run.[61] It is clear, however, that whatever process is followed here, the principles have to be ones that are capable of public contestation, and the process has to be understandable by the public as a search for the best moral-political reasons, a process warranted in its acceptability by its potential openness to wide-ranging debate. Nevertheless, once the right principles are found, constitutional review should proceed in a recognizably analogous fashion to ordinary practical judgment – a matter of conscientious moral reasoning – to enforce those convictions, especially against majoritarian decisions that violate those publicly shared principles. So with some sense of what, theoretically, we should expect to find in the opinion, let's turn to how the Supreme Court ruled on the justice of Andrade's two consecutive twenty-five-years-to-life sentences.

To the best of my nonlawyerly abilities to figure it out, here is how the Supreme Court addressed the question. According to Justice O'Connor, the Ninth Circuit Court erred in ruling that the sentence violated the Eighth Amendment, because: (1) the Ninth Circuit did not have jurisdiction to grant *habeas corpus* relief to Andrade, as (2) it did so on the theory that a Supreme Court doctrine of 'gross disproportionality' announced in *Solem v. Helm*[62] was 'clearly established law' under the terms of an unrelated federal statute (the Antiterrorism and Effective Death Penalty Act of 1996) and (3) had thus been objectively misapplied by the California Court of Appeals. However, (4) as the thicket of precedential "cases exhibit a lack of clarity regarding what factors may indicate gross disproportionality," the principle is fuzzy and so "applicable only in the 'exceedingly rare' and 'extreme' case,"[63] (5) the California Court of Appeals could not have made a clear error with respect to Supreme Court precedent as clearly established law, for (6) on the one hand, there was no precedential clarity, and (7) on the other, in citing precedent, the California Court of Appeals did not violate the rule of law by "confron[ting]

---

[61] Michelman's clearest formulations of these tasks come in the second half of Michelman, *Brennan and Democracy*, but this section of the book is dedicated to making the best sense out of Justice Brennan's jurisprudence from the vantage point of the judge's commitments to liberalism, democracy, and the office of Supreme Court Justice as he found it in his time, and so may not provide reliable evidence concerning the theoretical claims of Michelman's jurisprudence. Nevertheless, there are significant continuities, for example: "Justice Brennan's opinions and other writings are full of the idea that public respect for constitutional law will fail if the law is not kept responsive to the shifting controversies of social life that give concrete meaning to legal issues," 72. This suggests a process of principle detection akin to that employed by Eisgruber's judge. Further evidence that the process involves, for Michelman, looking to the norms and values embedded in the concrete sociohistorical ethical context of a specific nation state can be found at Frank I. Michelman, "Family Quarrel," *Cardozo Law Review* 17, no. 4–5 (1996): 1174–77.

[62] *Solem v. Helm*, 463 U.S. 277 (1983). [63] *Lockyer*, 9.

a set of facts that are materially indistinguishable from a decision of this Court and nevertheless arriv[ing] at a result different from [Supreme Court] precedent."[64] Finally, (8) the Ninth Circuit erred by incorrectly defining the controlling *habeas* relief standard of "objectively unreasonable" to mean "clear error."

One way of interpreting this kind of a decision is as an impressive employment of common law jurisprudential techniques in order precisely to avoid the substantive merits of the basic moral issue: is California's three-strikes law unjust? A different way is to point out that, as the apex of the federal appellate judiciary, and as the supreme constitutional court in the land, as well as being responsible for the elaboration of judicial doctrine relevant to the application of federal legal provisions (including those of the U.S. Constitution), the Supreme Court must ensure that reasons relevant to the specific character of the American legal system – most particularly, those reasons relevant to a common-law system of constitutional interpretation carried out by courts – are the decisive reasons in its decisions. The opinion in *Lockyer* is not, however, remotely akin to what our theories of juristic discourse as a model of principled reason would lead us to expect. It is, nevertheless, representative of the majority of the work-product of the Supreme Court, and even more so of that of appellate courts underneath it. Notably, many prominent legal theorists have built their careers by recommending that judges employ precisely these kind of legalistic techniques to avoid deciding substantive questions of justice. The motivation for such recommendations arises from the desire that courts not use up their legitimacy credit by appearing to be Platonic guardians of public morality: see, for instance, the bulk of Bickel's *The Least Dangerous Branch*, and much of the substantive jurisprudence advanced in Sunstein's *One Case at a Time*.[65] This is in stark contrast to the shared presupposition under examination here concerning the special suitability of Supreme Court discourse to moral-political reasoning. It is simply wide of the mark to suppose that *Lockyer* can provide positive evidence supporting the claim that the Court's decisions employ and crucially hinge on reasoning based in fundamental moral-political principles.

It seems that *Lockyer* cannot provide any evidence in support of the third framing question either, as it's hard to see how it could have salutary secondary effects on public reasoning about penal principles if there are no such easily identifiable principles to be found in the reasons supporting the actual judgment. *Lockyer* can't fairly be seen to support Rawls's claims that judicial review on controversial moral issues plays an educative

---

[64] Ibid.
[65] Bickel, *The Least Dangerous Branch*; Sunstein, *One Case at a Time: Judicial Minimalism on the Supreme Court*.

role with respect to public reason, or that it serves to heighten the quality of wide public moral deliberation and debate concerning the issue. And the actual juridical discourse of the *Lockyer* opinion is strikingly at odds with Eisgruber's inspiring claim: "When an issue moves to the Supreme Court, public argument does not die off; instead, it becomes more substantive, emphasizing the quality of reasons rather than their marketability."[66] Here, as in *Newdow*, there is some recognizable moral-political discussion in the nonmajority opinion, specifically where Justice Souter argues that the "gross disproportionality" of the defendant's sentence to his crime shows that the "three-strikes" sentencing rule is unjustly unreasonable and so unconstitutional. But even this straightforward moral argument is overwhelmed by a long and complicated discussion of supporting and distinguishable precedential holdings from previous Court cases in order to support the applicability of the moral principle of gross disproportionality to the case at hand in the first place, and in rebuttal of Justice O'Connor's majority dismissal of that principle's applicability (through a similar but even more convoluted discussion of precedential weight, applicability, and distinguishability). In sum, the actual juristic discourse employed in support of the *Lockyer* decision cannot be fairly held as exemplifying the use of public reason, representing the people's considered moral judgments, or even being capable of constituting a recognizable contribution to the spirited back-and-forth of public debate on matters of fundamental law subject to reasonable interpretive pluralism.

c. Individual Liberty: Physician Assisted Suicide and Homosexual Sex
Of course, laypersons as well as lawyers can selectively cite precedents supporting their positions, and perhaps my use of *Newdow* and *Lockyer* smacks of that. I am not arguing here that the Supreme Court, in exercising its power of judicial review, *always* avoids speaking directly to the substance of significant moral controversies. No more do I wish to claim that such court interventions *never* have the beneficial educative and deliberative effects on wide public debates claimed. The opposite is indeed sometimes the case, as I think consideration of how the Supreme Court treated physician-assisted suicide can show. In *Washington v. Glucksberg*[67] and *Vacco v. Quill*,[68] the Court refused to ban state laws outlawing physician-assisted suicide. Chief Justice Rehnquist's opinions in the cases, especially in *Vacco*, directly engaged in serious and difficult considerations of the substantive merits of the briefs presented by those both opposed to and in support of such state laws. And the other justices

---

[66] Eisgruber, *Constitutional Self-Government*, 98–99.
[67] *Washington v. Glucksberg*, 521 U.S. 702 (1997).
[68] *Vacco v. Quill*, 521 US 793 (1997).

in their various concurrences in the unanimous decision, further considered the twists and turns of diverse considerations, most of which are focused largely on the difficult moral issues involved, rather than strictly legal considerations. They were supported in this by a remarkable paragon of public reasoning in Rawls's sense: an *amicus* brief filed by seven of the most famous English-language moral philosophers – including Rawls himself – that was subsequently published as "Assisted Suicide: The Philosophers' Brief."[69] Thus the judicial decisions, in concert with "The Philosophers' Brief," were in this case clearly resting on principled moral arguments couched in an impartial public reason accessible and acceptable to many United States citizens, responsive to the public's convictions – and facially "striving to make themselves ever more effectively available to be influenced by public debates that are fully and fairly receptive to everyone's perceptions of situation and interest and, relatedly, to everyone's opinions about justice."[70] Finally, on the third framing question, the *Glucksberg* and *Vacco* decisions have one of the strongest claims as support for the educative and enlightening roles ascribed to Court decisions by Rawls and Eisgruber. Perhaps similar considerations, with respect to the three framing questions, would also ensue from looking at the Court's recent extension of constitutional protection to the private autonomy of gays and lesbians.[71] For Justice Kennedy's opinion in *Lawrence* strikes down state laws prohibiting homosexual sodomy on the grounds that they violate the fundamental autonomy and justified liberties of individuals – even as the opinion is also concerned with debates over the relative weight of *stare decisis* in constitutional adjudication, the dispositive status of historical understandings of legal principles, the dangers of Supreme Court flirtations with the doctrine of "substantive due process," and so on.

Assessing the claims of our three theorists with respect to the weight and import of reasoning and deliberation from fundamental moral-political principles, and the claims about the salutary effects of Court adjudication on democratic debate, is then a matter of judgment not of theoretical or empirical proof. The question, in short, is how representative episodes such as *Glucksberg*, *Vacco*, and (parts of) *Lawrence* are, and how representative episodes such as *Newdow* and *Lockyer* are.

---

[69] Ronald Dworkin et al., "Assisted Suicide: The Philosophers' Brief," *New York Review of Books*, March 27, 1997.

[70] Michelman, *Brennan and Democracy*, 59.

[71] *Lawrence et. al. v. Texas*, 539 US 558 (2003). See also parts of the majority opinion of *Romer* supporting the extension of some equal protection guarantees to gays and lesbians, in particular those parts unconcerned either with the weight and number of precedential citations or with the doctrinal history and usefulness of various judicially developed tests for violations of equal protection: *Romer, Governor of Colorado, et al. v. Evans et al.*, 517 U.S. 620 (1996).

Although this is an open empirical question, I doubt the former episode types are sufficiently numerous to justify the notion that the Supreme Court is either the exemplar of public reason within the U.S. separation of powers, or that it has the unique role of representing principled moral and political deliberation on behalf of the people, or even that citizens can accept its interventions as legitimate because the process of judicially finalizing contested interpretations of fundamental moral-political principle is seen to be open to the diverse reasons, opinions, and interpretations of legitimate interests evident in public culture.

d. Electoral Equality and the Redistricting Revolution
Perhaps after this consideration of various Supreme Court cases focused on some of the substantive individual rights thought necessary to secure a sphere of private autonomy and liberty, a deliberative democrat persuaded more by the proceduralist account of democratic legitimacy – and in particular, persuaded by a democratic justification for judicial review in proceduralist terms – might object to my arguments intended to loosen the seducements of juristic discourse. After all, she might say, we should be focusing first and foremost on the High Court's heightened deliberative and reasoning capacities with respect to those procedural rights that make legitimate democratic processes possible, not on their private autonomy jurisprudence. For, she might continue, if we are to take seriously worries about judicial paternalism, the democratic legitimacy of Court interventions in democratic processes must be tied to its role in maintaining the legitimacy conditions of the democratic process itself – not in making decisions about substantive values, decisions which should be left to democratic processes of opinion- and will-formation. Although I too find the procedural account of constitutional court legitimacy convincing, I do not think we should make the case by looking at the way in which Court jurisprudence either exemplifies, represents, or communicates with the people's principled considerations concerning the procedures of democracy. The argumentative link from the procedural legitimacy of democratic processes to the democratic justification of judicial review – if there is to be such a justification – cannot be made through the heightened reasoning powers of the judiciary concerning fundamental principles structuring the democratic process. Or, at least this is what I hope to be able to show now by turning to a series of U.S. cases over more than forty years concerned with legal rules aimed at securing the electoral equality of citizens. I believe this series of cases – specifically focused on whether there are limits to the disproportionality of electoral districts established by legislatures – show the same general predominance of legal principles over moral-political principles in the Court's jurisprudence as the earlier private autonomy cases, and so belie the seductive claims made on behalf of the specially principled character

of juridical discourse even with respect to rights concerned with the procedures securing public autonomy.

Establishing that all three theorists would conceive of the laws ensuring the voting equality of citizens as a fundamental matter of moral-political principle, and so appropriate for juridical exemplification, representation, or communication, is relatively straightforward. Turning first to Rawls's theory, it seems clear that issues concerning the relative equality of voting power fall under the aegis of public reason and so are ripe for treatment by a supreme constitutional court as an exemplar of that reason. Recall that, for Rawls, public reason is a specially tailored argot: it is designed to be the language in which citizens discuss the basic structural features of political life together. Said in Rawls's terms, public reason is the appropriate language for discussing the "basic structure" of society, concerning what exactly are to be the "fair terms of cooperation" free and equal citizens can agree to for their mutual consocation. Consider Rawls's conception of higher law: it "fixes once and for all certain constitutional essentials, for example, the equal basic political rights and liberties."[72] Voting rights and comparative voting power, it would seem, fall directly under the constitutional essentials of "equal basic political rights." If we then understand a constitution as the higher law under which ordinary law and ordinary political decisions must be made, as Rawls insists, then "a supreme court fits into this idea of dualist constitutional democracy as one of the institutional devices to protect the higher law. *By applying public reason* the court is to prevent that law from being eroded by the legislation of transient majorities, or more likely, by organized and well-situated narrow interests skilled at getting their way."[73] Equal voting rights are precisely the kinds of constitutional essentials that can be easily eroded by transient majorities and skilled partisan interest groups, and redistricting has proven to be one of the foremost vehicles for such an assault upon the basic political equality of citizens. The conclusion follows directly: if a supreme court is the exemplar of public reason, it should boldly step in to correct for majoritarian assaults on higher law. More important, it should do so strictly on the basis of non-sectarian considerations drawn from the overlapping consensus of reasonable comprehensive doctrines. That is, it should invoke clear political principles drawn from the distinctly *public* political reason of the society.

Eisgruber's argument for judicial review stresses the institutional features that make the Supreme Court "disinterested" and so capable of making decisions on principled moral grounds. It would therefore seem

---

[72] Rawls, *Political Liberalism*, 232.
[73] Ibid., 233, emphasis added. Rawls's conceptions here of the dualist character of constitutional democracy and the role of the Supreme Court in protecting higher law from erosion are both explicitly indebted to Bruce Ackerman's theory of judicial review.

that he would support judicial intervention in redistricting cases in order to protect the relative equality of voting power across citizens. After all, it's hard to think that the question "should each citizen have equal voting power or not?" is anything but a basic question of political fairness, turning on matters of principle, not a mere policy matter concerned with citizens' individual preferences, desires, and idiosyncratic interests. It is, in short, a fundamental issue of equality and how equal the political liberty of each individual should be. According to Eisgruber's principled argument, then, electoral districting would appear to be precisely the kind of issue that should be kept away from the lowly business of "legislative logrolling."[74] Here Eisgruber's reliance on arguments from the unique institutional location and incentives of courts would seem to require a verdict much like Ely's: because courts are uniquely positioned to be impartial referees of the procedures of democracy, they should ensure that no participants gain an unfair advantage by manipulating the rules of the political marketplace.[75]

In fact, however, Eisgruber has reservations about some of the Supreme Court's interventions in redistricting cases, in particular more recent ones concentrated on the interaction of legislative districting and racial minorities.[76] His worries here concern the complexity, messiness, and contingency of the issues a Court must competently handle in order to decide when race-based electoral districting plans are and are not permissible. Thus, even though the Court might be institutionally well located to render impartial judgments on democratic processes, it may not have the needed reasoning capacities for gathering relevant information, making balanced assessments of competing principles, evaluating the fairness of complex systems, and designing strategically successful remedies. Nevertheless, he endorses the core of the redistricting cases: "Cases like *Reynolds v. Sims* are undoubtedly among the Court's greatest achievements, and eliminating unfair election laws is an important part of the Court's constitutional job."[77] Hence, his theoretical argument clearly endorses the mainlines of the Court's so-called redistricting revolution, even as he expresses some reservations about the Court's capacities for oversight as it extended that revolution to the investigation of the interaction of race, geography, and electoral districting. The cases I consider in the following are the former mainstream redistricting cases Eisgruber endorses, and so they can be seen as clearly evidential with respect to his claim concerning the Court's representation of the people's principles.

<hr>

[74] Eisgruber, *Constitutional Self-Government*, 101.
[75] Ely, *Democracy and Distrust*, 73–104.
[76] Eisgruber, *Constitutional Self-Government*, 179–86.   [77] Ibid., 180.

Finally, it is also clear that Michelman takes his conception of communicatively open, and so democratically acceptable, judicial review to extend beyond substantive individual rights to the procedural rights structuring democracy itself. The Court's principled decisions on matters subject to reasonable interpretive pluralism can be seen as acceptably consistent with the practice of democratic self-government as long as they are widely open to the influence of the variety of public opinions "including, recursively, everyone's opinions about what sorts of arrangements really do make public deliberations fairly receptive to everyone's views and really do render official bodies available to the influence of those views."[78] That is, the Court's opinions, in order to be both epistemically reliable and free of paternalist worries about Platonic guardianship, should be open not only to the full variety of opinions and interests with respect to private autonomy rights but also to those concerning the very structures and processes of political consociation. I take it, then, that this would include broad public debates and opinions on whether in fact there are limits to political devices – including legislatively drawn voting districts – that would render citizens' comparative voting power significantly unequal.

We should be confident, then that the claims of all three theories about the principled character of juridical discourse can be tested by looking at issues of political procedure in general, and electoral districting in particular. Surveying the cases from the redistricting revolution inaugurated in 1962 by *Baker v. Carr*[79] to the 2004 term's *Vieth v. Jubelirer*[80] should give us pause on this score, however. Rather than manifest discussions about how the principle of political equality applies to questions about the relative voting power of citizens across electoral districts with significantly different sizes, the Court has focused on insulated and institutionally specific concerns with standing, jurisdiction, and, above all, justiciability. Hence, the overwhelming emphasis on apparently strictly juridical concerns: whether various proposed voting districts and questions about gerrymandering send the Court into a "political thicket," as Justice Frankfurter asserted in *Colegrove v. Green*;[81] if redistricting in general raises unfortunately "nonjusticiable political questions"; if court decisions would require judicially indiscernible and unmanageable standards; and so on. In fact, Justice Brennan's opinion in *Baker*, the case inaugurating the redistricting revolution, did not even go to the merits of the claim concerning the vast disproportionality of the Tennessee electoral districts, content rather to dwell on legalistic questions of jurisdiction,

---

[78] Michelman, *Brennan and Democracy*, 59.
[79] *Baker v. Carr*, 369 U.S. 186 (1962).
[80] *Vieth et al. v. Jubelirer*, 541 US 267 (2004).
[81] *Colegrove v. Green*, 328 U.S. 549 (1946).

standing, and justiciability. There is no surprise here, since in order to intervene, the Court had to overcome two obstacles given its common law methods. First, the extant doctrine of "nonjusticiable political questions" announced and followed since a mid-nineteenth-century Supreme Court case[82] had to be clarified and brought up to date to see whether it applied to state legislative districting. Second, any intervention had to overcome the directly contrary 1946 precedent in *Colegrove* holding that courts should not wade into such a "political thicket." This was achieved in *Baker* by claiming that what had been previously taken to be *Colegrove's* doctrine was actually mere *obiter dicta*. Justice Stewart's concurring opinion in *Baker* simply underlines the claim that the Court's holding concerned *only* issues of jurisdiction, standing, and justiciability. So much the worse apparently for the theories presupposing that, on matters of fundamental political principle, the Court is an exemplar of public reason, or speaks on behalf of the people's political principles, or is a public site for open contestation among citizens and consideration of the diverse opinions and interests on the matter.

In contrast, the next step in the reapportionment revolution – *Gray v. Sanders*[83] – facially appears to bolster the claims for the politically principled nature of judicial review. After all, there Justice Douglas pronounced, in the unmistakable overtones of principled political reason, that: "The conception of political equality from the Declaration of Independence, to Lincoln's Gettysburg Address, to the Fifteenth, Seventeenth, and Nineteenth Amendments can only mean one thing – one person, one vote."[84] However, as Justice Stewart insisted, again in concurrence, the case concerned only voting rights for officers representing the state as a whole, and should not be taken as having any implications for apportioning legislative districts within a state. This absence of implication was overcome in the following year by the group of reapportionment cases.

As the case that announced the central holdings and justifications of the reapportionment cases, *Reynolds v. Sims*,[85] like *Gray*, would seem to confirm the conception of the Supreme Court as a privileged site for principled argument. After all, not only did the case hold that the Equal Protection clause of the Fourteenth Amendment guarantees each citizen equal electoral weight in state legislative elections, but the controlling opinion contains evident examples of straightforward reasoning concerning political principle. As Chief Justice Warren memorably wrote "Legislators represent people, not trees or acres. Legislators are elected by voters, not farms or cities or economic interests."[86] However, I

[82] *Luther v. Borden*, 48 U.S. 1 (1849).   [83] *Gray v. Sanders*, 372 U.S. 368 (1963).
[84] Ibid., 381.   [85] *Reynolds v. Sims*, 377 U.S. 533 (1964).   [86] Ibid., 562.

believe that scrutiny of the arguments presented in *Reynolds* will show that this ringing rhetoric does not reflect the crucial turning points actually supporting the decision. Two moves proved decisive. First, Warren framed the issue of comparative legislative district size as a matter of an individual's right to vote. This allowed him to bring to bear older precedents protecting suffrage – as a fundamental right to vote and have that vote counted – while expanding their reach to cover the case. "The right of suffrage can be denied by a debasement or dilution of the weight of a citizen's vote just as effectively as by wholly prohibiting the free exercise of the franchise."[87] Thus, the first move was to legally reconstrue the presented issue to bring it within the ambit of a heretofore easily distinguishable precedent. The second crucial move was to reject the elephant-in-the-room analogy: the one between state legislatures, and federal Senatorial and Electoral College representation, which generate vast inequalities in voting power. Here Warren relied not on considerations of political principle that would investigate the import, scope, and limits of a federalist division of power – the kind of thing one would expect by a consideration of either Americans' "public reason" or their "convictions about justice" – but, rather, on selective histories concerning original state constitutions and the intentions of the framers of the Fourteenth Amendment. But, as Eisgruber reminds us repeatedly, history can't be dispositive for arguments of principle, as some historical practices are unjust, whereas others are not. Only moral-political argument can sort acceptable history from history we should overcome. In short, Warren's second and decisive argument in *Reynolds* turns not on political principles, but on legal ones. In fact, such an argument is almost required if one wants to simultaneously hold on to the precedential principle of 'one person, one vote' previously announced as a constitutional principle, and to the notion that the provisions of the Constitution (concerning Senatorial and Electoral College allocation) do not violate constitutional principles. Moral-political principles alone cannot square these two commitments.

A complex history of advance and retreat in Supreme Court interventions in legislative districting, with shifting standards and rationales, follows *Reynolds* for another four decades. I think it is accurate to say that this complex history is not generally one of battles over the fundamental principles governing democratic representation or electoral equality, but over legal *technicalia* of jurisdiction, standing, precedent, and, especially, justiciability. For instance, the central holding of *Davis v. Bandemer*[88] was that redistricting to serve partisan political interests is a justiciable issue.

---

[87] Ibid., 555.   [88] *Davis v. Bandemer*, 478 U.S. 109 (1986).

But after eighteen years of little agreement about what rule should properly be applied by courts to test for the permissibility of apparently partisan gerrymanders, the court in *Vieth* reversed the *Bandemer* doctrine, holding that partisan gerrymanders are simply nonjusticiable. The Court's aversion to using political principle here, and its enthusiasm for strictly juridical concerns, is nicely summarized in Justice Scalia's dismissive attitude towards the suggestion that the Supreme Court should even consider issues of basic electoral fairness in his controlling opinion:[89]

"Fairness" does not seem to us a judicially manageable standard.... Some criterion more solid and more demonstrably met than that seems to us necessary to enable the state legislatures to discern the limits of their districting discretion, to meaningfully constrain the discretion of the courts, and to win public acceptance for the courts' intrusion into a process that is the very foundation of democratic decisionmaking.[90]

With regard to Rawls, the question now is: do the redistricting cases show the Supreme Court as an exemplar of public reason? In one sense the answer is yes, for the Court intervened without overstepping the content restraints of public reason: it avoided, for instance, referring to our God-given rights to vote, or to the superiority of a rural form of life for achieving virtue and the good life, or to voting with one's co-religionists as a necessary condition for salvation, and so forth. But, in a more important sense, the answer must be no: in the main, it did not employ as decisive justifying reasons those basic principles affirmed, recognized, and employed by ordinary citizens to discuss fundamental issues of political fairness. The redistricting cases can fairly be read as grounded in legalistic considerations generated by the Supreme Court's role as an appellate court employing well-developed juridical principles, but not as grounded in the principled defense of the political principles of the Constitution or the public political overlapping consensus.

---

[89] Although Justice Kennedy joined in the judgment as the fifth justice, he did hold out the possibility that there might be some (quite remote) possible situation where a political gerrymander might be found unconstitutional as invidious *and* violating (a yet nonexistent) manageable judicial standard.

[90] *Vieth*, 291. Scalia's final claim here – that some solid standard is needed for the court to save public face after intervening into the "very foundation of democratic decision making"–is more than a bit ironic given the entirely evanescent equal protection standard invoked for the first time and then immediately revoked for the future to justify the Court's stunning intervention four years earlier in the 2000 presidential election in *Bush v. Gore*, 531 U.S. 98, 109 (2000): "Our consideration is limited to the present circumstances, for the problem of equal protection in election processes generally presents many complexities."

Similar considerations follow for Eisgruber's claim that the Supreme Court represents the principled convictions of the people. This simply doesn't seem to square with the justices' work-product as evinced by the redistricting cases. Even if we can retroactively extract principles from the decisions and hypothesize that these principles better explain the decision of the case than the actual opinions themselves do (a favorite pastime of constitutional law professors), it is hard to sustain the notion that reasoning about basic moral and political principles was solely or even largely decisive for the outcomes. We should rather consider what the justices produce, in their written opinions, as something more or less akin to what was decisive, rather than ignore it as so much papering-over of the "real" work we theorize must have gone on. In the redistricting cases, the Supreme Court has expended most of its effort on technical questions concerning the legal principles of jurisdiction, *stare decisis*, and justiciability, not straight arguments from fundamental moral-political principles.

Finally, it is simply hard to imagine how such legalistic concerns can be the basis of, or central topics in, a wide-ranging communicative back-and-forth between those experts formally trained to deal with questions of law and the vast legal laity that constitutes the bulk of the citizenry.[91] Given the argot, valence, and content of the crucial arguments made throughout this forty-year history of Supreme Court oversight of the conditions of democratic electoral processes, it is too far a stretch to imagining its "courtroom a site of democratically legitimating public participatory process – public discourse ... for contesting, reconsidering, and revising the rules of justice themselves."[92] Perhaps one can reconstructively imagine the history of advance, retreat, and changing rulings in this area as a more or less indirect response to the changing constellation and alignments of arguments in the broad public culture about electoral equality. But a law scholar's or political theorist's imaginative reconstruction cannot substitute here for the actual communicative interaction Michelman's theory requires. The democratic acceptability of judicial review – the "ground of its respect-worthiness" for citizens – hangs on features of the actual "process by which current major interpretations [of basic law] come to have the content they do":[93] namely, the fully and fairly open receptivity of that interpretive process to every citizen's opinions about matters of justice, a receptivity that underwrites the twin claims to the heightened

[91] No doubt my attempts here to understand and briefly summarize complex histories of American constitutional common law will be seen as naïve, simplistic, and often ignorant of the decisive moves in various cases by those more expert in the law – perhaps this could be considered a performative confirmation of my general point about the communicative insulation of juristic discourse.

[92] Michelman, *Brennan and Democracy*, 74.   [93] Ibid., 57.

epistemic reliability of the Court's interpretations and the moral respect nevertheless paid to the equal worth of each citizen in processes of self-government. Only actual communicative interchange could convince citizens that an institution that is not directly accountable is nevertheless both fully respectful of their equal claims to self-government, and, a more reliable mechanism for discerning the correct application and specification of the terms of self-government than other institutions. In sum, then, the Court's redistricting and reapportionment decisions are consistent with Rawls's, Eisgruber's, and Michelman's theories about where the Court should intervene, but not with their crucial presuppositions concerning how it should do so.

The third question to ask of these theorists vis-à-vis the redistricting cases concerns the extent to which, even if the opinions and decisions themselves did not turn on principled political arguments, they nevertheless might have spurred broader principled discussion and debate in the general public sphere. In Rawls's terms, did they fulfill the "educative role" of making public reason vital in the minds of citizens by demonstrating how to employ public reason to come to reasonable and fair terms of cooperation with other citizens who may hold different comprehensive worldviews? In Eisgruber's terms, can we see the redistricting cases "speaking on behalf" of the people's principles in such a way that lay citizens can recognize them as the principles they seek to live up to, and are willing to have trump their immediate desires? These are empirical questions, and theoretical arguments are largely speculative here.

Hazarding a judgment, on the whole I would answer these questions in the negative. Although the Supreme Court has been one among several official and nonofficial actors in the public sphere who have highlighted the importance and controversial character of issues concerning electoral equality, it has not been a shining beacon of public principle.[94] On the contrary, it seems to me to have served as a marker of the expertocratic insulation of such "messy" issues as legislative districting from wide public deliberation and debate, and precisely because it can only treat the basic issues in the more or less impenetrable garb of juristic discourse. Precisely because of the Court's rightful preoccupation with its institutionally and legally specific constraints, straightforward

---

[94] In reviewing U.S. opinion data and scholarship on it concerning public support of the redistricting decisions and, more importantly here, evidence concerning the salience of the issue for the public and their overall awareness of the Court's actions from 1964 to 1969, Gerald Rosenberg concludes that "the public was generally supportive of, but essentially oblivious to, the 'Reapportionment Revolution,'" Rosenberg, *The Hollow Hope: Can Courts Bring about Social Change?*, 299. This would seem a significant counter-indication to the exemplarity, educative, and catalyst claims.

public debate about the substantive merits of the policy and principle choices facing us as a self-governing collectivity is often seriously obscured.

I doubt that Rawls is right to claim that the Court's redistricting cases can be understood as exemplary in the educative sense that he hypothesizes ought to follow from placing an issue before a constitutional court. "In the midst of any great constitutional change, legitimate or otherwise, the Court is bound to be a center of controversy. Often its role forces political discussion to take a principled form so as to address the constitutional question in line with the political values of justice and public reason. Public discussion becomes more than a contest for power and position."[95] Assessing this claim is particularly difficult because it is an empirical counterfactual: it requires us to imagine what would have happened in the absence of Supreme Court intervention. Jeremy Waldron makes this point nicely with respect to Dworkin's similar claims for the invigorating effect on public debates of the constitutionalization of issues through judicial review.[96] But with respect to what did happen, it is hard to see how the everyday use of public reason is stimulated, invigorated, and guided by opinions concerned with federal appellate court jurisdiction, precedential distinguishability, and the doctrine of nonjusticiable political questions. Yes, juristic discourse is (often) suitably cleansed of contestable comprehensive doctrines, and yes, juristic discourse is a language of reasons, but it is not first and foremost a language of public moral argument. Rather, it is a language usually tailored to a specific legal context: common-law jurisprudence carried out by a constitutional court that is also the apex of various appellate court systems.

At one point, in fact, Rawls surprisingly seems to recognize the significant *disanalogy* between public reason and legal reason. In a later article reconsidering the concept of public reason, he makes an analogy that seems to point precisely to the difference between public reason as the argot of deliberating citizens, and juristic discourse as the specialized reason of lawyers and judges: "Public reason sees the office of citizen with its duty of civility as analogous to that of judge with its duty of deciding cases. Just as judges are to decide cases by *legal grounds* of precedent, recognized canons of statutory interpretation, and other relevant grounds, so citizens are to reason by public reason and to be guided by the criterion of reciprocity, whenever constitutional essentials and matters of basic justice are at stake."[97] Here we are presented with a picture of

---

[95] Rawls, *Political Liberalism*, 239.
[96] Waldron, "Judicial Review and the Conditions of Democracy."
[97] John Rawls, "The Idea of Public Reason Revisited," in *Collected Papers*, ed. Samuel Freeman (Cambridge, MA: Harvard University Press, 1999), 605, emphasis added.

judicial decisions more akin to what we actually saw in the cases discussed above. Even if we understand the catch-all of "other relevant grounds" to include the principles and canons constitutive of public reason, this still leaves us with a picture of judicial reason as largely a *nonpublic* reason of the law amalgamated with tinges of public reason. But Rawls doesn't seem to follow up on his analogy by recognizing that it is simply hard to put together the legalistic reasoning of case-based common law methods with principled moral and political reasoning about constitutional essentials. Perhaps it is the peculiar fate of those constitutional courts charged with being both the apex of a common-law appellate system and the supreme interpreter of ambiguous constitutional provisions to be forced to be competent in both legal and public reasoning.[98] But we should not mistake the one kind of reasoning for the other because of that peculiar fate.

Eisgruber also occasionally notices the gap between principled reasoning and legal reasoning in the U.S. legal context. For instance, he does note that the "cases and controversies" requirement for judicial presentment may significantly distort a just and fair consideration of the matters of principle at stake. First, as the court is only presented with the facts and considerations as offered by the parties to the case, there is a significant possibility that the interests of other affected parties may be disregarded.[99] The fact that principled controversies are only presented through the specific facts and parties to a determinate case in the United States system entails that courts will have limited capacities for gathering relevant information. Eisgruber does not notice, however, that this is a problem peculiar to the specific institutional practices of the United States Supreme Court. For a constitutional court with the power to perform "abstract review" of statutes and regulations independently of a specific case, as is the case for most European constitutional courts, there need be no information deficit imposed by party and controversy

---

[98] See Section C1 and Chapters 8 and 9 for further discussion.

[99] The deficiencies of court proceedings between two parties to a concrete controversy as a vehicle for principled reasoning is the centerpiece of Bennett's case that, because courts are counterconversational, the exercise of judicial review is in tension with (essentially conversational) democracy. "There is a dramatic difference in the conversational behavior of the courts, on the one hand, and of the political branches of government, on the other. The former engage in highly stylized interactions concentrated on limited private parties, while the latter have freely formed and diverse exchanges with all manner of constituencies.... The conversational difference between courts and the political branches of government is fundamentally attributable to the courts' self-conception as resolvers of disputes between the parties to litigation.... In democratic terms, however, this judicial conversation may be deep, but not broad. In the court context there is ... nothing comparable to the incentive of executive and legislative officials to figure out what might be of interest to those affected by decisions and then to take the initiative in talking to those constituencies," Robert W. Bennett, "Counter-Conversationalism and the Sense of Difficulty," *Northwestern University Law Review* 95, no. 3 (2001): 880–1.

restrictions.[100] Second, he argues that a reasoned judgment of principle may be thwarted or distorted by the limited solutions a court has to choose from based upon exactly what was litigated by the parties. Although a court may often seek to reach a different solution on separate grounds from those options presented in the controversy at hand, it still must decide the case as presented to it. This is a problem, however, peculiar to an institution that mixes common-law jurisprudential methods and constitutional adjudication invoking controversial moral and political principles. Eisgruber neither recognizes the provinciality of these problems nor takes more than passing notice of these gaps between moral-political and legal reasoning. More important here, he never acknowledges that these and other gaps may significantly distort the character of public sphere discussions about the controversial issues the Supreme Court has taken up.

An objector to my judgment about the less than salutary effects of Supreme Court decisions on the character of public sphere deliberations might point, however, to the redistricting cases as a directly contrary example. After all, these were the cases that introduced the clear rule of "one person, one vote" and elucidated for the populace the implications of the equality principle enshrined in the Fourteenth Amendment by showing how that abstract principle constrained state redistricting schemes. There is undoubtedly some truth to this, but I wonder how far it goes. For surely the American people have also learned what lawyers already know: simple, straightforward rules such as "one person, one vote" are actually shorthand for a long doctrinal rule stating a presumption in favor of electoral equality but then followed by a long series of exceptions, qualifications, and modifications. In other words, they know that when push comes to shove, the simple rule will only sometimes apply: it will disqualify some population inequality between districts, but not partisan gerrymandering; it will disqualify some race-based districts but not others; it will apply to state legislatures, but not federal legislatures, and so on. And, I suspect, we as ordinary citizens also know that the grand principle's precise incidence is controlled by the expert determinations of those trained in the niceties of precedent, standing, jurisdiction, justiciability, distinguishability, and so on. Even loudly announced and clear judicial rules may hurt the quality of public debate as much as help it.

---

[100] Roger Hartley pointed out to me that the party and controversy requirements are not as restrictive as they might appear at first glance, since the Court does welcome *amici* briefs and occasionally attends to extrajurisdictional precedents such as international law. Nevertheless, the use of such materials is still directed at resolving the particular controversy for the parties involved. Further discussion of the differences between abstract and concrete constitutional review can be found in Section B of Chapter 8.

C. LEGAL PRINCIPLES AND MORAL-POLITICAL REASONING

I've argued that deliberative democrats should avoid the seductions of conceiving of juridical reason as an exemplar of the kinds of reasoned deliberations they hope to promote and make decisive for at least some fundamental political issues. In particular, closer attention to the actual work product of judges should make us skeptical about Rawls's, Eisgruber's, and Michelman's claims concerning the principled character of juridical reasoning. But this raises more than a simple objection to the overly idealized picture of judicial reasoning presupposed by three theorists.[101] For if this chapter's arguments are successful, they cast significant doubts on major institutional recommendations made in favor of a division of labor between deliberative courts and populist legislative and executive organs. The seducements of juristic discourse include a hope to explain away the apparent democratic deficits of the practice of judicial review by pointing to courts as exemplars of what democracy is supposedly all about: reasoned deliberations about controversial moral and political matters in terms all citizens can recognize as morally compelling. We are enticed, thereby, to acquiesce in a division of labor between, on the one hand, populist-sensitive legislative and executive institutions that are to be concerned only with compromises and aggregations concerning our base interests and desires, and, on the other, expert institutions insulated from the vicissitudes of popular excitation and peopled by elites trained in the special task of fundamental reasoning on matters of principle. If the premise equating juristic reasoning with principled moral-political reasoning that motivates this division is false, we need to look to alternative institutions and fora for the kinds of wide-ranging, truly democratic deliberation, debate, and decision that deliberative democratic theory rightly stresses.[102] Deliberative democrats are right to stress the differences between deliberative and aggregative processes, and to insist that (at least) fundamental political decisions ought arise out of and follow from the reasoned deliberations of free and equal citizens. However, we should not take the short cut from the legitimacy criterion of

[101] Recall also the variety of theories briefly canvassed in Section A4 above, which, in different terms, ring the changes on the theme that judicial review as practiced in the United States is not antidemocratic but, rather, democratic precisely because of the way the reasoned deliberations of the Court are exemplary, representative, or communicative.

[102] A compelling and sufficiently capacious conception of the public as the fundamental institutional location for democratic discussion and debate concerning principled reasoning can be found in Habermas, *Between Facts and Norms*, especially in Chapters 7 and 8. However, I argue that Habermas is also seduced – although to a lesser extent than Rawls, Eisgruber, and Michelman – by the promise of the judiciary as a privileged site for reasoned argument in Chapter 7.

reasoned deliberation to expertocratic legal institutions, by way of an equation of juristic reason with public reason.

Let me now turn to three types of objections one might raise against the arguments I have developed in this chapter. First, one might object to the selection of cases I've presented here, in essence doubting that these are fairly and sufficiently representative of the work-product of the Supreme Court of the United States. In particular, this objection from "cherry-picking" continues, a different selection of cases could well be used to support the specific claims Rawls, Eisgruber, and Michelman make about the principled character of Court reasoning. I'd like to meet this objection by making my arguments at a more general level: namely, by claiming that the predominance of legal principles in the Court's reasoning is not just a contingent feature of a few or even the majority of cases, but is rather due to the specific legal and institutional contexts the Court occupies. The second objection takes issue with my argument's focus on judicial review in the United States: perhaps a celebration of the deliberative and thereby democratic qualities of constitutional review along the lines of Rawls's, Eisgruber's, and Michelman's claims is in fact more appropriate in other nation-states than in the United States. I'll address this objection from "provincialism" by very briefly considering alternative ways of institutionalizing the function of constitutional review. The third objection attacks the overly strong contrast between legal principles and moral-political principles my argument apparently relies on. This objection from "overdrawn contrasts" points out that legal principles might be considered as derivatives of moral-political principles tailored to the political virtues of the rule of law. I will address this objection by considering the relationship between the two kinds of principles, which in turn will raise issues of comparative institutional competence for democratic deliberation both within and across nation-states.

1.   The Institutional Determinants of Legalism in the U.S. Practice of Judicial Review

The first objection to the argumentative weight of the case examples I've investigated here is that they do not present a full and fair picture of the character and quality of the Court's deliberations. I agree here to the extent that no simple use of examples alone can carry the weight of arguing for or against the ideal of juristic discourse presupposed by the three focal theories. My use of these examples, however, was not intended to represent a complete assessment of the Court's work-product, but rather to remind those whose have read a tremendous number of such opinions of their actual character, and to invite those who haven't to compare theoretical claims with the data they are about. Anything less than a fully exhaustive cataloging and classification of the breadth of opinions where the Court has exercised its powers of constitutional review would be insufficient, in fact, to make a confident empirical assessment of the various claims made on behalf of or against the principled character of judicial review in the United States. And of course such legal research alone would not be enough, as the theories canvassed here aim to compare the judiciary favorably with other branches of government as constitutional interpreters. Hence, we would need to add sustained and serious comparisons of the judiciary's performance with like reasoning, deliberating, and communicating capacities and performance of other political actors and institutions in the U.S. political system.[103] Finally, of course, we would also need to do cross-national comparative studies between the United States and other constitutional and nonconstitutional democracies – especially attending to the differences between those with and those without institutions of judicial review – as a check on the often counterfactual nature of the claims advanced.[104] Perhaps then, and only then, could we confidently claim a sufficient empirical basis for assessing the claims concerning the character and content of juristic discourse in the U.S. context.

Perhaps, however, it is possible to strengthen the response to the cherry-picking objection in a different manner by considering the specific legal and institutional determinants of the predominance of legalistic reasoning in the U.S. system of constitutional adjudication. I have in mind here three broad types of features that constrain U.S. juridical reasoning and prevent it from exemplifying, representing, or communicating in the language of moral-political principles: (1) judicial review in the United States is only effected through particular cases, (2) by a Court that is simultaneously a constitutional court, at the apex of the national appellate system, and with significant authority within a complicated federalist division of political and judicial authority, and, (3) it is carried out through common law methods of adjudication. What the case examples can be taken to highlight then is the ways in which this peculiar

---

[103] An interesting part of such an empirical project of comparing constitutional reasoning in the various branches of government is presented in J. Mitchell Pickerill, *Constitutional Deliberation in Congress: The Impact of Judicial Review in a Separated System* (Durham, NC: Duke University Press, 2004).

[104] For instance, it makes some sense to assess counterfactual claims like 'If the Supreme Court hadn't taken up the principled defense of right X, then it would have been subject to erosion, or to legislative logrolling, or public would not have been sufficiently educated about political principles' by seeing how right X, its attendant political principles, and the broader public culture faired in sufficiently similar democracies that lack the power of judicial review. Jeremy Waldron, for instance, repeatedly points out the possibly heightened public deliberations occurring in British Commonwealth countries with Parliamentary sovereignty and no judicial review. See, for instance, Waldron, *Law and Disagreement*, 289–91.

institutional location with its particular legal practices, in a sense pre-structures the Court's deliberations in a legalistic way, a way that impedes their ability to exemplify, represent, or communicate with the people's deliberations on controversial but nevertheless inescapably fundamental moral-political issues.

Consider first the so-called cases and controversies requirements of Article III of the Constitution of the United States. As Eisgruber notes, but doesn't focus on, this restriction of the jurisdictional purview of the judicial power only to particular cases means that when the Court looks to exercise its powers of constitutional review, it must await a suitable vehicle in the form of a particular suit brought against a specific statute or regulation. And as Eisgruber notes, this will distort to some extent the Court's ability to gather relevant information, perhaps most important concerning the impact of likely decisions on the interests of all those affected. In addition, the necessity of resolving the case before it may constrain the set of solutions the Court may consider. But beyond this, attention to the particular review restriction on the Court can go some significant distance to explaining its focus on legal principles concerning issues such as standing, jurisdiction, ripeness, mootness, legal remediability and so on – principles that turned out to be decisive in the resolution of the *Newdow* and *Lockyer* cases concerning the Pledge and "three-strikes", respectively.

Consider, second, the complexities introduced by the fact that the Supreme Court must wear many judicial hats at once. Even as it has the power to review federal statues and regulations for constitutionality, it also has assumed a fair amount of authority to carry out the same kind of review with respect to many issues of individual state law, although the exact scope and limits of this second authority are hotly disputed.[105] Here it should be expected that such complexities will give rise to juristic principles governing authority and jurisdiction in order to rationally manage the employment of such powers. The Court also sits simultaneously at the apex of the federal appellate court system, and so it will have developed principles to manage when it is and is not willing to let stand inconsistencies between the rulings and doctrines of the various federal Appeals Courts. Recall the intricate interactions between common law considerations and the various relations between the Supreme Court, a federal Appeals Court, and the California Appeals Court central to

---

[105] The centerpiece of such disputes focus on the Court-developed doctrine of "incorporation," that is, the set of legal principles that determine how much of the original Bill of Rights constraining the powers of the federal Congress was, is, or should be made applicable also to the laws of the individuals states in the light of the 1868 Fourteenth Amendment – but the Fourteenth Amendment is by no means the only site of controversy about the Court's judicial review authority vis-à-vis state law.

O'Connor's decision in the "three-strikes" case *Lockyer*. The Court, despite what some of the more heated antijudicial rhetoric might lead one to believe, has not in fact arrogated to itself unlimited powers for passing on the constitutionality of governmental actions. It has, rather, developed a complex set of doctrines, principles, and presumptions intended to negotiate its interactions with the other branches of the federal government. Central to managing the limits of its power are doctrines such as "nonjusticiable political questions" whose changing incidence across the forty-year history of redistricting cases played such a central and decisive role in the Court's varied approaches to electoral equality.[106] Thus, specifically legal principles arise from the peculiar institutional location of the Supreme Court of the United States, and their associated intricacies understandably drive the predominance of legal over moral-political considerations even in cases that facially raise issues of the latter kind.

Finally, the Supreme Court's preoccupation with specifically legal issues like the weight and content of precedents, the incidence of the principle of *stare decisis* in different kinds of cases (e.g., in statutory vs. constitutional interpretation), distinguishability, the standing and content of judicial doctrines, methods for isolating holdings that add to precedent and shape doctrine from mere dicta, interpretive canons, and so on are basic features of a common-law method of adjudication. Such specifically juristic concerns were raised in every single case considered earlier and played an influential role in most. Yet labeling these concerns "specifically juristic" or "legalistic" is in no way intended to belittle or diminish their import, for they are neither accidental nor, more important, useless or troublesome features of juristic discourse. On the contrary, most if not all can be considered essential to or supportive of the basic values secured by the rule of law: that citizens can know their legal obligations, the predictability of legal decisions and the incidence of the use of coercive

---

[106] Of course, Court review of the scope and limits of the powers and actions of the federal legislative and executive branches also interacts with questions about the division of power between the national government and the states, since the Constitution allocates powers in a complex federalist scheme. This, too, is an area of high controversy in recent jurisprudence as the Court once again seems to be interested, for instance, in limiting the scope of Congress's legislative reach under the Commerce Clause. In a related vein, the Court's recent reinvigoration and extension to the individual states of the doctrine of "sovereign immunity" from suit has lead to a significant weakening of Congressional and federal government authority vis-à-vis the states in general, even as it may, somewhat counterintuitively, have led to a significant increase in the power of federal courts as overseers of federal law. For a critique of the recent development and use by the Court of the doctrine of state sovereign immunity and allied judicially developed doctrinal tests for Congressional action, see John T. Noonan, Jr., *Narrowing the Nation's Power: The Supreme Court Sides with the States* (Berkeley, CA: University of California Press, 2002).

force, systemwide consistency, legal stability, equal treatment of like cases, control of arbitrary official power, and so on. These specifically juristic features of common law methods serve, to use Fuller's felicitous phrase, the "internal morality" of law.[107] Of course, the internal morality of law can be served in other ways – and by other officials than judges – in alternative legal systems, such as civil law systems. Nevertheless, once a society entrusts constitutional review to a high court regularly employing the techniques of common law jurisprudence, significant constraints are placed on the abilities of constitutional judges to act either as exemplars of public reasoning about principle, or as impartial representatives of the people's principles, or even to clearly communicate with the legal laity of the citizenry in ways that might warrant democratic respect for the Court's interventions.

There may well be other legal and institutional determinants of the predominance of the use of legalistic over moral-political reasoning in the Supreme Court's judicial review cases. All I have sought to do here is point out some *general* features of the Court's actual institutional location and adjudicative practices that, I think, go a long way toward meeting the cherry-picking objection, namely, by explaining why we should generally expect to find significant disanalogies between actual Supreme Court discourse and the principled moral-political discourse presupposed by the three theories, much like the disanalogies evinced in the few example cases I've looked at here.

2.   Would a Kelsen-style Court do Better?

Once the specific structural determinants of the legalistic character of Supreme Court constitutional jurisprudence are made clear, however, the second objection from provincialism becomes even starker. For now one might object that my critique of the seducements of juristic discourse is too nation-state specific. What of the practice of constitutional review in other countries, and what of the different ways of institutionalizing the function – might not these theories fare better if we were to assess their claims in the context of other nations' institutions and practices? Here I am entirely in agreement with the general tenor and basic presuppositions of the objection: an adequate understanding and justification of the practice and institutionalization of constitutional review in terms of the normative ideals of deliberative democratic constitutionalism cannot avoid investigating and comparing a variety of potential ways the function can be realized, and this should surely include some cross-national comparisons of actual (and imagined) practices and institutional designs. It is to such tasks that Chapters 8 and 9 are largely devoted.

---

[107] Fuller, *The Morality of Law*.

A few brief remarks on the charge of provincialism as leveled at the debate concerning the specific claims of the three theories investigated here might be appropriate, as some light can be cast on the objection by various institutional thought experiments. To begin, consider the degree to which the theories themselves are provincial. Rawls is careful to point out that his comments about the character of Supreme Court reason as an exemplar of public reason are not intended to justify the specific institution of constitutional review in an independent judiciary, nor more concretely even to endorse the practice of judicial review as carried out in the history of the United States. Rawls is not putting forward a strong argument justifying judicial review but, rather, showing how one could understand extant U.S. institutions and practices as, at least, not objectionable from the point of view of the theory of political liberalism and its deliberative conception of democracy. It may then be that alternative institutions and practices may be even more unobjectionable insofar as they better exemplify the use of political public reason than the Supreme Court of the United States.

Eisgruber's and Michelman's theories are provincial in a stronger sense, as they both seek to give acceptably democratic justifications for the institutionalization of U.S. judicial review at its best, justifications that then also can be seen as the basis for discerning the best interpretive practices and sorting worthy from unworthy decisions in the Court's case history. This is no surprise, as both are law professors whose jobs require them to work within the historically specific set of extant institutions and practices that makes up the American legal system.[108] Of course, both explicitly claim that their arguments do not necessitate or require a system of constitutional review like the United States', and so both are in this sense also giving democratic excuses more than strong positive justifications for a provincial set of arrangements. And between the two, Eisgruber's theory is clearly more exculpatory than Michelman's theory, as the latter can reasonably be said to outline ideal conditions of democratic legitimacy for Supreme Court determinations of fundamental law, ideal conditions that are quite far from being fulfilled under contemporary conditions. Although each is then provincial in design, both seem structurally open to testing in different legal and institutional contexts.

Could it be that the three theories would fare better, then, where the function of constitutional review was not carried through particular cases

---

[108] Among the longer list of theories that seem similarly seduced by juristic discourse I mentioned in Section A4 earlier – especially those seduced by the claim that the Supreme Court is a democratic institution representative of the people's true or most basic moral-political principles – the overwhelming majority are the products of the United States legal academy. See also my concerns about the pathologies of *ad hoc* reasoning in American jurisprudence in Chapter 1.

and controversies by a multitasking superior appellate court employing the methods of common law jurisprudence to constitutional specification? The idea here would be that their claims to the exemplary, representative, or communicative character of constitutional court opinions might be not so much *false*, as *nationally misplaced*.[109] Perhaps a constitutional court of the structure preferred by Hans Kelsen and widely adopted since, especially in European constitutional democracies – namely, a court with the power for the direct "abstract review" of ordinary law independent of a concrete case, one specialized only in constitutional review and without other significant appellate duties, and perhaps even adjudicating without the legalistic requirements of common-law jurisprudence – could better exemplify, represent, and/or communicate in the public language of fundamental moral-political principles?[110] Such constitutional courts certainly seem less encumbered by the determinants of legalistic reasoning specific to the U.S. context.

The question this suggestion raises is: why require constitutional review to be carried out by a court? Why not look farther afield than judges? According to the theories under consideration, the reasoning and deliberating advantages accruing to the Supreme Court concern the complexity of the moral-political principles involved and the problems posed by generating more specific, justified moral-political principles from the abstract ones already constitutionally provided – but these are not first and foremost *legal* complexities. They are the complexities involved in the elaboration of any of the moral-political principles that are to legitimately regulate the collective life of democratic citizens – that is, they are the very same complexities faced at the level of constitutional design and ratification. If constitutional design and ratification is to be subject to the principle of reasons-responsive popular sovereignty – as deliberative democrats insist – then, *a fortiori*, the further development of constitutional principles must be likewise subject to that principle.

Once we step out of the specific legal and institutional context of United States judicial review, it seems we should also be considering noncourt institutionalizations of the function of constitutional review. If we want to design an institution that exemplifies, represents, and communicates in a public language of moral-political principles, we might consider, for instance, something along the lines of Rousseau's recommended "Tribunate": an institution focused on matters of contested fundamental moral-political principle and acting as an intermediary, properly balancing the relations between the people collectively

---

[109] My thanks to an anonymous reviewer for *The Journal of Political Philosophy* both for this formulation, and for insisting that I consider this possibility.

[110] Hans Kelsen, "Judicial Review of Legislation. A Comparative Study of the Austrian and the American Constitution," *Journal of Politics* 4, no. 2 (1942).

legislating in their sovereign capacity, the extant laws and constitution of the nation, the executive agencies of the government, and the citizens as private individuals.[111] On the model of the Roman Tribunes, Rousseau seems to envision the members of Tribunate as elected from the ranks of ordinary citizens (plebes not patricians), and he recommends term limits to control the body's enormous power, whereby a Tribunate would only exist for a set period of time before being shut down for a suitable interval and then convening a new one for another set term, and so on. The members of such a body would seem "better positioned to represent the people's convictions about what is right" (Eisgruber) than the legally trained and focused judges sitting on a Kelsen-style court, and certainly better positioned to be such representatives than Supreme Court justices. If we were to require, in addition, that the Tribunate determine and publicly justify its decisions through reasoned opinions focused on the public principles involved, we might also have good reason think such an institution much more exemplary of public reason than the present American Court. Finally, proper structuring of the electoral process for the Tribunate might well give individual citizens better reason to respect it than an independent constitutional court or the Supreme Court, since it could be understood as facially open to the full societal panoply of opinions and interests and thereby warrant its dual claims to epistemic reliability and respectful treatment of the equal political autonomy of each citizen. Perhaps given Eisgruber's claim about different institutional incentives, however, the members of such a court should be chosen by lot, rather than being buffeted by the ever-changing winds of electoral pressures. Or perhaps focused on the complexities of reasoning about moral principles and their application, we should randomly choose experts in political theory – philosopher-judges to keep the citizenry committed to their principles against the citizens' representatives anyone?

The point of such speculations is that they reveal that, in the absence of some theoretical explanation for why specifically *legal* forms of competence are indispensable to the good functioning of a system for constitutional review – once we go beyond the original provincial application of the three theories – each theory seems, in fact, to point *away* from courts as privileged sites of the reasoning and deliberation taken as criterial for democratic legitimacy. I take it that this supports, rather than

---

[111] "The Tribunate is the preserver of the laws and the legislative power.... The Tribunate is not a constitutive part of the City, and it ought to have no share of either the legislative or the executive power, but precisely because of this its power is all the greater: for while it can do nothing, it can prevent everything.... A wisely tempered Tribunate is the firmest bulwark of a good constitution," Book IV, Chapter 5 of Rousseau, *Of the Social Contract*, 136–7.

rebuts, the line of argument I have been running: deliberative democrats ought to resist both the seducements of juristic reasoning and the use of such seducements to underwrite an institutional division of labor between courts and electorally accountable political organs.

3. Legal Principles as Derivative Moral-Political Principles

That my critique of Rawls, Eisgruber, and Michelman relies on an over-drawn contrast between legal principles and moral-political principles constitutes the third line of objection.[112] Here, it might be said, as doctrinal legal principles are themselves the product of practical reasoning over time by courts looking for rational and reasonable ways to manage situations that they repeatedly run into, and to manage them in ways that are congruent with the overall moral and political values instantiated in a nation-state's particular legal system, we should conceive of such legal principles as justified in the light of moral-political principles, or as derived from the nation's moral-political principles, or, stronger still, as simply subsidiary moral-political principles. But if that is the case, then the objection to the disanalogy between juridical reasoning and the public reasoning about matters of fundamental moral-political principle collapses, and with it the worry about the seducements of juristic discourse for deliberative democracy.

In order to respond to this objection, we will need some more careful specification of terms. As a first step, note that what I have been calling "legal principles" might be better called "principles of adjudicative procedure," as they supply reasons for taking certain kinds of considerations into account, while avoiding other considerations, on the part of judges when they are looking to resolve particular cases or controversies before them. More than this, they are principles used almost exclusively in the adjudicative context. Thus, although many legal principles – from the most general and universal such as equality of persons before the law, to more concrete and context-specific ones such as the U.S. principle banning "cruel and unusual" punishments – are employed as reasons by judges, they also are employed by and accessible to other governmental actors and citizens in evaluating the actions of officials, actual and proposed legal rules, institutional transformations, policy proposals, and so on. Principles of adjudicative procedure might be thought of then as that subgroup of a system's legal principles employed almost exclusively by a specially trained group of experts (lawyers and judges), tailored to the institutional arrangement and specific hierarchical

---

[112] My thanks to both Victor Peterson and an anonymous reviewer for *The Journal of Political Philosophy* for forcing me to clarify my thoughts on this matter; each will no doubt be unsatisfied with the results.

structure of courts in that system, established to give structure, coherence, and regularity of incidence to the interpretive and applicative methods employed by courts, all in order to further the realization of basic rule of law values – to realize the "internal morality of law" – in the context of court business. So although it makes sense to see principles of adjudicative procedure as a subset of a nation's legal principles, it is a subset whose use and incidence are institutionally delimited, and so not *prima facie* the kinds of principles appropriately canvassed under Rawls's "political use of public reason," or Eisgruber's "moral convictions of the people," or used in Michelman's "legitimating public participatory process."

Second, note also that I have been rather loose concerning what is meant here by "moral-political" principles, and intentionally so, given the desire to challenge three different kinds of theoretical claims as all resting on the same presupposition concerning the suitability of juridical discourse for the wide public use of practical political reason. I have used the term "moral" largely here in deference to Eisgruber's usage.[113] Of course, the only principles we are talking about here – whether principles of adjudicative procedure or of political morality – are those that can reasonably be considered to be a part of a particular system of positive law. Thus, we can avoid here quite general debates about whether law is a mere subsidiary of morality, or about the correctness of natural law versus legal positivistic theories of the necessary relationship between law and morality, for the political systems we are concerned with are ones that have actually incorporated certain moral-political principles as legal principles. The subject of "political morality" is then those principles that are taken as fundamental to underwriting current political structures and the current regime of law, both ordinary and higher. The three theorists clearly differ about the appropriate scope of moral-political principles that should be a subject of Supreme Court constitutional adjudication – from Rawls's smaller set of "constitutional essentials" that make up the overlapping consensus, to Michelman's contested interpretations of fundamental law, to Eisgruber's full panoply of the people's convictions

[113] Eisgruber's references to morality are really to what might be better called "political morality," namely, that species of morality that we desire to model and realize in political structures and positive law. At any rate, the overriding contrast is for him between (alternatively) matters of "principle," "morality," "impartiality" or "justice" and (alternatively) matters of "desires," "interests," "collective self-interests," or "expediency." In one of the few passages in which he indicates the extension of his use of the term "morality," Eisgruber writes: "Many, if not all, of the Constitution's abstract provisions share an important feature: they refer to, or directly implicate, moral issues.... The Constitution's most significant rights-protecting provisions are drafted with explicit reference to freedom, equality, and other moral ideas; they speak, for example, of 'the free exercise of religion,' 'the freedom of speech,' and 'the equal protection of the laws,'" Eisgruber, *Constitutional Self-Government*, 52.

about principles of justice and morality. Nevertheless, each of them intends to assign an important degree of institutional control over the specification and application of such principles to courts on the theory that they have a unique claim to heightened deliberative powers for dealing reasonably with matters of principle.

To return then to the objection from overdrawn contrasts, its central motivating insight seems correct: namely, that principles of adjudicative procedure clearly can be justified in terms of more general political principles, the kinds of more general political principles that the three theories look to courts to exemplify, represent, and communicate with. So it might make some sense to agree with the objection's claim that we should understand principles of adjudicative procedure as subsidiary moral-political principles, or perhaps as derivatives of the more general legal principles instantiated in a nation-state's legal system. But the fact that there are these justificatory connections doesn't seem to undercut the main critical thrust of my argument. For even supposing that we could, for instance, explain why the doctrine of standing is important – in terms say of not overburdening the resources of courts, or of limiting the powers of the federal judiciary vis-à-vis matters of state law, or of ensuring a limited reach to court powers concerning constitutional questions – these justifications of standing in more general principled terms do little to assuage doubts that the actual work product in a case like *Newdow* exemplified, represented, or communicated with the public principles it facially engaged – those concerning the freedom of religion and the limits on governmental establishment of religion. The fact that principles of adjudicative procedure may be entailments of publicly shared, acknowledged, and accessible moral-political legal principles does not mean that the former are indistinct from the latter. Even less does it warrant the conclusion that the deliberative democratic character and consequences of judicial decisions and supporting opinions in cases such as *Lockyer*, where principles of adjudicative procedure predominated, are indistinct from that of cases such as *Vacco* and *Glucksberg*, where recognizably moral-political principles did.

To be sure, it may not always be as easy to assign a given principle to one end of the spectrum of legal principles or the other. Although the various procedural rules and doctrinal principles used to control the precise incidence of *stare decisis* clearly belong on the adjudicative end, and the principle of freedom of religious conscience clearly belongs on the moral-political end, some legal principles present more difficult cases. The adjudicative principle central to the redistricting cases – that realized in the doctrine of nonjusticiable political questions – is at one and the same time central to specifically juridical reasoning and clearly an entailment of some more general political principle governing the relationship between the various branches of government, a principle concerned with specifying the appropriate separation of powers for that nation-state. Furthermore, it is probably also the case that, when pressed, one could supply a plausible justification of even the most arcane and legalistic principles of adjudicative procedures in terms of some more recognizable and widely shared moral-political principle, or at least some value or set of values underlying such a principle. Nevertheless, neither imaginative *ex post facto* reconstructions of the 'real' moral-political principles doing the decisive work in a particular judicial opinion, nor pointing to the difficulty of bright-line distinctions between principle types is sufficient to undermine the case I have made here. For in order for the Supreme Court to be an exemplar of public reason, or the foremost representative of the people's convictions, or a communicator in the public participatory process of wide debate on fundamental political matters, its work-product must facially, and usually, trade in and rely upon a language of principled moral-political reasons that is publicly recognizable as such and cognizable by both the legal elite and the legal laity that make up the entire citizenry.

There is one more way in which the overdrawn contrast objection might be raised here. For even if one agrees that there are some important differences between principles of adjudicative procedure and moral-political principles, it seems that pointing out the differences in the work-product of courts alone is insufficient. After all, if there are analogues to adjudicative principles in other branches of government – that is, institutionally specific principles tailored to the peculiarities of that organ or branch – then the same phenomenon of the predominance of those institutional principles over moral-political principles could show up in those other branches as well. Surely there are manifold examples of legislatures resorting to principles of parliamentary procedure in order to avoid speaking to the merits of an issue, and the same is true for other governmental organs and actors. The issue this chapter raises is not simply one about the suitability of courts as forums of moral-political principle, but an issue of the comparative performance of various institutions and sites for the reasoned public discourse deliberative democrats hope to make the backbone of political practices. With this way of taking the objection, I find myself wholly in agreement.

It should then be a desideratum of an adequate theory concerning the appropriate sites for public discourse that it be comparative across the various branches of government and domains of society where such discourse might be located. The arguments in Chapters 8 and 9 explicitly rely on comparative assessments of deliberative competences available across institutions within a nation-state. Furthermore, we can extend the comparative desideratum across nation-states, especially across different ways of institutionalizing the function of constitutional review. In addition to assuaging worries about provincialism, this also may give us a way of gauging whether cherished justifications of certain U.S. principles of adjudicative procedure really hold true when tested. For instance, Lee Epstein suggests testing whether in fact the principles of justiciability actually facilitate judicial independence, as is commonly thought, by looking at European constitutional courts which have abstract review powers and so need no specific case or controversy to act.[114] Thus intra- and international and cross-institutional comparisons should be able to shed more light on the questions of the predominance of institutionally-specific principles over general moral-political principles in decision processes, and of the relations between various types of legal principles. Before taking up such issues however, I turn once again in the next chapter to normative political philosophy in order to lay out what I take to be the most convincing account of deliberative democratic constitutionalism – only with this account in hand can we ask the right questions of the mass of comparative and empirical data.

---

[114] Lee Epstein, "The Comparative Advantage," *Law and Courts* 9 (1999).

7

Constitutionalism as the Procedural Structuring of Deliberative Democracy

A.   A PROVISIONAL SUMMARY: CRITERIA FOR AN ADEQUATE THEORY OF CONSTITUTIONAL REVIEW

In the past five chapters, I have presented various arguments for and against the institutionalization of the function of constitutional review in an electorally independent judiciary. Part of the point was to critically evaluate the respective positions in the interest of supporting and developing the most cogent and compelling account of constitutional review and its judicial institutionalization. But another point was to investigate the extent to which more recent normative political theories focused on deliberative democracy might provide more adequate conceptual and normative means for addressing the core tension underlying more traditional accounts of judicial review: namely, the apparent tension between constitutionalism and democracy.

Chapter 1 noted the extent to which interesting American jurisprudential theories, in attempting to come to terms with the counter-majoritarian and quasi-paternalist character of judicial review as institutionalized and practiced in the United States, were led to develop normative political theories that significantly distorted the ideals of democracy and constitutionalism. I suggested there that a better approach to the problem would be one that started from the most plausible ideas of constitutional democracy and then proceeded to assess various arguments concerning how and where to locate the function of constitutional review, rather than attempting to significantly redefine the normative ideals of constitutional democracy in order to make them match the exact institutions and practices of constitutional review in a particular nation-state. As laid out in Chapter 2, traditional theories – whether of the Bickel/Choper or the Dahl/Ely varieties – understand constitutional democracy as a somewhat unstable amalgamation of two different principles: the principle of democratic popular sovereignty as aggregative responsiveness to citizen's prepolitical interests and desires, combined with the principle of constitutional limits intended to protect individuals and minorities in the light of putatively self-evident substantive truths about rights. But, I argued, this combination of majoritarian democracy and minoritarian constitutionalism is both descriptively and normatively inadequate. Empirically, such a conception of constitutional democracy seems deaf to the reasons-responsive deliberative interactions frequently witnessed among citizens and governmental officials in the formation of law and policy. This is not just a descriptive lacuna however, for ignoring the reason-responsive character of democracy also left the defense of aggregative majoritarianism relatively bereft of convincing justifications. Finally, I indicated how the natural-law inspired defense of minoritarian constitutionalism in terms of the preeminence of a constitution's substantive values faces increasing justificatory pressure under conditions of reasonable value pluralism and the demise of metaphysically grounded moral realism. Chapter 3 then laid out the conceptual groundwork for a new understanding of constitutional democracy that could compensate for the deficits of the older one.

Chapters 4 through 6 argued that a set of deliberative democratic argumentative strategies with respect to judicial review were unpersuasive. Substantialist defenses, such as those put forward by Dworkin and Perry, of a judicial institutionalization of constitutional review appear vulnerable to worries about judicial paternalism similar to those that bedeviled more traditional theories of minoritarian constitutionalism as well, particularly where they rested on empirically and morally dubious assumptions about the superior moral competences of judges vis-à-vis other officials and citizens. Theories such as those of Eisgruber, Michelman, and Rawls that attempt to redeem the claim to special moral competences in the judiciary by adverting not to the character of judges but, rather, to the representative character of juridical discourse – as the paradigmatic idiom for public reasoning amongst democratic citizens – seemed to fundamentally distort the actual technical and legalistic character of judicial reasoning. Recommendations for a division of labor between aggregative populist institutions and deliberative expertocratic institutions on the basis of the heightened moral reasoning powers of the judiciary appear, then, unconvincing. Finally, argumentative strategies like those adopted by Freeman of justifying judicial review as a potentially legitimate expression of the constitution-creating authority of popular sovereignty seemed to save the democratic legitimacy of constitutionalism at the level of an idealized original contract, but at the price of sacrificing the ongoing character of constitutional elaboration through actual democratic processes. Although in these three chapters, the prima facie objection to judicial review as paternalistic kept reappearing, I also tried to show that various aprioristic arguments advanced by Waldron that judicial review necessarily violates the fundamental democratic premise of the equal moral worth of citizens were, in the end, insufficient – the paternalist objection remained merely prima facie applicable, not dispositive.

However, the preceding chapters also revealed a number of important insights that one would want incorporated into an adequate account of deliberative democratic constitutional review: insights concerning the legitimacy, political processes, and institutions of constitutional democracy. To begin, it seems that the crucial fault lines in the debates concerning judicial review run mainly along the cleavages between different conceptions of the legitimacy of democracy, of constitutionalism, and of their interrelationships. They do not seem to run mainly along the lines – as jurisprudential scholarship often assumes – of different conceptions of judicial assertiveness and passivity, or of different methods of constitutional and statutory interpretation. One central pivot point here is whether or not the principles of democracy and constitutionalism are thought to be antithetical or complementary. I hope to have highlighted the attractiveness of a theory of deliberative democratic constitutionalism, one that conceives of the principles of democracy and constitutionalism as mutually reinforcing. In particular, if we are to take seriously the ideals of democratic self-determination, then democracy cannot be limited to ordinary politics, but must extend to the construction and ongoing elaboration of the constitution as well – a constitution that, in turn, structures the legitimate practice of democratic autonomy. Although the existence of persistent, good-faith disagreements among citizens about the substantive principles that are to be legally instantiated must be acknowledged, the extent of this disagreement should not be overemphasized lest we jeopardize the very project of normatively justifying any type of coercive law and ignore empirical evidence for some significant degree of democratic constitutional convergence. Thus, the existence of reasonable pluralism need not rule out a robust conception of political legitimacy from the get-go, at least if the latter is formulated along proceduralist lines. One particularly striking aspect of both historically effective constitutional agreements and the various deliberative democratic theories is the shared insistence that the fundamental rights required for democracy are much more extensive than those that are obviously entailed by the simple procedures of bare majoritarianism, such as individual franchise and expressive rights. Questions remain open here, however, concerning how exactly this more expansive catalogue of fundamental rights is to be understood theoretically.

Beyond these insights concerning the legitimacy conditions of constitutional democracy, the theories presented in the last few chapters also invite us to widen the purview of what counts as deliberative democratic politics. To begin, they show that the various forms of practical reason used in politics extend well beyond the instrumental and prudential use of reason focused on by aggregative and pluralist conceptions of politics: the use of reason concerned, that is, with the calculation of the preponderance of citizens' desires, the threat potentials of various groups and social powers, and the efficiency of various alternative policy means to achieving the ends determined by such preference aggregation and bargaining. For democratic politics is reasons-responsive in a much broader sense: it involves the political use of moral, ethical, and legal forms of practical reasoning, in addition to the prudential. The considerations presented in the last several chapters also point to a need to widen the scope of the public fora to which deliberative theories look for politically relevant discussion and debate. On the one hand, there are no good reasons for – and several good reasons against – restricting the search to judicial institutions. The "dignity of legislation" (Waldron) arises to the extent that it is the result of open, representative, structured, and reasons-responsive deliberation on pressing public matters. Deliberative democrats also should investigate the deliberative potentials in various other governmental institutions and arrangements beyond constitutional courts and national legislatures. On the other hand, the processes of political opinion and will-formation must not be unduly restricted to the formal organs of the state – legitimate and effective deliberative democracy requires and feeds off vibrant and politically influential informal public spheres. Deliberative democratic constitutionalism is therefore not only concerned with the diversity of political uses of practical reason but also with the diversity of fora in which it holds sway and becomes effective.

Finally, there seem to be some positive directions indicated as a result of the heretofore mostly negative arguments concerning the institutionalization of the function of constitutional review. First, it seems that the central considerations concerning how to institutionalize constitutional review will focus more on institutional location than comparative deliberative competence, even though comparative competence is not irrelevant. Second, it would seem essential to have some better sense of the comparative performance of various governmental and nongovernmental institutions within a nation-state – the needed arguments cannot stand solely on observations about one branch or institution. Third, such comparisons would be greatly strengthened by going beyond the limited domain of one nation-state and its possibly idiosyncratic structures and practices – we need to compare various governmental regimes across diverse, well-functioning constitutional democracies. Finally, it seems evident that the cogency and force of the democratic objection to constitutional review is sensitive to differences in institutional arrangements and practices. Before taking up these more inchoate insights concerning institutionalization in the next chapter, I focus in this chapter on issues of legitimacy and democratic process in the theory of constitutional democracy advanced by Jürgen Habermas.

These concerns can be focused by two questions central for any conception of constitutional democracy: How are laws enacted in a constitutional democracy legitimate? and, What is the proper characterization of democratic political processes? The considerations from the past several chapters I have just briefly summarized can be presented as a set of six adequacy criteria for a theory of constitutional review under the premises of deliberative democratic constitutionalism. If there is a theory that can fulfill these criteria – and thereby justify the function of constitutional review as a necessary component of legitimate deliberative democratic constitutionalism – it would seem best positioned to satisfyingly address the question of how to institutionalize such a function.

With respect to legitimacy such a theory should, first, be able to conceive of constitutional democracy, not as an uneasy combination of antithetical and unrelated principles, but rather as internally related and *mutually presupposing*. In particular, I suggest that constitutionalism should be conceived of as an ongoing democratic process of the elaboration of the higher law that instantiates the constitutive and regulative structures of democracy itself. Second, as substantivist accounts of democratic legitimacy appear to lead to worries about judicial paternalism – especially under conditions of value pluralism – it appears that we need a thoroughly *procedural* account of how constitutionally structured democratic politics can warrant the legitimacy of decisions; one without recourse to contestable substantivist checks such as natural law or the objective hierarchy of values. Third, we would still like to be able to account for the *deontic character* of fundamental rights ascribed to persons, without going beyond a procedural account of legitimacy. Thus approaches that understand fundamental rights merely as normal legal claims that are to be weighed against any other competing legal "rights" (that is, justiciable legal claims) in cases of conflict, or that reduce rights to values that must be weighed against each other and transitively ordered in each new conflicting situation, or that rely on deeply contested metaphysical claims about the natural grounds of human rights will all be unacceptable. Fourth, we would like this proceduralist account to be able to defend the *individual civil liberties* that make private autonomy possible, instead of being limited only to those political rights of participation that make public autonomy possible. This defense, moreover, should be articulable at the same level, and in the same terms, as the normative defense of constitutional democracy. This, then, rules out contingent and therefore relatively weak defenses of individual rights as the fortunate dispensations of a wise group of founders, of the normal paths of politics observed in most democratic societies, or of the contingent policies adopted by constitutionally unbound but good-faith parliamentarians.

With respect to democratic processes, it seems that we need, fifth, an account of the *diversity* of *forms* of political practical reason. Because each of the accounts of judicial review runs into problems when it ignores the variety of types of political interaction and reason-giving, we would like an account of democratic processes to be able to comprehend and distinguish between principled moral-political consensus, ethical-political self-clarification, interest aggregation, and bargained compromises. Given, further, that constitutions, statutes, and regulations are legal instruments, the account of political practical reason will also need to come to terms with specifically legal reasons, including those institutionally specific procedural reasons that interact in complex ways with less technical forms of practical reason. Sixth, democratic theory needs to pay more attention to the distinctions between, and the types of interaction among, *different* public fora. At the very least, we need to take seriously the potentially deliberative and reasons-responsive character of legislative processes – and of course, their predictable deficits. We also would need some account of the intergovernmental exchange of reasons of various types, and its role in determining governmental actions. But we also need to explain the connections between the informal publics peopled by citizens and the formal publics constituted by official actors. This entails a convincing account of the difference between formally organized and governmentally institutionalized public arenas of debate – paradigmatically, although not exclusively, legislative bodies – and informal, noninstitutionalized and heterogeneous arenas of debate – what is currently being called "civil society" or the "public sphere" – and of the interactions between the different arenas.

I turn now to Habermas's theory of deliberative democratic constitutional review, as it promises to fulfill many of these criteria. As I contend, however, his distinctive arguments in favor of a judicial institutionalization of constitutional review are unconvincing. I argue, rather, that stronger arguments are found in his further development of the basic justificatory strategy found in Dahl's and Ely's conceptions: an independent judiciary is institutionally well placed to policing the procedural legitimacy of democratic processes. Finally, I contend that the elaboration of this line of thought in terms of deliberative democratic constitutionalism threatens, once again, to overdraw on the legitimacy credit extended to a judicial institutionalization of constitutional review, precisely because of the greatly expanded tasks such review would need to fulfill given Habermas's more ambitious account of deliberative democratic processes in comparison with the earlier pluralist and majoritarian models. This will lead me, in Chapters 8 and 9, to consider a number of institutional innovations that could jointly fulfill the criteria of adequacy I enumerated earlier, even given the more capacious picture of democratic processes painted by deliberative democracy.

B. GUARDIANS OF THE CONDITIONS OF PROCEDURAL LEGITIMACY: HABERMAS

Habermas's theory of judicial review begins not from jurisprudential considerations, but from a combined normative and sociological theory of constitutional democracy oriented toward procedurally structured participatory deliberation. I begin by explicating the procedural conception of legitimacy that underlies Habermas's defense of constitutional democracy (1) and justifies the function of constitutional review (2). Then I turn to his differentiated account of democratic processes that prioritizes deliberations aimed at consensus on the principles of constitutional democracy structuring higher law, but that does not deny the import or place of pragmatic reasoning, ethical-political self-clarification, aggregation, and bargaining (3). Finally I examine his arguments for the institutionalization of the function of constitutional review in an electorally independent judiciary to assess the extent to which there might be lingering worries about paternalism in that account (4).[1]

1. Habermas on Democratic Legitimacy

According to Habermas, the fundamental normative idea of democracy can be modeled in a principle of democratic legitimacy: "only those statutes may claim legitimacy that can meet with the assent (*Zustimmung*) of all citizens in a discursive process of legislation that in turn has been legally constituted."[2] This principle of democratic legitimacy results from the "interpenetration" of the specific form of law as a medium for action coordination and the requirements for the justification of norms of

---

[1] Those familiar with the extensive secondary literature on Habermas's normative theories will note that, throughout my presentation, I emphasize the worth of proceduralism as a response to persistent, reasonable, and reasonably expectable disagreement amongst democratic citizens about the substantive values, principles, and ideals that are to be enshrined in or operationalized in positive law. Correspondingly, and in contrast to many commentators, I downplay the cognitivist idealization of all interlocutors coming to a full rational consensus on the basis of the same reasons shared by all, and the allied substantive ideal of impartiality as that which is in the equal interest of all. I tend to think of the attractiveness of Habermas's account of deliberative democracy in terms of its openness to contestation and disagreement and so I emphasize procedural fairness, rather than cognitive consensus, as central to deliberative democratic constitutionalism. In this, my reading of Habermas is decidedly influenced by that of Thomas McCarthy; see Thomas McCarthy, "Enlightenment and the Public Use of Reason," *European Journal of Philosophy* 3, no. 3 (1995), Thomas McCarthy, "Legitimacy and Diversity: Dialectical Reflections on Analytic Distinctions," *Cardozo Law Review* 17, no. 4–5 (1996), Thomas McCarthy, "Practical Discourse: On the Relation of Morality to Politics," in *Ideals and Illusions: On Reconstruction and Deconstruction in Contemporary Critical Theory* (Cambridge, MA: MIT Press, 1991).

[2] Habermas, *Between Facts and Norms*, 110.

action.[3] The crux of this democratic principle for my purposes here is that it points to a solely procedural test for the legitimacy of laws: statutory legitimacy hangs solely on whether a law has been enacted in the correct way, not on whether it fulfills some independent and antecedently specified substantive normative criteria for goodness or rightness. As can be seen in the principle itself, it combines two types of procedural requirements: that of a legal constitution of decision processes, and that of a moral-political requirement for the assent of all citizens secured through reasoned deliberation.

Turning first to the legal component of the democratic principle, it should be clear that it already contains, albeit only *in nuce* at this point, several components of three of the basic elements of constitutionalism identified in Chapter 3: the rule of law, entrenchment, and political structuration. First, the central components of a demand for the rule of law are already contained therein.[4] Citizens are to regulate their

---

[3] Habermas's analysis of the normative components of legal systems in *Between Facts and Norms* differs from his earlier analyses of the relation between law and morality, in which there was a danger of following Kant too closely by simply subordinating legal relations to moral demands. Whereas in his earlier work, Habermas had followed Kant both in the typology of legal versus moral action, and in the normative conception of the relationship between legal and moral norms, Habermas now agrees only with Kant's analysis of the legal form, while insisting that legal norms should not be conceived of as merely derived from more fundamental moral norms. Habermas now claims that the basic legal principle – the principle of democracy (quoted in the text above) – and the basic moral principle – the principle of universalization (U), "A norm is valid when the foreseeable consequences and side effects of its general observance for the interests and value-orientations of *each individual* could be *jointly* accepted by *all* concerned without coercion," Jürgen Habermas, *The Inclusion of the Other: Studies in Political Theory*, ed. Ciaran Cronin and Pablo De Greiff (Cambridge, MA: MIT Press, 1998), 42 – are *equiprimordial* specifications, tailored to the different forms of legal and moral norms, of a more general principle of discursive legitimacy (D): "Just those action norms are valid to which all possibly affected persons could agree as participants in rational discourse," Habermas, *Between Facts and Norms*, 107. That is to say, the principle of democratic legitimacy is no longer subsumed under the moral principle of universalization; the two rather stand at the same level, as separate instantiations of the basic justificatory principle of discourse, each specified for a different domain of interaction.

[4] Habermas's account of legality largely follows Kant's analysis of the differences between morally coordinated and legally coordinated action, although Habermas gives a significantly more "sociological" reading to legal relations, one informed by legal positivism. Law's basic function, according to Habermas, is to stabilize the behavioral expectations of socially interacting agents in a way that unburdens them from the high cognitive, motivational, and organizational demands of social action coordinated through face-to-face communicative interactions relying only on agents' moral competences. In this way, law allows for the development of domains of interaction (such as the economy) in which actors are free, within constraints, to treat others as merely facilitators of, or impediments to, the realization of their own desires – one may treat others as means to one's own end. Unlike morality, law addresses agents simply as purposive-rational actors rather than autonomous moral agents, and attends only to the external relations between social actors. As law contains publicly promulgated rules of action, it relieves actors of the

common lives together through the medium of positively enacted and enforced laws. Furthermore, those laws must themselves be created, changed, and applied according to legally regulated processes, requiring a fair amount of the structural elements of what Fuller called the "internal morality of law."[5] In particular, the democratic process itself – including whatever political institutions are necessary to it – must be legally structured, and presumably in such a way as to be relatively stable over time. Thus, the legal component of the democratic principle also seems to imply the requirements for a constitutional distinction between higher and ordinary law, whereby entrenched law is centrally concerned with political structuration.

Turning to the moral-political component, the crux of Habermas's idea here is the intuition that, if a social norm backed by the threat of coercive force – that is, a law – affects one, then one ought (ideally) to be able to reasonably consent to that law. But given the fact of reasonable pluralism, we can no longer assume that reasonable consent can be simply counter-factually ascribed to citizens on the basis of, say, philosophers' or theologians' lone insights into the demands of natural law or the cosmological order. Reasonable consent should be thought of, rather, as the outcome of actual processes of exchanging reasons and considerations with other actual individuals who will also be subject to the proposed norms, in an attempt to come to a common understanding on the best norms for regulating public matters, a common understanding, finally, that is based only on the "unforced force" of the better argument.[6] And this is just what Habermas's more general principle – the "discourse principle" (D) – for the justification of all social action

---

cognitive burdens of figuring out what the right thing to do is in typical situations, while giving reasonable assurance that they can expect like norm-conformative behavior from others and so increases the reliability of interactions. Furthermore, unlike morality, law abstracts from the reasons that motivate actors, demanding only that, for whatever reason, they comply. The only weakly motivating "force" of good moral reasons is replaced in law through the coercive threat of sanction. Finally, by structuring the emergence of organized forms of cooperation through secondary rules that allow for the production of primary rules, define jurisdictional powers, and found corporations, associations and so on, law relieves actors of the organizational demands that purely moral action would require, while creating the possibility for large-scale action coordination and regulation across complex and far-flung social institutions. See especially Habermas, *Between Facts and Norms*, 104–18.

[5] See the discussion of Fuller in Chapter 3.B. It may be helpful here to think of Hart's distinction between primary legal rules governing conduct and secondary rules that legally control the identification, introduction, modification, extinction, and adjudication of primary legal rules: Hart, *The Concept of Law*, 79–99.

[6] An excellent treatment of Habermas's practical philosophy, the basic ideals and intuitions that motivate it, and the arguments that support it can be found in William Rehg, *Insight and Solidarity: A Study in the Discourse Ethics of Jürgen Habermas* (Berkeley, CA: University of California Press, 1994).

norms (moral or legal or otherwise) claims: "Just those action norms are valid to which all possibly affected persons could agree as participants in rational discourse."[7] Avoiding counterfactual attributions of consent is particularly important in those situations – what Waldron calls the "circumstances of politics" – in which those foreseeably affected by the proposed norm do not agree with the reasons currently put forward but will nevertheless be equally subject to the coercive power of the state once a decision is made. Here, claims about what others would "reasonably consent" to, in the face of manifest evidence to the contrary, seem a particular affront to the ideal of the equal moral-political autonomy of citizens. The principle of democratic legitimacy is, then, a way of embedding the discourse principle governing the legitimate justification of social action norms in a specifically legal norm system: it insists that legally constituted democratic procedures themselves warrant the legitimacy of democratic decisions, rather than the consonance of the content of those decisions with some independent set of substantive values or principles.[8]

If we should next ask why democratic procedures alone grant legitimacy, Habermas's answer is that they warrant the (defeasible) expectation of rational outcomes.

The democratic procedure for the production of law evidently forms the only postmetaphysical source of legitimacy [for legal rules]. But what provides this procedure with its legitimating force?... Democratic procedure makes it possible for issues and contributions, information and reasons to float freely; it secures a

---

[7] Habermas, *Between Facts and Norms*, 107.

[8] A very clear presentation of this general procedural model of democratic legitimacy is put forward and defended against liberal, feminist, and political realist criticisms in Seyla Benhabib, "Toward a Deliberative Model of Democratic Legitimacy," in *Democracy and Difference: Contesting the Boundaries of the Political*, ed. Seyla Benhabib (Princeton, NJ: Princeton University Press, 1996), 68: "Legitimacy in complex democratic societies must be thought to result from the free and unconstrained public deliberation of all about matters of common concern.... Democracy, in my view, is best understood as a model for organizing the collective and public exercise of power in the major institutions of a society on the basis of the principle that decisions affecting the well-being of a collectivity be viewed as the outcome of a procedure of free and reasoned deliberation among individuals considered as moral and political equals." I have, however, reservations about the strong demands for the discovery or creation of a sense of common good, and of the strict impartiality of results of deliberation that Benhabib's conception seems to require: for example, "the basis of legitimacy in democratic institutions is to be traced back to the presumption that the instances which claim obligatory power for themselves do so because their decisions represent *an impartial standpoint said to be equally in the interests of all*," 69 (emphasis added). To my thinking, this latter idea depends on an overly moralized conception of politics, one that would unduly restrict the attribution of legitimacy only to those democratic outcomes strictly directed at realizing justice.

discursive character for political will-formation; and it thereby grounds the fallibilist assumption that results issuing from proper procedure are more or less reasonable.[9]

So a deliberative conception of popular sovereignty as the collective practice of reasoned and open debate, discussion, and decision concerning issues of public interest, rather than an aggregative conception of democracy as the accountability of representatives to electoral majorities, is at the heart of Habermas's procedural account of democratic legitimacy. In this way, Rousseau's central criterion for democracy as collective self-determination can be fulfilled: if the legally structured political community "constitutes itself on the basis of a discursively achieved agreement," then the resulting regime and its positive laws are legitimate according to "the idea of self-determination: [namely, that] citizens should always be able to understand themselves also as the authors of the law to which they are subject as addressees."[10] The crucial difference, however, is that whereas Rousseau's conception of legitimacy rather unrealistically required a full assembly of all citizens while relying only on the small size and extreme homogeneity of the population to generate reasonable laws, Habermas argues that a much more exacting specification of procedural requirements is required under conditions of value pluralism and in large, complex, modern nation-states in order to underwrite the expectation of generating reasonable laws.

In order to specify exactly what types of procedures could carry this weight of legitimation, Habermas explicates the pragmatic presuppositions of legally constituted democracy, drawing on both the requirements of the form of law and the normative ideal of self-government. This leads to a defense of constitutionally structured democracy whereby a system of five incompletely specified categories of rights indicate what types of rights individuals would need to legally grant each other if they wish to legitimately regulate their interactions through the medium of law. First,

---

[9] Habermas, *Between Facts and Norms*, 448. He continues, "The *democratic process* bears the entire burden of legitimation. It must simultaneously secure the private and public autonomy of legal subjects. This is because individual private rights cannot be adequately formulated, let alone politically implemented, if those affected have not first engaged in public discussions to clarify which features are relevant in treating typical cases as alike or different, and then mobilized communicative power for the consideration of their newly interpreted needs. The proceduralist understanding of law thus privileges the *communicative presuppositions and procedural conditions* of democratic opinion- and will-formation as the sole source of legitimation. The proceduralist view is ... incompatible with the Platonistic idea that positive law can draw its legitimacy from a higher law" (second emphasis added), 450. Of course, the same reasons underwrite the rejection of Platonism here and the rejection of Kant's direct derivation of legal norms from moral imperatives discussed in footnote 3.

[10] Ibid., 449.

as individuals who recognize each other as free and equal, persons coordinating their interactions through the medium of law would need to grant each other certain types of rights: (1) rights to the greatest amount of equal subjective liberties, (2) equal membership rights in the legal community, and (3) equal rights to the legal protection and actionability of their rights. These three categories of rights can, according to Habermas, be procedurally justified in terms of the meaning of legality and of the pragmatic presuppositions of raising and defending normative validity claims. The basic idea is that without such rights any individual's assent to legal enactments could not be assumed to rest on that individual's reasoned acceptance, but might be a result of distortion and exclusion through direct or indirect forms of force, coercion, fraud, and so on. The category of (4) equal rights to participation in processes of political opinion and will-formation then follows from the requirement that members of the legal community also be authors of the laws they are subject to. With this fourth category of rights, members first form themselves into a political community that must interpret and elaborate the more specific, "saturated" rights that will fill in the abstract categories of rights in a way tailored to particular political cultures and circumstances. Finally, the equal status of these four categories of rights can only be made more than a merely formal guarantee if citizens also ensure that all have an equal opportunity to utilize such rights through (5) "basic rights to the provision of living conditions that are socially, technologically, and ecologically safeguarded, insofar as the circumstances make this necessary."[11] Habermas claims that this last category of social and environmental rights is only instrumentally and contextually justified: they are those rights necessary for ensuring to citizens equal opportunities for utilizing their other civil, membership, legal, and political rights yet their sufficient provision is only required under contingent sociohistorical conditions where merely formal assurances of equal civil and political rights cannot alone secure an equal opportunity for their use among all citizens.[12]

It is important to see that this ambitious combination of political philosophy, legal analysis, and communicative pragmatics promises to provide a robust defense of the types of individual civil liberties apparently missing from Dahl's and Ely's contrasting procedural accounts of democratic legitimacy. For if it is correct, there is no fundamental

---

[11] Ibid., 123.

[12] I believe that this fifth category of social and environmental rights raises particular problems in formulating a legitimate method of constitutional interpretation, especially for contemporary legal systems that have become increasingly materialized in the wake of the development of the modern welfare state; but that is a subject for a book on interpretive methods.

contradiction between the principles of democracy and individual rights – that is, none at least at the justificatory level of political theory, as opposed to the everyday level of substantive political conflicts.[13] Thus, the Habermasian account should fulfill the third and fourth adequacy criteria I enumerated in Section A: it provides a proceduralist defense of individual private autonomy rights, deontically conceived.[14] To make this clear, it will help to contrast the varied procedural accounts of democratic legitimacy put forward by Dahl and Ely, on one side, and Habermas, on the other.

Recall Ely's inadequate responses to the objection that his defense of judicial review would allow the infringement of individual rights by duly-followed democratic procedures in those cases in which the right infringed is not clearly a requirement of proper political processes. On the one hand, he expressed confidence in the underlying libertarian content of traditional American political practice, and, on the other, he suggested that the justification for individual freedoms and democracy should both

---

[13] Like Habermas, Joshua Cohen, "Democracy and Liberty," in *Deliberative Democracy*, ed. Jon Elster (New York: Cambridge University Press, 1998), argues that there is not an intrinsic contradiction between individual liberties and the principle of democracy. In this article, Cohen uses the examples of liberties to free religious exercise, to wide freedoms of expression, and to pursue popularly denigrated moral tastes and pursuits. The key to his argument is the claim that democracy must be deliberative and not merely aggregative if it is to operationalize its basic aim that state power follow from collective decisions arising from citizens considered as equals. But deliberativeness implies that the proper conditions of public communication and the public reason conditions for public justification are both met. Finally, according to Cohen, these conditions require not just political liberties but individual liberties as well. So Cohen employs a structurally similar strategy to Habermas's: individual private autonomy rights are justified as parts of the legitimacy conditions for deliberative democracy. The most important difference is that although Habermas sees the internal connection between private and public autonomy in terms of the *legal order* that is required to structure democracy, Cohen sees the internal connection between deliberative democracy and the liberty of the moderns in terms of the requirements of *public reason*. And public reason is understood by Cohen in a largely Rawlsian manner, that is, as a set of substantive political principles that arise from the overlapping consensus of reasonable comprehensive doctrines, and that can be used to judge the reasonability of public interactions according to the degree to which their outcomes agree with the substance of the overlapping consensus. Thus Cohen uses a similar argumentative strategy to connect democracy and individual rights, but ends up with a much more substantive account of deliberative democratic legitimacy. This is particularly clear in Cohen, "Procedure and Substance in Deliberative Democracy."

[14] Kenneth Baynes, "Rights as Critique and the Critique of Rights: Karl Marx, Wendy Brown, and the Social Function of Rights," *Political Theory* 28, no. 4 (2000): especially 460–3, presents an excellent account of the claims and supporting arguments Habermas makes for the internal, reciprocal relation between democratic legitimacy and the system of rights. Baynes also helpfully shows how this conception can meet three kinds of skepticism concerning the putative naturalism of rights, the putatively exogenous character of preferences with respect to rights, and the ways in which institutionalizing rights may undermine their emancipatory potential.

be based in the same theory while merely hinting at the utilitarian roots of that theory. The first response suffers not only from historical amnesia but, more important, simply doesn't address the objection to his account of legitimacy. Dahl's more historically informed response along the same lines – namely that, in fact, democratic nations have done pretty well at providing rights – is no more helpful than Ely's in explaining the deontic character of rights, nor why we should think that individual private autonomy rights are theoretically justifiable in terms of, and so constitutional requirements for, democracy. The second response should worry the objector even more, as utilitarian theories notoriously appear able to save notions of the categorical character of individual rights only at the price of a certain *deus ex machina*: the invocation of certain substantive side-constraints on the operations of utility calculations, side-constraints justified arbitrarily either in the ungrounded private "intuitions" of philosophers or contingent social conventions captured in "our intuitions." Dahl"s more well-defined defense of aggregative democracy as maximizing individuals' chances for the fulfillment of their interests might take us some way toward the consideration of what is owed to individuals qua individuals, but it is quite unlikely to lead to a defense of individual rights as categorical claims that have a certain priority over aggregative goods. Rights, on this conception, are to be considered only as values to be weighed against other politically selected values, capable of being overridden by different weightings of other desirable political values. Recall that for Dahl, although there are many potentially important values that politics might serve, only the value of aggregative democracy has preeminence: all other values are to be at the disposition of majoritarian weightings and balances.[15]

In contrast, by basing a defense of rights to both individual liberty and political participation in the same proceduralist theory of constitutionally structured democracy, Habermas can offer a straightforward response to the rights-based objection to proceduralism. A clear violation of an individual right – such as the torturing of a person by officials – does violate the procedural conditions of democratic legitimacy once we see

---

[15] Recalling that Dahl understands questions of rights entirely in terms of personal interests, consider the following crucial passage: "What interests, then, can be justifiably claimed to be inviolable by the democratic process or, for that matter, any other process for making collective decisions? It seems to me highly reasonable to argue that *no* interests should be inviolable beyond those integral or essential to the democratic process.... Outside this [latter] domain a democratic people could freely choose the policies its members feel best; they could decide how best to balance freedom and control, how best to settle conflicts between the interests of some and the interests of others, how best to organize and control their economy, and so on. In short, outside the inviolable interests of a democratic people in the preservation of the democratic process would lie the proper sphere for political decisions," Dahl, *Democracy and Its Critics*, 182.

that such violations make it impossible for individual assent to laws to be understood as the result of reason, rather than force, coercion, fraud, manipulation, or exclusion from the opinion-forming and decision-making processes. If democratic legitimacy requires that individuals must be able to give their reasoned consent to those laws they are subject to, and that reasoned consent is impossible to secure without (1) maximal equal subjective liberty rights, (2) equal membership rights, and (3) equal rights to the legal protection and actionability of those rights, then popular sovereignty under law presupposes constitutionally guaranteed individual liberties. Of course, this theory of procedural legitimacy cannot show that *no* morally unacceptable rights-infringing law could *ever* be passed under our current best understanding of required procedures. But it seems equally correct to say that no substantivist theory of legitimacy could meet this extreme argumentative burden either: it is always possible that our best understanding of *ex-ante* moral constraints is not sufficient to protect against unforeseen possibilities of injustice.

Yet Habermas's argument avoids the recourse to substantivist defenses of rights in terms of natural law, religious truth, or other underwriters of substantive values that are subject to persistent, yet not unreasonable, disagreement in modern, pluralistic, and complex societies. This should ensure that Habermas's defense of constitutionalism – and by extension of constitutional review – does not fall prey to the problems of paternalism and partialism that substantivist accounts of legitimacy apparently lead to under conditions of value pluralism. In addition, Habermas claims to be able to capture the deontological character of rights because of their unconditional justification: rights to both private autonomy and political participation have the status of individuals' legal claims that may not be abrogated by considerations of the collective good and preferred policy initiatives, nor may be treated as merely one among other competing goods to be weighed and transitively ordered on a case-by-case basis. Thus, Habermas's account of the legitimacy requirements of constitutional democracy fulfills three of the conditions I outlined earlier: it can defend more than simply rights to political participation, it is proceduralist rather than substantivist, and, it understands rights deontologically rather than teleologically.

Finally, as should now be clear, it also fulfills the first criterion: constitutionalism and democracy mutually presuppose one another. The outcomes of democratic decisions processes cannot be considered legitimate unless those processes have adhered to stringent procedural conditions, conditions established by and regulated through constitutional entrenchment. Some of those entrenched constitutional conditions concern the regularity of a legal system and the rule of law, some concern the requisite political structures and governmental institutions, some concern the system of civil, political, and social rights – hence, Habermasian constitutionalism incorporates all four of the basic elements enumerated in Chapter 3. But democracy does not just presuppose constitutionalism; constitutionalism is illegitimate without deliberative democracy. This is because, in the end, the only warrant we have for the rightness or correctness of currently established constitutional provisions is that they provide the closest feasible approximation to what would be the outcome of unlimited deliberations under ideal conditions. Ideal conditions, however, never obtain, and so we must always be open to the possibility that current constitutional arrangements may be unjust, illegitimate, or even merely suboptimal, and so could be improved. But the only way we could know that – and the only way to legitimately decide upon improvements – is if we were open to a democratic elaboration of extant constitutional provisions, arrangements, and practices; if we were politically open to the deliberative contributions of all those possibly affected by the constitution. In a slogan, no legitimate constitutionalism without democracy; no legitimate democracy without constitutionalism.

2. Justifying the Function of Constitutional Review

But given this procedural concept of legitimacy that stresses the importance of citizens' reasoned deliberations about and decisions on substantive issues confronting the polity, it is not yet clear what unction constitutional review might play there, nor how it should be conceived of. For, if the substantive normative content of laws gains its legitimacy only by being enacted in accordance with the procedural requirements of popular sovereignty, why shouldn't *any and all* outcomes of proper legislative procedures have the force of law?[16] Like Dahl and Ely, Habermas answers this in terms of the need for the maintenance of exactly that system of rights that secures the legitimacy of the legal corpus through

---

[16] This is precisely the thought that motivates Rousseau to apparently reject all forms of constitutionalism in the name of popular sovereignty: "Public deliberation which can obligate all subjects toward the Sovereign ... cannot ... obligate the Sovereign toward itself, and it is therefore contrary to the nature of the body politic for the Sovereign to impose on itself a law which it cannot break," Rousseau, *"Of the Social Contract,"* Book I, Chapter 7, 51–52. One crucial difference here is that, whereas in Habermas's proceduralist republicanism the constitutional structuring of democracy is intended to *legally* insure political legitimacy, in Rousseau's civic republicanism the expectations of civic virtue, civic homogeneity, and small size carry an extremely heavy burden in ensuring that political deliberations are truly oriented toward the general will. In large modern, socially complex, and teleologically diverse nation-states, such heightened expectations are simply unwarranted. In fact, Rousseau himself was pessimistic about the possibility of realizing such expectations even in small, modern city-states: "All things considered, I do not see that among us the Sovereign can henceforth preserve the exercise of its rights unless the City is very small," Rousseau, *"Of the Social Contract,"* Book III, Chapter 15, 115–16.

procedural – that is to say, constitutional – correctness. Constitutional review is understood and justified as a surety for just those democratic procedures adherence to which confers legitimacy on positive laws. Because state actions are legitimate only on the condition that they have resulted from fair and open procedures, there must be some way of reviewing the correctness of those procedures, which includes ensuring individuals' procedurally required civil, membership, legal, political, and social rights.

According to Habermas, the constitutional review of ordinary statutes and governmental policies should be thought of, in ideal-typical terms, as a form of application discourse, not as a type of justification discourse.[17] In a discourse aiming at the justification of a general norm of action, all those potentially affected by the proposed norm must come to an agreement as participants in a rational discourse if the acceptance of the norm is to be valid. Parliamentary lawmaking can thus be understood as a type of justification discourse, where proposed statutes are debated and considered by representatives of all those potentially affected, before the law is decided on through a vote intended to secure finality under time and knowledge constraints. In contrast, application discourses do not aim at the justification of general norms of action tailored to standardized situations. Rather, they aim to apply already justified norms to the concrete features of a specific action situation. Because several valid norms may be *prima facie* relevant to the given situation, an application discourse aims to clarify the relevant features of the situation in order to make possible a determination of which of the potentially applicable norms is appropriate. Ordinary judicial proceedings can thus be understood as a type of application discourse, where a sufficiently exhaustive characterization of the facts of the case relevant from the point of view of potentially applicable legal norms should make possible an impartial judgment about the unique applicability of the appropriate, and hence decisive, legal norm. In the adjudicative context, of course, such an application discourse will often turn on a proper determination of the hierarchical relations between the potentially applicable legal norms, in which the decisive features of the situation actually concern the present state of the relevant law. Returning now to the constitutional review of statutes and policies, Habermas conceives of it as a type of application discourse, seeking an impartial application of already justified higher level constitutional norms to those legal norms justified through ordinary legislative procedures. In determining whether higher order constitutional

---

[17] In his distinction between justification and application discourse and his analysis of the latter, Habermas is heavily indebted to Klaus Günther, *The Sense of Appropriateness: Application Discourses in Morality and Law*, trans. John Farell (Albany: State University of New York Press, 1993).

norms are applicable to ordinary legal norms, constitutional review ensures that the procedural conditions of democratic legitimacy – basic rights to private and public autonomy – have been fulfilled.

Of course, at this point, no specific recommendations concerning how such review should be institutionalized follow from this account; all that is established is that some form of constitutional review is needed. Note also that for Habermas, unlike those who argue for judicial review as a distinctly antidemocratic counterweight required by constitutionalism's principle of individual rights, individual liberty and popular sovereignty are not competitive or antithetical principles whose conflict is to be resolved by an unaccountable judiciary.[18] On the contrary, legally constituted individual rights and legally constituted rights to political participation presuppose one another. Popular sovereignty is only legitimate if it respects the legal status of subjects as independent, so that their agreement can be supposed to rest on their autonomous consent and not on coercion. What, how, and with respect to what properties equal rights to private autonomy are to be equally enjoyed by all and legally enforced through the mechanisms of state coercion can, however, only be legitimately determined through citizens' use of their rights to political participation. Habermas has recently summarized this complex argument for the interdependence of private autonomy and public autonomy, and thus for the interdependence of constitutionalism and democracy:

> There is no law without the private autonomy of legal persons in general. Consequently, without basic rights that secure the private autonomy of citizens, there also is no medium for legally institutionalizing the conditions under which these citizens, as citizens of a state, can make use of their public autonomy. Thus private and public autonomy mutually presuppose each other in such a way that neither human rights nor popular sovereignty can claim primacy over its counterpart.[19]

The very processes of deliberative politics themselves that aim to transform conflicting opinions, desires, and interests into democratically sanctioned legal programs require that rationality-enhancing procedures and autonomy-ensuring conditions have been met if participants are to understand the results of such procedures – just because they are the results of such procedures – as legitimately binding on them. Thus, for Habermas, as for Dahl and Ely, constitutional review secures the legitimacy of political outcomes by insuring their procedural conditions.

---

[18] Recall that this antithesis between individual rights and democracy is the starting point for most theorists of judicial review who rely on a pluralist concept of democracy, for example, not only Bickel and Choper, but Dahl and Ely as well.

[19] Habermas, *The Inclusion of the Other: Studies in Political Theory*, 260–61.

In contrast to the majoritarian proceduralists, however, Habermas argues that much more activity is implied by this guarantor role, and so for whatever institutional organ or organs are to play the role.[20] Those reviewing the constitutionality of statues cannot simply be "antitrust" style referees in the political marketplace. As is already clear by the extensive system of rights Habermas takes as requisite for constitutional democracies, a reviewing body will have to scrutinize legislative processes and outcomes not only for violations of rights to political participation and adequate representation but also for violations of individual civil liberties, membership rights, rights to legal protection, and those social and ecological rights necessary for ensuring the equal opportunity of all citizens to actualize their legally ensured private and public autonomy. Hence, Habermas recommends a quite activist constitutional review precisely with respect to the procedural requirements for legitimate democracy:

> If one understands the constitution as an interpretation and elaboration of a system of rights in which private and public autonomy are internally related (and must be simultaneously enhanced), then a rather bold constitutional adjudication is even required in cases that concern the implementation of democratic procedure and the deliberative form of political opinion- and will-formation.[21]

In addition, because Habermas has a richer and more differentiated account of democratic politics than Ely and looks beyond the bare electoral relationship between representative bodies and the citizenry for the core circuit of democratic accountability, this also leads to an expansion of the purview of constitutional review over Ely's theory.

3. Habermas on Democratic Process

Rather than the Benthamite picture of politics as entirely a marketplace of competing individuals and groups trying to push their pre-political, private, and corporate interests through the legislature, Habermas develops a picture of politics as also including (at least sometimes) the Rousseauian, deliberative search for the general will. If this more expanded conception of democratic politics is warranted, it is no longer adequate to attend only to those processes of bargaining, compromise, and aggregation that exhaust the aggregative and pluralist models of democracy. Rather, democratic theory must be able to account for the *diversity* of forms of practical reasoning that can play different roles in political activity: not only the interest aggregation

---

[20] I leave Dahl's procedural justification for quasi guardianship out of consideration here, as he does not present a similarly well-elaborated jurisprudential position.

[21] Habermas, *Between Facts and Norms*, 279–80.

and fair bargaining that Dahl and Ely attend to, but also those consensus-oriented debates over what is in the equal interest of each
citizen that Dworkin points to in terms of principled morality, prudential reasoning about proper means to pregiven ends, as well as the
kind of ethical-political self-clarification and reflection on constitutive
histories that Perry focuses on. It will have to come to terms, as well,
with the complex role that institutionally specific legal principles and
reasons play in relation to the more overtly first-order practical considerations. Recalling the Chapter 6 discussion of the specifically legal
character of much juridical discourse in the United States, one must
contemplate the fact that legal principles encompass not only principles of adjudication specific to the form of legal system and the
institutional arrangements of courts but also analogous principles that
play a regulative role in legislative and administrative institutions as
well. Such technical and institutionally specific legal principles, broadly
construed, also play a significant role in the public use of practical
reason in complex constitutional democracies.

Often some or all of these different types of practical reasons are
bundled together in the justification discourses that constitutional conventions and legislatures engage in during enactment.

> Legal norms ... can be justified not only with moral but also with pragmatic and
> ethical-political reasons; if necessary, they must represent the outcome of a fair
> compromise as well. ... Valid legal norms indeed harmonize with moral norms [as
> just], but they are "legitimate" in the sense that they additionally express an
> authentic self-understanding of the legal community, the fair consideration of the
> values and interests distributed in it, and the purposive-rational choice of stra-
> tegies and means in the pursuit of policies.[22]

Once we attend to these different forms of practical reason, however,
it becomes clear that the normative content entrenched in constitutional, statutory, and regulatory law is quite complex, often comprising a
syndrome of justice, ethical-political, pragmatic, fairly bargained, and
technical legal claims. If constitutional review is thought of as the
application of already justified constitutional norms to legislatively justified statutory or regulatory norms, then, like any form of application
discourse, it often will involve unpacking a syndrome of different kinds
of practical reasons embedded in laws. Hence, the scope of activity for
purely procedural constitutional review is again increased from what Ely
recommends, moving beyond the latter's focus on the legislative con-
striction of participating parties and the governmental use of suspect

---

[22] Ibid., 155–6.

classifications, to include the quality and propriety of justifying reasons as well.[23]

The legitimating reasons available from the constitution are given to the constitutional court in advance from the perspective of the application of law – and not from the perspective of a legislation that elaborates and *develops* the system of rights in the pursuit of policies. The court reopens the package of reasons that legitimated legislative decisions so that it might mobilize them for a coherent ruling on the individual case in agreement with existing principles of law; it may not, however, use these reasons in an implicitly legislative manner that directly elaborates and develops the system of rights.[24]

Finally, the institutional scope of constitutional review is much greater on Habermas's model than on Ely's. Habermas claims that in order to ensure the procedural correctness of lawmaking activities, it is not enough to look only to formally organized legislative and quasi-legislative governmental bodies. These bodies are part of what Habermas calls the "strong public sphere," where decisive will-formation occurs. Besides this strong public sphere, there is a "weak public sphere" characterizable in terms of nongovernmental civil society that contributes information, diverse perspectives, opinions, and reasons to the collective processes of political debate.[25] Ideally, on Habermas's model, the legitimate circulation of power would operate by the formation of "communicative power" in the weak public spheres that identify and thematize problems, conflicts, and deficits in the everyday life of citizens, the taking-up of this public opinion into legislative contexts and its transformation into laws that can then direct the administrative power of the state to achieve the action coordination indicated. Ultimately, it is only the robust deliberative character of opinion formation in the "weak" public spheres that warrants the

---

[23] Strictly speaking, Ely *is* concerned with the propriety of some reasons used to justify some unequal distributions of the bounty of representative government, specifically with respect to whether such distributions are the results of mere animus, prejudice, or other unconstitutional motivation with respect to a society's habitual unequals. He in fact recommends, within the context of the history of American constitutional jurisprudence concerning the equal protection clause of the Fourteenth Amendment, that a series of differentiated suspect classifications can be employed to sniff out illicit reasons justifying certain legislation. However, the larger point I make in the text is that Habermas recommends a constitutional review of the quality and propriety of justifying reasons employed in legislative justification discourses across any number of issues, and recommends it not on the basis of a contingent constitutional development in the light of a specific history of racial subordination, but because such a review of justifying reasons is an inherent part of constitutional application discourses in the context of deliberative democracy.

[24] Habermas, *Between Facts and Norms*, 262.

[25] See especially Chapter 8 of ibid., 359–87.

expectation of rational outcomes from representative parliamentary procedures, and grants legitimacy to politically adopted programs.

Therefore, if constitutional review is to be oriented toward protecting and promoting participatory opinion and will-formation, it will need to be much more than an impartial referee between voters and their representative bodies: it will have to ensure that the "sluice-gates" through which public opinion gets channeled into the legally structured strong public sphere remain unobstructed.[26] And, finally, if we agree with Habermas's social-theoretic claim that obstructions to and distortions in these channels occur not only through governmental power but also from economic and social powers, then those entrusted with the power of constitutional review will have a great deal of work on their docket. According to Habermas, the function of constitutional review can be summarized as simply guaranteeing the procedural fairness and openness of democratic processes. Yet, concretely, the tasks involved are manifold: keeping open the channels of political change, guaranteeing that individuals' civil, membership, legal, political, and social rights are

---

[26] It is strange that the centrality of this two-track model of the public sphere, and in particular the way in which it combines a concern with rich and effective civic deliberation with a concern for legitimate institutional decisions mechanisms – a model that occupies over one-quarter of *Between Facts and Norms* – is completely elided in many readings of Habermas's recent political theory. On the one side are critics who dismiss Habermas's theory as a romantic call for turning politics into a philosophy seminar; on the other are critics who dismiss it as merely a repackaged defense of the traditional institutions of constitutionally limited majoritarianism. "There has been a renewed emphasis on *speech, discourse,* and *conversation* in recent political and legal theory, particularly in theory that has been influenced by the work of Jürgen Habermas. . . . Much of this is far-fetched in ways I cannot go into here – in its aestheticism, for example, or in its conception of discourse as an end in itself. . . . There is a constant temptation in modern discourse-jurisprudence to take as an implicit procedural ideal the model of an informal intimate conversation among friends," Waldron, *Law and Disagreement*, 69–70. "Law is treated as the main prop for moral and political discourse, not just the force for social control which an earlier Habermas would have stressed. Here Habermas sounds much like the American constitutional theorists I discussed earlier. . . . Habermas accepts key aspects of that [political] system, notably elections, law-making by legislatures, and lawful administrative implementation of policy. . . . These views would be regarded as old-fashioned by many political scientists (if not constitutional lawyers). . . . Setting aside the public sphere, Habermas's normative theory of the state is virtually identical to that proposed long ago by Theodore Lowi (1969) under the rubric of 'juridical democracy.' Lowi was widely criticized at the time for proposing a naïve civics-textbook version of democracy as an antidote to the ills of interest group domination of US politics and administration. Habermas's emphasis on elections as the main channel of influence from the public sphere to the state would also strike many political scientists as old-fashioned," Dryzek, *Deliberative Democracy and Beyond: Liberals, Critics, Contestations*, 26. A simple plea: those interested in Habermas's conception of democratic politics should read at least Chapters 4, 7, and 8 of *Between Facts and Norms*, before accepting the accuracy of such critiques.

respected, scrutinizing the constitutional quality and propriety of the reasons justifying governmental action, and ensuring that the channels of influence from independent civil society public spheres to the strong public sphere remain unobstructed and undistorted by administrative, economic, and social powers.

4. A Judicial Institutionalization of Constitutional Review?

The question now is what institutional arrangements would best carry out all of these various tasks of constitutional review, while being sensitive to the principle of popular sovereignty? Even if we accept that democracy, properly understood, requires a robust form of constitutional review, it is not clear that an electorally unaccountable body structured as a judicial panel is the best mechanism to carry out the manifold tasks of a procedural guardian of democracy. Habermas briefly considers alternative ways of institutionalizing constitutional review: for instance, in a special committee of the legislature or in the executive administration.[27] After categorically rejecting the latter as a subversion of the executive's proper constitutional role of being directed by legislatively enacted positive law, he notes that constitutional review "belongs without question among the functions of the legislature. Hence it is not entirely off track to reserve this function, even at a second level of appeal, to a legislative self-review that could be developed into a quasi-judicial procedure."[28] It is worth noting that this passage only claims that legislatures must take account of the constitutionality of proposed legal norms; since they may not simply pass off this task to others, it "belongs without question among the functions of the legislature." The passage does not recommend locating final and sole powers of constitutional review in the legislature since, as Habermas goes on to note, an ordinary legislative body – as opposed to a constitutional assembly – does not have the same disposition over the content of constitutional rights as it does with respect to ordinary statutory content.

However, he apparently drops further consideration of alternative designs in favor of an extended discussion of judicially institutionalized constitutional review and of various interpretive and methodological problems raised in the German and American contexts.[29] At this point,

---

[27] Habermas contemplates such options at Habermas, *Between Facts and Norms*, 241–2.
[28] Ibid., 242.
[29] Ten years after *Between Facts and Norms*, the same pattern continues: "Instead of dealing with the democratic legitimacy of the institution of judicial review, I will pursue the question of whether persisting disagreements in constitutional interpretation affect the legitimacy of the democratic system as a whole," Jürgen Habermas, "On Law and Disagreement: Some Comments On 'Interpretive Pluralism'," *Ratio Juris* 16, no. 2 (2003): 187.

I think, one might justly wonder whether Habermas has forsworn the utopian-critical potential of his broader project in favor of a type of ameliorist "justificatory liberalism" that merely intends to show why the way we do things around here is pretty much just fine as it is. Granted, his further discussion of the self-understanding of the adjudicative methodology of the German High Court is intended to move it from a value-balancing to a proceduralist jurisprudence, and this recommendation is motivated largely by worries about the judicial paternalism that can result from a method focused on reinforcing what the judiciary takes to be the ethical identity of its society. And his extended discussion of American jurisprudential debates about adjudicative methodology is likewise focused on worries about types of constitutional interpretation that lead to overreaching on the part of the Supreme Court. Yet these arguments about how a constitutional court should adjudicate already presuppose that the institutionalization question is settled. Perhaps the richness of the German and American jurisprudential debates simply distracts Habermas from a more wide-ranging consideration of issues concerning the separation of powers and institutional design.

Nevertheless, his theory must face the same problem raised by other theories: why isn't the common institutional arrangement of *judicial review* paternalistic? I believe that Habermas presents, rather obliquely, two distinctive kinds of considerations here, both of which, however, I find unconvincing. His first response is that a procedural understanding of the system of rights will not in fact lead to judicial paternalism, as judges reviewing the constitutionality of statutes need not have recourse to any substantive political or moral ideals justifiable apart from those already contained in constitutional provisions and legislatively enacted statutes. Although the rights specified in the constitution are to be understood as having substantive, deontic content, they are designed to be exactly (and no more than) those rights procedurally required for realizing the principle of popular sovereignty in a legal form, and so, exactly those rights individuals would have to grant each other if they intend to regulate their interactions as free and equal consociates under law. Because the system of rights is procedurally justified in the first place, whatever governmental organ is charged with interpreting that system does not need to rely on metaphysically secured theories of natural rights or objective value hierarchies. The basic idea is that the process of constitutional review does not itself require the *justification* of the normative content of the system of rights, but only requires the rational *application* of normative content already embodied in constitutional provisions; provisions that are already justified in terms of the legal and normative requirements of an association of free and equal citizens engaged in the process of ruling themselves.

In this sense, judges are in the same position with respect to the constitution as they are with respect to ordinary statutory application: they must unpack the normative reasons bundled together in relevant constitutional provisions or statutes in order to determine which of the relevant, potentially competing norms is applicable in a particular context. Above all, a constitutional court must avoid taking itself as trying to secure, through its jurisprudence, a substantive hierarchy of values or catalog of natural rights that ought to be, but are not currently, contained in the constitution: "By assuming that it should strive to realize substantive values pregiven in constitutional law, the constitutional court is transformed into an authoritarian agency."[30] In short, because the constitution itself is to be understood as largely procedural in character and because a constitutional court ought merely to apply that content, we need not worry about democratically unaccountable judges interpreting and imposing substantive normative content above and beyond what is already instantiated in law.

Of course, this response to the objection to a *judicial* instantiation of review puts the cart before the horse: it recommends an interpretive method to the judiciary, while presupposing a judicial institutionalization as given. The argument cannot itself establish the proper allocation of powers here; it presupposes that issue as settled. It may well be that a constitutional court *ought* to understand its work-product as merely an application of the already-justified normative content embedded in constitutional and statutory norms, but this self-understanding can only ward off the danger of particular paternalist decisions for a body that is – according to the objection – *institutionally* placed in such a way that it is constantly in danger of encroaching on the principle of popular sovereignty.

Habermas needs here some further argument to show that, compared to other branches of government, and to other possible forms of institutionalization, a supreme constitutional court, whose members are at most quite indirectly responsive to citizens' public use of reason, will have some higher degree of competence at performing constitutional review. His second response to the objection to judicial review from popular sovereignty aims more squarely at this argumentative burden. The institutionalization of constitutional review in a judicial body is recommended, according to this second argument, by an understanding of the separation of governmental powers along the lines of specialized discursive functions. Here Habermas relies on a form of the claim to judicial competence – one unlike Perry and Dworkin's claim that judges are better moral reasoners than elected officials, though structurally quite similar to the claims to the distinctive legal competence of judges witnessed at least in Eisgruber's and

---

[30] Habermas, *Between Facts and Norms*, 258.

Michelman's theories.[31] Whereas the legislature specializes in the function of *justifying* legal norms, the judiciary specializes in the rational *application* of *prima facie* justified legal norms to particular situations. The judiciary's competence is not based on judges' special character traits or particular capacity for moral reasoning, but on the judiciary's institutional competence for dealing with the specialized form of legal discourses of application – as opposed to pragmatic, moral, and ethical justification discourses. This special competence is established, maintained, and secured through the existence of an independent court system and a juridical form of argumentation through decisions backed by opinions.

Legal [juridical] discourse can lay claim to a comparatively high presumption of rationality, because application discourses are specialized for questions of norm application, and can thus be institutionalized within the surveyable framework of the classical distribution of roles between the involved parties and an impartial third party. For the same reasons, however, they cannot *substitute* for political discourses that, geared for the justification of norms and policies, demand the inclusion of all those affected.[32]

Because the review of legislatively enacted statutes for their constitutionality is still a matter of the rational application of already justified legal norms – those embodied in both constitutional provisions and ordinary legal enactments – the judiciary has the requisite competence for this function that other governmental bodies are lacking. Although legislative bodies are specialized in, and designed for, the justification discourses involved in making laws and establishing policy goals, and administrative bodies are specialized in, and designed for, the pragmatic discourses involved in the selection of efficient means to legislatively given policy goals, judicial bodies are specialized in, and designed for, the application discourses involved in determining the uniquely appropriate valid law applicable to concrete situations. Given the intricacies and difficulties of application discourses, only judicial bodies have the requisite competence to ensure a rational procedure of applying laws, especially as

---

[31] Recall also that it was the claim to the special *legal* competence of the judiciary that underwrote Hamilton's defense of judicial review in *Federalist 78*, and that Chief Justice John Marshall then memorably elaborated in *Marbury v. Madison*, 177–8: "It is emphatically the province and duty of the Judicial Department to say what the law is. Those who apply the rule to particular cases must, of necessity, expound and interpret that rule. If two laws conflict with each other, the Courts must decide on the operation of each. So, if a law be in opposition to the Constitution, if both the law and the Constitution apply to a particular case, so that the Court must either decide that case conformably to the law, disregarding the Constitution, or conformably to the Constitution, disregarding the law, the Court must determine which of these conflicting rules governs the case. This is of the very essence of judicial duty."

[32] Habermas, *Between Facts and Norms*, 266.

"the complex steps of a constructive interpretation" – as the central part of an impartial judicial application discourse – "certainly cannot be regulated through procedural norms." Courts are specialized in generating rational applications, even in the absence of the kinds of clear rules of decision and enactment that legislatures are subject to, as their verdicts are "subject to scrutiny according to the procedural rationality of legally institutionalized discourses of application."[33]

How strong an argument for *judicial* review is this? Much of the answer turns on the strength of the analogy between ordinary jurisprudence and constitutional review; that is to say, on Habermas's claim that both are instances of application discourse, and so justifiably judicial tasks as a result of the heightened rationality of juridical discourses specialized for resolving disputes impartially between involved parties. Although it is obscured in the U.S. context of concrete constitutional review – in which legislatively enacted statutes are reviewed for constitutionality by the Supreme Court only on the occasion of a test case with all of its concrete details – ordinary jurisprudence is clearly not directly analogous to constitutional review. To begin with, in ordinary jurisprudence, the question before the court is how to sufficiently describe the legally relevant facts of the situation so that exactly one of several *prima facie* relevant legal norms can be shown to be uniquely appropriate, and so dispositive of the case. In constitutional review, however, the question is whether lower-level legal norms, such as those embodied in statutes or administrative policies, can be made consistent with higher-level constitutional norms. In the former case, a semantically universal norm is being applied to particulars; in the latter, a semantically universal norm is being applied to another such norm.

One might use this difference to object to Habermas's argument by claiming that, since constitutional review involves a different form of practical reasoning than ordinary application discourses, it must be a form of justification discourse, and so properly carried out by a legislative body.[34] If, however, this objection proves anything, it proves too much.

---

[33] Ibid., 261. Here Habermas draws on some of the central idealizations of Dworkin's method of adjudication through constructive legal interpretation, but attempts to give it a dialogical twist, as it were, by subjecting Hercules's lonely considerations to the broader intersubjective scrutiny of a juridical public sphere. It remains an open question whether this multiplication of Hercules is sufficient to render the method of constructive interpretation sufficiently democratic.

[34] Vic Peterson, in personal correspondence, has pressed the disanalogy of constitutional review and application discourses. Although he claims that constitutional review follows the logic of a justification discourse, he also believes that this does not entail that it should not be performed by a judicial body. I don't see how a theory of constitutional review, committed to the principle of popular sovereignty, and to a procedural conception of democratic legitimacy could admit that a democratically unaccountable institution could *legitimately justify* new constitutional content, if in fact the ideal of justification requires the actual and reasoned assent of all affected. My thinking on these issues has been greatly

For surely any form of judicial discourse that hinges on ascertaining the proper hierarchy of valid legal norms – including the relationship between various positive rules and legal principles – also would not be in the strict form of an application discourse. Although a case may end by applying one legal norm to a fact situation, the decisive work is often done in properly ascertaining the relevant priority relationships between various legal norms, and this usually involves subsuming some semantically universal norms under others. If the special competence of judicial bodies does not extend to this form of reasoning about the hierarchical relationships between norms in a system of norms – if the logic of such reasoning is that of a justification discourse – then it is unclear why judicial bodies should ever have a legitimate say on such matters, irrespective of whether legal norm conflicts arise among ordinary legal norms or between these and constitutional norms. Perhaps we might reserve the term "application" for those cases in which a semantically universal norm is applied to particular facts, but then Habermas's argument should just be restated to say that judicial bodies have a specialized competence for "adjudicative" discourses, that is, those involving both norm application and norm prioritization.

Nevertheless, defending judicial review as merely an extension of the judiciary's ordinary capacities to the adjudication of norm conflicts between constitutional and statutory norms is insufficient to dispel worries about judicial paternalism. This is because crucial constitutional provisions are deliberately open-textured and the specific meaning of their content – usually debated in terms of their applicability to particular issues or controversies – is often the subject of reasonable and deep disagreement. This is precisely the problem of constitutional indeterminacy that forms the starting point for the competing theories of constitutional interpretation put forward by various jurisprudes: not only the specifically democratic jurisprudes focused on in the last several chapters – Dworkin, Eisgruber, Ely, Michelman, and Perry – but also almost all of those who put forward a determinate constitutional jurisprudence intended to guide judges in their specification of indeterminate provisions.

The worry about judicial paternalism arises once we combine the open-textured character of constitutional provisions with the structural fact that *no* normal governmental body has authority alone to act as a constitutional author. This is at the heart of the disanalogy between ordinary adjudication and constitutional review.[35] In both ordinary statutory

spurred by discussions with him, and by his notable criticisms of Habermas's and Günther's theory of moral application discourses in Victor Peterson, "A Discourse Theory of Moral Judgment" (Ph.D. dissertation, Northwestern University, 1998).

[35] Recall that Michelman makes the combined problems of constitutional indeterminacy and the contemporary fact of "reasonable interpretive pluralism" central to his account of

adjudication and constitutional review, the judiciary may well need to further specify the content of the relevant norms through some process of interpreting those norms. However, in the former case, the judiciary is on the same level as the legislature since, in a sense, the court is rendering to the legislature a rebuttable interpretation of the meaning of the original statutes, an interpretation that can be easily rejected by the legislature through a new enactment. (Like considerations seem to follow for regulatory adjudication.) In the case of constitutional review, by contrast, the court is only on the same level as a constitutional assembly, not the ordinary legislature. Here it is interpreting, through further specification, the relevant open-textured provisions of the constitution, yet it could only be rendering such a rebuttable specification to the people as a whole, understood, however, as a constitutional assembly. For, on the procedural account of democratic legitimacy and the deliberative account of democratic processes, the task of realizing the system of rights in concrete terms for an historically specific community is decidedly a matter for the people reasoning together as a whole, and not for any appointed set of wise tutors.

Another way of seeing the danger here is that in applying constitutional tests to statutes and policies, a constitutional court may engage in forms of constitutional specification that rely on reasons available legitimately only to democratic processes of self-government, and thereby surrender a court's ordinary claim to legitimacy based on its narrow specialization in legal discourse. Commenting on Robert Alexy's call for the judicial use of the full gamut of "general practical discourse" in ordinary judicial proceedings,[36] Habermas clearly recognizes this danger.

---

the legitimacy of judicial review. As long as the political procedures – including the procedures of judicial review – can be seen as making a good faith effort to correctly specify the abstract basic principles through mechanisms open "to the full blast of sundry opinions and interest-articulations in society," Michelman, *Brennan and Democracy*, 60, citizens can understand themselves as self-governing. Michelman also has argued that Habermas's solution to this problem of constitutional specification is to be found in his concept of a shared, nation-specific political identity arising out of a shared constitutional history. According to this reading of Habermas, "constitutional patriotism" provides citizens with the faith that, even though they vehemently disagree about their applicability, all are arguing about the *same* constitutional principles; what they disagree about is who they are as a people. See Frank I. Michelman, "Morality, Identity and 'Constitutional Patriotism'," *Denver University Law Review* 76, no. 4 (1999): 1022–8. Even if this is Habermas's 'solution' to the problem (which I don't think it is), I am wary of its implications for judicial interpretation. For if Michelman's account is right, then it appears that Habermas is recommending that a constitutional court see its decisions as hanging on historically contingent and ethically suffused visions of a nationality-specific good life; precisely the kind of "value jurisprudence" Habermas criticizes the German courts for employing.

[36] See Robert Alexy, "The Special Case Thesis," *Ratio Juris* 12, no. 4 (1999).

But it appears to me to be an even more pressing danger in the case of constitutional review:

I am still not quite clear about the role of what Alexy calls "general practical discourse." Here, different types of argument – prudential, ethical, moral, [and] legal arguments – are supposed to come in one package. I have the suspicion that this conception is not sufficiently sensitive for the desired separation of powers. Once a judge is allowed to move in the unrestrained space of reasons that such a "general practical discourse" offers, a "red line" that marks the division of powers between courts and legislation becomes blurred. In view of the application of a particular statute, the legal discourse of a judge should be confined to the set of reasons that legislators either in fact put forward or at least could have mobilized for the parliamentary justification of that norm. The judge, and the judiciary in general, would otherwise gain or appropriate a problematic independence from those bodies and procedures that provide the only guarantee for democratic legitimacy.[37]

Constitutional review, especially when it involves specifying the system of rights, observance of which grants legitimacy to positive law, may very well involve just this kind of a use of reasons that the judiciary does not have legitimate disposition over. In the end, if – to recall Rousseau's test of popular sovereignty – citizens are to understand themselves as both under positive law and free, they must be able to understand themselves simultaneously as authors of the system of rights and subjects of it.

Of course, the combination of judicial institutionalization and constitutional indeterminacy that proves threatening to citizens' political autonomy may indeed be mitigated by the adoption by constitutional courts of a form of constitutional interpretation that is oriented towards the reinforcement of deliberative democracy. And this is indeed what occupies Habermas's chapter called "Judiciary and Legislature: On the Role and Legitimacy of Constitutional Adjudication."[38] Nevertheless, the adoption of a mitigating form of constitutional jurisprudence cannot itself justify placing the power of constitutional review in a judicial body in the first place. In summary, neither of Habermas's two obliquely presented arguments for the institutionalization of constitutional review in an independent, politically unaccountable judiciary is compelling. First, his claim that a resolutely procedural form of legal interpretation would guard against judicial paternalism simply begs the question of how to institutionalize this power in the first place. His second argument hangs on the contention that the rationality of application discourses can be best ensured by an institutionally separated judicial power specialized in, and limited to the ambit of, such application discourses. Insofar as any

[37] Jürgen Habermas, "A Short Reply," *Ratio Juris* 12, no. 4 (1999).
[38] Habermas, *Between Facts and Norms*, 238.

controversies arise over how to specify indeterminate norms or prioritize competing norms, juridical resolutions can be safely offered, as rebuttable presumptions, to properly democratic actors specialized in justification discourses. Here, however, the analogy between ordinary and constitutional controversies breaks down, as in the former case the proper democratic actors are those with constitutionally delegated ordinary legislative powers, whereas, in the latter, the citizenry as a whole in their special configuration as a constitutional assembly.

It seems to me that the most cogent type of argument for entrusting a judicial panel with the power of constitutional review remains, then, the Dahl-Ely proposal based in institutional independence. In a controversy between political actors about the constitutive rules of political cooperation – the rules that, in a procedural conception of democracy carry significant weight for legitimation – none of the interested parties can be counted on for an impartial resolution of the controversy. In this way, a judiciary that is independent of normal political accountability is in a unique institutional position to guarantee that the procedural conditions of democratic processes are correctly fulfilled. However, the limitations of the majoritarian-proceduralist theories of judicial review result from the rather thin and partialistic conceptions of democracy and constitutionalism they employ, namely, that democratic self-government means merely a process of aggregating prepolitical preferences through elections in order to achieve overall social utility, subject to fortunately entrenched substantive side-constraints. Thus, we need to recognize, with Habermas, that an adequate guarantor of the legitimacy of the democratic process will need to take on tasks beyond policing elections and ensuring against monopolistic distributions disfavoring insular minorities. It will need to secure the full gamut of individuals' democratically elaborated constitutional rights to private and public autonomy, scrutinize the quality of reasons justifying governmental actions, and ensure that the circuit of communicative power from the weak public spheres through the strong public sphere and into administrative power remains undistorted by economic and social powers. Furthermore, the fact that constitutional review involves complicated adjudicative considerations concerning the application, specification, and prioritization of constitutional and statutory legal norms entails that rational outcomes of such review can not be warranted through a determinate set of procedural rules. Judicial bodies do, however, specialize in dealing with such adjudicative complexities, and so we might expect some heightened rationality from the outcomes of juridical discourses employed for constitutional review.[39] Yet this heightened rationality ultimately cannot

---

[39] It is important to remember here that judicial specialization creates its own perils – especially prevalent when dealing with fundamental constitutional questions – that

alone make up for the prima facie deficit in terms of the democratic practices of constitutionalism determined by the structural disanalogy between ordinary and constitutional adjudication.

As I have noted, it is surprising that Habermas displays somewhat of a lack of imagination concerning the institutional design of constitutional review, preferring to take currently prevalent structures for granted while focusing on the proper self-understanding of constitutional courts and the adjudicative methods that they should adopt. Yet I believe that his basic theory of constitutional review, especially since it properly conceives of the relationship between constitutionalism and deliberative democracy as mutually presuppositional rather than antithetical, gives us a solid basis for finding better forms of institutionalization. The arguments I have advanced so far, if successful, point to a set of criteria for whatever institutions might carry out the function of constitutional review. They should be: independent of ordinary political processes, open to the wide gamut of reasons and considerations presented by potentially affected citizens, capable of rationally cognizing complex adjudicative arguments concerning the internal coherence of a legal corpus and its appropriate application,[40] sensitive to the manifold tasks involved in securing the procedures of deliberative democracy in order to warrant the expectation of legitimate outcomes from ordinary political processes, capable of significant interventions in ordinary political processes when they malfunction, yet not capable of introducing substantive normative content into the system of rights without serious opportunities for citizens' participation and influence, nor capable of decisions with virtually indefeasible finality. Chapters 8 and 9 begin, then, to explore alternative institutional design strategies that might be able to meet these multiple and perhaps divergent criteria.

I meant to warn against in Chapter 6 under the heading of "the seducements of juristic discourse."

[40] It may be that the appropriate application of constitutional norms to particular cases should be a power withheld from an independent and specialized constitutional court, left instead to the ordinary courts to be carried out according to their ordinary juridical methods. This, at any rate, seems to be part of the idea behind institutional arrangements which permit constitutional courts only to perform abstract review of legal norms; institutional arrangements along the lines of France's *Conseil Constitutionnel*. I take up this question in Section B1 of the next chapter. Habermas, at any rate, clearly endorses the German arrangement whereby the *Bundesverfassungsgericht* has both concrete and abstract review powers.

8

The Institutions of Constitutional Review I

Design Problems and Judicial Review

This chapter and the next are more experimental and speculative than the preceding ones, proposing some institutional transformations for the processes of constitutional review in democratic societies. The proposals no doubt develop out of my own knowledge of and familiarity with the U.S. system of constitutional review – probably unavoidably also including my dissatisfactions with that system – but I do not intend them to be merely provincial in nature. At the very least, I believe the basic conception of deliberative democratic constitutionalism that I have been developing in this book supports the general spirit and aims animating the recommendations, even if the particular recommendations turn out to be problematic or questionable. They are meant, then, more as opening moves in an ongoing deliberative democratic project of constitutional government, rather than definitive conclusions about or claims to the indispensable requirements for constitutional democracy.

A. THE PROBLEMS OF DESIGNING INSTITUTIONS OF CONSTITUTIONAL REVIEW

Let me now present, in perhaps an overly schematized way, a set of considerations that can move the discussion forward from the ideal to the real, from purely normative considerations to more concrete and complex considerations of institutional design. In the first section I consider tensions between the ideals of deliberative democratic constitutionalism – in particular its conception of the function of constitutional review – and the unavoidable realities of ongoing constitutional elaboration within institutions intended to protect the constitutional structures of deliberative democracy. Motivated to manage these tensions through institutional design, the second section indicates the general strategy of dispersal and lays out a scheme for assessing the five institutional proposals considered in Section B of this chapter and in Chapter 9.

1.   Tensions between the Ideal and the Real

At the most abstract level, the function of constitutional review is easy to state: the protection of the constitutional framework within which government action occurs. According to the conception of deliberative democratic constitutionalism I have developed in the previous chapters, this function can be stated more exactly. Constitutional review discharges the function of procedurally protecting the political structures and the system of rights that make deliberative democracy possible, that is, protecting the constitutional structures that ultimately ground the supposition that the decisional outcomes of democratic processes are legitimate.[1]

Endorsing and developing lines of argument from Ely and Habermas, I have argued that the most convincing justification for placing the power of constitutional review in a politically independent constitutional court is twofold. First and foremost is the argument from structural independence. Insofar as constitutional review is intended to ensure the procedural correctness of political decision processes – that is, to police the rules of deliberative democracy – whatever organ or organs carry out the function should not be structurally under the control of particular disputants when the propriety of the procedures is called into question. Said another way, an organ independent of those in control of the legislature and the executive branches, as well as of various factions of the electorate, would be institutionally well situated to ensure the correctness of the procedures for democratic opinion and will-formation. For, on the proceduralist account of deliberative democratic legitimacy urged here, it is only the fact that those procedures have been followed that warrants the expectation that the outcomes will be sufficiently representative and reasonable to achieve legitimacy. Said another way, the following of suitably designed democratic procedures is the warrant that underwrites citizens' ability to understand themselves as simultaneously the subjects and authors of the law.

I have claimed that such an institutional location argument for an independent organ of constitutional review has important normative advantages over other forms of argument relying on the democratic nature of constitutional precommitments (as advanced by Freeman), or on heightened judicial competences either for moral reasoning (as advanced, for example, by Bickel, Choper, Dworkin, and Perry), or for representing democratic deliberation (as advanced, for instance, by Eisgruber,

---

[1] It is important to remember throughout this discussion that I use the term "legitimacy" and its cognates in its normative and not its descriptive sense (see, further, Chapter 3, Section A2). Thus, when I speak about, for instance, the legitimacy of constitutional court decisions or the legitimacy of its role, I am not referring to something like the degree to which they are socially accepted. I will save "social acceptance" and similar phrases for the sociological or factual senses.

Michelman, and Rawls). The generic argument that a democratic people could legitimately precommit themselves to judicial review fails to account for the ongoing and reciprocal relation between deliberative democracy and constitutionalism, an ongoing and reflexive dynamic that is crucial once we admit the persistence of apparently ineliminable but nevertheless reasonable substantive disagreement amongst democratic consociates. When the heightened moral competence of a constitutional court is invoked – as it is in substantialist defenses of constitutional courts as better at getting the right answers – it seems that the paternalist objection from democracy is inevitable. For what could be the warrant – given the basic democratic assumption of the political equality of citizens – for the claims that some citizens are not only better moral reasoners than others but also that this heightened moral competence allows them to know and represent the morally and politically relevant concerns of other citizens better than those citizens themselves could? Alternatively, the various arguments that a constitutional court could meet the paternalist objection by virtue of the fact that it best represents the kind of moral-political reasoning that the deliberative conception of democracy idealizes, fail to adequately distinguish different forms of the use of public reason. In particular, only by glossing over the significant distortions and evasions introduced into substantive moral-political argument through the technicalities of juristic discourses, I argued, could one make the claims that a constitutional court exemplifies the public use of reason, represents the people's moral commitments, or is communicatively open to the public use of reason, claims that could then be used in an exculpatory fashion to discharge worries about the counterdemocratic character of judicial review. Against arguments from the preemptive character of democratic fairness against any form of constitutional review (as advanced, for example, by Waldron) however, I claimed that they were both overly demanding and overly idealizing in ignoring constitutional arrangements intended to counteract foreseeable structural deformations that can make bare majoritarian political processes undemocratic and nonrepresentative.

The structural argument for an independent organ for the protection of democratic procedures does not of course, by itself, establish the claim that constitutional review should be placed in the hands of a *court* or quasi-judicial body. That claim is supported in part by the fact that a constitutional structuring of deliberative democracy is a *legal* structuring, and in part by the expanded tasks that a deliberative democratic constitutional court would have to take on. Here I relied on the Habermasian deliberative conception of democracy to show that the function of constitutional review includes a greatly expanded set of tasks beyond that involved in Ely's notion of the referees of electoral representative majoritarianism. Recall that this expanded set includes not only the bare procedures of electoral representation, but also scrutinizes the reasons justifying statutes, regulations and governmental actions, ensuring both the public autonomy and private autonomy rights necessary for procedural legitimacy, and, ensuring the nondistorted character of the "official" circulation of power from the communicative power of the weak public sphere, to the legislative and then administrative and judicial powers of the strong public sphere. There seems little doubt that this increased menu of tasks for constitutional review entails that whatever body or bodies are to carry it out would need to have significant capacities for comprehending and disambiguating the diversity of considerations, arguments, and types of public reasons supporting various decisions and actions. Furthermore, such a capacity for dealing with public reason would ideally be combined with an orientation toward maintaining and furthering a coherent system of law, constitutional, statutory, and regulatory. In the traditional separation of powers, by discharging the duty of a rational application of abstract norms to concrete cases, ordinary courts are specialized in both reason-sorting and maintaining legal systematicity. Given then the expansive tasks for constitutional review and the needs for cognizing complex reasoning discourses and maintaining legal systematicity, there is a strong *prima facie* case for constructing an independent constitutional review organ as a judicial or quasi-judicial body.

This heightened legal competence, however, should not be overemphasized. After all, we expect all of the normal branches of government to have capacities for understanding and abiding by the "internal morality" of law – if we didn't it would be very hard to explain how legislative and executive bodies, let alone the constituent power of the people exercised in both constitutional assemblies and ratification processes, could have any initiative or control over the shape and content of law. This concern about overselling legal competence in the justification of a constitutional court stood behind some of my reservations about Habermas's version of the separation of powers argument for judicial review, put forward by him in terms of the specialized capacities for handling application discourses inhering in judicial bodies. Said more generally, one should not mistake specifically juridical competence in the complexities of adjudication for legal competence *simpliciter*.

So far, the problem of institutional design looks relatively simple: the function of ensuring the procedural legitimacy of political decision making can be fulfilled by a politically independent protector of political procedures oriented toward maintaining the systematicity of constitutional law. However, the problem becomes considerably more complex once we recognize what might be called the "inevitability of transmutation" of the protection of constitutional provisions into their positive elaboration. The idea here is that, if the positive development of constitutional law and practice is an inevitable by-product of processes of enforcing procedural correctness, and if this process thereby occurs outside of the formally specified procedures for constitutional redesign (i.e., constitutional assemblies and amendment procedures), then an independent constitutional court becomes something much more than a simple referee of prespecified rules. It takes on, rather, the role of a constitutional legislator.[2] Let me suggest six kinds of mechanisms that contribute in part to the inevitability of protection-elaboration transmutation.

First is the difficulty in strictly separating the activities and results of justifying a general norm and applying that general norm to a concrete fact situation or a lower-level norm. Although we can analytically distinguish processes of justifying a general norm and applying a *prima facie* justified norm to a concrete situation, there is, nevertheless, a dialectical and reflexive relationship between the two processes.[3] For we could only accept the validity of a general norm in a justification discourse in the light of some expectations about how it will work in practice, that is, about how it will concretely affect various persons and their interests. Justification discourses, then, inevitably refer to application discourses. Likewise, as general norms are only provisionally justified in the absence of sufficiently countervailing reasons, new concrete fact situations can arise that cause us to call into question the *prima facie* justification of a general norm, thereby making the previously unproblematic general norm presumptively unjustified. Whether or not that presumption is correct – and so, whether or not the previously accepted norm is available to be applied to the new situation – is a question that can only be answered at the level of justification. Application discourses, then, inevitably refer back to justification discourses. If we then stylize constitution writing and enactment as a justification discourse, and constitutional protection as an application discourse, it seems that the general reflexive reciprocity between justification and application will result in the inevitable transmutation of constitutional protection into constitutional elaboration.[4]

---

[2] I mean this in the strong sense that a constitution-protecting organ will play a role in the positive elaboration of the structure and content of the law. If the following argument is correct, then, Kelsen's claim that a constitutional court could, in principle, be restricted only to a "negative" legislative function of annulling constitutionally problematic statutes and regulations is false: Kelsen, "Judicial Review of Legislation."

[3] Recall my discussion of justification, application, and adjudicative discourses in section B4 of Chapter 7. The dialectic between application and justification discourses is analyzed in the sympathetic but incisive criticism of Klaus Günther's discourse theory of norm application put forward in Peterson, "A Discourse Theory of Moral Judgment."

[4] The same point can be made independently of the Habermasian conceptual framework, as it reflects a general and pervasive problem of moral theory: the relation between general norms and particular instantiations. Consider, for instance, the debate between moral universalists and particularists as crystallized in Hegel's critique of Kantian moral theory for its empty formalism. The problem also crops up in debates between legal formalists and legal realists concerning whether legal rules have any semantic content apart from

Second, protection-elaboration transmutation will ensue simply from the peculiar semantic characteristics of many constitutional provisions: they are often written in quite general and abstract language. In contrast to structural provisions that straightforwardly spell out mechanical governmental provisions (electoral rules, eligibility rules for office holders, and so on), such generality and abstraction seems especially evident in various rights provisions, including not only fundamental individual rights but also the various positive duties of the state (duties, that is, that can be translated into the positive rights of citizens to forms of state action). Many structural provisions will also be quite general and abstract, namely, those concerning the precise scope of powers and duties of the relevant branches of government and, in a federal system, between the national and regional governments. This semantic character of constitutional provisions is, of course, the starting problem motivating the jurisprudential theories of judicial review I've canvassed here: those of Bickel, Choper, Dworkin, Eisgruber, Ely, and Perry. More broadly, one might say that the veritable outpouring of competing theories of the proper methodology for constitutional interpretation (and not just in the American context) should be seen as a response to the inevitability of the problem of protection-elaboration transmutation, where each theory attempts to control the deleterious effects of transmutation while channeling it in productive directions, guided by implicit conceptions of the proper role of judges in the separation of powers and intuitions about preferred judicial outcomes.

There is, third, another cause of transmutation tied to the practice of constitutionalism in modern pluralistic democracies. Given the persistence of unavoidable yet nevertheless reasonable disagreement amongst citizens with respect to ideals, values, and interests,[5] actual constitutional agreements are often achieved through what Cass Sunstein calls the dual methods of conceptual ascent (generalization and abstraction) and undertheorized agreement. Undertheorized agreements facilitate consensus on a textual formula in the absence of consensus on the

---

their applications to concrete cases; see Hart, *The Concept of Law*, especially 125–54 and 272–6. Finally, the same problem threatens the standard comparative law distinction between abstract and concrete modes of constitutional review. For an argument that the distinction collapses in practice – "as every architect knows, the abstract and the concrete are inseparable" – see Martin Shapiro and Alec Stone Sweet, "Abstract Review and Judicial Law-Making," in *On Law, Politics, and Judicialization*, ed. Martin Shapiro and Alec Stone Sweet (New York: Oxford University Press, 2002), 375.

[5] Recall that the problem of reasonable disagreement is central to both Waldron's and Michelman's quite different takes on the legitimacy of constitutional democracy. I hope to have given some reasons in Chapter 7 to think that the Habermasian strategy for a procedural conception of deliberative democratic constitutionalism persuasively combines a recognition of pluralism with an antiskeptical account of constitutional democracy.

reasons underlying that formula, whereas conceptual ascent facilitates agreement on text in the absence of agreement about the right answers in more concrete application contexts.[6] These kinds of strategies for getting the minimal constitutional agreement necessary for the ongoing democratic processes of discussion and decision will likely be used most in precisely those situations in which substantive controversies are most severe.[7] General or abstract constitutional provisions will of course give rise to more elaboration in the process of protection than less general or abstract ones. Likewise, those charged with authoritatively applying the results of undertheorized constitutional agreements, will have more interpretive room – and hence more elaborating effects – in the absence of accessible and agreed-on reasons underwriting the text of the provision. Constitutions, then, are susceptible to the transmutation problem not only because of the semantic characteristics of their provisions, but also because of the way in which the adoption of those provisions responds to the reasonable disagreement characteristic of modern value pluralism.

Although the first three sources of transmutation might be thought to inhere largely in the formal features of constitutional rules, the next three might be thought to arise from processes of social change. The fourth source is simply the ongoing development and elaboration of ordinary law, legislatively, administratively, and judicially. As the corpus of ordinary law changes and grows, its potential points of interaction with constitutional law likewise grow, producing new possibilities for conflict with higher-order constitutional norms. The potential for such conflicts is intensified not only through the production of law by legislatures and by delegated regulatory agencies, but also through responses to those developments by courts, which not only resolve conflicts but modify existing laws and establish new doctrinal rules and norms – rules and norms that will themselves further develop the corpus of ordinary law

---

[6] Conceptual descent – in which agreement is achieved on a quite specific norm without agreement on general norms or supporting arguments – is also a possibility for dealing with disagreement, but it is not particularly helpful in the context of drafting constitutional texts. See Sunstein, *Designing Democracy: What Constitutions Do*; Sunstein, *Legal Reasoning and Political Conflict*; and Sunstein, *One Case at a Time: Judicial Minimalism on the Supreme Court*. The general strategy for dealing with reasonable disagreement by achieving consensus on a determinate set of principles in the absence of agreement on the underlying reasons supporting those principles is forcefully defended in Rawls's notion of an overlapping consensus on political principles of justice: Rawls, *Political Liberalism*.

[7] Sweet's observation here is thus unsurprising: among the various problems faced by European constitution drafters after World War II, "the general problem of determining the exact content of rights provisions proved to be the most difficult aspect of constitutional negotiations in all countries," Sweet, *Governing with Judges*, 39.

where the doctrine of *stare decisis* is effective.[8] New potentials for constitutional conflicts in the hierarchy of law will, unsurprisingly, promote the elaboration of constitutional law.

To understand the fifth source of transmutation, recall my claim in Chapter 3: constitutions consist not only in the formal written text, and the elaboration of that text in various authoritative interpretations but also in those aspects of political institutions, governmental practices, and shared understandings that are entrenched in the sense of being more resistant to change than ordinary law: for example, the regnant political party system or the existing relationship between civilians and the military. Such features of a particular nation's political system should be thought of as constitutional – they are crucial to the particular functioning of that state and the use of political power, deeply entrenched, and part of the general procedures tied up with the legitimacy of lawmaking and execution – even though they may not be constitutionally specified, and are often not subject to direct judicial and or constitutional court control. They are, nevertheless, crucial parts of the overall constitutional system. Moreover, although they are the products of specific historical invention and development, such development usually does not occur through the formal channels of constitutional change: amendment or jurisprudence. If the constitutional structure is in this way elaborated outside of traditional modes of development, then whatever body is charged with constitutional protection will have to respond to those changes, and thereby reflexively solidify the resulting constitutional settlement, with likely additional elaboration.[9]

The sixth source of transmutation is simply the general process of change in the social contexts regulated by law. As this is an oft-repeated refrain in discussions of the fate of constitutions over time, it need not be

***

[8] Using a method intended to marry analyses of iterated strategic action with those of social rule systems – such as the law – Alec Stone Sweet has attempted to formalize the features both of processes of dispute resolution between two parties by independent judges within an existing rule system, and, of the path-dependent effects of precedent. For the former, see ibid., 1–30; for the latter Alec Stone Sweet, "Path Dependence, Precedent, and Judicial Power," in *On Law, Politics, and Judicialization*, ed. Martin Shapiro and Alec Stone Sweet (New York: Oxford University Press, 2002). In both cases, he argues, the processes will lead, over time, to increasing degrees of judicial rule-making – and, importantly for him, to the increasing role of judges in the development of governance structures: what he calls the "judicialization of politics."

[9] A concrete example of such dynamics is the rapid transformation of the United States electoral system – especially the increased focus on presidential candidates and their platforms, a newly developed two-party system, and an emerging regime of judicial review – that occurred from the original constitutional ratification in 1788, to Jefferson's "revolution of 1800," and through the apogee of Jackson's plebiscitary use of the presidential campaign. The story is intriguingly told in Ackerman, *We the People: Foundations*, 67–80.

belabored. It is perhaps worth noting, however, that the relevant changes here are not only in the extant set of social arrangements that law is applied to but also include scholarly and cultural changes that can systematically change the way law and society relationships are understood. Take, just as one prominent example, the profound changes wrought in the modes of both policy analysis and juridical decision once systematic social scientific data is taken to be relevant to understanding the predictable effects of various proposed legal regimes on the lives of those affected by them.[10] At any rate, we should expect such general processes of social change to be another contributing cause of the foreseeable transmutation from the function of protecting constitutional provisions into elaborating their content.[11]

The inevitability of transmutation from the protection of constitutional provisions into their elaboration means that, in practice, whatever organ or organs are charged with the function of constitutional review will have predominant control over the current state of constitutional law compared to the control exercisable by other organs authorized with lawmaking powers, even if the former are checked by the latter in various ways.[12] In part, this is a result simply of the more entrenched character of

[10] In jurisprudential theory, the American legal realists of the early twentieth century and the law and economics movement of the late twentieth century sought to systematically bring social scientific data to bear both on the study of law and on (at least) the future juridical development of law. In the American context, the use of social science by constitutional judges has figured especially prominently in high-profile, controversial, and consequential decisions. Two obvious examples are *Brown* and *Roe*.

[11] In a fascinating comparative analysis of constitutional amendment practices, Lutz distinguishes four reasons why a constitution needs to change. "Every political system needs to be altered over time as a result of some combination of: (1) changes in the environment within which the political system operates (including economics, technology, and demographics); (2) changes in the value system distributed across the population; (3) unwanted or unexpected institutional effects; and (4) the cumulative effect of decisions made by the legislature, executive, and judiciary," Lutz, "Toward a Theory of Constitutional Amendment," 242. His first two categories correspond to what I am here labeling general processes of social change, with his third and fourth roughly cutting across my fourth and fifth factors: the effects of the development of ordinary law and changes in the structure of the political system.

[12] In his illuminating study on the U.S. history of relations between the Supreme Court and Congress concerning issues of federalism, in particular the way in which constitutional jurisprudence can spur and shape debates and decisions taken by the legislature, Pickerill helpfully articulates a continuum between the supremacy of the Court over Congress and an equal role for both in constitutional elaboration. He argues for the actuality and desirability of judicial primacy, which lies between supremacy and equality, that is, "a theory of 'judicial primacy,' under which the Court has *the primary role in constitutional interpretation*, as opposed to a supreme role or (at the other extreme) an equal role. Under a theory of judicial primacy, the Court's constitutional interpretations will usually shape constitutional deliberation in other branches of government, and as such the Court will be the primary interpreter of the Constitution," Pickerill, *Constitutional Deliberation in*

constitutional law vis-à-vis ordinary law. The extent to which constitutional law is harder to change than other law determines the extent to which authorized constitutional elaborators will function effectively as veto players in the process of constitutional change. But the leading role of authorized constitutional decision makers is also in part because of the systematic path-dependence of a legal corpus organized as a system of social governance rules: earlier applications of general rules will have more effect than later ones simply because they establish precedents for those later cases, even in the absence of formal rules of *stare decisis* or other precedential doctrines. With such formal rules, of course, path-dependence is intensified. It seems clear, then, that if there is a constitutional court in a democratic system, it will have qualitatively greater control over the elaboration of constitutional law than other constitutional actors, both because of constitutional entrenchment and the court's own determinative role with respect to the paths of law.[13]

Here, however, is the ideal-real, norm-fact rub. From the pure normative point of view of democratic constitutionalism, the power of constitutional change inheres only in the people themselves, specially formed into a constituent assembly and exercising their constituent power.[14] From the realistic point of view of actual legal development over time – combined with the impracticability of endless constituent assemblies[15] – constitutional elaboration is a continuous process going on independently

---

Congress, 9. See, further, pages 133–53. My argument here is that this primary role is unavoidable when a constitutional court or the judicial system as a whole has disproportionate authority over constitutional meanings, and many of my institutional recommendations are intended, in part, to reduce this primacy.

[13] Given the combination of constitutionalism instituted through law, the requirements for internal legal systematicity and coherence, the path-dependent nature of the development of the legal corpus, and the causes of constitutional elaboration adumbrated above, it would seem that, even in the *absence* any authorized organ or organs for constitutional review, we should in fact expect an increasing density of constitutional law controlling the decisions and actions of ordinary political officials that would restrict their capacities for effecting legal change through ordinary political means. Such systematic dynamics might account for the ease with which we accord the honorific of "constitutional democracy" to political systems, such as that of the United Kingdom; it should also explain some of the obvious theoretical attractiveness of various accounts of "unwritten" constitutionalism such as Dicey's and David Strauss's – see my discussion in Chapter 3, Sections 2 and 3.

[14] A defense of the notion of the constituent power, and of its intrinsically democratic character, against skeptical challenges posed by Hannah Arendt and Hans Kelsen can be found in Andreas Kalyvas, "Popular Sovereignty, Democracy, and the Constituent Power," *Constellations* 12, no. 5 (2005).

[15] Even the most republican of civic republican theorists are skeptical about such possibilities. See, for instance, Rousseau's skepticism about full citizen assemblies (Book III, Chapter 15 – though see also Book III, Chapter 12), and his "solution" to the problem of a people writing their own fundamental laws by way of a "lawgiver" credited with mythic status and wholly independent of the people constituted as a sovereign assembly (Book II, Chapter 7), Rousseau, "*Of the Social Contract.*"

of the exercise of the people's constituent power; and even independently of their ordinary electoral powers. This constituent power cannot inhere in any ordinary branch of government, as those branches are intended to be authorized and controlled by constitutional law. One might object here that, just as the people can delegate various of their ordinary lawmaking powers to various representative bodies and official agencies, they should likewise be able to delegate the authority for constitutional elaboration to some authorized governmental organ. Although there is a glimpse of the truth in this objection – after all, it would seem that a constitutional court would have some important additional normative legitimacy to the extent that it was specifically provided for in a democratically ratified constitution – I think it should not be oversold. The problem here is that mere democratic choice of a given decision procedure or authoritative governmental body at the level of constitutional creation alone is insufficient to ensure the democratic operation of that procedure or body at the level of day-to-day governance. As Waldron clearly puts the point, there is an important "distinction between a democratic method of constitutional choice and the democratic character of the constitution that is chosen."[16]

The same point can be restated in terms of the insufficiency of classical conceptions of the separation of powers for accounting for the location of constitutional review. Traditional accounts of the separation of powers start with the notion of the supremacy of the legislative power that writes into general, prospective laws various policy choices, policy directives that the government then executes through administrative agencies and derivative regulations. The judiciary is then charged with applying those general and prospective legal norms retrospectively to particular fact situations – they are, as it were, "slaves" to the statutory and regulatory codes. Constitutionalism modifies this scheme by establishing a layer of higher-order legal norms, but its introduction is not supposed to fundamentally alter the separation of powers. In particular, there should still be a clear distinction between politics and law, reproduced on the constitutional level by the distinction between political powers of constitutional change and legal powers of constitutional enforcement.[17]

---

[16] Waldron, *Law and Disagreement*, 256. Recall the discussion of this point in the context of Freeman's argument for judicial review as a democratically legitimate decision at the level of constitutional precommitment, Chapter 5, section A4.

[17] The general formula of spelling out the separation of powers in terms of a dualistic distinction between politics and law is intended here, in part, to paper over the difficulties of saving the tripartite distinction's separation between legislative and executive functions in the light of the actual workings of modern constitutional democracies. The clear separation between legislative and executive powers has been substantially reduced both by, on the one hand, the significant legislative initiative power wielded by the executive branch in both presidential and parliamentary systems and, on the other hand, by the tremendous increase in law-writing performed through regulatory delegation. Reacting

If, however, any organ with the power of constitutional review is introduced into the system, and if the protection-elaboration dynamic is unavoidable, then the authorized constitutional review organ will be ineluctably involved with the generation of general and prospective constitutional norms, and thereby undermine the classical conception of the separation of powers. Thus, from the point of both ideal normative theory and realistic legal development, it seems much clearer to acknowledge that "constitutional courts ... occupy their own 'constitutional' space, a space neither clearly 'judicial' nor 'political'."[18] This conclusion fits well with the argument I advanced against one of Habermas's defenses of judicial review: namely, that which defended it as a simple extension of the judiciary's specialized function for handling application discourses. It should be evident that this is an updating of classical separation of powers arguments, and that it fails for the same reasons: the central analogy of a division of labor between legislatures and courts simply breaks down at the level of the constitutional convention. No ordinary organ of government can have a legitimate claim to exercise the constituent power of constitutional making, but constitution-making will nevertheless occur in the absence of the people's exercise of their constituent power.[19]

2.   Design Proposals and Assessment Values

To summarize then, the function of constitutional review is justified by the need to protect the procedures that grant legitimacy to the outcomes of democracy, and considerations of political distortions in democratic processes and the expanded tasks entailed by deliberative democratic constitutionalism recommend that the function be institutionalized in an independent constitutional court. However, the apparently inevitable

---

to the evident empirical weakness of the tripartite distinction, many still insist (unrealistically, in my view) on at least a dualistic conception of the separation of powers between the world of politics (dealt with by legislative and executive organs) and the world of law (dealt with by judicial organs): see Koopmans, *Courts and Political Institutions*, 245–51.

[18] Sweet, *Governing with Judges*, 34. Perhaps the major target of Sweet's work (and that of his frequent co-writer Martin Shapiro) are those theories, whether normative, jurisprudential, or empirical, that in some way or another still presuppose elements of classical conceptions of the separation of powers.

[19] See the discussion in Chapter 7, Section B4. The general conclusion also seems consonant with the widely felt and widely discussed insufficiency of Hamilton's argument in *Federalist Paper 78* for judicial review in terms of the separation of powers:Hamilton, Madison, and Jay, *The Federalist with Letters of "Brutus."* Most of the criticism of Hamilton's argument has been directed not at number 78 however, but the version of it put forward by Marshall in *Marbury* v. *Madison*, and memorably summed up in the phrase: "It is emphatically the province and duty of the Judicial Department to say what the law is," 177.

dynamic of transmutation from the function of constitutional protection to constitutional elaboration entails that a constitutional court will have a lead role in constitutional elaboration, even if, strictly speaking, that elaboration is only legitimately carried out through the constituent power of the people. So, the question for institutional design is how to negotiate the tensions between ideal demands and real constraints. In particular, it concerns how to structure extant and proposed institutions, and their interrelations, in order to maximize the possibilities for deliberative democratic input into and control over the processes of constitutional elaboration. After arguing for independent, specialized constitutional courts in Section B of this chapter, I will argue in the next chapter for four further reforms in institutional structures, beyond a constitutional court, that carry out the functions of constitutional elaboration. The basic intuition behind these suggestions is to multiply the sites of constitutional elaboration, specifically, to disperse the processes of constitutional review both horizontally across the various branches of national government, and vertically throughout the deliberative public sphere by connecting systematically the informal and more formal public sites of constitutional debate and development.[20] Hopefully such dispersal strategies should mitigate the ineliminable tensions between the ideal and the real, while at the same time improving actual processes of constitutional decision making by opening them to the diversity of relevant information and reasons available throughout the polity.

In order to get some theoretical purchase on the cogency of the various reform proposals, I suggest that they can be assessed on six independent value scales, each of which specifies one aspect that we would want institutions of constitutional review to positively support and/or promote. Ideally, such institutions in a deliberative democracy should (1) ensure the internal coherence of the system of legal of norms, (2) authoritatively settle constitutional disagreements and disputes, (3) be structurally independent of control by mechanisms of electoral accountability, (4) be sufficiently empowered to intervene in political processes to ensure their procedural legitimacy, (5) have the correct jurisdictional scope to promote the procedures of deliberative democratic decision without thereby injecting substantive content into fundamental law, and (6) be sensitive to the wide diversity of information and reasons relevant to constitutional decisions. Let me spell out each in turn, before taking up the question of the independence of the six assessment values.

---

[20] For clarity's sake I, once again, oversimplify by ignoring the complexities that might be introduced through a federalist division of powers between national and regional or other subnational authorities.

Systematicity – The promotion of the systematic nature of a legal corpus responds to the important value of an internally noncontradictory system of hierarchically ordered legal norms. Various philosophies of law will place more or less emphasis on this ideal, and will spell out the sources and desiderata of internal legal norm coherence in different ways.[21] I take it that it is, at any rate, uncontroversial that systematicity is a regulative ideal of a legal corpus: an ideal that regulates practice through its normativity and yet is not fully realizable in actual practice. Institutions of constitutional review should be oriented toward, at the least, not undermining the coherence of the legal systems and, at the most, at positively promoting increasing coherence over time.

Settlement – Given that constitutional law is fundamental law, institutions responsible for constitutional review should be designed in the light of the coordinative benefits to be gained from settled legal rules and sensitive to the fairness implications of various individuals' and social actors' reliance interests with respect to the predictability of the legal system.[22] Alexander and Schauer provide a clear conception of settlement – the authoritative determination of what is to be done in situations of conflict – that connects it with the general values of coordination and fairness that law serves, and with the important role it plays in the constitutional direction of the actions of officials: "It is as much a function of a constitution as of law in general to settle authoritatively what ought to be done, and to coordinate for the common good the self-interested and strategic behavior of individual officials.... A constitution exist[s] partly because of the value of uniform decisions on issues as to which people have divergent substantive views and personal agendas."[23] Although there are important connections between legal systematicity and settlement – both are centered around the notion of constitutionalism as a specifically legal practice – they are distinct. For although it would surely

---

[21] It may be that my specification of the ideal of legal systematicity is not sufficiently generic with respect to competing philosophies of the nature of law, particularly since it is quite close to the central animating concern of Kelsen's version of legal positivism: see, for instance Chapters 5 and 6 of Kelsen, *Introduction to the Problems of Legal Theory*, 55–89. I intend my formulation, however, to be agnostic with respect to the competing claims concerning the nature of law. Thus, for instance, both Hart and Fuller endorse the importance of noncontradiction between legal rules, even as they disagree about whether such contradictions can be established by the semantic hierarchy of rules alone or whether recourse to contextual moral, social, or technological factors also will be necessary: Hart, *The Concept of Law*, 95.; Fuller, *The Morality of Law*, 65–70.

[22] I draw here on the very clear articulation of the settlement function of law put forward in Larry Alexander and Frederick Schauer, "On Extrajudicial Constitutional Interpretation," *Harvard Law Review* 110 (1997), though I disagree with their overly strong conclusions that authoritative settlement is the *non plus ultra* of constitutional review – see later.

[23] Ibid.: 1376.

be hard to serve the settlement function through a massively incoherent complex of legal norms, a fully systematic legal corpus could leave much legally unsettled, both at the level of individual discretion, and at the political level.[24] A quite effective set of authoritative legal settlement institutions, alternatively, could produce and maintain a relatively contradictory body of law.[25]

It should be noted here that the virtues of legal settlement can be somewhat oversold, especially if they are taken as the only or even the pre-eminent virtue of a legal system. One might argue along the lines of Alexander and Schauer, for example, that the central function of the law is to coordinate individual behaviors in the absence of a preexisting consensus on values and in the face of recurrent collective action problems.[26] Accordingly, law serves this coordinative function through rules whose authority, and hence obligatory force, must be independent of the content of those rules, given ineliminable value and interest conflicts. Because coordination cannot occur without rules, and the authority of rules must be content-independent, there is a need for authorized rule makers and rule interpreters that effectively settle conflicts. Even if such authoritative settlement gives rise to a substantively suboptimal set of rules, some set of rules is better than no rules at all. Finally, if we presuppose – as Alexander and Schauer do – entirely strategic behavior on the part of nonjudicial actors while attributing to judges various forms of rule-governed behavior based purely on the internal normativity of legal rules, then it would seem best to ensure absolute deference to the authoritative interpretations of law put forward by exactly one highest constitutional court.[27]

---

[24] Federalist schemes often provide clear examples of the possibility of systematicity in the absence of uniform political settlements. Furthermore the varieties of processes of social and legal change will often yield situations where there is no legal settlement on a new problem, even though the legal corpus is internally coherent.

[25] Whether or not it is fully adequate to describe common-law systems, Karl Llewellyn's metaphor of the common law as a "bramble bush" should illustrate the possibility and frequency of settlement without systematicity.

[26] Alexander and Schauer, "On Extrajudicial Constitutional Interpretation."

[27] For the remarkably opposed accounts of the explanations of nonjudicial and judicial official behavior, compare especially ibid.: 1363–68 and 72–76, in which legislators are taken to act only strategically but judges are thought to bind themselves to the normativity of juridical reasons, such as precedent and constitutional principles. See, further, footnote 80 pages 1377–8 for more of the same. Here the kind of symmetry that Waldron rightly insists on would be most welcome: "Unlike law professors, [political scientists] have the good grace to match a cynical model of legislating with an equally cynical model of appellate and Supreme Court adjudication If legislators are rent seekers, what do judges maximize? ... Even if they support judicial review, most political scientists do not base that support on any asymmetry in the motivations they ascribe to judges and legislators, respectively," Waldron, *Law and Disagreement*, 32.

Deliberative Democracy and the Institutions of Judicial Review

As a normative consideration the value of settlement is important, but taking settlement as the preeminent and veritably exclusive virtue of a legal system[28] is subject to the exact same types of objections that Hobbes's original arguments for absolute monarchy as the only alternative to anarchic war of each against all are subject to. As memorably summarized by Rousseau – "The despot, it will be said, guarantees civil tranquility for his subjects.... Life is also tranquil in dungeons; is that enough to feel well in them?"[29] – there are two counter-arguments to such arguments. First, the settlement/peace arguments rely on a false dichotomy of institutional design options: either absolute concentrated authority or anarchy; either authoritative settlement or anarchy.[30] Second, it is often the case that the ignored institutional alternatives to concentrated authority and anarchy are arrangements that are responsive

[28] "Thus an important – perhaps *the* important – function of law is its ability to settle authoritatively what is to be done. That function is performed by all law; but because the Constitution governs all other law, it is especially important for the matters *it* covers to be settled. To the extent that the law is interpreted differently by different interpreters, an overwhelming probability for many socially important issues, it has failed to perform the settlement function," Alexander and Schauer, "On Extrajudicial Constitutional Interpretation," 1377.

[29] Rousseau, "*Of the Social Contract*," 45, Book I, Chapter 4.

[30] Calling such views "Protestant," Alexander and Schauer respond to relatively modest proposals for coordinate powers for constitutional interpretation shared by the three different branches of national government thusly: "This 'Protestant' view of constitutional interpretation entails not just parity of interpretive authority among the three branches of the federal government; it also entails parity of interpretive authority among the members of each branch; among all officials, state and local as well as federal; and indeed among all citizens. 'Protestantism' in constitutional interpretation – interpretive anarchy – produces no settled meaning of the Constitution and thus no settlement of what is to be done with respect to our most important affairs," Alexander and Schauer, "On Extrajudicial Constitutional Interpretation," 1378–9. Although it is likely they will not believe me, I think it unlikely that spreading out decisional authority concerning the constitution – exactly what my proposals are in part intended to do – inevitably leads, through a frictionless, nearly vertical slippery slope, to the anarchic specter of fully individualized and subjectivized constitutional interpretations, to a free-for-all of lawlessness. Its hard to think, for instance, that this specter of vast constitutional unsettlement and fully subjectivized interpretive anarchy adequately characterizes the state of constitutional law in a country such as France, where authoritative settlement of constitutional issues is distributed across various bodies: a specialized constitutional court, the supreme administrative court, the legislature, (to a small extent) the supreme appellate court, and, the developing transnational European Courts of Justice and of Human Rights. For a clear and concise account of the current French system see Doris Marie Provine, "Courts in the Political Process in France," in *Courts, Law, and Politics in Comparative Perspective*, ed. Herbert Jacob et al. (New Haven, CT: Yale University Press, 1996), especially 181–201; more in-depth treatments in the service of supporting the thesis of the judicialization of politics are in Alec Stone, *The Birth of Judicial Politics in France: The Constitutional Council in Comparative Perspective* (New York: Oxford University Press, 1992), and Sweet, *Governing with Judges*.

precisely to *other* values and concerns than the single and exclusivistic value appealed to as the contrast to anarchy. Were constitutional design a simple problem of optimization over one value, I submit that there would be little controversy over it. My list of assessment values is intended in part simply to show that there is more at stake in designing constitutional review than the value of authoritative and uniform settlement. Given the empirical dynamics of transmutation that I adumbrated earlier, furthermore, we should not be surprised when, as a matter of fact, actual constitutional court "settlements" turn out to be just the opposite: "Court rulings not only rarely 'settle' political conflicts; they often serve to encourage or generate further litigation on public issues.... The process of displacing controversial issues from electoral venues into judicial forums often ends up catalyzing as much as discouraging political mobilization around them among various political audiences."[31]

Independence – Hopefully I have said enough in previous chapters to explain why independence from direct political accountability is important for performing constitutional review in democratic representative systems.[32] Let me simply emphasize here that this value ideally requires not only independence from the formal branches of government whose officials are more directly politically accountable (legislatures and administrative agencies) but also from various forms of concentrated social powers. The latter is required to guard against analogues to what is often called "regulatory capture" – those situations where the regulatory agencies intended to set and enforce fair rules for competition in various sectors of society or the economy in fact become beholden to a subset of the interests they are supposed to regulate, generating rules and decisions that systematically favor that subset while effectively excluding fair

---

[31] Michael McCann, "How the Supreme Court Matters in American Politics: New Institutionalist Perspectives," in *The Supreme Court in American Politics: New Institutionalist Interpretations*, ed. Howard Gillman and Cornell Clayton (Lawrence: University Press of Kansas, 1999), 72. Sweet perhaps overemphasizes this point about the positively unsettling character of constitutional review mechanisms in his book (e.g., Sweet, *Governing with Judges*, 55, 74, 137–8, 95–96.) only rarely acknowledging that constitutional settlement does occur, effectively taking some issues and policy alternatives off of the list of possibilities for ordinary politics. In his reflections on precedential structures, however, he seems to vacillate between the opposing theses that path-dependent adjudication will, over time, lead to more and to less indeterminacy, that is more and less settlement. Contrast the summarized claims to increasing indeterminacy at Sweet, "Path Dependence, Precedent, and Judicial Power," 113 and 34, with the specific claims to decreasing indeterminacy at 129–31.

[32] Recall my endorsement of the various procedural referees justifications for independent organs for constitutional review given by Dahl and Ely, and by Habermas in Chapters 2 and 7 respectively. Recall also my answer to the most serious objections to such a justification in my rejoinders to Waldron's arguments from the democratic fairness of bare majoritarianism in Chapter 5.

consideration of the interests of other affected parties. Extending the analogy, then, organs of constitutional review should be sufficiently independent of capture by various forms of social power. It may be that if the function of constitutional review is carried out by institutions modeled closely on ordinary courts of law, a particular worry might be the analogous "capture" of constitutional courts by legal elites.[33] To the extent that other modes of constitutional review also are used in a political system, as I recommend, they, too, may well be subject to analogous forms of capture.

Empowerment – Whatever institutions are to carry out constitutional review must be not only politically independent but also sufficiently and relevantly empowered to be able to intervene in distortions of the legitimacy conferring democratic procedures. They must have sufficient capacity to actually intercede in decision making and policy implementation processes to correct for constitutional failures. Of course, sufficient power should not turn into overwhelming power, such that normal channels of democratic decision and implementation are effectively foreclosed. Relatedly, empowerment here must be relevant empowerment: that is, constitutional review institutions should have the capacity to control the procedures of democracy that are constitutionally germane. Unfortunately, I have no convenient formulas or metrics for evaluating the sufficiency and relevancy of empowerment at a general level. Much here would seem to turn on the specifics of the proposals, the way in which they are observed to function over time, and a manifold of contextual particularities concerning particular legal systems, cultural-historical variables, institutional peculiarities, and so on. Although the two assessment values of independence and empowerment are tightly connected to the institutional location justification for constitutional review, they are independent values. Consider a powerful constitutional court filled with political lackeys, or one that was fully depoliticized but that had no effective capacity to intervene.

---

[33] I'm unsure how far to push this insight, or how dangerous this in fact is. Perhaps some of my arguments against the seducements of juristic discourse in Chapter 6 could be reworked in terms of a metaphor of legalistic capture. At any rate, there would only be a problem if the analogy were fulsome: that is, if in fact legal elites (intentionally or unintentionally) influenced an independent constitutional court in a way sufficient to systematically distort the protection of the deliberative democratic procedures that warrant the legitimacy of political decisions. One way this might happen is if the threshold for the consideration of constitutional complaints presupposed such high degrees of legal competence that those with lesser degrees of cultural capital were effectively shut out of the process. Another might be the associated asymmetric threat potential of constitutional legal action, given the high price of securing the services of those with sufficient legal-cultural capital.

Jurisdiction – Institutions of constitutional review can be assessed, further, in terms of whether they have the proper jurisdictional scope. In terms of the theory I have advanced here, this means that they should be oriented towards ensuring, supporting, and reinforcing deliberative democratic processes, in the process of reviewing both constitutional and ordinary law. From the proceduralist perspective, this entails that, ideally, the work-product of such institutions would be entirely limited to protecting preestablished constitutional procedures that themselves are the product of the constituent power of the people – ideally, they would have no jurisdiction to inject new substantive content into the system of constitutional law through their decisions. Practically, the inevitability of transmutation would seem to make this impossible. Thus, in practice, the assessment value of proper jurisdictional scope apparently pushes toward institutional mechanisms such as multiple sites for constitutional review that can check one another, and, mechanisms that would reduce the finality, indefeasibility, or supremacy of any single institution's decisions. To put the problem in a slogan, on pain of infinite regress, there seems to be no way to find an infallible guardian of the jurisdiction of the guardians, yet some form of jurisdictionally restricted constitutional review appears indissociable from the project of deliberative democratic constitutionalism.

Sensitivity – Together with the assessment value of proper jurisdiction, the value of sensitivity is most closely connected to the deliberative democratic components of the conception of constitutional review. As a regulative ideal, it entails that review institutions remain as open as possible to the relevant reasons, values, and interests of the wide spectrum of citizens that will be affected by their decisions. Such institutions must be reasons-responsive, and responsive to the full gamut of potentially relevant reasons of the whole citizenry. As Michelman rightly emphasizes, the institutional legitimacy of an organ with significant powers for determining matters of fundamental law, especially when those matters are subject to reasonable but persistent disagreement throughout society, should be tied to its openness and sensitivity to inputs from the wide, informal public sphere. The institutional structures of review "would have to include arrangements for exposing the empowered basic-law interpreters to the full blast of sundry opinions and interest-articulations in society, including on a fair basis everyone's opinions and articulations of interests."[34] Institutions of constitutional review are not themselves immune to the deliberative democratic criterion of legitimacy, spelled out as a regulative ideal by Habermas: "Only those [laws] may claim legitimacy that can meet with the assent of all citizens in a discursive process of legislation that in turn has been

---

[34] Michelman, *Brennan and Democracy*, 60.

legally constituted."[35] Insofar as such institutions assume some of the people's constituent power for the coauthorship of the constitutional laws they are subject to – namely, through the inevitable nonconstituent elaboration of constitutional law – the legitimacy of such institutions depends on their degree of openness to and responsiveness to the people's constitutionally relevant reasons, values, and interests.

The principal inputs here will be reasons and information germane to who various different constitutional policy regimes would affect and how they would be affected, but more reflexive and technical forms of information also will be needed: about the foreseeable legal consequences for the internal coherence and structure of the legal corpus, the likely effects for reshaping political decision-making structures, the likely impact on legally structured but nonpolitical domains of social life, and so on. Even though these latter forms of reflexive input may have an expertocratic cast, in the end, the various considerations must be internally connected back to the kinds of reasons that could convince citizens that the option chosen is acceptable to them on the basis of good arguments. Obviously, then, this assessment value (like all of the others) is a regulative ideal, structuring the normative understanding of the practice even if not fully realizable in actuality.

It seems clear that the six assessment values I have proposed are independent of one another in the sense that each could be promoted or demoted by institutional arrangements without the covariance of the others. Rather than argue systematically for their independence, however, I hope that consideration of different applicability of the assessment values to the various proposals will be sufficient to show their noncovariance. Another way to think about the claim of independence is to say that the values are in tension with one another. For example, attempts to fully realize the ideal of systematicity may undermine the value of settlement, as apparently settled legal issues in one area of law are

---

[35] Habermas, *Between Facts and Norms*, 110. I have modified Habermas's original formulation by substituting "laws" here, where the original has "statutes." This prevents unduly narrowing the democratic legitimacy criterion only to the legislative production of ordinary statutes. This seems justified to me on the simple grounds that Habermas repeatedly insists that constitution-writing is itself a process of democratic self-legislation, and he conceives the project of constitutionalism as an ongoing deliberative democratic project. As an example: "The character of constitutional foundings, which often seal the success of political revolutions, deceptively suggests that norms outside of time and resistant to historical change are simply 'stated.' The technical priority of the constitution to ordinary laws belongs to the systematic elucidation of the rule of law, but it only means that the content of constitutional norms is *relatively* fixed. As we will see, every constitution is a living project that can *endure* only as an ongoing interpretation continually carried forward at all levels of the production of law," Habermas, *Between Facts and Norms*, 129. See also ibid., 384, 410, and 444, and Habermas, "Constitutional Democracy: A Paradoxical Union of Contradictory Principles?"

disturbed by the need to overcome potential contradictions or conflicts with other areas of law. Alternatively, settlement of constitutional issues in a system of constitutional review diffused throughout the appellate judiciary may lead to a decrease of systematicity. Another example is the tension between political independence and popular sensitivity. At least if the only available institutional locations are the three major branches of national government, placement of the function of constitutional review seems to involve an unavoidable trade-off between independence and sensitivity. On the standard supposition that electoral accountability increases the sensitivity of a branch to the reasons, values, and interests of the people, as well as to the likely impact of various decisions on them, the assessment values of sensitivity and independence seem to be directly and inversely correlated. However, as I hope to suggest with the recommendations for civic constitutional fora, this inverse proportionality is not inevitable, but can be significantly mitigated. Simply put, the idea is that by locating some powers for constitutional consideration in the broader, informal public sphere, there is a possibility of promoting popular sensitivity while simultaneously maintaining independence from potentially distorted processes of formal political governance in the official public sphere. Whether such changes would turn out to be realistic or effective, it seems to me that one of the more exciting elements of the move to deliberative conceptions of democracy is that, by refusing to model all political interactions as strategic bargaining situations and by expanding the conception and location of "politics" beyond the formal organs of government, deliberative models at least open up the scope of possibilities for productive and innovative institutional design.

The actual effectiveness of the recommendations for meeting their goals is another, obviously crucial, dimension of assessment for the various proposals. Effectiveness is, however, a different kind of consideration: it is not a value to be optimized or promoted, and assessed by reference to the structural characteristics of the institution proposed. Rather it is an empirical matter concerning whether or not those values could actually be promoted by the institution proposed, given what we know about the workings of various legal and political systems. Relevant evidence then is most likely to come from historical and comparative studies that attempt to assess the independent impact of various distinct constitutional arrangements across various extant constitutional democracies (and across nonconstitutional and/or nondemocratic legal and political systems when probative). This is a relatively nascent but exciting field of literature, and I refer to it where I have found its findings particularly pertinent to the institutional proposals I recommend. Given the volume, specificity, and complexity of the empirical studies, however, the effectiveness of the proposals made here can't be definitively established. The proposals should be read, then, as exploratory conversation openers, rather than the definitive conclusions of an overconfident and overidealizing political philosophy.

B.   INDEPENDENT CONSTITUTIONAL COURTS IN A CONCENTRATED REVIEW SYSTEM

In a spirit of speculative experimentalism, I now propose five general types of institutional reforms that I believe more in concert with the spirit of deliberative democratic constitutionalism than many extant arrangements. The proposals are intended to respond to the evident tension between the idealizations concerning the people's constituent power for constitutional elaboration and the realities of the dynamics of actual constitutional systems by, in general, both structuring broad and responsive constitutional debates and deliberations and dispersing the authoritative powers for constitutional elaboration horizontally across the branches of government and vertically throughout the links between the informal and formal public spheres. The proposals are: (1) the establishment of independent constitutional courts in a concentrated system of review, (2) self-review panels in legislatures and regulatory agencies, (3) mechanisms for interbranch debate and decisional dispersal, (4) easing formal amendability requirements, and (5) establishing civic constitutional fora. This section focuses on constitutional courts; the next chapter takes up the remaining four proposals.

The first reform proposal, then, is to place significant powers for constitutional review in the hands of an independent quasi-judicial body, specialized in questions of constitutionality, in a legal system where such powers are concentrated in such a court, rather than diffused throughout the ordinary judiciary.[36] The model is basically akin to the institution proposed by Hans Kelsen in the 1920s and enacted in the Austrian

---

[36] As well as general texts that give a comparative overview of national constitutions such as Robert E. Maddex, *Constitutions of the World* (Washington, DC: Congressional Quarterly, Inc., 2001), I have relied on comparative texts – both jurisprudential and political scientific – that focus more specifically on comparing constitutional courts: Allan R. Brewer-Carías, *Judicial Review in Comparative Law* (New York: Cambridge University Press, 1989), Mauro Cappelletti, *Judicial Review in the Contemporary World* (Indianapolis, IN: Bobbs-Merrill, 1971), Louis Favoreu, "Constitutional Review in Europe," in *Constitutionalism and Rights: The Influence of the United States Constitution Abroad*, ed. Louis Henkin and Albert J. Rosenthal (New York: Columbia University Press, 1990), Hirschl, *Towards Juristocracy*, Herbert Jacob et al., *Courts, Law, and Politics in Comparative Perspective* (New Haven: Yale University Press, 1996), Koopmans, *Courts and Political Institutions*, Arne Mavcic, *A Tabular Presentation of Constitutional/Judicial Review around the World* (concourts.net, March 1, 2004 [cited December 21, 2004]); available from http:// www.concourts.net/index.html, Sweet, *Governing with Judges*. Needless to say, any errors or fallacious judgments that might be encountered in the following are my sole responsibility. The significant simplifications encountered throughout are a by-product

Constitution of 1929, and widely adopted with many variations in European countries after the end of World War II. Such a concentrated or centralized system can be usefully contrasted to the diffuse or decentralized system developed in the United States, where constitutional review powers may be exercised by any ordinary court in the course of its resolution of specific cases.[37] Although there are a host of both possible analytic contrasts and ways of structuring constitutional courts, I focus here on three aspects as crucial to my proposal: structural independence, the use of juridical techniques, and specialization in constitutional issues within a concentrated system. I also will have some comments on questions of jurisdiction and the various modalities of referral, but these latter issues seem to me to concern more contextually specific judgments that could not be adequately made at the level of abstraction employed here.[38]

---

of my intention to evaluate various proposals in the light of a normative theory of deliberative democratic constitutionalism.

[37] Brewer-Carías, *Judicial Review in Comparative Law* makes the contrast between diffuse and centralized systems of constitutional review the central organizing principle of his work, introducing as a third category various "mixed" systems of review.

[38] In the history of debates about how to institutionalize judicial constitutional review – beginning with Kelsen's work in the 1920s and intensifying especially in the second half of the twentieth century, especially with the accelerating adoption of democratic constitutions – a set of dichotomous contrasts have been employed in the stylization of the so-called American and European systems, whereby one half of each contrast is traditionally mapped to one system, the other to the contrasting system: diffuse versus concentrated systems, a posteriori versus a priori review, concrete versus abstract review, positive powers of constitutional legislation versus merely negative powers, common-law style doctrines of *stare decisis* and precedent versus their absence in civil or Roman law–style legal systems. Theoretical parsimony recommends such contrasts but, as often as not, empirical considerations require the analysis to retract much of the claim for the actual relevance of the contrasts. This latter move is furthered by some of the actual convergence, over time, noted between the systems (not to mention the existence of various "mixed systems"). The concentrated/diffuse contrast is central to my argument, and so I will try to develop its import. I also will claim that it is important for a constitutional court to be able to review legislation both before (a priori) and after (a posteriori) it is put into effect. (Notably, even in France, where constitutional review is formally only allowed a priori by the Constitutional Council, the a posteriori use of constitutional principles by the Council of State has increased, breaking down the neat dichotomy: see Provine, "Courts in the Political Process in France," and Sweet, *Governing with Judges.*) The distinction between concrete and abstract modalities of review – that between the review of a legal norm incidental to a concrete "case or controversy" involving at least one affected private litigant, and the review of a legal norm in "abstraction" from any particular court case – is analytically sustainable, even as it is no longer a distinguishing contrast between the American and the European systems. For the claim to the importance of abstract review in the United States, see Shapiro and Sweet, "Abstract Review and Judicial Law-Making"; for the corresponding claims about the existence of concrete review in, say, France where it is not a formally recognized review modality, see Sweet, *Governing with Judges.* The distinction nevertheless has, I think, important implications from the point of view of deliberative democracy, yet I will

1. Structural Independence

A constitutional court ought to be independent of political accountability if it is to be able to fairly correct violations of the political procedures that warrant the legitimacy of the decisional outcomes of democratic processes. The crux of such independence is that the constitutional court and its members are institutionally independent of political accountability. I should stress here that this does not mean that the court is somehow wholly apolitical, or that its membership should be determined through nonpolitical processes. The point, rather is that, once selected to serve on the court, appointees should not be subject to ongoing political pressures as they carry out their duties, and the internal administration of the court should likewise be independent of direct control by politically accountable officials.

This point can be made clearer by contrasting the basically political processes of recruitment and selection for members, with the politically-independent conditions of their retention. In most constitutional democracies with forms of judicial review, members are drawn not only from the ranks of jurists, but also from other careers and professions.[39] Perhaps more important, the various selection mechanisms adopted all seem oriented to the recognition that, in practice (even if not in theory), constitutional court judges are to be selected with an eye toward both their ideological and their jurisprudential tendencies. Whether structured by appointment or election mechanisms, selection of members is invariably

---

not be able to do justice to the complexities of the issue. If the transmutation of provision protection into provision elaboration is inevitable, then Kelsen's belief that a distinction could be institutionally maintained between the merely negative legislative function of a constitutional court, and more substantive positive legislative contributions seems to have been mistaken (Sweet, *Governing with Judges*, argues that the negative/positive legislation distinction is doomed by the introduction of individual rights provisions into contemporary constitutions, and by the inevitability of employing balancing and rationality tests when fundamental rights conflict). Finally, the exclusivistic association of diffuse systems with common-law legal traditions and concentrated systems with civil code traditions appears to be – when considering public law and especially constitutional law – both unnecessary conceptually (see Brewer-Carías, *Judicial Review in Comparative Law*, 128–31 and 86–8), and increasingly unhelpful empirically (Brewer-Carías, *Judicial Review in Comparative Law*, Herbert Jacob, "Introduction," in *Courts, Law, and Politics in Comparative Perspective*, ed. Herbert Jacob et al. (New Haven: Yale University Press, 1996), 3–6, and Koopmans, *Courts and Political Institutions*, 40).

[39] Formal and informal recruitment rules range from having virtually no formal qualifications stipulated for constitutional court members (as in France), to informal but long-standing traditions of favoring jurists but not excluding other prominent citizens and former political officials (as in the United States), to stricter formal rules restricting membership to well-experienced judges or tenured law professors (as in Italy). A helpful chart comparing France, Germany, Italy, and Spain on the recruitment to and composition of the constitutional court can be found at Sweet, *Governing with Judges*, 49. Details concerning recruitment and selection can be found in Maddex, *Constitutions of the World*.

controlled by diverse organs of the national government, with significant powers given not only to the ruling majority or coalition but also to various minority players in the national government. These various forms of recruitment and selection are, as it were, institutional responses to the fact that constitutional courts play a crucial role in a fundamentally political task: the further elaboration of constitutional law. Obviously, their decisions will be highly consequential not only for the future of constitutional law but also for the possibilities and limitations of future ordinary legislation, regulation and administration, ordinary adjudication, and the overall structures and dynamics of politics itself.

Hence the role of politics in the recruitment and selection of constitutional court members is a response to the democratic demand for sensitivity in the elaboration of constitutional law. Consider, for instance, Perry's argument that term rather than life appointments would make the U.S. Supreme Court more accountable to the electorate through more frequent judicial appointments. For if "'We the people' now living, who, after all, unlike our dead political ancestors, are supposed to be politically sovereign," and constitutional specification involves elaboration of the constitution, then the principle of democratic sovereignty pushes towards reducing potential lag-times between changes in considered public opinion and in the opinions of constitutional court judges.[40] Agreeing that term appointments would reduce the problem of "drift" between a constitutional court and the political branches, Ferejohn also argues that consensus-oriented political appointments mechanisms (for instance, supermajority rules) should result in the selection of more moderate judges, both in terms of their jurisprudence and their underlying political values and ideology.[41]

Yet for all of their broadly political impact, the members of effective constitutional courts should not be dependent on the political branches once in office and carrying out the duties of constitutional review. This rules out forms of electoral or political branch control such as standing for reelection or subjection to recall mechanisms, once in office. It also requires significant guaranteed funding for such a court to carry on its on administrative duties independently of political control. Finally, court membership should not be seen as a stepping stone to elected or other high political offices after the end of a term, although it seems there is no felt need to formalize such requirements.[42]

[40] Perry, *The Constitution in the Courts: Law or Politics?*, 196.
[41] John Ferejohn, "Constitutional Review in the Global Context," *New York University Journal of Legislation and Public Policy* 6 (2002–2003), John Ferejohn, "Judicializing Politics, Politicizing Law," *Hoover Digest* (2003).
[42] This worry about postterm expectations and incentives seems to have contributed to Hamilton's insistence that federal judges must have life, rather than term, appointments in order to be sufficiently independent, in *Federalist No. 78*. Note also that he recognized

2. The Use of Juridical Techniques

If the argument that a constitutional court must be politically independent hangs on the structural role it is to play in policing the procedures of constitutional democracy, the argument that it be a court, or at least employ quasi-juridical methods, stems from the basic deliberative democratic insistence on reasons-responsiveness.[43] On the most fundamental concerns that structure the practice of democratic self-rule through the medium of law, deliberative democracy insists that reasons and arguments are to play the central and decisive role in decision making. Here it seems that judicial methods of decision making are preferred because they forefront careful consideration of the competing claims and supporting arguments put forward, insist on consistent applications of norms and principles invoked in one area to other areas (where appropriate), are sensitive to analogies and disanalogies and the relevancy criteria that govern such, develop systematic rules and principles that carry over from one set of decisions to another, are (usually) compelled to produce and publicize the reasons and arguments that support their decisions rather than just announcing the decisions, and so on. Recalling the criteria I laid out for an adequate theory of constitutional review at the end of Chapter 7, it is important to remember that the function involves more than simply deciding – more than authoritatively settling norm conflicts and intervening in defective political processes. Decisions must be based on specific forms of reasoned considerations: unpacking of the syndrome of justifying reasons supporting legal norms, attending to the diversity and relative importance of the different types of reasons required, subjecting those different types of reasons to various appropriate tests of rationality or reasonableness, all within the ambit of an ideally coherent hierarchical system of legal rules, norms, and principles. It should be added here that courts, although not unique in their use of precedential reasoning, have developed well-understood techniques for increasing the rationality of decisional outcomes over time in the context of complex rule systems by reference to a developing set of second-order doctrines for the interpretation and application of first-order norms.[44] It would seem then, that even if not composed entirely of judges

---

the need for monetary independence –"Next to permanency in office, nothing can contribute more to the independence of the judges than a fixed provision for their support," Hamilton, Madison, and Jay, *The Federalist with Letters of "Brutus,"* Number 79, 384. To be independent, a court – as a modern bureaucracy – also will need internal administrative independence.

[43] See Chapter 3, Section A.

[44] One might object here that I have, by invoking the virtues of precedentialism, unreasonably favored a common-law style of constitutional review, where that may be inappropriate (as in civil law systems) or undesired (for instance, from a theory that understands constitutionalism as the practice of rigidly specifying, from the outset and

and lawyers, an independent constitutional review organ should be established as a quasi-judicial body and may be well-served by the use of juristic techniques.

One might expect Jeremy Waldron to explode at this point. After all, he would argue, why portray legislators as incapable of being reasons-responsive? They strenuously and openly debate and deliberate about how to structure and shape the law, their deliberations are formalized and shaped by rules that encourage the give and take of good-faith reasoning amongst large, diverse, and representative assemblies, and they – just like constitutional court judges – ultimately make their final decisions by the simple mechanisms of majoritarian voting. Finally, if one is inclined to be cynical of legislative argument as a mere cover for some less reputable modes of decision making, then the principle of theoretical parsimony gives one no reasons not to extend the same cynicism to judicial motivations and behavior.[45]

The proper answer to this objection begins by conceding both the point about attributive parsimony and that about the dignity of legislation – after all, without at least some degree of noncynicism about the role of reason in politics generally, there would be little point of pursuing the normative project of deliberative democratic constitutionalism. It is important, next, to recall at what point in the overall argument the question about judicial versus other forms of decision-making comes in. The point here is *not* to hang the justification for an independent constitutional court on the peculiarities of judicial reason.[46] Rather, having already justified the need for an independent organ or organs that is to protect the constitutional processes that make legitimate democracy possible, the question of whether judicial or quasi-judicial

---

for the future, certain bright-line formal rules that could limit all exercises of power, see Scalia, "Common-Law Courts in a Civil-Law System: The Role of United States Federal Courts in Interpreting the Constitution and the Laws.") In answer to the objection, I defer to the empirical scholars: "Even in civil law cultures where *stare decisis* is not formally acknowledged, constitutional law almost invariably becomes case law employing precedential reasoning even when the court's opinions do not formally announce such reasoning," Martin Shapiro, "The Success of Judicial Review and Democracy," in *On Law, Politics, and Judicialization*, ed. Martin Shapiro and Alec Stone Sweet (New York: Oxford University Press, 2002), 168. To this I would only add the observation that precedential techniques are employed in most kinds of bureaucratic organizations, once their internal rule systems have become sufficiently complex and have been in use for extended periods of time, simply because such precedential techniques both greatly decrease the decision costs of information gathering and reduce decisional uncertainty concerning concrete applications of the rules.

[45] See generally Waldron, *Law and Disagreement*, and Waldron, *The Dignity of Legislation*.

[46] One way of understanding many of my arguments against various justifications for judicial review throughout this book – see, for instance, Chapters 2, 4, 6, and 7 – is as critical objections to the notion that heightened judicial competence vis-à-vis other political actors could in fact underwrite judicial review.

reasons-responsiveness is to be desired comes in once we are trying to consider how the decision making of that body is to be structured. Should it be allowed to decide through simple majority vote, or does this inappropriately import a concern for representative fairness into an institution whose members shouldn't reasonably be thought to represent various sectors or populations or interests in society? Would it be better for the institution to seek consensus in its decisions rather than extending ideological polarization into constitutional review by means of majoritarian decisions backed up with the publication of the full panoply of possible dissents?[47] The key point in deciding such issues is that we want whatever mechanisms adopted to be sensitive to the internal normativity of a legal system of rules, and responsive to the substantive normative content of the system of constitutional principles that a people has given itself over time. Surely there are alternative ways for doing this, but juridical methods – attention to argumentative force, capacity for dealing with a variety of different types of reasons, attention to precedential norms and principles, capable of adhering to the demands of the rule of law including the internal systematicity of the legal corpus, and so on – seem to be particularly appropriate to the function of constitutional review. The question then could be turned back against the Waldron objection: shorn of pressures for reelection and the demand for societal representativeness, and no longer subject to simple majoritarian decision rules, wouldn't the "dignity of legislation" look an awful lot like the "majesty of jurisprudence"?

There is, however, a different objection that might be made to the recommendation of a constitutional court, one motivated by worries about the increasing effects of the so-called judicialization of politics. There are divergent understandings of this phenomenon, and overall assessments of both its actual extent and the degree to which democratic theorists should worry about it vary considerably.[48] For my purposes here, I adopt Sweet's rather clear definition: "By *judicialization*, I mean (a) the production, by constitutional judges, of a formal normative discourse that serves to clarify, on an on-going basis, the constitutional rules governing the exercise of legislative power, and (b) the reception of these rules, and of the terms of this discourse, by legislators."[49] Although he is intent on

---

[47] John Ferejohn and Pasquale Pasquino, "Constitutional Adjudication: Lessons from Europe," *Texas Law Review* 82 (2004).

[48] An influential collection of papers developing the specific themes of judicialization is Neal Tate and Thorsten Vallinder, eds., *The Global Expansion of Judicial Power* (New York: New York University Press, 1995). Hirschl, *Towards Juristocracy* is an important empirical study of the phenomenon in Canada, Israel, New Zealand, and South Africa. Support for the thesis is drawn from both theoretical considerations and empirical cases studies in four European constitutional democracies in Sweet, *Governing with Judges*.

[49] Sweet, *Governing with Judges*, 195.

showing that traditional continental notions of the separation of powers and the supremacy of legislation have been rendered obsolete through judicial control of traditional political lawmakers (both in legislatures and regulatory agencies) – that is, on showing the effect of the dynamics collected under heading (a) – it is really the phenomenon indicated in clause (b) that appears to rankle. The worry seems to be that, to the extent that lawmakers are put under the control of judicially interpreted and elaborated constitutional provisions, ordinary political law-makers increasingly adopt the discourse, modes of reasoning, and conceptual structures elaborated by constitutional courts. I certainly cannot do justice to the welter of issues raised by this facet of judicialization. Granting that it is an observable phenomenon tightly tied to the judicial practice of constitutional review,[50] the question here is whether the use of a quasi-judicial body for constitutional review is recommended over other approaches. On the one hand, to the extent that judicialization can be seen as a way in which politically accountable officials are given strong incentives to take seriously the constitutional aspects of their actions and decisions, the phenomenon is, rather than worrisome, to be applauded. On the other hand, to the extent that free and open discussion and debate about the substantive principles and values enshrined in constitutional law is distorted by its juristic packaging – as I suggested in Chapter 6 is often evident in the U.S. context – then judicialization is a worrisome phenomenon. There may then be both beneficial and deleterious consequences of having a quasi-juridical independent organ of constitutional review. Let me note here, however, that to the extent that processes of constitutional review are dispersed, we should expect a mitigation of the juristic constraining of constitutional discussion, as reasons and arguments are introduced from other quarters and perspectives. That is, the worry about judicialization is increased to the extent that an independent constitutional court is taken not only as the preeminent determiner of the meaning and content of constitutional law but also its single, final, and authoritative source.

3. Specialization in a Concentrated Review System

Not only should the body be an independent constitutional court, but it should be specialized only in the function of constitutional review and be the exclusive court responsible for deciding constitutional complaints.

---

[50] Employing quite a different methodology than Sweet, Pickerill, *Constitutional Deliberation in Congress*, suggests a similar conclusion in the United States context: the threat of judicial review by the Supreme Court and its actual exercise both provoke and promote constitutional deliberation and debate in Congress, and this debate is significantly shaped by the judiciary's discourse and framing of the issues.

This arrangement is motivated, first, by the peculiar position of a constitutional reviewer in terms of its leading role in the development of constitutional law, a development ideally only exercised through the constituent power of the people themselves. Distributing the power of constitutional review throughout the ordinary court system obscures the peculiarity that, strictly speaking, this power belongs to none of the ordinary branches of government. Second, the inevitability of the development of constitutional law outside of formal exercises of the people's constituent power suggests that the necessary internal systematicity of the legal corpus could be promoted through the existence of a centralized quasi-judicial organ responsible for the coherence of a multitiered legal hierarchy. Third, separating the function of constitutional review from the duties of a supreme court at the apex of the ordinary appellate judiciary should reduce confusions about what it is the constitutional court does and what it is that ordinary judicial organs do. This would improve the conditions for processes of democratic deliberation and debate about constitutional issues, as there would be less confusion between constitutional issues and the technical legalisms they often come wrapped within in diffuse systems of constitutional review.[51] A specialized constitutional court in a centralized system could not pick and choose between constitutional principles and various juridical principles pertaining to appellate justiciability in grounding its decisions. By the same token, ordinary courts could not announce new or substantively elaborated principles of constitutional law in order to decide individual cases and controversies. They would be limited to those which were already established by the extant system of higher-law elaboration.[52]

One might object here that, in practice, the distinction between concentrated and diffuse systems, between the "European" and "American"

---

[51] Recall the discussions of the four examples of areas of United States constitutional jurisprudence in Chapter 6. Although it appeared that the Supreme Court's decisions managed to break free of juristic distortions in the case of some rights to individual liberty (physician-assisted suicide and sexual activities), the central moral-political issues raised by constitutional conflicts in three other areas (religious freedom, criminal punishment, and electoral redistricting) were systematically distorted by confusing those issues with technical juristic considerations arising from the intertwining of constitutional and appellate review functions.

[52] One might worry here about what ordinary courts are to do when, in the light of a new fact situation presented in a concrete case, they are faced with a hitherto unnoticed conflict between constitutional norms with *prima facie* equal hierarchical status. The standard solution is to employ a mechanism whereby ordinary courts can submit constitutional controversies to the constitutional court. I return to this later in the consideration of concrete referral modalities. At this point, it is important to notice that such a mode of referral does not entail that a formally concentrated systems of review suddenly becomes diffuse, as the ordinary court does not have the authority to further elaborate constitutional law through the resolution of constitutional conflicts.

systems, is breaking down. There are at least two forms of this objection: one coming from developmental considerations from the U.S. perspective, the other from the European considerations. From the former, one might contend that the Supreme Court of the United States has, *de facto*, become a court specialized in constitutional jurisprudence.[53] Koopmans, for instance, claims that the Supreme Court is much like a specialized court since its discretionary control over its own docket has allowed it to focus increasingly only on constitutional matters, leaving the business of ordinary appellate review to the rest of the federal appellate system.[54] Although there is some truth to this as a mitigation of the starkness of the contrast, it avoids at least two important disanalogies. First, as a matter of fact, the Court only exercises judicial review – in the strong sense of checking federal statutes for their constitutionality – in a relatively small percentage of cases a year. Even when the Court's consideration of local and state laws is added to the mix, the degree of constitutional nullification appears to be around 10 percent or less of their yearly decisions.[55]

So the Supreme Court may be more specialized in constitutional matters than other federal courts, but it is certainly not one whose docket is largely dedicated to constitutional review. Second, and perhaps more important, even when the Court is dealing with constitutional issues, there is still a basic confusion of roles in its treatment of them. As I argued

---

[53] Already in 1971, Cappelletti noted the trend of the United States Supreme Court toward becoming increasingly specialized in constitutional questions: Cappelletti, *Judicial Review in the Contemporary World*, 67.

[54] Koopmans, *Courts and Political Institutions*, 35–36 and 63.

[55] My numbers concerning the Supreme Court are arrived at in the following manner. Baum, *The Supreme Court*, 105, states that "between the mid-1980s and the late 1990s, the number of decisions with full, signed opinions dropped from 140 per term to 80. Since then the Court has maintained these lower caseloads." In the thirteen years from 1990 through 2002, thirty-four federal statutes were held unconstitutional (historical chart on page 170), and seventy-three state laws and local ordinances were held unconstitutional (historical chart on page 173), for a total of 107 nullifications, or an average of 8.23 per year. If the Court's decision rate dropped suddenly in 1990, which seems unlikely, then the percentage of constitutional nullifications would be just above 10 percent. One might think that a better measure of the Court's constitutional specialization is the percentage of their cases where there is a constitutional issue present, which for the 2001 term was 51 percent (chart on page 163). Yet even ordinary courts in a concentrated system will regularly hear cases where a constitutional issue is present, since constitutional law is a part of the law that courts must apply to ordinary cases. A relevant measure of specialization cannot be then simply that a constitutional issue was present; it would have to be something like a measure of the percentage of cases where a court not only considered and decided on the basis of constitutional considerations, but where that decision positively elaborated the system of constitutional law. Given the difficulty of gauging this – especially once one considers that a judgment of elaboration will in part turn on the observer's jurisprudential and evaluative predispositions – it is not surprising that such measures are hard to find. See also footnote 39 of Chapter 1.

in Chapter 6, this creates problems not only for the clarity of constitutional jurisprudence itself – as the relevant constitutional issues are systematically distorted by their consistent entanglement with the technical legal principles designed for the management of appellate adjudication – but also for the broader public sphere generally. Crucial constitutional decisions are routinely shrouded in technicalia of adjudicative doctrine which is impenetrable by the legal laity, and nonconstitutional but nevertheless controversial decisions are understood as invading the jurisdiction of democratic constitutional elaboration on the misplaced assumption that the Court's work product is almost exclusively constitutional. There are, then, clear benefits from the point of view of a deliberative democratic consideration of constitutional fundamentals to having the work and results of a constitutional court clearly separated from that of the ordinary appellate systems.

The distinction between concentrated and diffuse systems might seem to break down when considered from the perspective of the existing "European" systems. Captured in the phrase "the constitutionalization of the legal order," Sweet identifies the phenomenon as "the process through which (1) constitutional norms come to constitute a source of law, capable of being invoked by litigators and applied by ordinary judges to resolve legal disputes, and (2) the techniques of constitutional decision-making become an important mode of argumentation and decision-making in the [ordinary] judicial system."[56] To the extent that "constitutionalization" has occurred in concentrated systems, the distinction between the methods, work-product, and jurisdiction of specialized constitutional and ordinary courts has gradually diminished. Although this trend might mitigate the starkness of the contrast between constitutional courts and the ordinary judiciary, it does not mean that the distinction has no practical differences or has broken down altogether. Furthermore, as Sweet himself demonstrates, rates of constitutionalization are themselves sensitive to the particular structure and jurisdiction of the system of constitutional review: "Cross-national differences in the scope, pace, and intensity of constitutionalization appear to be closely tied to the existence, or non-existence, of particular modes of review."[57]

More important here, however, is the evaluative question: is constitutionalization a process that deliberative democratic constitutionalism

---

[56] Sweet, *Governing with Judges*, 114. See especially 114–26 for discussion.

[57] Ibid., 116. In particular, Sweet links accelerated and intensified processes of constitutionalization to those systems – extant in Germany and Spain – where the constitutional court employs both abstract and concrete modes of review (discussed later), and where concrete review referrals can be made both by ordinary courts, and by individual litigants (as well as by a constitutional ombudsperson in Spain).

should be worried about?[58] From the normative perspective adopted here, the changes seem, at least *prima facie*, to be beneficial rather than deleterious. For what Sweet describes as constitutionalization is, at least in part, a process of bringing coherence to the system of law by unifying disparate areas of law and various distinct codes under the constitution: "constitutional law unifies these domains into a more or less coherent legal order."[59] On the normative assumptions that a constitution structures the processes of deliberative democratic self-government, and that those processes themselves must carry the weight of legitimation for those subject to law, the requirement that disparate areas of the law must respect constitutional law is not something to be bemoaned – quite the contrary. If there is a normative worry here, one caused by the constitutional unification and structuring of ordinary legal processes, it would have to concern the extent to which ordinary adjudicative dispute resolution involves the elaboration of constitutional law, and simultaneously displaces or forecloses the possibility of nonjuridical elaborations of constitutional law. And here, Sweet's empirical work gives us a fair amount of evidence that this is not in fact the case; what we witness instead is a complex interplay between various actors across the spectrum of formal and informal public spheres who, through reflexive and mutually reinforcing processes, build up the internal complexity of constitutional law over time through participatory, more or less, "political" processes.[60]

---

[58] Here Sweet's work is not as helpful, nor is its evaluative rhetoric particularly clear. For although throughout his treatment of constitutionalization he employs a somewhat alarmist tone about the radicality of these changes, the tone is directed at (unnamed) jurisprudential theories that remain tied to traditional notions of a cognizable and legally effective distinction between the work of constitutional courts and ordinary courts, and especially to traditional conceptions of the separation of powers that stress the supremacy of the statute over other forms and sources of law and, as a corollary, tend to conceive of ordinary adjudication as a relatively mechanical and formal process through which the judge is subservient to statutory code. His critical animus, then, is directed at empirical and theoretical models of actual judicial practices; it is not evaluative in the sense I'm interested here – or at least is not intended to be so. Rather, his critical targets are those jurisprudential theories and general conceptions of distinct governmental functions that do not yet acknowledge the substantial changes in the paradigm of law and governance that accompany a constitutional structuring of the legal code.

[59] Sweet, *Governing with Judges*, 115.

[60] Using "legitimacy" in the sense of social acceptance, Sweet argues in general that "the legitimacy of constitutional review is a product of the participatory nature of constitutional adjudication," ibid. In particular, he claims that "Realists argue that the constitutional law is developed within interpretive communities, comprised not only of constitutional judges, but also of legislators, administrators, ordinary judges, scholars, and the interested public. The monopoly of the constitutional judge, presumed by the Kelsenians, is therefore rejected. The perspective is broadly congruent with my own, to the extent that realists see the building of the constitutional law as a participatory process, involving a wide range of actors, public and private," 132.

In summary, the distinction between concentrated and diffuse systems of constitutional review is neither rendered irrelevant by the practice of the Supreme Court of the United States nor vitiated by the fact that constitutional principles become important in other branches of government than the constitutional courts in concentrated systems. Hence the normative advantages of a concentrated system should not be dismissed.

4. Jurisdiction and Referral Modalities

If there is to be an independent constitutional court with exclusive powers for constitutional elaboration in a concentrated system of review, what kinds of constitutional issues should it adjudicate? This simple question raises quite difficult problems, precisely at that point of interface between the ideal and the real. On the one hand, the normative political theoretic answer to the question appears simple: the constitution is the fundamental law that makes possible legitimate democracy, and if a constitutional court is justified in such a system, then there should be no areas of constitutional law in principle off limits to a constitutional court. On the other hand, although barred ideally from constitutional elaboration, such elaboration appears inevitable, and so a constitutional court will encroach on the constituent power of the people in any jurisdictional area in which it is authorized to intervene. Furthermore, the complexities of the interactions between various actors and institutions, and the contextual particularities of their developmental tendencies make generalizations in this area particularly problematic.

The particular proceduralist conception of deliberative democratic constitutionalism developed here suggests that there are five or six core jurisdictional areas in which a constitutional court should (ideally) play the role of a protector of legitimacy-guaranteeing constitutional rules. It should be able to review, first, statutes passed by the national legislature, second, other legal norms such as regulations or directives issuing from agencies with properly delegated powers, and, if the nation has a federalist system, third, any subnational constitutions, statutes, and regulations passed by subnational authorities. These three forms of review follow directly from the notion of a constitution as structurally higher law regulating the production and content of all other law; in all cases, the court's jurisdiction is limited to the constitutionality of legal norms. Fourth, constitutionally protected fundamental right guarantees – including those to both private and public autonomy – are required for the outcomes of democratic decisional procedures between free and equal political consociates to be legitimate. Because they constitute part of the demanding conditions required for citizens to understand themselves simultaneously as the authors and subjects of legal norms, a constitutional court ought to have the ability to protect against their violations. Fifth, as part of the constitutional structure is the division of powers between various branches, authorities, and agencies in government, a court would ideally have jurisdiction over policing boundary disputes between official agencies according to established constitutional norms. Sixth, a constitutional court ought to have some significant capacities for policing the rules of the democratic process narrowly construed: that is, rules concerning voting qualifications, districting, electoral requirements, party formation, campaign financing, referenda rules, and so on. After all, it is this "participation-oriented, representation-reinforcing approach to judicial review"[61] that gets the structural independence justification for a constitutional court going in the first place. Although this is an extensive jurisdiction, it is important to remember what it leaves out, namely, control over: the internal coherence of the decisions and doctrinal developments of diverse branches of the ordinary judiciaries and of the subconstitutional legal corpus (the court is not the apex of the ordinary appellate system), review of the specific actions of officials for consistency with ordinary law and clearly established constitutional law, and, review of any subnational legal systems for internal coherence and of official actions taken according to them.

So much for ideal theory. Historically and empirically sensitive accounts of the actual workings of constitutional review in many different legal contexts will surely be able to show problematic uses by constitutional courts of these and other forms of jurisdictional authority. Furthermore, in each area, one can predict significant conflicts between a robust practice of constitutional review and political actors of various kinds. This is especially true in the two latter categories of policing political boundaries between branches and protecting the integrity of political processes – even if these functions appear from the ideal point of view to be the core of the court's jurisdiction.[62] Such potentially explosive conflicts risk undermining the social acceptance of the constitutional court, no matter what its ideal legitimacy consists in. Given the contextual particularities involved in predicting when, where, and

---

[61] Ely, *Democracy and Distrust*, 87.

[62] From the proceduralist perspective adopted here, constitutional review as carried out in the French and U.S. systems are particularly deficient. The French Constitutional Council has no discernible powers for policing political process violations. The Supreme Court of the United States, although in theory having just as much legitimate authority here as in other areas of judicial review (that is, whether one thinks the practice is legally valid or not), has developed a series of judicial doctrines intended to limit its treatment of political process violations, with the lead doctrine being that of "nonjusticiable political questions." See Chapter 6, Section B2 for more discussion. It is somewhat remarkable that a Court that takes so much time in considering its own tenuous role and location within a general scheme for a "republican form of government" is unwilling to enforce any concrete requirements concerning that republican form of government.

how such potential breakdowns of bare social and political acceptance of constitutional court jurisdiction might occur, not much can be said at a general level. Recommendations, rather, would have to be tailored to the specific history, political structures, social conditions, and legal systems of individual nation-states.

The second area of institutional design in which there are few possibilities for convincing generalization concerns the various ways that issues may be brought before such a court. There are at least three separate issues about referral modalities: whether review is possible only before (*a priori*) or also after (*a posteriori*) a normal legal rule has been adopted by political authorities, abstract versus concrete review, and who has the authority to refer issues to the court. The French system that derived historically from an insistence on the superiority of the statute, allows the Constitutional Council only to check the constitutionality of a proposed law before it is promulgated epitomizes *a priori* review. If a bill is referred to the court, and the court finds it constitutional, then it not only goes into effect, but it is also immune from subsequent review. In effect, the court acts like a third legislative chamber giving a final reading to a bill, albeit a chamber that is independent of direct political control.[63] The disadvantage of such a system is clear: in those situations in which empirically ungrounded predictions about the likely effects and consequences of the statute turn out to be wrong – in particular when the statute's actual effects come into unforeseen conflict with extant constitutional norms – there is no formal provision for controlling it once promulgated. Such considerations incline toward granting a constitutional court *a posteriori* review powers, as well as *priori* powers. Although the former can reduce error costs, the latter should not be denied, particularly where we can expect that *a priori* review will not only improve legislative deliberations but also lessen possible tensions between a constitutional court and politically accountable officials.

European Kelsen-style constitutional courts are often associated with abstract review processes, whereas American-style diffuse review systems are associated with concrete review. Concrete review of the constitutionality of a legal norm is carried out incidental to a specific judicial case or controversy between affected parties; abstract review involves the consideration of the constitutionality of a legal norm in the absence of a concrete case or controversy. With abstract review, the issue is brought

---

[63] "Constitutional courts ought to be conceptualized as specialized third legislative chambers, specialized because their legislative powers are meaningfully restricted to decisions on constitutionality," Alec Stone Sweet, "Constitutional Politics in France and Germany," in *On Law, Politics, and Judicialization*, ed. Martin Shapiro and Alec Stone Sweet (New York: Oxford University Press, 2002), 201. Originally published in 1994 as "Judging Socialist Reform: The Politics of Coordinate Construction in France and Germany," *Comparative Political Studies*, 26 (194), 443ff.

before a constitutional court by various government officials (usually but not exclusively by legislators) through formalized referral mechanisms.[64] Although the empirical sustainability of strict distinctions and exclusivistic associations is (once again) subject to serious empirical doubts,[65] the issue is also somewhat sticky from a normative point of view. In general, I find the limitation to abstract review to be preferable from the point of view of deliberative democracy. The overtly political mechanisms by which abstract review is initiated manifest, as does the concentrated and specialized system of review in general, the special and peculiar place of constitutional review in the ordinary division of powers. It is an explicit signal that what is at stake is a fundamental matter of constitutional law, and that there are reasonable disagreements about such fundamental matters that nevertheless need to be settled. Thus, rather than implying that what is at issue is a technical matter of the law where there is supposed to be some clear and correct answer dictated by the extant internal structure of the legal corpus itself – as concrete practices do – abstract review foregrounds the constitutional character of the dispute: the disagreement is about the terms of mutual consociation that are, ideally, at the disposition of the constituent powers of the people themselves. The overtly political character of initiating abstract review recognizes that the people's current political representatives have considered opinions on the matter which should be taken seriously. By contrast, concrete review, at least on the surface, depoliticizes what is manifestly a problem of deliberative politics: the ongoing democratic elaboration of the terms of citizens' legitimate consociation.

That, at least, is the ideal normative argument for a limitation to abstract review powers. Not surprisingly, the move toward the real makes the situation more ambiguous. The central complexities concern the information collection and processing capacities of constitutional courts. Recall here Michelman's apt criterion for a respect-worthy system of

---

[64] Cappelletti, *Judicial Review in the Contemporary World*, 69–77, distinguishes these as "review incidenter" and "review principaliter" on the grounds that concrete review is incidental to a case or controversy, whereas abstract review is initiated by government officials (principals) through special procedures.

[65] For the assumption by the Supreme Court of the United States of significant aspects of abstract review, see Shapiro and Sweet, "Abstract Review and Judicial Law-Making." Although not put in these terms, the extreme version of Sweet's thesis of constitutionalization can be understood as breaking down the distinction from the other side of the dichotomy: "As constitutionalization deepens, ordinary judges necessarily behave as constitutional judges – they engage in principled constitutional reasoning and resolve disputes by applying constitutional norms. And, as constitutionalization deepens, constitutional judges become more deeply involved in what is, theoretically, in the purview of the judiciary: they interpret facts in a given dispute, and they review the relationship between these facts and the legality of infraconstitutional norms." Sweet, *Governing with Judges*, 115.

constitutional elaboration: it must expose "basic-law interpreters to the full blast of sundry opinions and interest-articulations in society, including on a fair basis everyone's opinions and articulations of interests."[66] On the one hand, concrete review appears more adept at such information collection and evaluation for a number of reasons. Actual cases and controversies may reveal heretofore unforeseen consequences of constitutional norms and potential norm conflicts; the adversarial system of ordinary jurisprudence focuses extensively on the real effects of law on persons' interests; and concrete review may allow for those who are relatively politically powerless to get their interests taken into account in constitutional elaboration. Furthermore, to the extent that concrete review takes place in a diffuse system of constitutional review, there will be more courts collecting relevant information and reasons; that information and argumentation will be more richly textured and develop over longer periods of time; and diffuse systems allow time for issues to ripen and their complexities to be considered before decisive constitutional elaboration takes place. On the other hand, the collection of information and reasons in concrete review systems is contingent upon the cases and controversies actually brought before courts; that contingency may in addition lead to unrepresentative and biased presentations of the relevant issues;[67] there may be systematic distortions introduced by the significant costs of retaining legal counsel and litigating constitutional complaints, and by the role of specialized legal elites in influencing the information available to constitutional courts;[68] and it will be very difficult to disentangle the business of elaborating constitutional principles from the juridical necessities of dealing with principles of adjudicative

---

[66] Michelman, *Brennan and Democracy*, 60.

[67] I made analogous arguments about the limitations of the cases and controversies requirement for the consideration of the moral-political issues at stake in my discussion of Eisgruber's theory in Chapter 6. Hans Kelsen appeared to be getting at a similar problem when he remarked that "it is in principle only the violation of a party-interest which puts in motion the procedure of the judicial review of legislation [in the United States system]. The interest in the constitutionality of legislation is, however, a public one which does not necessarily coincide with the private interest of the parties concerned. It is a public interest which deserves protection by a special procedure in conformity with its special character." Kelsen, "Judicial Review of Legislation," 193.

[68] Consider, for instance, the informational influence wielded by the so-called Washington bar (the small group of specialized constitutional lawyers who have formed strong trust relationships with the Supreme Court) in the United States: Kevin T. McGuire, "The Supreme Court Bar and Institutional Relationships," in *The Supreme Court in American Politics: New Institutionalist Interpretations*, ed. Howard Gillman and Cornell Clayton (Lawrence: University Press of Kansas, 1999). According to McGuire's findings, the Court is strongly influenced by these few legal elites in controlling the flow of decision-relevant information, somewhat strongly in terms of setting the agenda through case selection, and perhaps only weakly in terms of decisions on the merits of the case.

procedure (as emphasized in Chapter 6). Each system, then seems to have both comparative advantages and disadvantages.

One way of incorporating the apparently superior informational capacities of a concrete review system, while retaining the normative clarity concerning the peculiarity of constitutional review as a constituent legislative power would be to allow for referrals to the specialized constitutional court by ordinary courts, when difficult constitutional issues arise incidental to the settlement of specific cases and controversies.[69] This should mitigate some of the informational deficits possible with respect to pure abstract review in a concentrated system, without subverting the normative and institutional acknowledgment that the power of constitutional review is peculiar, not simply an extension of the "emphatic province and duty of the judiciary."[70]

Three objections might be raised to this proposed scheme. First, a concrete review system might be said to better ensure that individual rights violations are protected than would an abstract review system, but I believe this is an illusion partly created by assumptions underwriting various substantialist justifications for judicial review. The idea here would be that, on the assumption that courts are to be more trusted with detecting individual rights violations than legislatures and other accountable policy makers, concrete review modalities would result in a more perfect protection of the system of rights and hence better guarantors of justice.[71] But notice that this idea assumes not only that there are single correct answers to a range of substantive questions about rights – how rights are to be exactly protected in specific cases, how various

---

[69] Simplifying, there appear to be three main referral modalities to constitutional courts: referral by political officials (abstract review), by ordinary judges (concrete), or by individual litigants (concrete). One other interesting arrangement is the authorization of a constitutional "ombudsperson" to refer individual controversies and or suspect laws to a constitutional court. As an electorally independent official, the ombud would seem, in principle, to nicely complement the structural independence of the constitutional court, while taking on some of the (often quite heavy) caseload faced by constitutional court judges who must sift through thousands of individual petitions a year in concrete review systems. Spain has such an ombud, whose office accounts for about 2.5 percent of the nonlitigant initiated constitutional complaints. During its first decade of existence (1981–90), the Spanish Constitutional Tribunal faced thirteen hundred referrals from private litigants, eighty-three referrals from ordinary courts, and 143 referrals from government officials or agencies, including six from the ombud: Sweet, *Governing with Judges*, 64–65.

[70] Again, these arguments should be considered provisional and *ceteris paribus*. I am indebted to participants at the Philosophy and Social Sciences Colloquium at the Institute of Philosophy of the Czech Academy of Sciences in Prague, the Czech Republic (May 20, 2005), particularly Frank Michelman, for forcing me to think more about the virtues of concrete review procedures from a deliberative democratic perspective.

[71] This is the substantialist argument for the United States system of judicial review put forward, for example, in Sager, *Justice in Plainclothes*.

conflicting rights are to be properly balanced or otherwise hierarchically ordered in a given case, what the best rulelike interpretations of abstract rights principles are, and so on – but also that judicial institutions are systematically superior in discovering and implementing those substantive truths than other political institutions. However, even granting the cognitivist assumptions concerning correct answers on fundamental rights questions – cognitivist assumptions that are pragmatic presuppositions of engaging in good faith argument concerning rights in the first place – the arguments I have advanced against substantialist defenses of judicial review throughout this book should caution us against faith in the superiority of judicial institutions for finding them. The core argument, recall, arises from the combination of the principle of democratic political equality, the deliberative interpretation of that principle, and recognition of the facts of modern pluralism with respect to substantive principles and values. To put it briefly, the only warrant we can have – under conditions of modern pluralism and the postmetaphysical loss of faith in objectivistic groundings of a system of political morality – that we have in fact correctly interpreted the system of rights necessary for constitutional democracy is the fallibilist assumption that our current interpretations and specifications have, so far, withstood demanding tests for democratic justification, suitably structured through the medium of constitutional law. On the assumption that abstract legal norms are legitimate – that is, have ensued from constitutionally correct democratic processes – then their proper application to concrete cases is all the warrant that we can have that the correct individual rights of citizens and subjects have been correctly protected. The objection that concrete review better protects individual rights countenanced here, however, goes further. It says that though the extant system of rights may have been upheld for individuals, the extant system is normatively deficient, and judges in individual cases are better at correctly ascertaining and ensuring those rights than others. This latter idea, I have argued throughout this book, is the exact and correct target of the paternalist objection to judicial review.

Let me be clear. I do not endorse a ban on individuals seeking to have their fundamental constitutional rights protected in specific cases and controversies. This is nothing more than ensuring to individuals that their cognizable legal claims, in light of the current state of the legal corpus, are vindicated. In cases of adjudicating ordinary legal norms, this is a function of the normal judicial system, and I see no reason why ordinary courts should be restricted only to subconstitutional legal norms. My argument does preclude, however, ordinary courts from exercising jurisdiction over the constitutional validity of extant legal norms and hence over the content of the constitutional norms themselves. It recommends, in other words, separating analytically and institutionally (as far as possible) two different functions: the assurance of individual litigants' legal rights – constitutional and otherwise – in any particular case or controversy, and, the testing of extant legal norms for constitutionality.[72]

Second, some object to abstract review for employing politically accountable officials to initiate review processes. The worry, in brief, is simply that electoral losers will routinely resort to constitutional courts to secure policy preferences that they could not get adopted through democratic means. This will be a particular danger, according to the objection, to the extent that referral to a court is relatively costless – and, the political costs of such referrals will decrease over time to the extent that constitutional review becomes a normal part of the ordinary legislative practices. It seems to me, however, that much of the force of this objection hangs on the assumption that democracy is essentially majoritarian, and when the majority can't get what it wants, then democracy is constrained or foreclosed. If we reject this aggregative conception of democracy in favor of a deliberative one, as I have urged, then we cannot simply read a diminution of democracy off of the fact that the minority party seeks to have its policy preferences implemented elsewhere than in the ordinary processes of legislation. The outcomes of majoritarian legislative process may be the result of legitimate majoritarian decision procedures adopted under time and knowledge constraints, or they may be the result of distortions in those very procedures. And it is this question of procedural legitimacy that the constitutional court is asked to adjudicate. Without a check on the constitutional legitimacy of the procedures, the fact that legislative losers have been able to prevail through a

---

[72] The conflation of these two roles under the broad term "judicial review" has, I believe done much to confuse various debates over judicial review. For instance, in his otherwise quite illuminating and wide-ranging discussion of various democratic arguments brought against judicial review, Spector consistently slides from the uncontroversial claim that individuals ought to have their constitutional rights secured by courts – because courts are impartial arbiters of disputes between individuals – to the much stronger claim that independent courts ought to have full powers of constitutional review: Spector, "Judicial Review, Rights, and Democracy." However, the impartial adjudication of an individual's claim to have her extant constitutional rights properly vindicated in a particular case is simply the fulfillment of the ordinary judicial function, one which must take into account the entire legal corpus, including extant higher-order – that is, constitutional – legal norms. But this is quite different from the review of a statute or regulation for constitutionality, which involves several competing interpretations of the same legally extant constitutional right proffered by legislators, various judges, litigants, lawyers, the public, and so on. The question of the proper institutional design of organs for constitutional review in the strict sense, is the question of how to allocate the authority to decide between the various competing positive legal schemes that are going to operationalize those constitutional rights that are already a part of the extant legal corpus. One cannot simply infer the latter authority from a defense of the need to protect impartially an individual's constitutional rights claims through judicial bodies.

nonmajoritarian procedure tells us little about the democratic pedigree or character of the decision.

A third objection to this proposal is that, by opening the door to some forms of concrete review on referral from ordinary courts, this will open the floodgates to constitutional elaboration diffused throughout the judicial system. Although Sweet's analyses suggest that this inevitably happens – as it is part of the wider process he calls the "constitutionalization" of ordinary law – I have the impression that the account fails to adequately distinguish two senses of constitutionalization.[73] On the one hand, there is the general subservience of ordinary judiciaries to the constitutional law, above and beyond their traditional specialized areas of the legal code – what he refers to as the unification of disparate areas of the law under a higher-order constitutional scheme – and, on the other, the positive production of constitutional norms by ordinary courts. If the judiciary has the power to refer legal norms to a constitutional court when there is a controversy incidental to the case before them, this means that they are part of a broader institutional system involved with the elaboration of constitutional law, but it does not imply that they have a leading or primary role in its actual elaboration. At any rate, when Sweet does produce evidence to support the stronger sense of constitutionalization, the phenomenon does not appear inevitably bound to the unifying effects of constitutional law, but to the specifically supervisory role some constitutional courts have taken in overseeing the various balancing, reasonability, and proportionality tests they have delegated to lower courts.[74] Even if not inevitable, however, the

---

[73] See especially Sweet, *Governing with Judges*, 114–26.

[74] Sweet's leading example here is the German jurisprudence that has grown up around the interaction of free speech rights and private law, starting with the landmark 1958 case called *Lüth* (*BverfGE* 1958, volume 8, page 51). In general, with respect to fundamental individual rights, the German Federal Constitutional Court has not only developed a doctrinal set of balancing and proportionality tests for determining whether a statute's infringement on a constitutionally protected right is significant enough to invalidate all or a portion of that statute but, more important, it also has required ordinary courts to apply these balancing tests in individual cases. It is precisely this latter move that leads to the elaboration, by ordinary courts, of constitutional law, as they are thereby empowered (and required) to operate as quasi-constitutional courts. To this extent, the officially "concentrated" system of review in Germany has become effectively diffuse, and by means of a set of judicially developed and imposed interpretive doctrines. Habermas's overwhelming worry about the use of balancing tests and other judicial doctrines of interpretation, to the detriment of questions of institutional design, is then perhaps unsurprising (see Chapter 7, Section B4). Although Sweet's use of the German example supports the stronger sense of constitutionalization whereby ordinary courts are induced to act like constitutional courts, his Italian and Spanish examples support only the weaker sense that ordinary courts find that the decisions of a constitutional court are binding on them. Given the history of his scholarship, his evidence in the French case is the most extensive, and does support the strong sense of constitutionalization. Yet the need for

actual diffusion of constitutional rule-making powers throughout the judiciary is worrisome enough to take measures ensuring that a concentrated system of constitutional review does not practically develop into a diffuse system simply through the introduction of concrete referral mechanism and the adoption of judicial doctrines that turn ordinary courts into constitutional elaborators.

5. Assessment

If we now return to the six assessment values I elucidated at the end of Section A, they should be able to generate an overview summary of the potential advantages and disadvantages of my proposal for a specialized, independent court in a concentrated system of constitutional review. The proposal can be productively assessed by comparing it to two other (ideal-typical) arrangements: a system of constitutional review diffused throughout the ordinary judiciary with powers for review effectively limited only by the development of jurisprudential doctrine, and a system in which the only checks for constitutionality are internal to each of the various branches of government effectively yielding a system of pure coordinate construction. For the sake of convenience in this discussion I will label these the "concentrated," "diffuse," and "coordinate" systems respectively. Turning first to the value of systematicity, the concentrated and diffuse systems would seem to perform equally well at ensuring the internal coherence of the legal corpus as a whole, while the coordinate system might fare a bit worse than those. One way to think about the degree of systematicity is to consider the proportional number and persistence over time of conflicts between laws, whether between lower-order and higher-order legal norms or between those at the same level. Assuming that all three systems have, on the one hand, functioning hierarchical court systems that effectively reduce conflicts of ordinary legal norms and thus contribute to systematicity and, on the other, effective procedures in the other branches to ensure that newly enacted legal norms are consistent with the extant legal corpus, the only remaining difference concerns those situations in which there are conflicts between different branches's varied specifications of well-established constitutional norms or principles. In those cases, the systems with judicial review would seem to fare a bit better, as they delegate to the constitutional court or courts the power to resolve conflicts of law concerning

---

many different lower courts to take on the tasks and techniques of constitutional elaboration is not, in this case, due to an ordinary court referral mechanism – after all, there is no formal concrete review at all in France. It seems, rather, to be a result of the peculiar arrangement of having a constitutional court limited not only to abstract review but also only to the *a priori* review of statutes and other legal norms.

constitutional provisions. The coordinate system, by contrast, must live with the conflict between the varying constitutional constructions until such a time as the various branches come into concord of their own accord. This difference should not be overplayed, however, as it is to be expected that various forms of settled practices and shared under-standings will mitigate the frequency and intensity of such conflicts.

It might seem that the differences between the constitutional review systems and the coordinate one concerning systematicity are really due to disparities in the extent to which the settlement function can be per-formed with respect to constitutional law. After all, the slightly decreased systematicity in the coordinate system appears entirely due to the lack of any authoritative finality with respect to constitutional law: each branch is authoritative only over its own constitutional interpretations. This is not quite correct, however, as can be seen once we compare the diffuse and the concentrated systems. Ideally the concentrated system would do better on settlement than the coordinate, but perhaps surprisingly, it would also seem to settle issues better than the diffuse system. For in a diffuse system, constitutional conflicts are "settled" only for specific cases and controversies before particular courts. Yet different courts across the national judiciary will settle similar controversies differently and by invoking different bits of controlling law and doctrine, resulting in the very real and typical situation that, in fact, the area of constitutional law is quite unsettled from the point of view of the nation as a whole. By con-trast, in a concentrated system, the state of constitutional law is clearly settled by one authoritative court. None of these points however, which rest on an ideal-typical contrast between the three systems, comes to terms, further, with the actual possibility of constitutional unsettlement through political reactions against disfavored rulings of a constitutional court or courts. From this perspective, it may be the case that the coor-dinate system actually turns out to perform better on the settlement scale, as it may be less prone to setting off high-stakes, high-profile con-frontations between the political branches and the judiciary over com-peting visions of the proper way to legally operationalize constitutional principles. At any rate, reliable judgments here must be based on more than speculation and ideal-typical analyses: solid empirical data, suitably controlled to focus on the structural differences between concentrated, diffuse, and coordinate constructions systems of judicial review would be necessary.[75]

---

[75] These comparative judgments concerning settlement and systematicity, then, must be understood as quite tentative, especially in the absence of serious empirical support. At the very least, judgments here must be made from a comparative perspective, rather than attending only to the particularities of one legal system. It may be that "without a written constitution as a stabilizing force, there is a risk that too many issues needing at least

Turning to the value of independence, it should not be surprising that the concentrated system has significant advantages over the coordinate system with respect to its independence from the politically accountable branches (given appropriate selection and retention mechanisms as discussed earlier). The comparison with the diffuse system is not as clear. It may appear equally independent when considering only its structural location vis-à-vis the other branches, but a diffuse system may improve independence to the extent that there are many more sites throughout the entire judiciary that could ensure the procedural legitimacy of democratic processes. Furthermore, a diffuse system may perform more independently because private litigants, and not politically accountable officials, are the central initiators of constitutional complaints. One problem of independence that constitutional courts in both systems seem vulnerable to arises from the fact that they employ quasi-juridical procedures, thus building in access asymmetries based on the technical legal competence and knowledge needed to effectively contest constitutional issues before them. This is the problem I earlier formulated, on the analogue to regulatory capture, as the capture of constitutional courts by legal elites. Finally, it is important to remember that constitutional courts in either concentrated or diffuse systems are rightly not, in fact, wholly apolitical institutions – as indicated by the political nature of the various appointments processes. Once composed, however, they are designed to function relatively independently of the political branches, whatever the origins of their membership. In sum, a concentrated system fares much better on the independence scale than a coordinate system, but perhaps not quite as well as a diffuse system.

Concentrated constitutional courts seem to me to be a significant improvement over both coordinate and diffuse systems with respect to the assessment value of empowerment. In a coordinate system, by definition, there is no organ sufficiently empowered to intervene in ordinary political processes that violate constitutional norms. Although the courts in a diffuse system are sufficiently empowered to intervene, given the confusion between their constitutional and ordinary jurisdictional powers, there may well be a tendency for sufficient empowerment to turn into

---

intermediate term settlement will remain excessively uncertain," Alexander and Schauer, "On Extrajudicial Constitutional Interpretation," 1376, but it also may be that, in fact, such systems without a written constitution actually display *greater* settlement than systems with both a written constitution and authorized judicial finality with respect to its interpretation. Is it really true that, for instance, the British legal system has historically been significantly unsettled with respect to constitutional norms? And is its settlement value increasing now that the Human Rights Act of 1998 has brought the British system closer to a diffuse system of judicial review? The questions cannot be "settled" at the level of abstract argument and in the absence of any *comparative* considerations concerning different legal systems as Alexander and Schauer attempt to do.

overempowerment.[76] Even more important, the specificity of a specialized constitutional court means that it may be more relevantly empowered than the courts in a diffuse system. By giving the function of constitutional review an explicit institutional place in the political system, the court need not pretend to find a formalistic and specifically juridical doctrine for its decisions, nor need it await a concrete case presenting the issue in just the right way to address evident constitutional violations. Constitutional courts are hybrid legal-political institutions and, to the extent that the diffuse system attempts to assimilate them entirely to a formalistic model of legal adjudication, courts may be unwilling to intervene precisely where they are most needed: in policing the boundaries between the various political agencies, and especially in ensuring the constitutionality of democratic processes narrowly construed.[77]

The discussion of relevant empowerment thus, in this case, leads directly to jurisdictional issues. Constitutional courts of both stripes will perform better than coordinate systems with respect to the constitutionality of national statues, fundamental rights guarantees, interbranch border disputes, and the rules of the democratic process, precisely because courts in a coordinate system would not have jurisdiction over such issues. They are not sufficiently empowered because of jurisdictional constraints. All three systems, however, might perform equally well with respect to the constitutional review of other nonstatutory national legal norms (such as those ensuing from administrative agencies), and subnational legal norms of all types.[78] Concentrated systems, I would think,

---

[76] This is one way of formulating the worry that drives many jurisprudential debates in the United States, as scholars and judges seek to find appropriate methods of constitutional interpretation that will sufficiently but only relevantly empower the courts, and the Supreme Court in particular. It seems unlikely that a particular recommended interpretive methodology, however, will make a significant empirical difference, because debates over the correctness of various interpretive approaches will simply add a meta-legal layer of uncertainty to the significant legal uncertainty already encountered in the domain of constitutional law. Said another way, institutional prospects for limiting overempowerment problems seem more promising than interpretive strategies for self-limitation, however warranted the latter might be in specific contexts.

[77] Perhaps this concern is stimulated more by peculiarities of the United States system, than by the structural differences between concentrated and diffuse systems, in particular by the peculiar reticence of American courts to police even the most egregious inequalities in the basic electoral system, a reticence fostered by the self-imposed juridical doctrine of "nonjusticiable political questions." By contrast, American appellate courts, especially the Supreme Court, seem to have no compunctions about extensive judicial elaboration of the constitution with respect to individual private autonomy rights. This seems to me to get things the wrong way around.

[78] For instance, what classically counts as "judicial review" in the Untied Kingdom is precisely such review of nonstatutory law at the national level, and manifold forms of law at subnational level, all of course in the light of the supremacy of statutes enacted by Parliament. English courts have been particularly effective in policing the legality of

should perform better than diffuse systems as the former's jurisdiction will be both properly restricted and properly expanded. A specialized constitutional court is, first and foremost, only a *constitutional* court and its jurisdictional reach will, as it were, be constitutionally mandated to respect that restriction. But, unlike courts in a diffuse system, a concentrated court could robustly exercise its powers to guard all of the constitution, rather than doctrinally slicing it up into pieces justiciable and nonjusticiable. With respect to the assessment value of proper jurisdiction, then, a concentrated system promises notable improvements over a diffuse one, and quite significant improvement over a coordinate system,

Both systems of judicial review, however, trade off their advantages for settlement, independence, empowerment, and jurisdiction for a significant decrease in their sensitivity to the full blast of constitutionally relevant reasons and information, when compared with a coordinate system. Relying as it does on manifold sites for the collection of reasons and information, rather than being limited to the relatively meager resources and capabilities of the judiciary alone, a coordinate system is much more likely to collect considerations from a wide diversity of society's members and sectors. Not only is the governmental body most specialized for such sensitivity involved – the representative legislature – but all of the other organs of government also serve as "sluice gates" through which the opinions, arguments, and interests expressed in the broad informal public sphere can be filtered and worked up into the system of constitutional elaboration. When we turn to comparing the two judicial review systems, it appears that the diffuse system will be somewhat better off than a concentrated system. Although a diffuse system may systematically distort the constitutionally relevant deliberative inputs it receives because of the cases and controversies restriction and the requirement for expert legal representation of the private interests involved, this deficit will be offset by the numerous cases that can be heard on similar issues throughout the judiciary. Recall that the informational restrictions on a concentrated system were part of the reason I advocated a limited role for concrete review, in the form of judicial referrals to the constitutional court. Nevertheless, even this remedial mechanism seems inadequate to make up the difference from the expanded sensitivity of a

---

specific administrative actions and the details of regulatory schemes. Herbert M. Kritzer, "Courts, Justice, and Politics in England," in *Courts, Law, and Politics in Comparative Perspective*, ed. Herbert Jacob et al. (New Haven, CT: Yale University Press, 1996). Clearly this traditional conception of judicial review within a system of Parliamentary sovereignty is breaking down with the incorporation of European human rights law, by statute, into British law. An intriguing consideration of this change can be found in Stephen Gardbaum, "The New Commonwealth Model of Constitutionalism," *American Journal of Comparative Law* 49, no. 4 (2001).

diffuse system. In sum, with respect to the value of sensitivity, the concentrated system will be the worst of the three here, with a diffuse systems doing perhaps a bit better, and a coordinate system quite significantly outperforming both.

Finally, I should add that if we restrict our vision only to the two options of constitutional courts or no such courts, it would appear that the trade-offs in designing an overall constitutional review and elaboration system are rather binary: either independence and relevant empowerment or sensitivity; either legal but unresponsive elaboration or democratic but anarchic elaboration. Thus the age-old dichotomous debate between the virtues of the rule of law versus those of democracy seem simply reformulated. Only by looking at other institutional options for carrying the functions of constitutional review can we see that the trade-offs faced are not simple dichotomies in a zero-sum game. By considering how we might institutionally structure constitutional deliberation and decisional dispersal both horizontally across the branches of national government and vertically through connections between informal and formal public spheres, I contend, these traditional binaries can be seen as the false dichotomies they are.

9

The Institutions of Constitutional Review II

Horizontal Dispersal and Vertical Empowerment

This chapter continues the institutional design proposals started in the previous, turning to four different types of modification in the system of constitutional review. I consider, in turn, the establishment of self-review panels in the legislative and executive branches of national governments (A), various mechanisms for interbranch debate and decisional dispersal concerning constitutional elaboration (B), easing constitutional amendability requirements in overly obdurate systems (C), and finally establishing civic constitutional fora as replacements for traditional amendment procedures (D). In each case, the proposals are motivated by the problems of judicial review I identified in the previous chapter, and their design is oriented to the fullest realization of the six assessment values I specified there. I assume throughout that some form of judicial review is extant in the political system, and for the most part I assume the concentrated system with specialized constitutional courts argued for there. Where something important hangs on the difference between a concentrated and diffuse system of constitutional courts for the design of these other mechanisms for constitutional elaboration, I take that up in the discussion.

Let me turn now to some simpler proposals that could help to mitigate the various kinds of structural sensitivity deficits and potential jurisdictional and empowerment pathologies of constitutional courts. Recall that the basic idea here is to disperse the inevitable processes of constitutional elaboration both horizontally across the various organs of government and vertically throughout the various levels of the formal and informal public spheres. The next two proposals of self-review panels and interbranch constitutional dialogue can both be thought of in terms of the former horizontal dispersal; the final two of easing amendability requirements and institutionalizing civic constitutional fora can be thought of in terms of vertical dispersal. As I will argue, only the vertical dispersion solutions really overcome the standard trade-offs witnessed in other mechanisms between the values of independence and sensitivity and thereby promise to actually realize the high ideals of deliberative democratic constitutionalism.

A.   SELF-REVIEW PANELS IN THE LEGISLATURE AND REGULATORY AGENCIES

As a first step in horizontal dispersion, I recommend formalized procedures for the official rule-making branches of government to institutionalize their own constitutional review. The idea is to establish panels in both the legislative and the executive branches that would have responsibility for considering the constitutionality of proposed statutes and regulations before they are formally enacted into law, and resubmitting them for revision should they be found deficient.[1] The supporting arguments here are fourfold. First, from an ideal point of view, the proposal is recommended from the simple fact that all government officials have preeminent duties to uphold, support, and further the constitution and its inherent rules and principles. As entrenched, higher-order law, the constitution binds all government officials equally.[2] Furthermore, as an ongoing project of self-government, the practice of constitutionalism is to be carried by the constituent power of the people and, because the legislative and executive branches are official representatives of the people,

---

[1] Other institutional variations are possible. In New Zealand, for example, the Attorney-General has the explicit duty of screening legislative bills for possible conflicts with a bill of rights, and bringing these to the attention of the legislature before passage. This way of institutionalizing review processes, by introducing interbranch checks, may strengthen the *a priori* review process along the dimension of political independence.

[2] This is essentially the same normative idea that has undergirded proposals in the United States for so-called coordinate construction of the constitution. The idea stretches at least as far back as the antifederalist arguments against judicial powers of review that would render final and supreme "constructions" of constitutional meaning. See Brutus's letters XI through XV: Brutus, "Letters of 'Brutus'," in *The Federalist with Letters of "Brutus,"* ed. Terence Ball (New York: Cambridge University Press, 2003), 501–29, especially 507–08 and 527–9. Allied arguments for coordinate construction have repeatedly arisen in American political history, advanced by (among others) Thomas Jefferson, Andrew Jackson, Abraham Lincoln, Franklin Roosevelt, and Richard Nixon. They are also now particularly resurgent in United States legal scholarship: Kramer, *The People Themselves*, Michael Stokes Paulsen, "The Irrepressible Myth of *Marbury*," *Michigan Law Review* 101 (2003), Terri Jennings Peretti, *In Defense of a Political Court* (Princeton, NJ: Princeton University Press, 1999), Thomas, "Recovering the Political Constitution: The Madisonian Vision", Tushnet, *Taking the Constitution Away from the Courts*, Whittington, *Constitutional Construction: Divided Powers and Constitutional Meaning.* The overly stringent argument for the pre-eminence of constitutional "settlement" that I criticized in Chapter 8, Section A7 is largely directed against these newly resurgent arguments for coordinate construction in the United States context: Alexander and Schauer, "On Extrajudicial Constitutional Interpretation."

those branches ought to play a central role in whatever constitutional elaboration happens outside of formal procedures for constitutional opinion and will-formation. Third, given the greater reason and information collecting capacities of the larger and more representative branches of government, some of the sensitivity deficits of a constitutional court might be addressed by the proposal. Finally, as a practical matter, I believe that such self-review panels should positively influence the character and quality of constitutionally relevant debate, discussion, and decision making in the various branches. By formally connecting official decision-making processes with an awareness of constitutional issues, it is to be hoped that politically accountable officials can no longer off-load onto the judiciary, as it were, the difficult work of squaring policy proposals with the demands of constitutionality.[3] By making such officials responsible for the constitutional dimensions of their duties, such panels might be able to reduce the prevalence of a phenomenon apparent where an unaccountable court is taken as not only the final but also as the only arbiter of the meaning and import of constitutional provisions. For, when constitutional review is entirely entrusted to the judiciary, it appears that politically accountable officials routinely take advantage of what might be called a "double demagoguery" credit: enacting laws (statutory or regulatory) that are known to be unconstitutional but nevertheless sound appealing in a sound-bite polemic (credit one), and then attacking a constitutional court as un- and antidemocratic when the law is predictably struck down (credit two). The point of such panels, then, is to bring the relevance and specific shape of constitutional rules and principles into ordinary processes of legislative and regulatory lawmaking.

Assessment of this proposal according to the six values can proceed by thinking of the contrasting situation, where the are no such internal constitutional self-review panels (but there are independent constitutional courts). Such self-review panels should improve somewhat the internal systematicity of the legal corpus, since it can be expected that the work of the panels will be in part oriented toward possible conflicts between existing law and the pending law under consideration. This would reduce, to some extent, the burden on ordinary and constitutional courts of detecting and correcting for inconsistencies. I would expect no significant effect one way or another on the scale of settlement, as the panels are not conceived of as having final or dispositive control over the constitutionality of the legal norms they find constitutionally acceptable. As panels internal to the politically accountable branches, they will not have the kind of independence desired for guaranteeing procedural correctness, and this

---

[3] See the classic empirical study of this phenomenon in the United States: Mark A. Graber, "The Nonmajoritarian Difficulty: Legislative Deference to the Judiciary," *Studies in American Political Development* 7 (1993).

is a central reason for denying them final and dispositive control over the constitutionality of the decisions of the relevant branch.[4] This also means that, although they would be relevantly empowered to intervene in decision-making processes that ensue in unconstitutional results, their jurisdiction will not be able to extend to the full gamut of the six areas that a constitutional court would ideally handle. A legislative self-review panel would review statutes but not regulations; an executive panel the contrary. Although there might be relevant opinions concerning laws ensuing from other national branches, subnational laws, and boundary disputes between the national branches, neither type of self-review panel could have control over such areas. I see no reason, however, why such panels would not have the capacity to consider seriously fundamental constitutional rights, and in particular how they are to be specified, secured, and operationalized through concrete legal schemes. After all, it is precisely here that we can expect a significant degree of reasonable disagreement among citizens, such that the epistemic benefits of wide exposure to those disagreements is directly relevant to the legitimacy of the final decision. Such panels would, however, be poorly located structurally to adequately police the rules of the democratic process narrowly construed. As to the last assessment value of sensitivity, it would seem that given both the heightened electoral accountability and the vastly superior reason and information collection capabilities and resources of the legislative and executive branches in comparison with a constitutional court or courts, such self-review panels would be quite a bit more sensitive to constitutionally relevant opinions, arguments, and information encountered throughout the diverse sectors of society.

One more important point. It is clear that, even in the absence of such panels, constitutional politics and positive constitutional elaboration do occur in the ordinary course of legislative and regulatory lawmaking. Blinded by a one-sided focus on the supremacy and finality of constitutional court decisions, there is sometimes a tendency, especially in legal scholarship, to identify the production of constitutional law entirely with the juridical production of decisions and accompanying doctrine.[5] This identification makes it quite hard to explain how it is, for instance, that there could be effectively entrenched legal rules that were, nevertheless,

---

[4] This also points to the basic problem of strict schemes of coordinate construction. To the extent that a political branch has final authority over its own procedures for lawmaking, the worries about its ability for systematically distorting democratic processes are greatly magnified. As a concrete example, consider the practical upshot of allowing the current legislative majority to have control over the rules for drawing legislative districts: those currently in power can effectively render their own positions immune to electoral vulnerability.

[5] Recall the discussion of the pathological concepts of constitutionalism often employed in the United States in Chapter 1, Section B3.

enacted through ordinary legislative channels. In the United States, for instance, signal achievements of the democratic practice of constitutionalism include the legislative extension of equal protection and antidiscrimination principles to African Americans, women, and handicapped persons,[6] although none of these elaborations of constitutional principles, entrenched above the level of ordinary statutory law, are the exclusive products of juridical rule-making. Self-review panels are a way of formalizing the constitutional responsibilities of politically accountable officials, and thereby hopefully improving the character, quality, and outcomes of already existing practices of democratic constitutional elaboration.

B. MECHANISMS FOR INTERBRANCH DEBATE AND DECISIONAL DISPERSAL

The next proposal, or rather type of proposal, is to structure interbranch debate concerning proposed constitutional elaborations that occur outside of formal amendment modalities, in part by injecting time for interbranch deliberations on issues before full settlement and in part by dispersing constitutional decisional powers beyond the constitutional court alone.[7] The kinds of institutional arrangements I have in mind here include devices such as the Canadian "notwithstanding" clause, requirements for legislative specification and elaboration of constitutional provisions, and various jurisprudential doctrines that cede significant decisional room to politically accountable officials in specified constitutional areas.

As discussed in Chapter 4, the Canadian constitution scheme allows the legislative branch to pass a statute that would be otherwise be in conflict

---

[6] I am thinking here especially of the signal Civil Rights Act of 1964, which, among other things, prohibited discrimination in many areas of economic and social life on the basis of race, religion, national origin, and sex. Also important are the later extensions of Title VII of that act to include government employers; Title IX of the Education Amendments Act of 1972 concerning sex discrimination in educational institutions; the Americans with Disabilities Act of 1990; and numerous regulations both establishing new agencies for oversight of antidiscrimination compliance and providing further substantive content to the various acts and provisions.

[7] Pickerill, *Constitutional Deliberation in Congress*, and Jeffrey K. Tullis, "Deliberation between Institutions," in *Debating Deliberative Democracy*, ed. James S. Fishkin and Peter Laslett (Malden, MA: Blackwell, 2003), give important empirical evidence that such processes of interbranch debate on constitutional essentials exist in the U.S. context. While Pickerill focuses on interbranch debates about principles of federalism, Tullis gives a focused case study of a particular type of back-and-forth between the executive and the legislature practiced in the late eighteenth and nineteenth centuries. I think there are significant benefits to be achieved by formalizing such processes. See Gardbaum, "The New Commonwealth Model of Constitutionalism," 719–39, for an illuminating discussion of three different ways of institutionalizing interbranch debates concerning individual rights in Canada, New Zealand, and the United Kingdom.

with specific judicial decisions concerning the requirements of fundamental freedoms, legal rights, and equality rights, though not concerning democratic rights and mobility rights. Such an exceptional act by the legislature in passing a law "notwithstanding" existing judicial specifications of rights becomes inoperative after five years unless legislatively restated (for yet another five years).[8] In principle, such mechanisms are intended to allow the legislature to temporarily block the final interpretive judgments of the constitutional court, and thereby have sufficient time for initiating and carrying out a formal amendment process that would overrule the court's interpretation. Although, then, the mechanism is in principle consistent with the court's interpretive finality (and with the people's supreme constitutional powers), in practice the mechanism would seem to decrease the court's interpretive finality, ceding some significant powers of constitutional-decision making to the political branches. More important, from a normative point of view, such a mechanism can play a positively catalytic role in spurring further democratic debate and discussion about the precise meaning and import of the constitutional terms of mutual consociation. This is especially important on questions of fundamental individual rights where their precise specification, as well as the exact terms of their legal interactions with other rights provisions, are both open to persistent, reasonable disagreement amongst citizens.[9] The exceptional nature of such a mechanism, when invoked, should be expected to signal to the broader informal public spheres that significant issues of fundamental law are at stake, hopefully catalyzing there as well-focused consideration and debate on the constitutional terms of consociation. In summary then, such mechanisms would ideally promote both the participatory and deliberative values of deliberative democratic constitutionalism.[10]

---

[8] Section 33 of the Canadian Charter of Rights and Freedoms. It is a bit odd that, in phrasing the notwithstanding clause, the Charter makes a distressing semantic elision between the actual content of the Charter and judicial decisions concerning its meaning. Though the provision is specifically intended to give the legislature a formal response mechanism to constitutional court rulings, the court is nowhere mentioned: "33. (1) Parliament or the legislature of a province may expressly declare in an Act of Parliament or of the legislature, as the case may be, that the Act or a provision thereof shall operate notwithstanding a provision included in section 2 or sections 7 to 15 of this Charter."

[9] Recall that the clause exempts democratic and mobility rights from the mechanism, recognizing that there needs to be a politically independent body in order to adequately protect the very processes of political representation. The provision, in other words, seems to precisely embody a proceduralist conception of the place of independent constitutional courts, not a substantialist one.

[10] Perhaps such mechanisms for generating interbranch dialogue are also recommended in those cases in which we have reason to think that both legislative and judicial processes of constitutional specification may have simultaneous defects on a particular issue: for instance, where we have reason to think that the information gathering capacities of the

The second kind of mechanism allocating constitutional elaboration powers horizontally across the branches of government I have in mind are explicit clauses in a constitutional provision for legislative elaboration and specification of the particular legal means that are to be used to put the provision into force.[11] Such requirements for legislative specification are a way of explicitly acknowledging that constitutional provisions are neither self-evidently self-interpreting, nor legally operationalizable without tailoring less abstract legal norms to contextually specific cultural, historic, social, and economic conditions. They also acknowledge that the ongoing democratic character of constitutional elaboration, outside of formal amendment procedures, is a power of self-government to be carried out through the closest approximation to a constituent assembly: the people's elected representatives. Another way of thinking of this point is to consider possible reasons one might want to constitutionally enact such provisions in the first place. There may well exist, at the point of constitutional enactment, clear and well-established agreement on what abstract principles a people wants enshrined in its constitution. It may, nevertheless, be helpful in various ways both to forestall specific elaboration to the future and to make the content of such elaborations subject to easier change than the abstract principles of the provision themselves. The original agreement on a constitutional provision may be the result of an undertheorized agreement, that is, an agreement on an abstract textual formula over disagreement about appropriate specifications or grounding reasons.[12] Drafters and ratifiers may have insufficient information to comprehend how concrete applications might work. There may be some expected benefits from experimenting with different legal regimes for the realization of the provisions' principles. There

---

legislature are superior to those of the courts, but we also have worries about normal political pressures closing out relevant groups or cutting off the channels of change.

[11] Most European constitutions contain not only individual rights provisions but also positive duties provisions that operate in effect as commands for constitutional elaboration by legislatures and regulatory agencies. Not only do citizens have constitutionally specified duties (say, to military service) but, central for the considerations here, so do states (say, to provide public education or protect the environment): for a clear chart comparing the rights and duties of various parties in the French, German, Italian, and Spanish constitutional systems, see Sweet, *Governing with Judges*, 42–43. Of the twelve amendments to the Constitution of the United States before the Civil War in the second half of the nineteenth century, none contained any provisions for legislative specification. Of the fifteen post–Civil War amendments, eight contain explicit provisions that (with minor syntactical variations) "Congress shall have power to enforce this article by appropriate legislation." It seems then that American amendment practices after the Civil War, and post–World War II European constitutional settlements are fully in line with the proposal put forward here. The situation is much more ambiguous, however, once one includes jurisprudence in the overall picture of constitutional practice.

[12] See for instance Sunstein, *Designing Democracy: What Constitutions Do*, 49–66.

might be a reasonable expectation that the relevant social and political conditions will continue to change over time in such a way that it would be unwise to specify at the time of ratification determinate solutions for all future situations.[13]

Of course, there are real questions concerning the extent to which a constitutional court might in fact allow legislatures to actively employ these provisions and whether a legislature might actually exercise (and exercise appropriately) such allocated powers, but these are not problems generated by the structure of the proposal, but by the standard political problem of getting any branch of government to properly carry out its constitutionally allocated powers.[14] The language of the provisions should, at any rate, go some way toward limiting encroachments on such delegated legislative powers and toward encouraging legislatures to use them appropriately.

The third kind of interbranch dialogue and decisional dispersal mechanisms are various doctrines imposed on a constitutional court, either through explicit constitutional provision or by the court's own jurisprudence, that would require the court to defer certain kinds of judgments to the more politically accountable branches. Examples here include the German constitutional court's practice of ruling some laws "not compatible" with the constitution rather than strictly "unconstitutional," thereby permitting the law to remain in effect for some period of time with the understanding that it will be suitably revised by the legislature; the Italian constitutional court's similar practice of declaring that a law will be struck down in the future if not properly changed by the legislature in the meantime; the U.S. judicial doctrine of constitutional issues that pose "nonjusticiable political questions"; and, the widespread constitutional court practice of selectively amputating, as it were, offending sections of a statute rather than annulling the law as a whole. Mention also should be made here of the recently inaugurated arrangements in New Zealand and the United Kingdom that, on the one hand, require courts to interpret laws in accordance with fundamental rights

---

[13] Two examples that might make these points vivid include free speech and intellectual property regimes. In both cases, all four reasons might be adduced for legislative specification provisions: there are competing justifications and understandings of free speech and property principles under wide agreement on their basic value and significance, insufficient information at ratification might be caused by the large variety of contexts in which free speech and intellectual property principles are relevant, such information deficits are virtually guaranteed by future transformations of relevant socioeconomic, technological, and political conditions, and so there may well be strong benefits accruing from a more experimental approach to various specification regimes.

[14] The overall historical record of the United States Supreme Court, especially with regard to Section 5 of the Fourteenth Amendment, should give one serious pause here. For a striking recent example, see *City of Boerne v. Flores*, 521 U.S. 507 (1997).

laws but, on the other, do not allow such courts the power to nullify or significantly rewrite ordinary laws, ceding to legislatures final authority for significant rewriting of ordinary laws and the elaboration of the system of fundamental rights.[15] Constitutional law scholars can no doubt point to many other such strategies. Both the actual effectiveness and the normative worth of such strategies in any particular national context will, of course, depend on the content of the particular doctrines, the individual history, traditions, and current membership of the court, and the relative power and assertiveness of the various branches. At any rate, they do promise some degree of interbranch debate and decisional diffusion of constitutional elaboration processes.

Given the diversity of mechanisms canvassed here, and their particular interactions with specific national cultures, political arrangements, and legal systems, the possibilities for reliable general assessments are limited. Nevertheless, to the extent that each type of proposal aims at stimulating interbranch discussion and dispersing decisional authority, some general tendencies are observable when comparing systems with such arrangements against ones without. To begin, the proposals would appear to have no significant effect with respect to the internal systematicity of the legal

---

[15] The scheme inaugurated by the New Zealand Bill of Rights Act of 1990 is particularly interesting in this regard. Effectively, this subconstitutional ordinary statute established a set of individual fundamental rights that do not have their effect through their status as higher-law vis-à-vis ordinary law. Quite the contrary: Section 4 of the Act specifically establishes that it does not function to override and invalidate conflicting laws, and bars courts from so ruling. What the Act does do in Section 6, however, is establish a judicial duty to attempt to construe statutes in accordance with the rights listed. The Act, then, operates as a set of (legislatively mandated) substantive interpretive canons for the judiciary. See the discussion at Gardbaum, "The New Commonwealth Model of Constitutionalism," 727–32. Section 3 of the newly inaugurated Human Rights Act of 1998 in the United Kingdom – yet another statutory elaboration of a constitutional system – also requires judges to construct ordinary laws, as far as possible, in accordance with the provisions of the European Convention of Human Rights: Gardbaum, "The New Commonwealth Model of Constitutionalism," 732–9. What is particularly interesting about the Untied Kingdom scheme is what happens when such an accommodating construction of a law cannot be achieved, when, that is, the law is facially incompatible with the ECHR. At that point, the relevant higher court must formally declare to Parliament that the law is incompatible (Section 4), though that declaration has no nullifying force. The scheme thus analytically and institutionally separates the function of detecting conflicts – placed in the appellate judiciary – from the function of correcting the problem – which, in accordance with traditional notions of parliamentary sovereignty, is reserved to the legislature. Both the New Zealand and the United Kingdom arrangements, then, mandate fundamental rights-conforming interpretive powers to the judiciary, but ultimately leave the final power of rights specification to politically accountable branches. Both schemes also, it should be noted, are restricted to the domain of individual fundamental rights; they thus do not address or affect the other jurisdictional areas with which I have suggested independent constitutional courts should be concerned.

corpus. Allowing a greater role for legislative constitutional elaboration in legal systems where independent constitutional courts play an important role in detecting conflicts of laws would increase legal incoherence only where legislatures were incapable of responsibly considering the legal effects of proposals in addition to their other consequences. But if legislatures are systematically incapable of that, then it's hard to imagine how they can play any role in the elaboration of the ordinary legal system. The proposals do, however, promise to decrease to some extent the degree of authoritative settlement of constitutional law. To the extent that there is back-and-forth between variously authorized constitutional elaborators, there will be some greater uncertainty over time about the specific shape and implications of constitutional law. Although a system employing only provisions requiring legislative elaboration would not affect settlement significantly – after all, the state of the law is authoritatively determined – systems employing doctrinal deference mechanisms will involve decisional exchanges between branches and thereby decrease settlement somewhat, with the greatest decrease occurring in systems with formal notwithstanding type mechanisms. Notably, however, even in the latter case, the actual arrangements can mitigate this problem by setting relatively long time frames for the interbranch interaction: settlement, it should be noted, is temporally indexed.[16] Clearly all three solutions will be weakly detrimental with respect to political independence. We should not expect the proposals, then, to work well for the review or constitutional elaboration of interbranch branch boundaries and laws directly affecting democratic participation. Depending on the specific arrangements adopted and numerous variables affecting the way they would actually function, the proposals could relevantly and sufficiently empower the legislature to participate actively in a system of constitutional elaboration where constitutional courts also play a significant role. Of course, to the extent that such courts are involved, the empowerment increase should not be expected to be either tremendous or overwhelming – these are not systems of pure coordinate construction after all. As already indicated, such proposals are well tailored only to a subset of the jurisdiction recommended earlier for independent constitutional courts and, should they be so limited, we can expect them to perform well on the jurisdictional assessment scale.[17] Finally, important

---

[16] Recall that the Canadian system allows a law resulting from a notwithstanding response by the legislature to stand for five years.

[17] Recall that the Canadian notwithstanding clause, and the New Zealand and United Kingdom doctrinal schemes are specifically focused on private autonomy rights but are not extended to rights to democratic participation and the criteria of national citizenship. Recall that a similar distinction underlies the doctrinal recommendations that Ely makes with respect to where and when the U.S. Supreme Court should and should not be comparatively deferential to the judgments of Congress. Ely bases his preferred

improvements on the sensitivity scale should be discernible with the various arrangements. Given that we should expect legislatures to have significantly greater information and relevant reason collecting resources and capabilities than courts – not only because of their much greater staffs but also because of their representative makeup, the diversity of their membership, and their structural sensitivity to public input – the proposals are specifically tailored to taking advantage of these differences. They are designed to ensure that the elaboration of constitutional law, especially with respect to fundamental private autonomy rights, is better capable of fulfilling the demanding requirements for the justification of democratic law. In normative terms, laws are illegitimate to the extent that their processes of justification ignore the expected consequences and side-effects such laws can be foreseen to have on the interests of all affected by them. At least in principle, legislatures are structurally more open to the "full blast of sundry opinions and interest-articulations" than courts, and such sensitivity is a primary reason to increase interbranch debate and decisional dispersal concerning constitutional essentials.

A few comments on the potential effectiveness of such mechanisms – however inadequate – seem apropos. First, with respect to the Canadian innovation, it should be noted that, in practice, it has not worked as foreseen here. To make a long story short, the regional legislature of Quebec made "a blanket and preemptive use of Section 33 to immunize itself as much as possible against the constitutionalized Charter."[18] After the Canadian Supreme Court upheld this extraordinarily assertive use of the notwithstanding clause, it has not been used again. There appears to have arisen, therefore, a sort of informal convention among political officials in Canada against the further use of the provision, arising out of the background particularities of the rather polarized interregional politics in Canada. It remains an open question, however, to what extent this unfortunate history is a result of structural and procedural deficiencies inherent in any such provision, as opposed to the general difficulties of transregional constitutionalism in a nation-state deeply divided into culturally differentiated regions. The effectiveness of the two other

---

interpretive strategy, and resulting doctrinal recommendations, on Justice Stone's famous footnote 4 to *Carolene Products*, which reads in part: "It is unnecessary to consider now [for the present case] whether legislation which restricts those political processes which can ordinarily be expected to bring repeal of undesirable legislation, is to be subjected to more exact judicial scrutiny under the general prohibitions of the Fourteenth Amendment than are most other types of legislation," 152. See, further, discussion in Chapter 2, Section B1.

[18] Gardbaum, "The New Commonwealth Model of Constitutionalism," 724. I rely here on Gardbaum's telling of the story; citations to more extensive literature can be found at 724–6.

interbranch proposals is, to some extent, intertwined. This is because the degree to which legislative-specification provisions will be effective depends on the assertiveness of constitutional courts, and the latter is tied at least in part to the particular doctrines that courts take themselves to be bound to. In general, I am more hopeful concerning arrangements that not only formally structure interbranch dialogue and decisional authority but also that provide institutionally based incentives for their effective operation. Conversely, strategies that rely on either the individual self-limitation of officials or more informal conventions appear less promising.[19] It should go without saying, of course, that institutional structures do not run themselves, but depend upon, among other factors, "the support of an accommodating political culture."[20] They do not, in other words, guarantee the results desired theoretically. Finally, note should be taken of the empirical dynamics of the authoritative elaboration of rule-systems themselves, in particular the apparent tendency of constitutional courts, when given the power to selectively interpret and amputate statutes in the light of their own understandings of constitutional provisions, to adopt a somewhat tutelary role toward legislatures, more or less dictating to the latter the results and policy regimes desired.[21] This final point should not be taken, however, as a demonization of constitutional courts, for the dynamic only plays out to the extent that electorally accountable political officials are unwilling to challenge that tutelage, happy, rather, to delegate their duties for making laws that are constitutional and for constitutional elaboration itself. The problem then is not simply designing structures for possible interbranch constitutionalism, but structuring institutional incentives for those structures to operate in the manner intended.[22]

C.   EASING FORMAL AMENDABILITY REQUIREMENTS

Thus far the three types of proposal considered have dealt with the allocation of powers for constitutional elaboration at the horizontal level

---

[19] In an interesting consideration of contrasts between the U.S. system of constitutional review and the Canadian from the point of view of sensitivity to wide public reasons and information, Tushnet renders this contrast as one between relying on psychological factors versus structural or institutional features: Mark Tushnet, "Forms of Judicial Review as Expressions of Constitutional Patriotism," *Law and Philosophy* 22, no. 3–4 (2003).

[20] Habermas, *Between Facts and Norms*, 487.

[21] Sweet, *Governing with Judges*, 63–114, gives numerous examples of this phenomenon in four European nations; many could be added from U.S. history. I doubt it is localized only to these five nations.

[22] Unfortunately on this latter problem of incentive design, I've no concrete ideas that seem both workable and normatively acceptable.

of the national government. Although they have been designed with an eye to the character of the interactions between the informal public spheres and the formally institutionalized public spheres of state decision, they have not systematically tried to establish a reliable vertical link between the two. If we recall Habermas's "two-track" conception of deliberative democratic politics I endorsed in Chapter 7, however, we can see that such links are absolutely crucial to ensuring the legitimacy of exercises of political power. On the rich deliberative model of democratic processes, it is not enough to simply secure the electoral accountability of public officials who are then licensed with basically plenary powers to decide upon policy choices, which choices are taken as consented to in the absence of electoral revolt. This thin conception of democracy relies on an aggregative conception of the public good and is, as I argued in Chapters 2 and 3, not particularly convincing on either normative or empirical grounds. Even if we "thicken" up this conception by structuring certain intragovernmental processes of deliberation and dispersed decision making – say by adopting various separation of powers or federalist schemes – this still leaves deliberative democracy largely up to the interactions between variously positioned and incentivized political elites and the diverse holders of expert knowledge they may rely on in choosing amongst policy alternatives. In order, however, for democratic processes to meet the demanding idealized condition that their outcomes be based upon a sufficient gathering of information and serious, reasons-responsive consideration of the likely consequences and side-effects for all affected by policy choices, there must be a set of vertical channels through which those affected can not only have their arguments and concerns heard but can expect that they will have some significant effect on the agenda, procedures, and outcomes of official processes of political decision. To put the point in Habermas's suggestive metaphors, there must be a way in which the communicative power of the citizens can be collected and channeled in the broad, diverse, and relatively anarchic realm of the informal public spheres, and forced through the sluice gates of the official policy-making processes, thereby transforming communicative into legitimate political power through the medium of law. The administrative power of the state – which is necessarily coercive at many points – is then legitimated to the extent to which it is directed by political power in the form of legitimate statutes and regulations, where this power in turn has been constituted and directed by communicative power of the citizenry.

To be sure, this idealization of a legitimate circulation of power is overly demanding as an empirical description of reality, and so as a normative criterion for everyday exercises of state power. Here Habermas, rightly to my mind, suggests that as long as this circuit can in fact be mobilized by citizens – as evidenced by its more or less frequent use by a national public when sufficiently motivated and mobilized – the fact that some exercises of power might exhibit a top-down "countercirculation" from political elites and experts does not invalidate the democratic character of the political system as a whole. The relation that this picture of the circulation of power has to a constitutional democracy's system of constitutional elaboration becomes clear once we consider the basic modalities of constitutional change. As Lutz succinctly puts it, "a constitution may be altered by means of (1) a formal amendment process; (2) periodic replacement of the entire document; (3) judicial interpretation; and (4) legislative revision."[23] Assuming the soundness of the argument for a constitutional court, and even adopting the various horizontal proposals earlier, formal amendment procedures that are relatively easy to use leave open a crucial option for the people to assume their constituent power and thereby actuate, as it were, the official circulation of constitution-making power.[24] Amendment procedures, that is to say, formally institutionalize the possibility of a vertical employment of the people's constituent power, in particular to correct for deficiencies in the horizontal system of normal constitutional elaboration. On the one hand, they allow for the democratic development of fundamental law and, on the other, they can ease the democratic deficits caused by the transmutation of constitutional protection into elaboration.

If then formal amendment procedures provide a mode by which the people's constituent power can actuate the official democratic circulation of power with respect to constitutional essentials, how exactly should they be designed? Here, given the complexity of the issues involved, I have no specific metrics, only some general suggestions.[25] Centrally relevant complexities here concern, at the least, structural factors such as the length of the constitution itself, the variety and specificity of government functions covered in the constitution, the various initiative and ratification modalities allowed by the amendment procedures, and the roles and

---

[23] Lutz, "Toward a Theory of Constitutional Amendment," 237.

[24] I leave out of consideration here the possibility of entirely new constitutional beginnings for reasons of complexity. Nevertheless, it should be clear that the criteria of deliberative democratic legitimacy retain their force even for originary constitutional conventions, requiring real democracy not only in the selection of a constituent assembly, but in the ratification process as well. Perhaps the widely noted "democratic deficit" in the writing of the proposed European Constitution explains, to some extent, its recent apparent defeat at the ratification stage through the popular rejection, by referenda, in France and the Netherlands. As of this writing (March 2006), the future of that political project is quite uncertain. There remains a set of interesting conceptual, normative, and factual questions concerning whether a constitution should include, in itself, specified procedures for its own overcoming through the writing of a new constitution.

[25] Even these suggestions are undoubtedly colored by my provincial understanding as a citizen of the United States, one who finds his own nation's constitution much too difficult to amend.

techniques adopted by various governmental agencies in the processes of informal constitutional elaboration outside of formal amendment processes.[26] But there are also a host of external factors to consider, concerning, for instance, the degree of ideological and political polarization in the nation, levels of inequality as they relate especially to individuals' resources and capacities for civic competence, the character of the nation's political culture broadly construed (including officials' adherence to rule of law values, the social acceptance of various forms of rule, and the degree of enthusiasm for democratic as opposed to autocratic institutions and officials), the prospects for constitutional sustainability over time, the relative levels of power between government and other sectors of society such as the economy, the military, civil society, and various forms of secondary associations – just to name a few.[27]

Given these complexities, the following insufficient platitudes will have to substitute here for what should be a more robust theory of constitutional amendment that could fully warrant a recommendation for relatively easy amendment procedures. To begin with, it is clear that the central issue is striking an appropriate balance between unchangeable obduracy and mercurial transformability. On the one hand, a constitution has to be sufficiently difficult to change in order to maintain a basic distinction between constitutional higher-law and the subordinate status of ordinary law. On the other hand, it cannot be so hard to change that democratically achieved changes to the constitution are effectively foreclosed, except through wholesale constitutional replacement. Some attention also should be paid to differences in the way in which the relevant difficulties of formal amendment are set up. I have in mind here, in particular, a distinction between the procedural hurdles established by various levels of supermajoritarian rules, and those hurdles which are established either by extending the amendment process over time or by increasing the diversity of representative points of view. Although in terms of a numerical metric of difficulty of amendability both may be equivalent,[28] from a deliberative perspective, the constitution is not

---

[26] This is a distillation of the many factors that Lutz considers in his very important theoretical and empirical analysis of constitutional amendments: Lutz, "Toward a Theory of Constitutional Amendment."

[27] Several of these factors are distilled out of the rather surprising advice rendered from a deliberative democratic perspective to constitutional designers in a set of newly emergent constitutional democracies, by Stephen Holmes and Cass R. Sunstein, "The Politics of Constitutional Revision in Eastern Europe," in *Responding to Imperfection: The Theory and Practice of Constitutional Amendment*, ed. Sanford Levinson (Princeton, NJ: Princeton University Press, 1995).

[28] See Lutz, "Toward a Theory of Constitutional Amendment," 254–60, for his derivation of an index measuring the relative difficulty of various amendment procedures, and his assignment of a value to various mechanisms.

conceived of as a simple counter-majoritarian instrument, but as a facil-itator of legitimate democratic decisions procedures. Thus amendment hurdles that encourage the collection and rational assessment of relevant reasons and information are to be favored over ones that simply make it difficult for a majority to get its way, even as any amendment hurdles will undoubtedly do that as well.[29] Finally, the normative framework embraced here would also appear to favor popular referenda mechanisms for the initiation of constitutional amendment processes in general, though legislative initiative procedures also would be acceptable. Popular ratification procedures should be the norm, although this does not exclude adding representative institutions to the ratification mix on top of popular ones.

But designing amendment procedures is not just a matter of linking up normative theory with structural data at an abstract level; one must also take into account the particular dynamics of constitutional elaboration fostered by different amendment schemas. From the proceduralist con-ception of deliberative democratic constitutionalism adopted here, it appears that there may be good reasons for differential levels of entrenchment correlated to different kinds of issues constitutions deal with. Ideally, the system of rights, rights to both private and public autonomy, should be equally strong and resistant to change. But, in practice, it is quite difficult to strike the correct semantic balance, when writing constitutional provisions, between requisite abstract formulation and controlling determinacy. And this difficulty seems significantly increased for adequately guaranteeing the substance of many individual private liberty rights, as opposed, say, to the more procedural character of the guarantees necessary to ensure equal individual rights to democratic participation. It is precisely in the former case that constitutional courts have been particularly assertive in taking on the tasks of constitutional elaboration, to the detriment of the people's constituent power for the same. When a constitution is particularly difficult to amend, the pressures for constitutional elaboration outside of the normal amendment process will grow and, to the extent that this task is taken on by a constitutional

---

[29] Compare, for instance, the equivalent values Lutz assigns for difficulty in amendment approval modalities where those modalities nevertheless would promise different deliberative benefits, ibid., Table 10, 258–59. Although an absolute majority popular referendum should be as hard to pass as (bicameral) legislative approval twice by an absolute majority with an intervening election, the latter seems recommended by its longer time frame allowing for greater deliberation. Greater deliberative benefits also should flow from having approval follow from a majority of state (subnational) legislatures as opposed to from a combination of executive action plus a two-thirds majority of the national legislature, even though both receive closely equivalent scores on the difficulty index. In this case, the former solution is recommended by the possibility for a greater diversity of viewpoints represented.

court, a positive feedback loop is created between court specification, doctrinal elaboration of various balancing tests, and the unwarranted judicial injection of substantive content into the constitutional system.[30] In short, as constitutional provisions protecting individual liberty rights are increasingly entrenched, it seems that the problem of the transmutation of constitutional protection into elaboration is reciprocally increased over time.[31] It's an open empirical question whether or not similar effects can be detected with respect to a constitutional court's enforcement of provisions concerning governmental structure and individual rights of democratic participation; my sense is to the contrary. If that is correct, then different degrees of amendability might be tailored to different kinds of constitutional provisions.[32]

Turning to the assessment values, much will depend on the specific details of the schemes being compared and the sociopolitical and legal contexts in which they are employed. Having left much of this detail out, it still seems possible to say that easing or restructuring formal amend processes, if properly carried out, should have no discernible effect on systematicity, since normal amendment procedures incorporate various methods for vetting the specific text proposed in amendments by relevant legal and policy experts. Perhaps overly permissive procedures would lead to a constitution turning into something akin to an overly fulsome and specific civil code, thereby engendering increased numbers of potential legal conflicts at the constitutional level.[33] This potential systematicity deficit should, then, be a consideration against setting the difficulty of amendability too low. Amendments may, in addition, have a small but important positive effect in terms of settlement, since they

---

[30] Sweet, *Governing with Judges*, 92–126.

[31] My considerations here suggest that combining open-textured constitutional provisions with their, as it were, superconstitutional entrenchment against amendability, whether through explicit constitutional text or developing judicial doctrine, is not advisable. This combination – as evinced for instance in much European jurisprudence with respect to rights – has led, in practice, to the use of judicial construction methodologies that invite expansive judicial lawmaking in the area. See Sweet, ibid.

[32] This provides one way of thinking about the justification of the structure of the Canadian notwithstanding clause. By allowing legislative responses to constitutional elaboration by constitutional courts in the areas of substantive individual liberties, but barring such responses with respect to membership and democratic rights, the provision recognizes the special democratic danger of juridical elaboration with respect to the former.

[33] Lutz, "Toward a Theory of Constitutional Amendment," 247–50 and 60–61, presents compelling evidence from comparisons between both United States state constitutions and across thirty nation-state constitutions, that the length of the constitutional text is strongly correlated to the rate at which it is amended over time. He also provides the standard explanation for this strong correlation: "Commentators frequently note that the more provisions a constitution has, the more targets there are for amendment, and the more likely the constitution will be targeted because it deals with too many details that are subject to change," 244.

definitively decide certain constitutional issues, rather than leaving them open to various and potentially competing official constitutional elaborators.

Amendments processes should, in principle, have just the kind of independence from political officials that the proceduralist model of constitutional review prizes. If we want especially to ensure that the rules of the democratic process, especially in their constitutional form, are not being systematically deformed, abused, or ignored by those currently in office to either close off the channels of political change or systematically disfavor the interests of underrepresented subsections of society, then the structural dependence of amendment procedures on the people, not on their governmental agents, seems particularly appropriate. To put it in a slogan, in a system of constitutional elaboration including constitutional courts, amendments look like the way that "the guardians of democracy" can themselves be guarded. Of course, this ideal picture of independence does not entirely match up with reality. After all, if amendment proposals are initiated by legislative bodies or other forms of special bodies of governmental officials, then independence is undercut. Furthermore, the need for vetting the text of amendment proposals may provide significant room for "recapture" of the proposal by political officials. Perhaps, however, the real threat to the necessary independence of the amendment procedure is the apparent ease and success by which it can be captured by social powers looking to promote their own sectional interests to the detriment of others. I return to this important issue later in considering the assessment value of sensitivity, as some of the most prevalent mechanisms for such capture result from the structural transformations of the informal public sphere that have made widespread, high-quality public deliberation so hard to achieve.

In a political system in which the full gamut of the constitution is amendable, easing overly obdurate amendment procedures would have clear benefits with respect to sufficient and relevant empowerment. One might be worried here, however, about the costs of overempowerment promised by relatively easy amendability, as repeated and continuous changes in the overall constitutional system may produce deleterious consequences from the point of view of both systematicity and settlement. It should be noted, however, that the problem of overempowerment does not derive from the fact that amendments are directly subject to popular will. Although there is a frequent invocation of the specter of unbridled populism, especially evident in many debates over ordinary referenda, Lutz's data from a decade of American state amendment patterns make clear that the more "populist" route for initiating a constitutional amendment – namely through various popular referenda, rather than through the legislature or through special constitutional convention – has not been notably easy or successful.[34] Worries, then, about amendments and mercurial populism, and the resulting threat of overempowerment, seem overstated and perhaps misplaced. Furthermore, easing amendability is clearly recommended from the point of view of jurisdiction: constitutional elaboration is rightly the province and duty of democratic citizens themselves.

Ideally, it would seem that the same strong positive conclusion would follow on the sensitivity scale as well, as the legitimacy of the process of constitutional elaboration itself depends crucially on the extent to which its outcomes are responsive to relevant reasons and information stemming from the people themselves. What better way to be sensitive to the people's inputs, then, than a direct vote or series of votes by them? Elaboration by amendment need not, for instance, be defended through any circuitous, counterfactual, or hypothetical accounts of how the people themselves are better represented by their governmental agents than by their own explicit vote.[35] And this sensitivity would entail that constitutional elaboration through amendment is not susceptible to the paternalist worries about judicial elaboration, canvassed throughout this book, that arise from the evident gap between the people's will as expressed in the constitution and the particular use made of that "constitutional will" by judicial interpreters.[36]

[34] "Many believe that the initiative, by making the process of proposing an amendment too easy, has led to a flood of proposals that are then more readily adopted by the electorate that initiated them....As Table 7 shows, during the period 1970–79, relatively few amendments [8.5%, with only 2.2% by popular initiative] were proposed by other than a legislature [91.5%]. One-third of the states use popular initiative as a method of proposing amendments, and yet even in these states the legislative method was greatly preferred. The popular initiative has received a lot of attention, especially in California, but in fact it has thus far had a minimal impact. What has been the relative success of these competing modes of proposing constitutions? Table 8 shows that the relatively few amendments proposed through popular initiative have a success rate [32%] roughly half that of the two prominent alternatives [64% initiated by legislatures, 71% by special conventions]. The popular initiative is in fact more difficult to use than legislative initiative," ibid., 254. Extension of Lutz's research to cross-national comparisons, and over a longer time frame, would be quite welcome.

[35] Recall that this is a common strategy for justifying both representative government by virtuous elites, and judicial review itself, where judges are taken to be more representative of (some crucial, fundamental, and theory-specific aspect of) the will of the people. See the venerable line of such arguments canvassed in Chapter 6, Section A4.

[36] A classic denial of this gap is contained, for instance, in Hamilton's justification for judicial review as merely securing the will of the people as expressed in the constitution. The argument for judicial review does not "by any means suppose a superiority of the judicial to the legislative power. It only supposes that the power of the people is superior to both; and that where the will of the legislature declared in its statutes, stands in opposition to that of the people declared in the constitution, the judges ought to be governed by the latter, rather than the former." Hamilton, Madison, and Jay, *The Federalist with Letters of "Brutus,"* #78, 380.

As any astute observer of contemporary politics realizes, however, sensitivity to the simple electoral desires of the public is, quite often, not sensitivity to the people's considered opinions, but rather sensitivity to those who can most effectively make use of the myriad techniques of "the scientific marketing of candidates [and amendment proposals!] by soundbite specialists."[37] The problem with the ideal account of the sensitivity of amendment procedures presupposed in the previous paragraph is that it attends only to the aggregative mechanism of voting as a measure of sensitivity. But, to adopt the terminology I laid out in Chapter 3, this is a one-sided focus on whether the structures of accountability are more populist or expertocratic; it entirely leaves out the notion that democratic processes ought to be sufficiently deliberative. As currently institutionalized and practiced, amendment procedures take for granted that there is an effectively functioning informal deliberative public sphere that can be expected to help and encourage citizens collectively to weigh amendment proposals in the light of relevant information and reasons. Thanks, however, to the work of deliberative democratic scholars from many different research traditions and domains, we can now be fairly certain that this presupposition is seriously undermined by any number of actual "deliberative troubles."[38]

The kinds and sources of such deliberative troubles are manifold, and I do not propose to review them all here. But even a partial list would have to start with a problem that lies at the level of individual citizen incentives. What Anthony Downs memorably termed "rational ignorance" refers to the strategic calculations that an individual might make with respect to becoming informed about complex political questions and proposals currently before the public. On the one hand, in polities with high populations, my single vote will not make much of a difference to the outcome of an election. On the other hand, the personal costs of sorting the various facts, values, reasons, and so on that ought ideally to be taken into account are quite high. Thus I have strong "rational" incentives to remain ignorant about them.[39] However, this should not be considered an atemporal general phenomenon of all circumstances of political citizenship, for it is quite clear that individuals have a diversity of motivations and incentives that may override the two identified by Downs, and changes in social context may significantly alter the relevant personal "calculations."

It is precisely here, in identifying the historic structural changes in the informal public spheres and the ways they have shaped individuals'

---

[37] Ackerman and Fishkin, *Deliberation Day*, 10.

[38] The phrase is from Sunstein, *Designing Democracy: What Constitutions Do*, but I use it here to pick out a wider variety of phenomena than he analyzes.

[39] Anthony Downs, *An Economic Theory of Democracy* (New York: The Free Press, 1957).

incentive structure and environment, that much of the most interesting applied work in deliberative democratic theory has occurred.[40] To begin, the rise and refinement of modern opinion polling, and its close connection to the commodified packaging of candidates and proposals in superficial but motivationally effective advertising packages – think sound-bites – have significantly raised the political salience of reasons-unresponsive or even reasons-resistant desires, fears, biases, ideologies, and mythologies. This is further fostered, of course, by the fact that modern mass media are more-or-less push phenomena, disseminating the soundbites that political elites, socially powerful actors and groups, and their image consultants desire to have disseminated. Such mass media are driven, in addition, not by any interests in promoting public discussion but by selling advertising. Furthermore, the increasing diversification of outlets and venues for politically relevant information and opinion – both in the old media markets of newspapers, radio, and television, and through the development of the Internet – leads to the segmentation of broader public spheres into limited "deliberative enclaves" (Sunstein) of those with like-minded values and opinions. Such deliberative enclaves become increasingly insensitive to the information, opinions, and arguments coming from other quarters of society, and simultaneously more likely to reinforce the prediscussion errors and biases of the group members. The diversification of society itself, in particular value pluralization, also may contribute to such deliberative troubles, at the same time that increases in the overall degree of social complexity – with clear analogues in the internal development of a constitutionally structured legal corpus – make it more difficult to comprehend and evaluate relevant political alternatives. Finally, all of these various phenomena are overlaid with and permeated by the existing social inequalities in a society. Not only are the agenda, content, and character of public flows of information, opinions, and arguments highly structured by asymmetrical distributions of wealth and power but also – precisely because the distribution of deliberative capacities and resources is strongly correlated with such material asymmetries – the "deliberative" outcomes of public opinion tend to promote policies and alternatives that reinforce asymmetries of wealth and power. Mere sensitivity to the pre- or nondeliberative opinions of the public, then, may be a form of populist sensitivity, but it does not adequately attend to the deliberative troubles extant under current social conditions, or to the

---

[40] I draw the following account from a variety of sources. However, four crucial works in the area deserve special mention as particularly important and insightful: Bohman, *Public Deliberation: Pluralism, Complexity, and Democracy*, Fishkin, *Democracy and Deliberation*, Jürgen Habermas, *The Structural Transformation of the Public Sphere: An Inquiry into a Category of Bourgeois Society*, trans. Thomas Burger (Cambridge, MA: The MIT Press, 1989), and Sunstein, *Designing Democracy: What Constitutions Do*.

ideals of a reasons-responsive employment of the state's coercive power.[41] It is important that one not draw overly pessimistic conclusions from these contemporary obstacles. For, in fact, high-quality, widely dispersed popular constitutional debate and decision making can and has occurred, even if usually only under propitious and extraordinary historical conditions.[42]

Amendment proposal and ratification processes as currently structured, then, are sensitive to popular opinion in its raw or unfiltered form, but this is not the full type of sensitivity a theory of deliberative democratic constitutionalism should be concerned to rely on, especially when considering the fundamental procedures that structure democratic forms of consociation – when citizens are called on, that is, to continue to carry on the process of constitutional elaboration. What Ackerman and Fishkin say in the context of candidate elections seems even more important when it comes to constitutional matters:

> Raw opinion of the entire mass public is the realization of plebiscitary democracy. The long-term trajectory of American democracy, and indeed of most democracies around the world, has been to consult the mass public more and more directly. This process has brought power to the people – with referendums and other plebiscites, with primaries in candidate selection, with the elimination of indirect modes of election of some office-holders, and with the expansion of the office-holders who are directly elected, etc. The end result has been that innumerable decisions that were once made ... through a select or elite group deliberating, are now subject to the incentives for rational ignorance on the part of the mass public. Increasingly, we have brought power to the people under conditions where the people have little reason to think about the power we would have them exercise.[43]

Well-structured amendment procedures are designed to reflect the diversity and disagreement evident amongst citizens seeking to mediate

---

[41] The quote from Dewey that I discussed in Chapter 2 is worth quoting here again: "Majority rule, just as majority rule, is as foolish as its critics charge it with being. But it is never *merely* majority rule. As a practical politician, Samuel J. Tilden, said a long time ago: 'The means by which a majority comes to be a majority is the more important thing': antecedent debates, modification of views to meet the opinions of minorities, the relative satisfaction given to the latter by the fact that it has had a chance and that next time it may be successful in becoming a majority.... The essential need, in other words, is the improvement of the methods and conditions of debate, discussion and persuasion. That is *the* problem of the public," Dewey, *The Public and Its Problems*, 365.

[42] Ackerman's sweeping and compelling history of extended periods of "higher lawmaking" in United States history punctuating much longer periods of politics as usual provides much evidence to support the claim that high-quality popular constitutional deliberation is possible: Ackerman, *We the People: Foundations*, Ackerman, *We the People: Transformations*.

[43] Ackerman and Fishkin, *Deliberation Day*, 29.

their social life through legitimate law, and to provide an effective means for citizens to employ their constituent power in the light of the inevitable elaboration of a constitutional scheme in the normal course of everyday processes of lawmaking and law-applying. I doubt however that, in their present form, they can be particularly effective in achieving these laudable goals, unless they are transformed to take account of the deliberative troubles which undermine the supposition that sensitivity to popular voting is enough to ensure the democratic character of constitutionalism. The problem of institutional design is, once again, one of mediating between the ideal and the real.

D. ESTABLISHING CIVIC CONSTITUTIONAL FORA

I mentioned at the end of Section A of Chapter 8 that we should expect tensions and tradeoffs between the various assessment values as realized in different institutional mechanisms for constitutional review. Having worked through four types of proposals, some general patterns emerge. First, all four proposals appear to have either no substantial effect or a moderate positive effect on the overall systematicity of the legal corpus. Second, with the exception of some modes of interbranch decisional dispersal (particularly temporary legislative overrides of constitutional court decisions), the same can be said with respect to settlement: either no effect or a moderate positive effect. If correct, these two findings should go a fair way to rebutting claims for locating extraordinarily strong powers of constitutional decision exclusively in the judiciary, claims that are based on the specter of lawlessness, anarchy, and confusion said to ensue in the absence of such rigorous and exclusive control. All four proposals sufficiently and relevantly empower various different actors to have a role in the scheme of constitutional elaboration. Empowerment, however, is often tied to the jurisdictional reach of each proposal: although I claim that none of the proposals overstep their proper jurisdiction, the reach of each is variable, from the more extensive jurisdiction over the constitutional corpus as a whole granted to constitutional courts and amendment procedures, to the more limited domain of authority granted to self-review panels and interbranch mechanisms of decision. In sum, on the four measures of systematicity, settlement, empowerment, and jurisdiction there do not seem to be the kinds of trade-offs and compromises that we might have suspected in the absence of a more thorough consideration of each proposal.

However, the predicted tensions between independence and sensitivity do repeatedly surface. Thus, the scheme that does well in terms of independence – constitutional courts – turns out to have serious deficits with respect to sensitivity. Conversely, the schemes that do well on the sensitivity scale – self-review panels and interbranch mechanisms – do poorly on the independence scale, and apparently precisely because of their electoral sensitivity. The one proposal that held out the promise for achieving both requisite independence and sensitivity – easing amendability – does not achieve it: its ideal promise wilts significantly in the light of the real conditions of current democratic politics. What looked to be not only an independent mechanism for guarding the guardians of the procedures of democracy but also the one mechanism most closely tied to the will of the people, seems to be neither sufficiently independent nor sensitive in the right way. Should we then resign ourselves to an irreconcilable tension between the ideal and the real, and give up hopes for a fully democratic process of constitutional self-government? I think not, and precisely because the actual independence and sensitivity deficits of amendment procedures as currently structured are, in fact, linked to one another. The hinge is the character and quality of public democratic deliberation witnessed in modern informal political public spheres. On both assessment scales, although amendment procedures look good ideally, in reality it seems that they will be subject to just the kind of mercurial and uninformed populism that has always lingered as the spectral foil to more elitist forms of organizing governmental decisions. If, however, there are achievable and effective ways of significantly improving public democratic deliberation, then there is the prospect for transforming processes of constitutional elaboration in ways to avoid the independence–sensitivity trade-off, thus belying its apparent inevitability.

The same point can be made another way: the independence–sensitivity trade-off looks inevitable at the horizontal level of government because, no matter how reasons-responsive various government organs are, independence and sensitivity are both structurally tied to the influence of elections at the horizontal level of national government. The move to the vertical relationship between the constituent power of the people, the constitution, and the organs of government – via the amendment process – ideally promised to change the independence–sensitivity dynamic but fails to do so because of deliberative troubles. We need not accept the current state of political public spheres as an unchangeable given, however. Diverse avenues of contemporary institutional design for improving deliberation – and the empirical research that provisionally supports its effectiveness – promise ways of overcoming or mitigating much of the deliberative trouble, and thereby reinvigorating the promise of truly deliberative democratic constitutionalism.[44] As

---

[44] An excellent overview of much of the empirical literature concerning the effects of public deliberation is provided by Delli Carpini, Cook, and Jacobs, "Public Deliberation, Discursive Participation, and Citizen Engagement." The authors conclude that deliberation in and of itself is not always an unalloyed good, or even a good at all when poorly structured, carried out under suboptimal circumstances, or insufficiently topically

an exploratory set of proposals, then, I suggest the establishment of various kinds of civic constitutional fora: intentionally structured locations for focused and high-quality citizen deliberation and decision making concerning constitutional matters, especially those that arise from the ongoing processes of constitutional elaboration, but not necessarily limited to those. To get an idea of the shape of these proposals, I turn first to some very exciting work ensuing from deliberative democrats.

The most promising directions begin with Fishkin's proposals for deliberative public opinion polls, and the research and testing supporting their effectiveness.[45] I summarize these polls just enough to familiarize one with their basic ideas, processes, and results – abjuring a full analysis here. Fishkin summarizes the basic process as follows:

The Problem – Citizens are often uninformed about key public issues. Conventional polls represent the public's surface impressions of sound bites and headlines. The public, subject to what social scientists have called "rational ignorance," has little reason to confront trade-offs or invest time and effort in acquiring information or coming to a considered judgment.

The Process – Deliberative Polling® is an attempt to use television and public opinion research in a new and constructive way. A random, representative sample is first polled on the targeted issues. After this baseline poll, members of the sample are invited to gather at a single place for a weekend in order to discuss the issues. Carefully balanced briefing materials are sent to the participants and are also made publicly available. The participants engage in dialogue with competing experts and political leaders based on questions they develop in small group discussions with trained moderators. Parts of the weekend events are broadcast on television, either live or in taped and edited form. After the deliberations, the sample is again asked the original questions. The resulting changes in opinion represent the conclusions the public would reach, if people had opportunity to become more informed and more engaged by the issues.[46]

---

focused. My proposals for well-structured civic constitutional fora are specifically tailored to optimizing the circumstances of deliberation for the consideration and ratification of constitutional amendments. For a clear overview of various institutional design choices and how they affect the diverse functions and goals deliberative democratic public fora are intended to promote, supported in the light of five actual "minipublic" experiments, see Fung, "Recipes for Public Spheres."

[45] An early formulation can be found in Fishkin, *Democracy and Deliberation*, 1–10, 82–104. Much more extensive treatment, including empirical data collected in running numerous deliberative polls in diverse policy and national conditions, can be found in James S. Fishkin, *The Voice of the People: Public Opinion and Democracy*, expanded ed. (New Haven, CT: Yale University Press, 1997); James S. Fishkin and Robert C. Luskin, *Experimenting with a Democratic Ideal: Deliberative Polling and Public Opinion* (2004 [cited June 15 2005]), available from http://cdd.stanford.edu/research/index.html, and at the Web site for The Center for Deliberative Democracy.

[46] James S. Fishkin, *Deliberative Polling®: Toward a Better-Informed Democracy* (2004 [cited June 15, 2005]), available from http://cdd.stanford.edu/polls/docs/summary/.

A few more details: the whole group usually ranges between two hundred and five hundred participants (similar in size to modern representative legislatures); participants are given material incentives for participation; small group deliberations occur among twelve to fifteen persons with procedural moderators looking to ensure civility and balanced equality between the contributions of members and between the major arguments canvassed in the briefing documents. Fishkin and Luskin summarize the results of comparing preevent polls (both of the participants and often a different, larger control group) to exit polls conducted after deliberations:

1 The participants are representative....
2 Opinions often change....
3 Vote intentions often change....
4 The participants gain information....
5 The changes in opinions and votes and the information gains are related....
6 The changes in opinions and votes are unrelated to social location....
7 Policy attitudes and vote intentions tend to be more predictable, and predictable on the basis of normatively preferable criteria after deliberation than before. Thus regressions of policy attitudes on collections of values and empirical premises that ought to affect them carry bigger adjusted R^2s after deliberation than before. Similarly, U.S. primary election voters tend to give much greater weight than the control group to the candidates' policy positions in deciding how to vote.
8 Single-Peakedness increases.... The participants may not agree more after deliberating, but they do seem to agree more in this sense about what they are agreeing or disagreeing about....
9 The increases in single-peakedness and information gains are related. The increases in single-peakedness stem primarily from those participants emerging most informed.
10 Preferences do not necessarily "polarize" across discussion groups....
11 Preferences do not necessarily homogenize within groups....
12 Balanced deliberation tends to promote balanced learning.[47]

In short, remarkable increases in the quality of the outcomes of opinion-formation processes can be achieved through the astute institutional design of deliberations among a representative cross-section of ordinary

---

[47] Fishkin and Luskin, *Experimenting with a Democratic Ideal: Deliberative Polling and Public Opinion* (references omitted).

citizens. Although the results, to some extent speak for themselves, a few comments are particularly relevant here. First, result 6 is quite significant as a rebuttal to claims (now unfashionable to make explicitly) that deliberation is the special province of elite, well-off, or well-educated citizens alone: "That the changes of opinion and vote intention are largely uninfluenced by sociodemographic factors, including education suggests that the process seems accessible to all social strata."[48] Second, result 7 can be reformulated in terms of the notion of reasons-responsiveness: after engaging in the deliberative polls, participants' policy preferences were brought into much closer line with the information, values, and reasons that they found to be directly relevant to supporting or undermining those preferences. Given that a large measure of the structure of deliberative polling is oriented toward civic education this should not be surprising, but it is important to underline in the face of skepticism about the worth or import of deliberation when compared to other factors motivating belief and preference formation: preferences may not be fully reasons-responsive, but they are not fully insensitive to reasons either. Results 8 and 9 go a fair way to answering charges about the mercurial and unstable nature of public opinion, at least when the latter has been anchored in robust, actual processes of deliberation: "deliberation lessens the collective confusions of mass democracy, creating a shared public space for public opinion.... If anything, the desirability of avoiding preference cycles argues *for* deliberation."[49] Finally, results 10 and 11 follow from the facts that communication in deliberative polls occurs across lines that typically separate citizens in their ordinary lives, and that the pool of available information and arguments that participants must contend with is not limited to the socially and ideologically bounded pools increasingly produced in niche-marketed mass-media productions and through deliberative enclaving.

This is related to one final important point. We should *not* expect high quality deliberation to result in or tend towards consensus on policy alternatives, or, more grandly yet, on questions of basic values, worldviews, and moral systems. "In the Deliberative Polls we have found that the items that change are not fundamental values, but rather specific policy attitudes, factual knowledge and what we have called 'empirical premises' (typically, assumptions about causal connections between policy choices and valued outputs). Fundamental values seem to have greater stability than any of the items just mentioned."[50] To put the same point another way, deliberation is not a panacea for reasonable, persistent disagreement tied to modern conditions of value pluralism, nor can we expect it to produce a utopia of unanimous consent on substantive principles of justice. It is, rather, a process by which citizens' fundamental

[48] Ibid.   [49] Ibid.   [50] Ackerman and Fishkin, *Deliberation Day*, 30, footnote 9.

disagreements can become clear, while stripping away the confusions caused by myths, false beliefs, and simple lack of relevant information. As I have been arguing throughout this book, it is precisely the problem of reasonable substantive disagreement, coupled with the fact that the use of state power is inevitably coercive and so demands justification, which should encourage us to adopt a proceduralist conception of democratic constitutional legitimacy. Deliberative polls give us no empirical reasons, additional to the standard theoretical ones,[51] to believe that consensus on relatively specific fundamental values or on encompassing value systems would be forthcoming, if we could only deliberate better together.

Returning now to the design problem concerning institutions of constitutional elaboration, is there any place for deliberative polls or their derivatives, and if so where? Fishkin's original design for deliberative polls was specifically structured to improve the public opinion that policy makers rely on in the ordinary course of politics. The idea was to move from the raw and unfiltered preferences that traditional opinion polls gauge to well-formed preferences that are reasons-responsive and the outcome of a fair confrontation with the opinions, beliefs, and arguments of other citizens from diverse sectors of society. It was hoped that such deliberative polls would not only have beneficial effects for the participants, however, but might also be able to go some way toward restructuring the broader informal public spheres. In principle they seem well suited to correcting the kinds of deliberative troubles undermining the ideal independence and sensitivity of actual amendment procedures.

Deliberative opinion polls could easily focus on constitutional issues, without any changes in their current format. They might then play a consultative role in extant structures for constitutional elaboration: constitutional courts, self-review panels, and interbranch constitutional decision makers could all draw on their results (perhaps in different ways and with respect to different jurisdictional areas) to gauge "the conclusions the public would reach, if people had opportunity to become more informed and more engaged by the issues."[52] Of course, the claim that the outcomes of one or several deliberative opinion polls each involving five-hundred-odd citizens are the opinions of the public at large are counterfactual. This might lead to some skepticism concerning both their actual representativeness and, as a consequence, the degree to which the opinions of a small sample of the public fulfill the democratic demand for political equality. Fishkin's central rejoinder here is that contemporary scientific survey techniques, employing robust random sampling, enable a high degree of confidence in the representativeness of the participants of

---

[51] A canonical formulation of such theoretical reasons is Rawls's list of the "burdens of judgment": Rawls, *Political Liberalism*, 54–58.

[52] Fishkin, *Deliberative Polling®: Toward a Better-Informed Democracy.*

deliberative polls. This is then tied to an equal impact standard of formal political equality: the preferences of each citizen are to have an equal chance at affecting outcomes.[53] Majority rule in mass elections is only one way of operationalizing this conception of political equality – of special importance here, so are random samples and lottery systems (discussed later). Although it is true that deliberative democracy employs a more robust notion of political equality centered on the reasons-responsiveness of government action, in particular its responsiveness to a full consideration of the interests of all affected, this does not undermine the claim of constitutional consultation polling to adequately model political equality. If, in fact, all that we want out of such a process is a good idea of what the public would think if sufficiently informed and given the opportunity to deliberate adequately, and the representativeness of deliberative polling is sufficiently robust, then it seems that we achieve as much political equality as needed in this consultative context. There is one remaining element that might undermine our confidence in that representativeness however, and that is the problem of self-selection. Participation in deliberative polling is voluntary, and although encouraged by material incentives for partaking, we should expect a higher-degree of participation by "political junkies" and other active citizens instead of a full cross-section of the population. As we have no reason to think that the distribution of the effects of constitutional decisions mirrors the self-selection distributions of deliberative poll participants, relevant representativeness might be undermined and thereby the political equality that random selection was intended to ensure. To put it in terms of the assessment values, relevant sensitivity may be undermined not by the small number of participants, but by the self-selection problem.[54]

---

[53] Fishkin defines formal political equality thus: "a procedure which gives equal consideration to the preferences of each citizen. . . . The basic idea is that formal political equality is achieved when every voter has an equal probability of being the decisive voter, assuming that we know nothing about the actual distribution of preferences of other voters (and so that every alternative is equally likely). The definition captures the root notion of various formal indexes for equal voting power," Fishkin, *Democracy and Deliberation*, 31. It is important to note here that he does not think that political equality can be fully secured through formal procedures alone: certain conditions for insulating individuals from external threats or rewards for voting compliance, and for an effective hearing of the full range of interests involved must also be met. Nevertheless, his conception of political equality is essentially akin to the aggregative conceptions that underlie majoritarian conceptions of democratic political equality, conceptions I distinguished from deliberative conceptions in Chapter 3, Section A.

[54] Here one should note that the voluntary participation evinced in deliberative polling – in part an artifact of the civil society form of Fishkin's experiments – is one significant disanalogy from the ancient Athenian practices of large, randomly selected deliberative assemblies of all citizens, with mandatory participation, that Fishkin often refers to as a model for combining political equality with high-quality deliberation.

There are two more significant concerns about deliberative opinion polls that concern their actual effectiveness, but may mitigate our hopes for them as means for correcting the deliberative troubles identified earlier. First, they have not had a significant impact, at least in the United States, in the broader informal public spheres through which facts, opinions and reasons circulate, especially with respect to the mass media.[55] Political events are still, if not to an even greater degree than before, covered and reported in terms of horseraces between political personalities, rather than in terms of the substantive issues and relevant considerations. If deliberative opinion polls do not receive significant uptake in the mass media and the informal public spheres more generally, their salubrious deliberative effects will be limited mostly to participants themselves. Not surprisingly, this also means that their impact on decision makers in the formal public sphere also will be attenuated. Their effects on decisional outcomes may be magnified in the case of constitutional consultation polling, however, as they are specifically initiated by political officials. Where analogous initiatives have been taken by decision makers to employ deliberative polling techniques, there do seem to have been discernible impacts on policy decisions.[56]

More recently, in collaboration with Ackerman, Fishkin has extended the basic structure of deliberative opinion polling into a much more ambitious call for:

Deliberation Day – a new national holiday [in the United States]. It will be held one week before major national elections. Registered voters will be called together in neighborhood meeting places, in small groups of 15, and larger groups of 500, to discuss the central issues raised by the campaign. Each deliberator will be paid \$150 for the day's work of citizenship, on condition that he or she shows up at the polls the next week. All other work, except the most essential, will be prohibited by law.[57]

Clearly this proposal also focuses on the educative effects on individual voters to be expected from structured deliberations with other citizens.

---

[55] I say at least in the United States because the evidence from other countries looks a bit better, especially concerning the extensive coverage of the deliberative opinion poll in Denmark focused on adoption of the Euro currency, the various British polls on crime, European membership, and the monarchy, and the Australian polls on constitutional transformation toward a republican form of government and on Aboriginal issues. Much would seem to depend on the current state of the mass media and the public spheres in general in specific countries.

[56] See the summary of eight regional deliberative polls commissioned by public utility companies in the U.S. state of Texas, especially at page 10: Robert C. Luskin, James S. Fishkin, and Dennis L. Plane, *Deliberative Polling and Policy Outcomes: Electric Utility Issues in Texas* (1999 [cited June 16 2005]), available from http://cdd.stanford.edu/research/index.html.

[57] Ackerman and Fishkin, *Deliberation Day*, 7.

The major increase in scale, however, supports their hope that it would have significant transformative effects not only on individual citizens but also on the broader political public spheres: the structure of campaign strategies for information dissemination, advertising, and spending, the revitalization of local political organizations, the character and quality of mass-media coverage of campaigns, and so on. Hopes for significant structural transformations of the political public spheres are much more secure here than in the case of small group deliberative opinion polls, no matter how great the uptake the latter receive in the informal public spheres. Furthermore, the extensive citizen participation mandated for deliberation day – secured through the requirement of deliberative participation in order to vote – would vitiate the worry about self-selection biases that threaten the fully representative character of deliberative opinion polls.

Deliberation day could easily be adopted in the run-up to voting for constitutional amendments, while leaving the rest of the formal procedures for amendment unchanged. Adoption of deliberation day at first only for constitutional amendments might even be considered as an experiment for testing its worth and experimenting with details on the way to full adoption of the innovation for general elections.[58] I believe such a proposal would go a long way to ameliorating the most egregious deliberative troubles plaguing current formal amendment procedures. Recall that one problem is simply the structure of incentives for voters in ordinary elections that lead to rational ignorance. Deliberative polling techniques undermine this incentive structure by providing a set of incentives for becoming informed, most of which operate directly or indirectly through participants' concern with maintaining social recognition in the interpersonal context of the small groups. They also combat rational ignorance incentives by providing opportunities for learning about the relevant issues through the briefing materials, one's communicative interlocutors, and relevant policy experts, candidates, party representatives or special interest representatives. The face-to-face

---

[58] Ackerman and Fishkin estimate that deliberation day, held biannually for all major national elections, would cost about $15 billion annually, ibid., 26. Deliberation day only for constitutional amendments, assuming continuation of the United States annual amendment rate of 0.13 (Lutz, "Toward a Theory of Constitutional Amendment," 261) would be significantly less. Even factoring in a significantly eased amendment requirement and the additional deliberation days needed for failed amendment proposals, I would expect the annual rate of amendment deliberation days to remain below 0.5. Moreover, as Ackerman and Fishkin rightly note "instead of measuring the benefits of Deliberation Day in terms of dollars [through the narrow lens of standard cost-benefit analysis], we should instead measure the legitimacy of the present distribution of dollars in terms of its capacity to gain the deliberative consent of citizens on Deliberation Day," Ackerman and Fishkin, *Deliberation Day*, 26.

structure of the small groups, furthermore, greatly reduces the salience, for opinion- and preference-formation, of reasons-unresponsive forms of advertising and political persuasion. The contemporary constellation of traditional opinion polls feeding into candidate packaging that then drives mass-media campaign coverage is, then, much less likely to be effective in the face of deliberating citizens. The deleterious effects of deliberative enclaving and the contribution of media segmentation to such, should both be significantly decreased by means of deliberative interactions across the standard lines of social division and ideology. Deliberative polling techniques open up much broader argument pools for interlocutors than they might otherwise encounter through self-selected media consumption, and they foster a context that supports taking important considerations and arguments seriously. Deliberation between individuals of heterogeneous backgrounds and class positions also should undermine some of the positive feedback cycles often noted between inequalities in deliberative capacities and resources and inequalities in the distributive mechanisms of government. Finally, the required association of deliberation day with elections on amendment proposals will dispel the need to wait upon exceptional "constitutional moments" (Ackerman) and propitious historical conditions for realizing the benefits of citizen deliberation on the fundamental structures of their political consociation. Even if preamendment deliberation days cannot solve or eliminate all of these deliberative troubles – especially those deeply rooted in social cleavages and inequalities – they do promise some quantum improvement by mitigating their deleterious effects.

Both deliberative polling and deliberation day are focused almost entirely on political opinion-formation, leaving intact extant structures for decisive will-formation. They are focused, then, on changing the environment of opinion within which candidates or policies are chosen by normal electoral majorities, not on changing the basic structures of decision making themselves. If a constitutional amendment deliberation day were adopted, it might well contribute to ameliorating the independence and sensitivity deficits of standard amendment practices. I think that their advantages could be leveraged further, however, by exploring how such deliberative structures might become empowered: using them, that is, not only for opinion-formation but also decisive will-formation as well. I start with Leib's intriguing proposal to use deliberative polling techniques in a new form of ordinary lawmaking, in order to highlight some specific challenges of adapting the techniques to the system of democratic constitutional elaboration.

In his proposal for a new "popular" branch of government to add to the other three branches of government in the United States, Leib takes the idea of deliberative polls one step further, by giving them decisive

legislative powers.[59] The basic idea is to replace existing procedures for
national initiatives and referenda with a mechanism for periodic meetings of 525 randomly selected citizens, who are required to come together
to deliberate about and decide on legislative proposals. Although they
would employ many of the techniques developed for deliberative polls –
small group interactions guided by trained and impartial mediators,
feeding into larger plenary sessions, briefings by political representatives
and experts, and so on – the key difference is that, at the end of their
sessions, they must make a decision on the proposal before them by
voting (under various supermajority rules) and thereby enact new
national law. Leib rightly emphasizes that requiring a decision by the
deliberative assemblies should have significant salubrious effects on the
deliberations themselves: the change from mere talk to action restruc-
tures the expectations and orientations of participants, and the need for a
decision significantly increases the focus of the discussions.[60] I can't begin
to do justice to his thoroughly elaborated and detailed proposal here –
I use it rather as a springboard to articulate some of the key design issues
posed in attempting to conceive of civic constitutional fora as having
authorized powers for constitutional amendment and elaboration.

   Their first issue concerns jurisdiction: while Leib's popular branch is
specifically designed to produce ordinary law, my aim is to think about
how to influence and produce constitutional law. He does speculate
briefly about a possible role for the popular branch in extant U.S.
amendment procedures, but his focus is elsewhere.[61] This focus on the
production of ordinary law leads him to envision an entirely new branch
of government, and to consider many important details about how this
would be integrated into standard separation of powers arrangements. As
I want to think about how to use structured deliberations in the context of
a system of constitutional elaboration, there is not as great a need to go
into such details – the proposal is to rethink and redesign constitutional
amendment procedures. As pressures for amendment should be somewhat rarer than correcting for felt failures of the ordinary legislative
process, a separate new branch of government is unnecessary. However,
as we are tailoring structured deliberation to constitutional issues, we
cannot have the constant recourse, as Leib does, to the backstop of
judicial review as a response to worries about getting bad outcomes from

[59] Leib, "Towards a Practice of Deliberative Democracy." His proposed fourth popular
branch has other functions than producing national legislation, although I don't focus on
those here.

[60] Delli Carpini, Cook, and Jacobs, "Public Deliberation, Discursive Participation, and
Citizen Engagement," 333, also note that mere deliberative talk without a need for
decision can often lead to worse outcomes, through frustration and disenchantment, than
would be expected in the absence of deliberation.

[61] Leib, "Towards a Practice of Deliberative Democracy," 413–14.

given decision procedures.[62] If Fishkin-style techniques are going to be applied in the system of constitutional elaboration, constitutional review is not an option: what is at issue may well be the limitation or overruling of the judgments of constitutional court or other constitutional actors about the correct way to carry out constitutional elaboration.

Given that changes in fundamental law are at stake, how can the institutions mirror the significance of this jurisdiction? In part, this raises similar issues as arose with respect to normal amendment procedures: a matter of tailoring the degree of obduracy to constitutional significance. I've no more substantive details to add here to the discussion earlier: adopted decision rules will need to be obdurate but not too obdurate, depending on the other particularities of a nation's system of constitutional elaboration. It is, however, worth taking up again one aspect of the problem: how to model political equality in decision procedures. Recall that Fishkin's original design for deliberative opinion polling employed an equal impact standard to argue for random selection as a guarantor of requisite political equality. Although there are clear self-selection problems with the polls, these don't seem so important when we are using them in civic constitutional *consultation* fora, where other such fora are simply supplying information to other constitutional actors. But if we expect such civic fora to have some degree of *control* over amendment decisions, the problem is more acute. Leib's solution is to adopt the ancient Greek modeling of political equality in the form of mandatory duties for serving on randomly selected juries in his popular branch. It thus uses random sampling – choice by lottery – to achieve political equality, while correcting for self-selection through mandatory service.[63] To this general scheme, he simply adds in more and fancier forms of supermajority rules for those decisions when amendment proposals are on the agenda of the popular branch.[64]

---

[62] For all of his careful attention to the potential benefits of citizen deliberation, Leib consistently presupposes the standard American conception of constitutional democracy as majoritarian aggregation restrained by minoritarian side-constraints. Unsurprisingly, he then consistently endorses the substantivist defense of judicial review as better at getting the right answers with respect to the minoritarian side constraints. And like the substantivist defenses encountered in Chapter 2, he also vacillates about where those side-constraints come from and what they are intended to protect. See ibid.: 369–70, 374–5, 408–14, 422, where almost the full gamut of "democratic" specters canvassed in the history of American defenses of judicial review is included.

[63] Another interesting proposal drawing on the notion of lottery to model political equality is put forward by Spector: use of randomly selected juries (of twelve, thirty-six, or more citizens) for the function of constitutional review, Spector, "Judicial Review, Rights, and Democracy," 331–3. I take it that this proposal has the same problems as those I identify presently with respect to Leib's juries.

[64] Leib, "Towards a Practice of Deliberative Democracy," 413–14. As I discussed earlier with respect to ordinary amendment procedures, I find this focus on supermajoritarianism as

Mandatory service does correct for self-selection biases, and selection by lot is one plausible theoretical way to model a conception of political equality in terms of equal impact, but I find the proposal insufficient. There is first a concern about whether any small group of citizens – whether in a random jury or in a body of elected representatives – can really be expected to fully represent that "full blast" of the opinions, values, interests, and reasons in a large heterogeneous nation-state. Perhaps "scientific random selection" and the astute collection of relevant briefing materials and selection of experts that deliberative juries would be exposed to go some way toward mitigating this worry while acknowledging the impossibility of full citizen assemblies. But there is a deeper problem, one located in the notion of conceiving of political equality in terms of equal impact in the first place. Recall Learned Hand's formulation of the paternalist objection to judicial review: "If [a bevy of Platonic Guardians] were in charge, I should miss the stimulus of living in a society where I have, at least theoretically, some part in the direction of public affairs. Of course I know how illusory would be the belief that my vote determined anything; but nevertheless when I go to the polls I have a satisfaction in the sense that we are all engaged in a common venture."[65]

One way to take Hand's notion of democratic satisfaction is to see it as pointing out a crucial connection between a subjective sense of being involved in a decision-making process and the legitimacy of the process of democratic government itself. Exposure to the full blast of sundry considerations of one's fellow citizens is then, not something that can be entirely or satisfactorily fulfilled virtually, through the theoretical abstractions of randomized sampling or lotteries. If exercises of government power are legitimated to the extent that their decision procedures are reasons-responsive to a full consideration of the interests of all affected, and if this can only occur democratically to the extent that citizens are ultimately responsible for that reasons-responsiveness, then there is an inexpugnable normative element of mutual consociation involved in constitutional democracy. As thinkers as diverse as Rousseau, Dewey, Hand, Dworkin, and Habermas – and many others as well – point out in diverse ways, democracy is a common venture, a form of mutual consociation through law. It is precisely this interactive, participatory, and common character of democracy that gets left out of Leib's popular

---

the way to think about obduracy somewhat misplaced. To be sure, we will need more difficult procedures for amendments than for ordinary laws, but its not simply a numbers game of allowing more minority vetoes or making it harder for majorities to win. Difficulty should be tailored rather to the deliberative virtues of allowing sufficient time for deliberation, encouraging the deliberative inputs of heterogeneous actors and agencies with diverse viewpoints and specialized competencies, and, spreading out decisional authority across those heterogeneous actors and agencies.

[65] Hand, *The Bill of Rights*, 73–74.

branch, no matter how participatory, interactive, and common it is for the small fraction of the population selected for service.

Traditional forms of civic republicanism, and their contemporary descendents in participatory democracy and communitarianism, have been centrally concerned with fostering this particular sense of democracy as a joint venture. Their institutional solutions for achieving it have, however, suffered from a certain degree of unreality. In particular, there seems little hope for reconstituting political communities on the scale of the Greek *polis* or Rousseau's beloved Geneva under contemporary sociopolitical conditions, nor is devolution of democracy to locally autonomous communities acceptable given the scale and scope of contemporary coordination problems.[66] Deliberation day, does however, hold out the promise of realizing the sense of being involved in a common venture through small-group deliberative interactions, all the while maintaining most of the efficiency and simplicity of normal electoral mechanisms. I propose, speculatively then, to combine Leib's civic juries with Ackerman and Fishkin's deliberation day into a new type of process for constitutional amendment. The basic idea is that we can use randomly selected deliberative juries for certifying amendment proposals for the ballot, and require national deliberation days for the ratification or rejection of those amendment proposals. Without getting overly specific about detailed mechanisms, let me suggest that there are three important stages that institutional design would need to focus on in working out the details: *selection* of amendment proposals, *certification* of proposals for voter consideration, and *ratification* or rejection of the proposals.

The selection stage is one of the more difficult ones from the perspective of deliberative democratic constitutionalism. Rather than delineating new procedures here, I take mostly for granted standard ways of initiating national amendment proposals, for instance, by garnering a sufficient number of citizen signatures (perhaps geographically distributed) or on referral from national legislatures. Given that civic constitutional fora are intended in part to act as a check on constitutional elaboration carried out by the various branches of the government, it is crucial to maintain the popular initiation route, although I see no reason why government initiated proposals should be excluded. It is often the case that, for instance, legislators recognize that there are

---

[66] One might legitimately wonder here whether the nation-state is sufficiently capacious to deal with these coordination problems. Here again, the limitations of this study to constitutional democracy in extant nation-states come to the fore. The limitations of the nation-state concern not only empirical worries about feasibility but also serious normative worries given the contingent historical reasons for its particular way of drawing boundaries between citizens, subjects, and outsiders – boundaries which increasingly widen the disconnect between the sets of those affected by national law and those with authoritative power over the content of that law.

changes needed in the procedures of democratic representation even though they face insurmountable political obstacles to solution in legislatures themselves: procedures for political districting are a good example here.

If the selection phase is considered as embodying the problem of agenda-setting, then there are at least two quite different kinds of worries about the initiative process that puts an amendment proposal to deliberative constitutional juries. First, from a more expertocratic direction, there is a worry about the quality of whatever proposal makes it through. Because what is being considered is a law that will change the conditions of democratic law-making itself – a constitutional amendment – the proposal ought to be carefully considered from the viewpoint of its foreseeable impact, including its specifically legal impact on the overall systematicity of constitutional and ordinary law, and its long-term institutional and substantive consequences for society in general. From this perspective, we would want any proposal to receive some legal consideration and vetting to prevent, at least, proposals that are sloppily drafted or would destabilize the legal system. However, a constitution is not simply a lawyer's document; it is the people's structuring of the procedural conditions for their mutual consociation through higher law. There is, then, a second worry coming from a more populist direction about a preselection of the agenda by lawyers or other elites. And this worry will be increased to the extent that the vetting process extends into consideration of the substantive consequences of such a proposal for society in general. My intuition here, at least, is that at the selection stage we should err on the side of allowing proposals to go forward that might look unwise, trusting in the deliberative qualities of the later two stages of certification and ratification to weed out ones that turn out so to be, in the light of the considered judgment of democratic citizens themselves. Thus, perhaps all that is needed at this early selection phase is a politically independent panel of legal experts – including, say, appointed national judges and law professors – to vet proposals for minimal legal soundness and clarity.

Perhaps there is a different worry about agenda-setting at the initial selection stage, one focused on the popular proposal means of setting the agenda of constitutional juries. The same concerns about the outsized influence of social powers and deep-pocketed private interests that arise in normal popular referenda – and that troubled ideal claims for the independence and sensitivity of normal amendment processes – might be thought to arise with the modified system I am recommending here. There are two important reasons I think this worry is misplaced however. First, the popular initiative does not put a proposal directly on the ballot, it, rather, selects a proposal for constitutional deliberative juries to consider. My proposal then interposes a deliberative filter between the selection and ballot certification stages. In order to fully utilize the deliberative advantages of the system, I recommend further that three successive constitutional juries would be required to certify an amendment proposal for the national ballot. The three juries should be spaced out over a significant time span, and each should be composed of a different group of randomly selected jurors. The relative obduracy of this proposal is not recommended simply to make the process difficult, but to draw on the extensive deliberative resources of informal public spheres, extended over the time period from the original selection of the proposal until its possible certification. There will need to be, then, rather extensive mechanisms for postdeliberation reporting on and education about the work of the certification juries, although this need not be formally institutionalized if there are robust informal public sphere institutions that could carry this function.[67] The remarkable information and argument collecting resources of public spheres – and in particular those of the diverse civil society associations that support its vibrancy and effectiveness – should not be discounted simply because of worries about the possibly deleterious influence of social powers and moneyed interests. At the end of the day, what should determine whether a proposal is selected for the ballot is the quality and strength of the reasons and arguments that can be marshaled in support of it – and it is precisely the task of certification juries to figure this out.[68] Said another way, amendment proposals cannot be simply dismissed out of hand because of who they were originated by or how they first came before the public. In sum, worries about the character of the agenda-setting process are to be largely addressed through the reasons-responsiveness of the certification and ratification stages.

Might similar problems reappear, however, once an amendment proposal has been certified for the ballot by three successive constitutional juries? Shouldn't we expect a return of all of the deliberative troubles of mass-mediated informal public spheres and the disproportionate influence of well-funded pressure groups utilizing the techniques of modern political slogan advertising? Such worries are a significant part of the reason for requiring a national deliberation day before voting on a constitutional amendment. Recall that Ackerman and Fishkin's arguments for deliberation day are not only focused on changing the current incentives for rational ignorance on the part of individual voters.

---

[67] The importance of such post-deliberation activity is stressed at Ryfe, "Does Deliberative Democracy Work?," 60–62.

[68] See the thoughtful discussion of the way in which deliberative assemblies change the political incentives for interest groups operating in the informal public spheres, and thus their role in setting the agenda of deliberative juries, at Leib, "Towards a Practice of Deliberative Democracy," 441–56.

They also hope – a reasonable hope I believe, given the available evidence – that there will be significant changes in the incentive structures for information providers in the public sphere generally. Political officials, civil society groups, moneyed interests, and the mass media will all need to reorient their current dissemination and persuasion mechanisms and techniques with a view to reasonably well-informed voters, who would be much more aware of the difference between fact and hyperbole, substance and soundbite, strong reasons and weak reasons.[69] In short, hopes for the democratic worth and quality of civic constitutional fora are ultimately based in part in hopes for a structural transformation of the public sphere and in part in a belief in the capacity of democratic citizens to actually set their own constitutional terms of mutual consociation. To be sure, such considerations will never sufficiently satisfy those who, for normative or empirical reasons, have a hypertrophied distrust of the reasoning powers of ordinary people or of the capacity for even well-informed citizens to govern themselves, but then no democratic theory – deliberative, constitutional, or otherwise – could.

By way of a recapitulation, it helps to see how the elements of this proposal for civic constitutional fora support the six assessment values set out for mechanisms of constitutional review. First, I expect it to have no significant effect on the overall systematicity of the legal corpus, as those amendment proposals that make it onto the ballot and are ratified would be analyzed at each step along the way for their legal effects. Expert legal opinions would play a role not only in the minimal vetting process of selecting proposals for consideration by constitutional juries but also would surely be injected in the general argumentation processes carried on both in the public spheres and within deliberative assemblies themselves – both constitutional juries and deliberation day assemblies. With respect to settlement, we might well expect the same modest positive effect witnessed by standard amendment procedures, where unresolved constitutional issues are definitively settled by authority of the people's constituent power. Or perhaps the relative ease of the procedure would lead to its frequent use, thus somewhat undercutting settlement as measured over a long time span. At any rate, such modest settlement deficits, were they to occur, would not themselves be cause for

---

[69] This is what is referred to as the "leveraging strategy" that deliberation day would employ, in Ackerman and Fishkin, *Deliberation Day*, 13. Leib shares the same idea: "Since the aggregation of uninformed votes would no longer win policy elections, it is no longer in the media-manipulator's interest to use techniques that avoid intelligent and more detailed information," Leib, "Towards a Practice of Deliberative Democracy," 455. Perhaps such hopes will turn out to be overly optimistic. In that case, it might become important to establish public institutions for extensive postcertification reporting and civic education concerning the relevant issues and arguments arising out of the selection and certification processes.

concern: democratic constitutionalism is a process of permanent, peace-
ful, procedurally structured revolution that does not rely solely or significantly on legal stability and its associated values for legitimacy.[70] Like
normal amendment procedures, civic constitutional fora would be
strongly contributory with respect both to empowerment – it would allow
democratic citizens to take the powers of constitutional elaboration into
their own hands – and to jurisdiction – exercising the constituent power
to set the procedural conditions of lawmaking, citizens would have the
same jurisdiction as ordinary constitutional assemblies.

The real improvement over traditional amendment mechanisms
comes from drawing on and leveraging the techniques of deliberative
polling in order to operationalize a practice of deliberative democratic
constitutionalism. By making amendment processes systematically
reasons-responsive to the full blast of information, opinions, values,
and arguments available in the informal and formal public spheres,
the deliberative troubles that appear to actually undermine the ideal
sensitivity and independence of normal amendment mechanisms can be
largely mitigated. Rather than placing gag rules on public sphere com-
municators, they employ basic techniques for improving the processes
of considering and weighing those communications that would greatly
reduce the salience of hype, sound bites, fictions, pandering, threats, and
so on. Deliberation then addresses worries about social powers capturing
normal amendment referenda and rendering them insufficiently independent. But civic constitutional fora also should greatly increase the
sensitivity of amendment processes to the wide diversity of information
and reasons available in the public spheres, and change what that sensitivity is to: not the raw voting power of the citizenry, but their voting
power as reflective citizens engaged in the common venture of coordinating their mutual political lives through the medium of constitutional
law. This entails finally that, unlike in the case of the other three types of
proposals I endorsed that operate at the horizontal level of formal government – concentrated judicial review, self-review panels, and interbranch dispersal – civic constitutional fora could overcome the otherwise
intractable tension between political independence and popular sensitivity. Drawing on the vertical relationship between the informal and
formal public spheres, we can institutionally structure a truly independent
"guardianship of the guardians" of the constitution that is, at the same
time, much more sensitive to the interests, opinions, and values of all
affected than any form of elite platonic guardians.

---

[70] For example, would it have been better to prefer settlement over the U.S. people's
capacity to repeal the Eighteenth Amendment (prohibiting the manufacture, sale, and
commerce of alcohol) only fourteen years later through the Twenty-First Amendment?

Let me be clear: I am not claiming that civic constitutional fora can solve all of the ills of contemporary political public spheres, nor more grandly yet, that it can solve all of the problems of constitutional self-government. I don't think, for instance, that such proposals will lead to enlightened unanimity or near-consensus throughout a diverse nation-state on obviously rational political goals and clear and indubitable policy implementations. Deliberation alone cannot liquefy the facts of reasonable pluralism or social complexity, or the difficulties of practical reasoning in general, through the solvent of unfettered Reason. I am claiming, however, that significant improvements can be made through relatively modest changes in current incentive structures for citizens, political actors, and the supporting political public spheres, and that these changes can be implemented through modest proposals to improve the procedures of democratic constitutional elaboration. After all, if deliberative democratic legitimacy aims at a system of law where citizens can understand themselves as both subjects and authors of that law, and if that is only achievable under modern conditions on the supposition that democratic procedures alone warrant the expectation of better decisions, then we cannot simply take inherited procedures for granted as the best possible. And this is precisely what democratic constitutions acknowledge explicitly by allowing for amendment in the first place: it may well be that there are mechanisms for improving the basic procedures of democratic lawmaking itself. We owe it to ourselves as democratic citizens to seek out and foster those procedures that can best fulfill the aspirations of deliberative democratic constitutionalism.

Bibliography

Ackerman, Bruce. *We the People: Foundations*. Cambridge, MA: Harvard University Press, 1991.
　We the People: Transformations. Cambridge, MA: Harvard University Press, 1998.
Ackerman, Bruce, and James S. Fishkin. *Deliberation Day*. New Haven, CT: Yale University Press, 2004.
Alexander, Larry. "Introduction." In *Constitutionalism: Philosophical Foundations*, edited by Larry Alexander, 1–13. New York: Cambridge University Press, 1998.
　"Is Judicial Review Democratic? A Comment on Harel." *Law and Philosophy* 22, no. 3–4 (2003): 277–83.
　"The Constitution as Law." *Constitutional Commentary* 6 (1989): 103ff.
Alexander, Larry, and Frederick Schauer. "On Extrajudicial Constitutional Interpretation." *Harvard Law Review* 110 (1997): 1359–87.
Alexander, Larry, and Lawrence B. Solum. "Popular? Constitutionalism? A Book Review of *the People Themselves* by Larry D. Kramer." *Harvard Law Review* 118, no. 5 (2005): 1594–640.
Alexy, Robert. "The Special Case Thesis." *Ratio Juris* 12, no. 4 (1999): 374–84.
Amar, Akhil Reed. *The Bill of Rights: Creation and Reconstruction*. New Haven, CT: Yale University Press, 1998.
Ankersmit, F. R. *Aesthetic Politics: Political Philosophy beyond Fact and Value*. Stanford, CA: Stanford University Press, 1997.
Apel, Karl-Otto. "The a Priori of the Communication Community and the Foundations of Ethics." In *Towards a Transformation of Philosophy*, 225–300. London: Routledge & Kegan Paul, 1980.
Aquinas, Saint Thomas. *Summa Theologiae*. 60 vols. Vol. 43. New York: McGraw-Hill, 1964.
Arato, Andrew. *Civil Society, Constitution, and Legitimacy*. Lanham, MD: Rowman & Littlefield, 2000.
Aristotle. *Politics*. Translated by Benjamin Jowett. New York: Random House, 1943.
　The Complete Works of Aristotle. Translated by Jonathan Barnes. 2 vols, *Bollingen Series*. Princeton, NJ: Princeton University Press, 1984.

Arrow, Kenneth J. *Social Choice and Individual Values*. Second ed. New Haven: Yale University Press, 1963.

Baker v. Carr, 369 U.S. 186 (1962).

Barber, Benjamin J. *Strong Democracy: Participatory Politics for a New Age*. Berkeley: University of California Press, 1984.

Barber, Sotirios A., and Robert P. George, eds. *Constitutional Politics: Essays on Constitution Making, Maintenance, and Change*. Princeton, NJ: Princeton University Press, 2001.

Barnett, Randy E. *Restoring the Lost Constitution: The Presumption of Liberty*. Princeton, NJ: Princeton University Press, 2004.

Baum, Lawrence. *The Supreme Court*. Eighth ed. Washington, DC: CQ Press, 2004.

Baynes, Kenneth. "Rights as Critique and the Critique of Rights: Karl Marx, Wendy Brown, and the Social Function of Rights." *Political Theory* 28, no. 4 (2000): 451–68.

Bellamy, Richard. "The Political Form of the Constitution: The Separation of Powers, Rights and Representative Government." *Political Studies* XLIV (1996): 436–56.

Bellamy, Richard, and Dario Castiglione. "Introduction: Constitutions and Politics." *Political Studies* XLIV (1996): 413–16.

Benhabib, Seyla. "Toward a Deliberative Model of Democratic Legitimacy." In *Democracy and Difference: Contesting the Boundaries of the Political*, edited by Seyla Benhabib, 67–94. Princeton, NJ: Princeton University Press, 1996.

Bennett, Robert W. "Counter-Conversationalism and the Sense of Difficulty." *Northwestern University Law Review* 95, no. 3 (2001): 845–906.

Talking It Through: Puzzles of American Democracy. Ithaca, NY: Cornell University Press, 2003.

Bickel, Alexander M. *The Least Dangerous Branch: The Supreme Court at the Bar of Politics*. Second ed. New Haven, CT: Yale University Press, 1986.

Bogdanor, Vernon. "Constitutional Reform in Britain: The Quiet Revolution." *Annual Review of Political Science* 8, no. 1 (2005): 73–98.

Bohman, James. *Public Deliberation: Pluralism, Complexity, and Democracy*. Cambridge, MA: MIT Press, 1996.

"Survey Article: The Coming of Age of Deliberative Democracy." *The Journal of Political Philosophy* 6, no. 4 (1998): 400–25.

Bork, Robert H. "Neutral Principles and Some First Amendment Problems." *Indiana Law Journal* 47 (1971).

Brewer-Carías, Allan R. *Judicial Review in Comparative Law*. New York: Cambridge University Press, 1989.

Brigham, John. "The Constitution of the Supreme Court." In *The Supreme Court in American Politics: New Institutionalist Interpretations*, edited by Howard Gillman and Cornell Clayton, 15–27. Lawrence: University Press of Kansas, 1999.

Brown v. Board of Education, 347 U.S. 483 (1954).

Brutus. "Letters Of "Brutus"." In *The Federalist with Letters of "Brutus,"* edited by Terence Ball, 433–533. New York: Cambridge University Press, 2003.

Bush v. Gore, 531 U.S. 98 (2000).

Cappelletti, Mauro. *Judicial Review in the Contemporary World*. Indianapolis, IN: Bobbs-Merrill, 1971.

Castiglione, Dario. "The Political Theory of the Constitution." *Political Studies* XLIV (1996): 417–35.

Chambers, Simone. "Deliberative Democratic Theory." *Annual Review of Political Science* 6, no. 1 (2003): 307–26.

"Democracy, Popular Sovereignty, and Constitutional Legitimacy." *Constellations* 11, no. 2 (2004): 153–73.

Cheeves, John. "Committee OKs Ban on Nude Club Dancing." *Lexington Herald-Leader*, February 11, 2000, B 1.

Chemerinsky, Erwin. "The Supreme Court, 1988 Term – Foreword: The Vanishing Constitution." *Harvard Law Review* 103 (1989): 43–104.

Choper, Jesse H. *Judicial Review and the National Political Process*. Chicago, IL: University of Chicago Press, 1980.

Christiano, Thomas. "Waldron on Law and Disagreement." *Law and Philosophy* 19, no. 4 (2000): 513–43.

City of Boerne v. Flores, 521 U.S. 507 (1997).

Clayton, Cornell, and Howard Gillman, eds. *Supreme Court Decision-Making: New Institutionalist Approaches*. Chicago: University of Chicago Press, 1999.

Clinton, Robert Lowry. "How the Court Became Supreme." *First Things* 89 (1998): 13–19.

Cohen, Joshua. "An Epistemic Conception of Democracy." *Ethics* 97 (1986): 26–38.

1998. Dahl on Democracy and Equal Consideration. In, http://web.mit.edu/ polisci/research/cohen/dahl_on_democracy.pdf (accessed March 31, 2005).

"Democracy and Liberty." In *Deliberative Democracy*, edited by Jon Elster, 185–231. New York: Cambridge University Press, 1998.

"For a Democratic Society." In *The Cambridge Companion to Rawls*, edited by Samuel Freeman, 86–138. New York: Cambridge University Press, 2003.

"Procedure and Substance in Deliberative Democracy." In *Democracy and Difference: Contesting the Boundaries of the Political*, edited by Seyla Benhabib, 95–119. Princeton, NJ: Princeton University Press, 1996.

Cohen, Joshua, and Joel Rogers. *Associations and Democracy*. London: Verso, 1995.

Colegrove v. Green, 328 U.S. 549 (1946).

Constant, Benjamin. "The Liberty of the Ancients Compared with That of the Moderns." In *The Political Writings of Benjamin Constant*, edited by Biancamaria Fontana, 307–28. New York: Cambridge University Press, 1988.

Cooper v. Aaron, 358 U.S. 1 (1958).

Corwin, Edward S. *The "Higher Law" Background of American Constitutional Law*. Binghamton, NY: Cornell University Press, 1955 (1928).

Dahl, Robert A. *A Preface to Democratic Theory*. Chicago, IL: University of Chicago Press, 1956.

"Decision-Making in a Democracy: The Supreme Court as a National Policy-Maker." *Journal of Public Law* 6 (1957): 279–95.

"Decision-Making in a Democracy: The Supreme Court as a National Policy-Maker." In *The Democracy Sourcebook*, edited by Robert A. Dahl, Ian Shapiro, and José Antonio Cheibub, 246–51. Cambridge, MA: MIT Press, 2003 (1957).

Democracy and Its Critics. New Haven, CT: Yale University Press, 1989.

How Democratic Is the American Constitution? New Haven, CT: Yale University Press, 2001.

On Democracy. New Haven, CT: Yale University Press, 1998.

Dahl, Robert A., Ian Shapiro, and José Antonio Cheibub, eds. *The Democracy Sourcebook.* Cambridge, MA: MIT Press, 2003.

Davis v. Bandemer, 478 U.S. 109 (1986).

Delli Carpini, Michael X., Fay Lomax Cook, and Lawrence R. Jacobs. "Public Deliberation, Discursive Participation, and Citizen Engagement: A Review of the Empirical Literature." *Annual Review of Political Science* 7, no. 1 (2004): 315–44.

Dewey, John. *The Public and Its Problems.* Edited by Jo Ann Boydston. Vol. 2: 1925–1927, *The Later Works of John Dewey, 1925–1953.* Carbondale: Southern Illinois University Press, 1984.

Dicey, A. V. *An Introduction to the Study of the Law of the Constitution.* 10th ed. New York: St. Martin's Press, 1965 (1908).

Downs, Anthony. *An Economic Theory of Democracy.* New York: The Free Press, 1957.

Dred Scott v. Sandford, 60 U.S. 393 (1857).

Dryzek, John S. *Deliberative Democracy and Beyond: Liberals, Critics, Contestations.* New York: Oxford University Press, 2000.

Discursive Democracy: Politics, Policy and Political Science. New York: Cambridge University Press, 1990.

Dworkin, Ronald. *A Matter of Principle.* Cambridge, MA: Harvard University Press, 1985.

"Constitutionalism and Democracy." *European Journal of Philosophy* 3, no. 1 (1995): 2–11.

Freedom's Law: The Moral Reading of the American Constitution. Cambridge, MA: Harvard University Press, 1996.

Law's Empire. Cambridge, MA: Harvard University Press, 1986.

Sovereign Virtue: The Theory and Practice of Equality. Cambridge, MA: Harvard University Press, 2000.

Taking Rights Seriously. Cambridge, MA: Harvard University Press, 1978.

"The Model of Rules." *University of Chicago Law Review* 35 (1967).

Dworkin, Ronald, Thomas Nagel, Robert Nozick, John Rawls, Thomas Scanlon, and Judith Jarvis Thomson. "Assisted Suicide: The Philosophers' Brief." *New York Review of Books*, March 27 1997, 41–47.

Eisgruber, Christopher L. *Constitutional Self-Government.* Cambridge, MA: Harvard University Press, 2001.

"Disagreeable People." *Stanford Law Review* 43 (1990): 275ff.

Elk Grove Unified School District et al. v. Newdow et al., 542 U.S. 1 (2004).

Elster, Jon. "The Market and the Forum: Three Varieties of Political Theory." In *Deliberative Democracy: Essays on Reason and Politics*, edited by James Bohman and William Rehg, 3–33. Cambridge, MA: MIT Press, 1997.

Ely, John Hart. "Another Such Victory: Constitutional Theory and Practice in a
    World Where Courts Are No Different from Legislatures." *Virginia Law
    Review* 77 (1991): 833–79.
    Democracy and Distrust: A Theory of Judicial Review. Cambridge, MA: Harvard
    University Press, 1980.
    On Constitutional Ground. Princeton, NJ: Princeton University Press, 1996.
Epstein, Lee. "Judicial Decision Making." In *Encyclopedia of Law & Society*, edited
    by David C. Clark. Thousand Oaks, CA: Sage, 2005.
    "The Comparative Advantage." *Law and Courts* 9 (1999): 1–6.
Eskridge, William N., Jr., and John Ferejohn. "Politics, Interpretation, and
    the Rule of Law." In *The Rule of Law: Nomos XXXVI*, edited by Ian Shapiro,
    265–2894. New York: New York University Press, 1994.
Estlund, David M. "Beyond Fairness and Deliberation: The Epistemic Dimension
    of Democratic Authority." In *Deliberative Democracy: Essays on Reason and
    Politics*, edited by James Bohman and William Rehg, 173–204. Cambridge,
    MA: MIT Press, 1997.
Fabre, Cécile. "A Philosophical Argument for a Bill of Rights." *British Journal of
    Political Science* 30 (2000): 77–98.
Fallon, Richard H., Jr. "Legitimacy and the Constitution." *Harvard Law Review*
    118, no. 6 (2005): 1787–1853.
Favoreu, Louis. "Constitutional Review in Europe." In *Constitutionalism and Rights:
    The Influence of the United States Constitution Abroad*, edited by Louis Henkin
    and Albert J. Rosenthal, 38–62. New York: Columbia University Press,
    1990.
Ferejohn, John. "Constitutional Review in the Global Context." *New York
    University Journal of Legislation and Public Policy* 6 (2002–2003): 49–59.
    "Instituting Deliberative Democracy." In *Designing Democratic Institutions*,
    edited by Ian Shapiro and Stephen Macedo, 75–104. New York: New York
    University Press, 2000.
    "Judicializing Politics, Politicizing Law." *Hoover Digest* (2003).
Ferejohn, John, and Pasquale Pasquino. "Constitutional Adjudication: Lessons
    from Europe." *Texas Law Review* 82 (2004): 1671–1704.
Ferejohn, John, Jack N. Rakove, and Jonathan Riley. "Editors' Introduction." In
    Constitutional Culture and Democratic Rule, edited by John Ferejohn, Jack N.
    Rakove and Jonathan Riley, 1–37. New York: Cambridge University Press,
    2001.
Finn, John E. "The Civic Constitution: Some Preliminaries." In *Constitutional
    Politics: Essays on Constitution Making, Maintenance, and Change*, edited by
    Sotirios A. Barber and Robert P. George, 41–69. Princeton, NJ: Princeton
    University Press, 2001.
Finnis, John. *Natural Law and Natural Rights.* London: Oxford University Press,
    1980.
Fishkin, James S. 2004. Deliberative Polling®: Toward a Better-Informed
    Democracy. In, http://cdd.stanford.edu/polls/docs/summary/ (accessed June
    15, 2005).
    Democracy and Deliberation: New Directions for Democratic Reform. New Haven, CT:
    Yale University Press, 1992.

The Voice of the People: Public Opinion and Democracy. expanded ed. New Haven, CT: Yale University Press, 1997.

Fishkin, James S., and Robert C. Luskin. 2004. Experimenting with a Democratic Ideal: Deliberative Polling and Public Opinion. In, http://cdd.stanford.edu/research/index.html (accessed June 15, 2005).

Forst, Rainer. "The Rule of Reasons: Three Models of Deliberative Democracy." *Ratio Juris* 14, no. 4 (2001): 345–78.

Freeman, Samuel. "Constitutional Democracy and the Legitimacy of Judicial Review." *Law and Philosophy* 9 (1990–1991): 327–70.

"Deliberative Democracy: A Sympathetic Critique." *Philosophy and Public Affairs* 29, no. 4 (2000): 371–418.

Fuller, Lon L. *The Morality of Law.* Revised ed. New Haven, CT: Yale University Press, 1969.

Fung, Archon. "Recipes for Public Spheres: Eight Institutional Design Choices and Their Consequences." *The Journal of Political Philosophy* 11, no. 3 (2003): 338–67.

Gardbaum, Stephen. "The New Commonwealth Model of Constitutionalism." *American Journal of Comparative Law* 49, no. 4 (2001): 707–60.

Ginsburg, Tom. *Judicial Review in New Democracies: Constitutional Courts in Asian Cases.* New York: Cambridge University Press, 2003.

Goodin, Robert E. "Democratic Deliberation within." In *Debating Deliberative Democracy,* edited by James S. Fishkin and Peter Laslett, 54–79. Malden, MA: Blackwell, 2003.

Gordon, Scott. *Controlling the State: Constitutionalism from Ancient Athens to Today.* Cambridge, MA: Harvard University Press, 1999.

Graber, Mark A. "The Nonmajoritarian Difficulty: Legislative Deference to the Judiciary." *Studies in American Political Development* 7 (1993): 35–73.

Gray v. Sanders, 372 U.S. 368 (1963).

Grey, Thomas C. "Constitutionalism: An Analytic Framework." In *Constitutionalism,* edited by J. Roland Pennock and John W. Chapman, 189–209. New York: New York University Press, 1979.

Griffin, Stephen M. *American Constitutionalism: From Theory to Politics.* Princeton, NJ: Princeton University Press, 1996.

Griswold v. Connecticut, 381 U.S. 479 (1965).

Günther, Klaus. *The Sense of Appropriateness: Application Discourses in Morality and Law.* Translated by John Farell. Albany: State University of New York Press, 1993.

Gutmann, Amy, and Dennis Thompson. *Democracy and Disagreement.* Cambridge, MA: Harvard University Press, 1996.

Habermas, Jürgen. "A Short Reply." *Ratio Juris* 12, no. 4 (1999): 445–53.

Between Facts and Norms: Contributions to a Discourse Theory of Law and Democracy. Translated by William Rehg. Cambridge, MA: MIT Press, 1996.

"Constitutional Democracy: A Paradoxical Union of Contradictory Principles?" *Political Theory* 29, no. 6 (2001): 766–81.

"On Law and Disagreement: Some Comments On 'Interpretive Pluralism'." *Ratio Juris* 16, no. 2 (2003): 187–94.

The Inclusion of the Other: Studies in Political Theory. Edited by Ciaran Cronin and Pablo De Greiff. Cambridge, MA: MIT Press, 1998.

The Structural Transformation of the Public Sphere: An Inquiry into a Category of Bourgeois Society. Translated by Thomas Burger. Cambridge, MA: MIT Press, 1989.

Hamilton, Alexander, James Madison, and John Jay. *The Federalist with Letters of "Brutus," Cambridge Texts in the History of Political Thought*. New York: Cambridge University Press, 2003.

Hand, Learned. "Democracy: Its Presumptions and Realities." In *The Spirit of Liberty: Papers and Addresses of Learned Hand*, edited by Irving Dilliard, 90–102. New York: Alfred A. Knopf, 1960 [1932].

The Bill of Rights. Cambridge, MA: Harvard University Press, 1958.

Harel, Alon. "Rights-Based Judicial Review: A Democratic Justification." *Law and Philosophy* 22, no. 3–4 (2003): 247–76.

Hart, H. L. A. *The Concept of Law*. Second ed. Oxford: Clarendon Press, 1994.

Hayek, Friedrich A. *The Constitution of Liberty*. Chicago: University of Chicago Press, 1960.

Hirschl, Ran. *Towards Juristocracy: The Origins and Consequences of the New Constitutionalism*. Cambridge, MA: Harvard University Press, 2004.

Hobbes, Thomas. *Leviathan*. Edited by Richard Tuck, *Cambridge Texts in the History of Political Thought*. New York: Cambridge University Press, 1991.

Holmes, Stephen. "Gag Rules or the Politics of Omission." In *Constitutionalism and Democracy*, edited by Jon Elster and Rune Slagstad, 19–58. New York: Cambridge University Press, 1988.

Passions and Constraint: On the Theory of Liberal Democracy. Chicago: University of Chicago Press, 1995.

"Precommitment and the Paradox of Democracy." In *Constitutionalism and Democracy*, edited by Jon Elster and Rune Slagstad, 195–240. New York: Cambridge University Press, 1988.

Holmes, Stephen, and Cass R. Sunstein. "The Politics of Constitutional Revision in Eastern Europe." In *Responding to Imperfection: The Theory and Practice of Constitutional Amendment*, edited by Sanford Levinson, 275–306. Princeton, NJ: Princeton University Press, 1995.

Hume, David. "An Enquiry Concerning the Principles of Morals." In *Enquiries Concerning Human Understanding and Concerning the Principles of Human Morals*, edited by P. H. Nidditch. New York: Clarendon Press, 1975.

Jacob, Herbert. "Introduction." In *Courts, Law, and Politics in Comparative Perspective*, edited by Herbert Jacob, Erhard Blankenberg, Herbert M. Kritzer, Doris Marie Provine and Joseph Sanders, 1–15. New Haven, CT: Yale University Press, 1996.

Jacob, Herbert, Erhard Blankenberg, Herbert M. Kritzer, Doris Marie Provine, and Joseph Sanders. *Courts, Law, and Politics in Comparative Perspective*. New Haven, CT: Yale University Press, 1996.

Kalyvas, Andreas. "Popular Sovereignty, Democracy, and the Constituent Power." *Constellations* 12, no. 5 (2005): 223–44.

Kant, Immanuel. "Idea for a Universal History with a Cosmopolitan Purpose." In *Kant's Political Writings*, edited by Hans Reiss, 41–53. New York: Cambridge University Press, 1980.

Kavanagh, Aileen. "Participation and Judicial Review: A Reply to Jeremy Waldron." *Law and Philosophy* 22, no. 5 (2003): 451–86.

Kelsen, Hans. *Introduction to the Problems of Legal Theory*. Translated by Bonnie Litschewski Paulson and Stanley L. Paulson. New York: Clarendon Press, 1992.

"Judicial Review of Legislation. A Comparative Study of the Austrian and the American Constitution." *Journal of Politics* 4, no. 2 (1942): 183–200.

Klarman, Michael J. *From Jim Crow to Civil Rights: The Supreme Court and the Struggle for Racial Equality*. New York: Oxford University Press, 2003.

Koopmans, Tim. *Courts and Political Institutions: A Comparative View*. Cambridge: Cambridge University Press, 2003.

Kramer, Larry D. *The People Themselves: Popular Constitutionalism and Judicial Review*. New York: Oxford University Press, 2004.

Kritzer, Herbert M. "Courts, Justice, and Politics in England." In *Courts, Law, and Politics in Comparative Perspective*, edited by Herbert Jacob, Erhard Blankenburg, Herbert M. Kritzer, Doris Marie Provine and Joseph Sanders, 81–176. New Haven, CT: Yale University Press, 1996.

Lawrence et al. v. Texas, 539 US 558 (2003).

Leib, Ethan J. "Towards a Practice of Deliberative Democracy: A Proposal for a Popular Branch." *Rutgers Law Journal* 33 (2002): 359–456.

Levinson, Sanford, ed. *Responding to Imperfection: The Theory and Practice of Constitutional Amendment*. Princeton, NJ: Princeton University Press, 1995.

Lijphart, Arend. *Patterns of Democracy: Government Forms and Performance in Thirty-Six Countries*. New Haven, CT: Yale University Press, 1999.

Lochner v. New York, 198 U.S. 45 (1905).

Locke, John. "The Second Treatise of Government." In *Two Treatises of Government*, edited by Peter Laslett, 265–428. New York: Cambridge University Press, 1988.

Two Treatises of Government. Edited by Peter Laslett. New York: Cambridge University Press, 1988.

Lockyer v. Andrade, 538 U.S. 63 (2003).

Luskin, Robert C., James S. Fishkin, and Dennis L. Plane. 1999. Deliberative Polling and Policy Outcomes: Electric Utility Issues in Texas. In, http://cdd.stanford.edu/research/index.html. (accessed June 16, 2005).

Luther v. Borden, 48 U.S. 1 (1849).

Lutz, Donald S. "Toward a Theory of Constitutional Amendment." In *Responding to Imperfection: The Theory and Practice of Constitutional Amendment*, edited by Sanford Levinson, 237–74. Princeton, NJ: Princeton University Press, 1995.

MacCormick, Neil. "The Relative Heteronomy of Law." *European Journal of Philosophy* 3, no. 1 (1995): 69–85.

Maddex, Robert E. *Constitutions of the World*. Washington, DC: Congressional Quarterly, Inc., 2001.

Manin, Bernard. "On Legitimacy and Political Deliberation." *Political Theory* 15, no. 3 (1987): 338–68.

Mansbridge, Jane. *Beyond Adversary Democracy*. Chicago: University of Chicago Press, 1983.

Marbury v. Madison, 5 U.S. 137 (1803).

Marmor, Andrei. "The Rule of Law and Its Limits." *Law and Philosophy* 23, no. 1 (2004): 1–43.

Marshall, T. H. *Citizenship and Social Class.* London: Cambridge University Press, 1950.

Mavcic, Arne. 2004. A Tabular Presentation of Constitutional/Judicial Review around the World. In http://www.concourts.net/index.html (accessed December 21, 2004).

McCann, Michael. "How the Supreme Court Matters in American Politics: New Institutionalist Perspectives." In *The Supreme Court in American Politics: New Institutionalist Interpretations,* edited by Howard Gillman and Cornell Clayton, 63–97. Lawrence: University Press of Kansas, 1999.

McCarthy, Thomas. "Enlightenment and the Public Use of Reason." *European Journal of Philosophy* 3, no. 3 (1995): 242–56.

——— "Legitimacy and Diversity: Dialectical Reflections on Analytic Distinctions." *Cardozo Law Review* 17, no. 4–5 (1996): 1083–125.

——— "Practical Discourse: On the Relation of Morality to Politics." In *Ideals and Illusions: On Reconstruction and Deconstruction in Contemporary Critical Theory,* 181–99. Cambridge, MA: The MIT Press, 1991.

McCulloch v. Maryland, 17 U.S. 316 (1819).

McGuire, Kevin T. "The Supreme Court Bar and Institutional Relationships." In *The Supreme Court in American Politics: New Institutionalist Interpretations,* edited by Howard Gillman and Cornell Clayton, 115–32. Lawrence: University Press of Kansas, 1999.

Michelman, Frank I. *Brennan and Democracy.* Princeton, NJ: Princeton University Press, 1999.

——— "Constitutional Authorship." In *Constitutionalism: Philosophical Foundations,* edited by Larry Alexander, 64–98. New York: Cambridge University Press, 1998.

——— "Family Quarrel." *Cardozo Law Review* 17, no. 4–5 (1996): 1163–77.

——— "Morality, Identity and 'Constitutional Patriotism.'" *Denver University Law Review* 76, no. 4 (1999): 1009–28.

——— "The Problem of Constitutional Interpretive Disagreement: Can 'Discourses of Application' Help?" In *Habermas and Pragmatism,* edited by Mitchell Aboulafia, Myra Bookman and Catherine Kemp, 113–38. New York: Routledge, 2002.

——— "The Supreme Court, 1985 Term – Forward: Traces of Self-Government." *Harvard Law Review* 100, no. 4 (1986): 4–77.

Miranda v. Arizona, 384 U.S. 436 (1966).

Moon, J. Donald. "Rawls and Habermas on Public Reason: Human Rights and Global Justice." *Annual Review of Political Science* 6, no. 1 (2003): 257–74.

Murphy, Coleen. "Lon Fuller and the Moral Value of the Rule of Law." *Law and Philosophy* 24, no. 3 (2005): 239–62.

Nagel, Robert F. "Interpretation and Importance in Constitutional Law: A Re-Assessment of Judicial Restraint." In *Liberal Democracy,* edited by J. Roland Pennock and John W. Chapman, 181–207. New York: New York University Press, 1983.

Nino, Carlos Santiago. *The Constitution of Deliberative Democracy*. New Haven, CT: Yale University Press, 1996.

Noonan, John T., Jr *Narrowing the Nation's Power: The Supreme Court Sides with the States*. Berkeley: University of California Press, 2002.

O'Connor, Sandra Day, and Pete Williams. "The Majesty of the Law: An Interview with Justice Sandra Day O'Connor." In *University of Louisville Kentucky Author Forum*. Louisville, KY: WFPL, 2003.

Paulsen, Michael Stokes. "The Irrepressible Myth of *Marbury*." *Michigan Law Review* 101 (2003): 601–37.

Peretti, Terri Jennings. *In Defense of a Political Court*. Princeton, NJ: Princeton University Press, 1999.

Perry, Michael J. *The Constitution in the Courts: Law or Politics?* New York: Oxford University Press, 1994.

The Constitution, the Courts, and Human Rights: An Inquiry into the Legitimacy of Constitutional Policymaking by the Judiciary. New Haven, CT: Yale University Press, 1982.

The Idea of Human Rights: Four Inquiries. New York: Oxford University Press, 1998.

"What Is 'the Constitution'? (and Other Fundamental Questions)." In *Constitutionalism: Philosophical Foundations*, edited by Larry Alexander, 99–151. New York: Cambridge University Press, 1998.

Peterson, Victor. "A Discourse Theory of Moral Judgment." Ph.D. dissertation, Northwestern University, 1998.

Pickerill, J. Mitchell. *Constitutional Deliberation in Congress: The Impact of Judicial Review in a Separated System*. Durham, NC: Duke University Press, 2004.

Planned Parenthood v. Casey, 505 U.S. 833 (1992).

Plessy v. Ferguson, 163 U.S. 537 (1895).

Posner, Richard A. *Law, Pragmatism, and Democracy*. Cambridge, MA: Harvard University Press, 2003.

Preuß, Ulrich K. "Constitutionalism." In *Routledge Encyclopedia of Philosophy*, edited by Edward Craig, 618–22. New York: Routledge, 1998.

Provine, Doris Marie. "Courts in the Political Process in France." In *Courts, Law, and Politics in Comparative Perspective*, edited by Herbert Jacob, Erhard Blankenburg, Herbert M. Kritzer, Doris Marie Provine and Joseph Sanders, 177–248. New Haven, CT: Yale University Press, 1996.

Przeworski, Adam. "Minimalist Conception of Democracy: A Defense." In *Democracy's Value*, edited by Ian Shapiro and Hacker-Cordón Casiano, 23–55. New York: Cambridge University Press, 1999.

Radin, Jane. "Reconsidering the Rule of Law." *Boston University Law Review* 69 (1989): 785ff.

Railton, Peter. "Judicial Review, Elites, and Liberal Democracy." In *Liberal Democracy*, edited by J. Roland Pennock and John W. Chapman, 153–80. New York: New York University Press, 1983.

Rawls, John. *A Theory of Justice*. Revised ed. Cambridge, MA: Harvard University Press, 1999.

Political Liberalism. Paperback ed. New York: Columbia University Press, 1996.

"The Idea of Public Reason Revisited." In *Collected Papers*, edited by Samuel Freeman, 573–615. Cambridge, MA: Harvard University Press, 1999.

Raz, Joseph. "On the Authority and Interpretation of Constitutions: Some Preliminaries." In *Constitutionalism: Philosophical Foundations*, edited by Larry Alexander, 152–93. New York: Cambridge University Press, 1998.

"The Rule of Law and Its Virtue." In *The Authority of Law: Essays on Law and Morality*. Oxford: Clarendon Press, 1979.

Rehg, William. *Insight and Solidarity: A Study in the Discourse Ethics of Jürgen Habermas*. Berkeley: University of California Press, 1994.

Reynolds v. Sims, 377 U.S. 533 (1964).

Riker, William H. *Liberalism against Populism: A Confrontation between the Theory of Democracy and the Theory of Social Choice*. Prospect Heights, IL: Waveland Press, 1982.

Roe v. Wade, 410 U.S. 113 (1973).

Romer, Governor of Colorado, et al. v. Evans et al., 517 U.S. 620 (1996).

Rosenbaum, Alan S. "Introduction." In *Constitutionalism: The Philosophical Dimension*, edited by Alan S. Rosenbaum, 1–6. New York: Greenwood Press, 1988.

Rosenberg, Gerald N. *The Hollow Hope: Can Courts Bring about Social Change?* Chicago: University of Chicago Press, 1991.

Rosenfeld, Michel. "The Rule of Law and the Legitimacy of Constitutional Democracy." *Southern California Law Review* 74, no. 5 (2001): 1307–51.

Rostow, Eugene V. "The Democratic Character of Judicial Review." *Harvard Law Review* 66 (1952): 193–224.

Rousseau, Jean-Jacques. *Discourse on Political Economy and the Social Contract*. Translated by Christopher Betts. New York: Oxford University Press, 1994.

"Of the Social Contract." In *The Social Contract and Other Later Political Writings*, edited by Victor Gourevitch. New York: Cambridge University Press, 1997.

Rubenfeld, Jed. *Freedom and Time: A Theory of Constitutional Self-Government*. New Haven, CT: Yale University Press, 2001.

Ryfe, David M. "Does Deliberative Democracy Work?" *Annual Review of Political Science* 8, no. 1 (2005): 49–71.

Sager, Lawrence G. *Justice in Plainclothes: A Theory of Constitutional Practice*. New Haven, CT: Yale University Press, 2004.

Saward, Michael. *The Terms of Democracy*. Malden, MA: Blackwell, 1998.

Scalia, Antonin. "Common-Law Courts in a Civil-Law System: The Role of United States Federal Courts in Interpreting the Constitution and the Laws." In *A Matter of Interpretation: Federal Courts and the Law*, edited by Amy Gutmann, 3–47. Princeton, NJ: Princeton University Press, 1997.

Schumpeter, Joseph A. *Capitalism, Socialism, and Democracy*. London: George Allen & Unwin, 1943.

Shapiro, Martin. "The Success of Judicial Review and Democracy." In *On Law, Politics, and Judicialization*, edited by Martin Shapiro and Alec Stone Sweet, 149–83. New York: Oxford University Press, 2002.

Shapiro, Martin, and Alec Stone Sweet. "Abstract Review and Judicial Law-Making." In *On Law, Politics, and Judicialization*, edited by Martin Shapiro and Alec Stone Sweet, 343–75. New York: Oxford University Press, 2002.

On Law, Politics, and Judicialization. New York: Oxford University Press, 2002.

Solem v. Helm, 463 U.S. 277 (1983).

Spaeth, Harold J. 1998. United States Supreme Court Judicial Database, 1953–1997 Terms. In, Michigan State University, Dept. of Political Science, http://webapp.icpsr.umich.edu/cocoon/ICPSR-STUDY/09422.xml. (accessed January 10, 2005).

Spector, Horacio. "Judicial Review, Rights, and Democracy." *Law and Philosophy* 22, no. 3–4 (2003): 285–334.

Stone, Alec. *The Birth of Judicial Politics in France: The Constitutional Council in Comparative Perspective*. New York: Oxford University Press, 1992.

Strauss, David A. "Constitutions, Written and Otherwise." *Law and Philosophy* 19, no. 4 (2000): 451–64.

Sunstein, Cass R. *Designing Democracy: What Constitutions Do*. New York: Oxford University Press, 2001.

Legal Reasoning and Political Conflict. New York: Oxford University Press, 1996.

One Case at a Time: Judicial Minimalism on the Supreme Court. Cambridge, MA: Harvard University Press, 1999.

The Partial Constitution. Cambridge, MA: Harvard University Press, 1993.

Sweet, Alec Stone. "Constitutional Politics in France and Germany." In *On Law, Politics, and Judicialization*, edited by Martin Shapiro and Alec Stone Sweet, 184–208. New York: Oxford University Press, 2002.

Governing with Judges: Constitutional Politics in Europe. New York: Oxford University Press, 2000.

"Path Dependence, Precedent, and Judicial Power." In *On Law, Politics, and Judicialization*, edited by Martin Shapiro and Alec Stone Sweet, 113–35. New York: Oxford University Press, 2002.

Tate, Neal, and Thorsten Vallinder, eds. *The Global Expansion of Judicial Power*. New York: New York University Press, 1995.

Thomas, George. "Recovering the Political Constitution: The Madisonian Vision." *The Review of Politics* 66, no. 2 (2004): 233–56.

Tribe, Lawrence H. "The Puzzling Persistence of Process-Based Constitutional Theories." *Yale Law Journal* 89, no. 6 (1980): 1063–80.

Tullis, Jeffrey K. "Deliberation between Institutions." In *Debating Deliberative Democracy*, edited by James S. Fishkin and Peter Laslett, 200–11. Malden, MA: Blackwell, 2003.

Tushnet, Mark. "Forms of Judicial Review as Expressions of Constitutional Patriotism." *Law and Philosophy* 22, no. 3–4 (2003): 353–79.

Taking the Constitution away from the Courts. Princeton, NJ: Princeton University Press, 1999.

United States v. Carolene Products Co., 304 U.S. 144 (1938).

Vacco v. Quill, 521 US 793 (1997).

Vieth et al. v. Jubelirer, 541 US 267 (2004).

Waldron, Jeremy. "A Right-Based Critique of Constitutional Rights." *Oxford Journal of Legal Studies* 13 (1993): 18–51.

"Freeman's Defense of Judicial Review." *Law and Philosophy* 13 (1994): 27–41.

"Is the Rule of Law an Essentially Contested Concept (in Florida)?" *Law and Philosophy* 21 (2002): 137–64.

"Judicial Review and the Conditions of Democracy." *The Journal of Political Philosophy* 6, no. 4 (1998): 335–55.

Law and Disagreement. New York: Oxford University Press, 1999.

"Rights and Majorities: Rousseau Revisited." In *Liberal Rights: Collected Papers 1981–1991*, 392–421. New York: Cambridge University Press, 1993.

The Dignity of Legislation. New York: Cambridge University Press, 1999.

Walker, Neil. "The Idea of Constitutional Pluralism." *The Modern Law Review* 65, no. 3 (2002): 317–59.

Washington v. Glucksberg, 521 U.S. 702 (1997).

Whittington, Keith E. *Constitutional Construction: Divided Powers and Constitutional Meaning*. Cambridge, MA: Harvard University Press, 1999.

Wolin, Sheldon S. "The Liberal/Democratic Divide: On Rawls's *Political Liberalism*." *Political Theory* 24, no. 1 (1996): 97–119.

Zurn, Christopher F. "Deliberative Democracy and Constitutional Review." *Law and Philosophy* 21 (2002): 467–542.

Index

Ackerman, Bruce, 19–21, 53, 83, 92,
   171, 175, 182, 196, 260, 320, 322,
   330, 332, 336, 338, 339
administrative bodies, 246
Alexander, Larry, 10, 94, 182, 266–9,
   297, 302
Alexy, Robert, 249
Amar, Akhil Reed, 50, 53, 60, 102, 135
Americans with Disabilities Act of 1990
   (U.S.), 305
analytic distinctions, 75, 78–80
anarchism, 126
Ankersmit, F. R., 155
Apel, Karl-Otto, 16
Aquians, 80, 116
Arto, Andrew, 95
Arendt, Hannah, 262
Aristotle, 83, 96, 103–5, 108, 109, 112,
   116
Arrow, Kenneth J., 65
Australia, 330
Austrian Constitution of 1929, 274
autonomy
   see also constitutionalism and
   democracy; constitutionalism and
   constituent power; constitutionalism
   and individual independence;
   constitutionalism and rights;
   democracy and political equality;
   democracy and popular sovereignty;
   democracy and rights; rights
   collective, 5, 71
   equal, 230

individual, 4, 123
and practical reasoning, 5
relation of collective and individual,
   233, 238

Barber, Benjamin J., 68
Barber, Sotirios A., 96
Barnett, Randy J., 42
Baum, Lawrence, 28, 283
Baynes, Kenneth, 233
Belgium, 24
Bellamy, Richard, 23, 96, 101
Benhabib, Seyla, 230
Bennett, Robert W., 71, 205
Bentham, Jeremy, 73, 143, 205
Bickel, Alexander, 2, 3–4, 13, 19, 32–7,
   39, 44, 46, 49, 54, 63, 65, 94,
   100, 104, 118, 120, 124, 126, 148,
   172, 173, 174, 180, 192, 221, 254,
   258
Bogdanor, Vernon, 90
Bohman, James, 68, 72, 321
Bork, Robert, 15–17, 42, 43, 135
Brennan, Justice William J., Jr., 191, 198
Brewer-Caras, Allan R., 274, 275, 276
"Brutus," 302

Canada, 24, 46, 280, 305
   Charter of Rights and Freedoms, 41,
   46, 110
   'notwithstanding clause', 110–11,
   305–6, 310, 311, 317
Cappelletti, Mauro, 274, 283, 289

356   *Index*

Castiglione, Dario, 88, 96, 97
Chambers, Simone, 72, 83, 96
Chemerinsky, Erwin, 14–15
Choper, Jesse, 32, 36–9, 45, 48, 49, 54,
   63, 65, 94, 100, 104, 124, 126, 174,
   221, 254, 258
Christiano, Thomas, 124, 126, 127,
   147, 149, 155
circumstances of politics, 57, 127, 142,
   230
civic constitutional fora, 273, 325–41
   see also deliberative opinion polls;
     constitutional amendment
   and amendment certification, 336,
     338
   and amendment ratification, 336,
     338–9
   and amendment selection, 336
   as consultative, 328–30, 334
   and deliberation day, 330–2
   and mandatory service, 334
   and political equality, 328–9, 334–6
civil law and common law systems, 75,
   91–2, 212, 214, 267, 278–9, 120–1
Civil Rights Act of 1964 (U.S.), 305
Clinton, Robert Lowry, 28
Cohen, Joshua, 55, 68, 70, 83, 166, 233
communicative power, 241, 313
communitarianism, 85, 336
Constant, Benjamin, 101
constitutional amendment, 90, 306
   see also civic constitutional fora;
     constitutionalism
   easing requirements for, 314–23, 324
   factors in designing processes for,
     314–15
   frequency of
   initiation of, 316, 318, 336
   obduracy and, 89, 315–16, 334
constitutional court, 274–300, 323
   see also constitutional review;
     judicial review
   a priori vs. a posteriori review, 288,
     302
   assessment of, 258–9, 301, 340
   and constitution ombudsperson, 291
   decision mechanisms of, 278–81
   as deliberative, 35, 38

   as educative, 170, 171, 180, 188, 189,
     194, 204
   as exemplar of public reason, 170,
     171, 201
   informational capacities of, 289–91,
     303
   and judicialization of politics, 260,
     280–1
   juridical techniques in, 275, 278–9
   jurisdiction of, 275, 286–8
   justification for, 255–6, 274–81
   Kelsen-style (European), 215, 257,
     266, 275, 285, 288
   member recruitment and selection,
     276–7
   member retention, 276, 277
   and ordinary courts, 282, 287, 291
   political independence of, 3, 35, 38,
     47, 55, 64, 103, 173, 251, 254–5,
     275, 276–7
   referral authority, 288, 291
   referral modalities for, 275, 288–95
   and social acceptance, 287
   specialization of, 214, 252, 275, 281
   terms vs. life appointments, 110, 277
   unique location of, 264, 282
   United States-style, 275–6,
     282–4, 288
constitutional politics, 25, 96, 97, 258,
   261–2, 285, 304
constitutional provisions, 79
   disagreement about, 248
   generality of, 40, 113, 151, 176, 307,
     316
   indeterminacy of, 43, 94, 107, 113,
     131, 140, 150, 248, 316, 317
   justification of, 240, 244, 257
   legislative specification of, 305, 312
   as moral principles, 114
   rights, 258
   state duties, 258
   structural, 258
constitutional review
   see also civic constitutional fora;
     constitutional court; judicial
     review; institutional design
   as analogous to ordinary
     adjudication, 247–51

as application discourse, 240, 244–5, 257, 264
assessing institutions of, 265–74, 295–300
assessment vales for
  effectiveness, 273–4, 308, 311–12, 330
  empowerment, 270, 297–8, 304, 310, 318–19, 323, 332, 340
  independence, 269–70, 273, 297, 303, 310, 318, 323–4, 332, 337, 340
  jurisdiction, 271, 298–9, 304, 310, 319, 323, 333, 340
  relation of, 272–3, 300, 301, 323–4, 340
  sensitivity, 271–2, 273, 277, 299–300, 304, 311, 319–23, 323–4, 329, 332, 337
  settlement, 266–9, 272, 278, 296, 303, 310, 317, 318, 323, 339, 340
  systematicity, 266, 272, 282, 295–6, 303, 309, 317, 318, 323, 337, 339
and balancing tests, 294
and constitutionalization of legal order, 284–5, 288, 289
in coordinate, concentrated, and diffuse systems, 295–300
designing institutions for, 2, 7–8, 134–5, 208, 212–15, 252, 256, 265, 274
and democracy reinforcement, 271
in executive branch, 243–4
  see also constitutional review by self-review panels
  function of, 235, 236–8, 243, 254, 264
function vs. institutions of, 7, 29, 134, 156
and horizontal dispersal, 265, 281, 301, 302–12, 324, 340
ideal-real tension of, 7, 262–4, 286
interbranch mechanisms for, 24, 305–12, 313, 323, 340
see also Canada, "notwithstanding clause"; constitutional provisions,

legislative specification of; judicial review and doctrines of deference
and lead role in constitutional development, 261–2, 265
in legislative branch, 243
  see also constitutional review by self-review panels
procedural justification of, 2
and protection-elaboration application-justification dialectic and, 257
  as inevitable, 256–61, 264, 282, 286
  informal constitutional development and, 260
  legal development and, 259–60
  minimal constitutional agreement and, 258–9
  semantic generality and, 258
  social change and, 260–1
transmutation, 314, 317
as reasons-responsive, 271, 290
and Rousseau's Tribunate, 214–15
by self-review panels, 302–5, 323, 340
and social powers, 242, 251, 270, 297, 318, 337
tasks of, 2, 239–43, 251–2, 255–6, 278
and vertical empowerment, 265, 273, 281, 301, 313–41, 324
constitutionalism
  see also all 'constitutional…' entries; natural; law rights; rule of law
  as result of bargaining, 94
  and conceptual ascent, 258
  and constituent power, 19, 92, 122, 130, 133–4, 137, 140, 151, 214, 222, 249, 256, 262, 264, 265, 272, 282, 286, 302, 307, 314, 316, 323
  contortions of ideals of, 21–5, 304
  and democracy, 1, 7, 38, 48, 57, 59, 92, 95, 103–5, 122, 130, 131, 138, 140–1, 161–2, 225, 238, 255–6, 306, 314, 316, 339
  and disagreement, 136–7, 258–9, 289, 327–8

constitutionalism *(Cont.)*
  elements of, 84–103
  and entrenchment, 58, 89–95,
    146–7, 229, 260, 261, 302, 304,
    316–17
  equated with judicial review, 21, 23
  as higher law, 19, 58, 89–95, 93, 255,
    259, 263, 286, 315
  and individual independence, 79, 132
  as limiting power, 98–9
  minoritarian, 7, 49, 63, 80, 126, 222,
    316
  in nations without judicial review, 24
  and ongoing development, 131,
    139–41, 214, 222, 223, 260, 262,
    272, 289, 302, 304, 323, 340
  and original enactment, 131, 138,
    139, 140, 263, 314
  and political culture, 157
  as political practices, 57, 90, 262
  and political structuration, 7, 95–9,
    146–7, 157, 229
  as positive law, 88, 89, 91, 97
  and religious neutrality, 79
  and rights, 7, 23, 36–7, 48, 58–9, 79,
    99–103, 125–6, 147, 244
  and rule of law, 58, 88, 146, 228
  settlement function of, 94, 302
  and status quo, 152, 154
  and substantive principles, 34–5, 94,
    98, 116, 302, 304, 310
coordinate constitutional construction,
    261, 307
  see also constitutional review,
    inter-branch mechanism of;
    constitutional review, in coordinate,
    concentrated, and diffuse systems;
    constitutional review, horizontal
    dispersal of; constitutional review
    by self-review panels
Corwin, Edward S., 89
critical legal theory, 120

Dahl, Robert, 33, 39, 41, 51, 54–63, 66,
    75, 81, 82, 92, 95, 100, 101, 102,
    104, 106, 126, 142, 174, 221, 226,
    232–4, 236, 238, 240, 251, 269

deliberation
  and deliberative enclaves, 321, 327,
    332
  in deliberative polling, 83, 325–8
  and deliberative troubles, 320–2,
    324, 328, 331–2, 338, 340
  as discussion, 69–70, 333
  in judiciary, 107–8, 110, 111, 163,
    245–7
  in legislatures, 110, 111, 224, 303
  in public spheres, 110, 163, 224,
    320–3, 324
  and social struggle, 62
deliberative democracy, 5, 6–7, 51–2,
    68–84, 131, 143, 165, 231, 239,
    273, 292, 293
  see also deliberation, democracy,
    deliberative democratic
    constitutionalism
  and circulation of power, 241–3, 251,
    313–14
  as a common venture, 335–6
  majoritarian, 75, 143
  legitimacy criterion of, 81, 82–4,
    139–40, 231, 254, 271, 311, 313,
    335
  political equality vs. reasons-
    responsiveness in, 165–6
  as reasons-responsive, 53, 70–1, 81,
    222, 254, 271, 311, 313, 335
deliberative democratic
    constitutionalism, 2, 7, 26, 95, 140,
    162, 223, 225–6, 235–6, 254, 284,
    286, 306
deliberative opinion polls, 325–30
  and a new 'popular' branch, 332–3
  and representative sampling, 328–9,
    334
Delli Carpini, Michael X., Fay Lomax
    Cook, and Lawrence R. Jacobs, 53,
    72, 324
democratic accountability
  expertocratic versus populist, 81,
    82–4, 145, 165–6
democratic legitimacy
  connected to institutional processes
    and accountability, 139–40

and consent, 137
    proceduralist, 40, 41, 46, 77–80, 123,
        144, 195, 223, 225, 228, 230, 254,
        328
    substantialist, 17, 77–80, 107, 115,
        116–17, 123, 131, 168, 183, 230, 233
democratic process
    aggregative, 46, 51, 56, 73–6, 114,
        170, 320
    content of, 74
    deliberative, 66, 73–6, 107–22, 111,
        115, 170, 173, 223, 226, 230, 320
    distortions in, 45–6, 48, 60–1, 95,
        127–9, 136, 157–60, 242, 255
    institutional division of, 166–8, 171–2,
        174, 176–8, 207–8, 222
    majority rule, 151–5
    mechanisms of, 74, 76, 120, 131
    supermajoritarian, 58–9, 146, 152–4,
        334
democratic worth of institutions, 133–4,
        137–40
    instrumental versus intrinsic, 80–2,
        117, 132, 144–5, 183
democracy
    aggregative, 5, 63, 73, 81, 82, 131,
        227–36, 313
    and anti-constitutionalism, 141,
        145–7, 161, 236
    as arbitrary, 65, 142
    and civil society, 69, 83
    and common good, 51, 73–4, 85
    as a common venture, 5, 335–6
    and complexity, 82, 84, 144, 321, 341
    and constituent power,
        see constitutionalism and
        constituent power
    and constitutionalism, 1, 38, 57, 59,
        103–5, 122, 130, 140–1, 161–2,
        225, 238, 255–6
    denigration of, 15–21
    and devolution, 336
    direct, 82, 152, 154
    and disagreement, 40, 64, 84, 123,
        131, 134, 136–7, 141, 142, 149–51,
        223, 235, 255, 322, 341
    distortions of ideals of, 13–21
    and elections, 73, 313

and factionalism, 51
and fairness, 82, 131, 143–4, 152–3,
    255
forum models of, 74
and individual independence, 81,
    116
and information exchange, 69
and interests and preferences,
    15–16, 33–5, 38, 47, 51–3, 56–8,
    62, 65, 71, 73, 74, 89, 115
and justice, 132
majoritarian, 3, 7, 15, 32–3, 36, 49,
    63, 65–6, 71, 73, 80, 136–7, 222,
    251, 293
market models of, 33–4, 46, 62, 74,
    81, 239
minimalist, 81
and obligation, 65
and opinion polls, 321, 325, 327,
    328, 332
and participation, 69, 82, 124
plebiscitary, 322
pluralistic, 34
and political equality, 5, 14, 40, 45,
    61, 64, 71, 73, 81, 115, 123–4, 128,
    132, 138, 144, 199, 255, 292
and popular sovereignty, 106, 109,
    116, 122, 130, 133–4, 140, 250
    see also constitutionalism and
    constituent power, precommitment
as pre-eminent value, 38, 58, 154,
    234, 254, 255
radical, 84
and rational ignorance, 320, 322,
    325, 331
and reasons-responsiveness, 70–1
    see also deliberative democracy;
    legislatures as reasons-responsive
and rights, 14, 60–2, 101, 126, 132,
    143, 150, 223, 232
    see also rights
and social inequality, 321, 327,
    332
and tolerance, 69
and virtues, 69
and voting, 52, 81
and wealth, 83
Denmark, 330

Dewey, John, 66, 142, 322, 335
Dicey, A. V., 57, 90, 96, 262
dictatorship, temporary, 138
diffidence, moderate, 127
Douglas, Justice William O., 199
Downs, Anthony, 320
Dryzek, John S., 69, 242
duty of civility, 169
Dworkin, Ronald, 17–18, 23, 44, 49,
    86, 94, 99, 102, 104, 108, 113–18,
    130, 131, 132, 135, 175, 176, 180,
    182, 194, 204, 222, 240, 245, 247,
    248, 254, 258, 335

Education Amendments Act of 1972
    (U.S.), 305
Eisgruber, Christopher, 104, 132,
    164, 166–8, 172–5, 177, 178, 180,
    181, 187, 190, 193, 194, 196–7,
    200, 202–6, 210, 213, 215,
    217, 222, 245, 248, 254–5, 258,
    290
electoral districts and equality, 186,
    195–206
Elster, Jon, 33, 65, 74
Ely, John Hart, 12, 36, 41–53, 54, 57,
    63, 66, 76, 100, 103, 104, 106, 109,
    112, 128, 156, 157, 158–60, 197,
    221, 226, 232–4, 236, 237, 238,
    239, 240, 248, 251, 254, 255, 258,
    262, 269, 310
Epstein, Lee, 185, 220
Eskridge, William N. Jr., 87
Estlund, David M., 77
European Constitution (Treaty
    Establishing a Constitution for
    Europe), 314
European Union, 29
European Convention on Human
    Rights, 93, 309
European Court of Human Rights, 268
European Court of Justice, 268

Fabre, Cécile, 124, 126, 132, 147,
    149
Fallon, Richard H., 76
Favoreu, Louis, 274

federalism, 27, 55, 200, 258, 261, 265,
    267, 305, 318
Federalist Papers, The 25, 37, 51
    see also "Brutus," Hamilton,
    Alexander
Ferejohn, John, 74, 83, 87, 96, 98, 277,
    280
Finland, 24
Finn, John E., 96
Finnis, John, 77
Fishkin, James S., 69, 72, 83, 320, 321,
    322, 325–32, 334, 336, 338, 339
Forst, Rainer, 70
France, 119, 268, 275, 276, 294, 307,
    314
    Conseil Constitutionnel, 252, 275,
        287, 288
    Conseil d'État, 275
Frankfurter, Justice Felix, 198
Freeman, Samuel, 38, 95, 105, 131–41,
    161, 166, 182, 222, 254, 263
Fuller, Lon, 77, 86, 87, 207, 212, 229,
    266
Fung, Archon, 72, 325

Gardbaum, Stephen, 299, 305, 309,
    311
Germany, 284, 307
    Basic Law, 89
    Bundesverfassungsgericht, 244, 252,
        276, 294, 308
Ginsburg, Tom, 94
Goodin, Robert E., 70
Gordon, Scott, 95, 98
Graber, Mark A., 303
Grey, Thomas C., 85, 92
Griffin, Stephen M., 96
Günther, Klaus, 237, 248, 257
Gutmann, Amy and Dennis
    Thompson, 69

Habermas, Jürgen, 41, 69, 76, 78, 95,
    101, 105, 113, 150, 162, 177, 181,
    207, 225, 226–52, 254, 255, 256,
    258, 264, 269, 271, 294, 312, 313,
    321, 335
    and constitutional patriotism, 249

on democracy, principle of, 227,
  231–6, 228
on discourse, principle of, 228
interpretations of, 227
on law, 227, 228–9
on law and mortality, 228
on norm justification, 227, 229–30, 237
on norm application, 237
on universalization, principle of, 228
Hamilton, Alexander, 38, 131, 181,
  246, 264, 277, 319
Hand, Learned, 3, 4–5, 13, 32, 109,
  130, 335
Harel, Alon, 182
Hart, H. L. A., 43, 76, 229, 258, 266
Hartley, Roger, 206
Hayek, Friedrich A., 77
Hegel, Georg Wilhelm Friedrich, 257
Hirschl, Ran, 40, 94, 274, 280
Hobbes, Thomas, 86, 100, 112, 138,
  268
Holmes, Stephen, 81, 105, 132, 169,
  315
homosexual sex, 186, 194
Hume, David, 127

incorporation, doctrine of, 210
institutional design
  see also constitutional amendment;
    constitutional court; constitutional
    review
  considerations in, 7–8, 83, 127–9,
    219–20, 224, 323, 155–60
Israel, 24, 280
Italy, 276, 294, 307, 308

Jackson, Andrew, 302
Jacob, Herbert, 274, 276
Jefferson, Thomas, 302
judicial decisions
  as application discourses, 237, 246
  factors in, 185–6
judicial interpretation, 41–2, 223
  and dilemma of strict interpretivism,
    43–4
  proceduralist as nonpaternalist,
    244–5

theories of, in jurisprudence, 11, 12,
  135, 140, 192, 248, 250, 298
judicial review
  see also constitutional court;
    constitutional review
  of administrative action, 27, 287
  and common-law methods, 120–1
  concentrated versus diffuse, 24, 281–6
  concrete versus abstract review, 257,
    275, 288
  versus constitutional review,
    see constitutional review, functions vs.
      institutions of
  as counter-majoritarian, 3, 19, 32,
    36–9, 39–40, 148
  as democratic, 20, 162, 163–4, 174–5,
    179
  of democratic process rules, 287,
    298
  as diminishing democratic capacities,
    32, 119, 303
  and doctrines of deference, 305,
    308–9, 312
  and federalism, 286, 287
  and justice, 291
  and legal competence, 38, 103, 118,
    119, 123, 215, 245–51
  and moral competence, 17, 35, 40,
    47, 52, 106, 108, 109, 111–12, 120,
    122, 123, 145, 164, 177, 222, 245,
    254–5, 292
  narrowly defined as constitutional
    review, 27–8
  as paternalist, 4–5, 32, 43, 52–3,
    54–5, 64, 65, 109, 110, 122, 124,
    141, 148, 178, 179, 222, 245,
    248–9, 255, 292, 319, 335
  and principled reasoning, 17,
    35–6, 114, 118, 172–4, 183,
    197, 207
  procedural legitimacy of, 40, 41, 44–7,
    55, 80, 106, 306
  and public reasoning, 19, 118–19,
    192–3, 203–6
  of regulations, 286
  as representation-reinforcing, 45,
    108, 158, 287

judicial review *(Cont.)*
  and rights, 57, 59–60, 103, 108, 121,
    286, 291–3, 316
  of separation of powers, 287, 298
  of statutes, 27, 286
  substantialist legitimacy of,
    39–41, 63, 107, 108, 117–18,
    124, 126, 132, 222, 255–6, 291,
    334
  tutelary role of, 312
  Waldron's formal argument against,
    147–9
judicial supremacy, 21, 93, 150, 261,
    267, 281, 302, 306, 323
jurisprudence
  see also judicial interpretation
  firmament and favorite cases in,
    11–12
  and ideals of constitutional
    democracy, 9
  institutional panglossianism in, 9–11,
    13, 24, 243–4
  parochialism of, 6, 15–21, 24, 53–4, 213
  social science in, 262–4
  theories of judicial review in U.S.,
    8–25, 221, 244, 258
  triangulation pathologies of, 8–12
juristic discourse
  as specialized application discourse,
    246–7, 255–6
  as communicative, 167, 175, 177–8,
    180, 198, 202–3, 219
  as deliberative, 163, 214
  as democratic, 18, 162, 222
  as distorting democratic
    deliberation, 281
  as exemplifying public reason, 167,
    180, 219
  as institutionally constrained, 184,
    190, 198–201, 209–12
  as legal language, 222, 255–6
  and legal principles, 184, 188–9, 192
  and moral-political principles, 184,
    190–1, 193–4, 196–7
  as representing people's moral
    reason, 167, 175, 181–3, 187–8,
    202, 219, 319

justiciability, 7, 21, 198, 199, 211, 218,
    220, 282, 287, 299, 308

Kalyvas, Andreas, 262
Kant, Immanuel, 99, 122, 127, 133,
    228, 231, 257
Kavanagh, Aileen, 128, 132, 149
Kelsen, Hans, 76, 94, 214, 257, 262,
    266, 274, 275, 285, 290
Kennedy, Justice Anthony, 22, 194, 201
Klarman, Michael J., 40, 181
Koopmans, Tim, 25, 119, 264, 274,
    276, 283
Kramer, Larry D., 10, 96, 302
Kritzer, Herbert M., 299

learning processes, 8, 60–2, 107, 108,
    109, 151
law and economics, 261
legal formalism, 257
legal positivism, 74–89, 76, 86, 217, 266
legal realism, 120, 185, 257, 261, 285
legislatures, 33, 81
  bicameral, 153
  dignity of, 144
  and electoral accountability, 128, 173
  and fiduciary power, 138
  and justification discourses, 236–7, 246
  and moral competence, 107, 117
  and parliamentary sovereignty, 141,
    145, 150, 263, 281, 299
  and policy, 35–6
  as reasons-responsive, 279
  and representation, 154–6
  and social powers, 128
  and strategic action, 267
legitimacy, 76–7, 85, 223, 225, 254
Leib, Ethan J., 83, 332–6, 338, 339
liberalism, 85, 101, 104
libertarianism, 85, 94, 233
Lijphart, Arendt, 40, 60, 151
Lincoln, Abraham, 199, 302
Lelwellyn, Karl, 267
Locke, John, 77, 92, 100, 102, 106,
    107, 115, 116, 120, 133, 138, 139,
    143, 156
Luskin, Robert C., 325, 326

Lutz, Donald S., 90, 261, 314, 315, 316, 317, 331
Luxembourg, 24

MacCormick, Neil, 123
Maddex, Robert E., 274, 276
Madison, James, 34, 37
Manin, Bernard, 69, 74
Mansbridge, Jane, 69
Marmor, Andrei, 86
Marshall, Justice John, 246, 264
Marshall, T. H., 62
mass media, 83, 321, 327, 330, 332
Mavcic, Arne, 274
McCann, Michael, 269
McCarthy, Thomas, 227
McGuire, Kevin T., 290
Michelman, Frank, 104, 105, 164, 166–8, 175–8, 180, 187, 190, 198, 202–6, 213, 217, 222, 245, 248, 254, 255, 258, 271, 289
Mill, John Stuart, 152, 156
monarchy, 135–8, 268
Moon, J. Donald, 78
Murphy, Coleen, 87

Nagel, Robert F., 92
natural law, 9, 44, 76, 77, 80, 86, 89, 94, 100, 102, 108, 116, 140, 156, 217, 222, 235
Netherlands, The, 7, 40, 314
New Zealand, 40, 119, 280, 302, 305, 308, 310
    Bill of Rights Act of 1990, 309
Nino, Carlos Santiago, 52, 69, 95, 105, 106, 177
Nixon, Richard M., 302
Noonan, John T. Jr.
normative political theory, 1–2
    limits of, 7, 26
    and empirical theory, 135
    and political institutions, 6–8, 9–11, 12, 25–6
    instrumental use of, 8–9, 13, 14
    tacit reliance on, 2–6
norm hierarchies in law, 247–8, 266, 282
Norway, 40

O'Connor, Justice Sandra Day, 22–3, 189, 191, 193, 210
oppression, fact of, 65
    see also state coercive power
overlapping consensus, 168–9, 259

Pasquino, Pasquale, 280
path dependence, 260, 262, 269
Paulsen, Michael Stokes, 302
Peretti, Terri Jennings, 302
Perry, Michael J., 10, 42, 104, 107–13, 114, 117, 124, 130, 131, 132, 156, 182, 222, 240, 245, 248, 254, 258, 277
Peterson, Victor, 216, 247, 257
Pickerill, J. Mitchell, 209, 261, 281, 305
Platonism, 231
Pledge of Allegiance, the, 187
pluralism
    see also democracy and disagreement; constitutionalism and disagreement
    evaluative, 40, 69, 112–13, 124, 141, 222, 258, 292, 321, 327
    fact of reasonable, 50, 71, 112–13, 135, 136, 168, 175, 223, 229, 341
    reasonable interpretative, 176, 248
Posner, Richard A., 82
Post, Robert, 176
practical reason
    defects of, 177
    different forms of, 223–4, 226, 239–40, 257
    ethical forms of, 107, 109, 112–13
    legal forms of, 226, 240
    phronesis and, 108
    religion and, 108, 112
precedent, 218, 278–9
    see also civil law and common law systems; judicial review and common-law methods; path dependence; Supreme Court of the United States and common law methods
precommitment, 95, 133–4, 254–5, 263
Preuß, Ulrich K., 105

principles, legal and moral-political
vs. policy, 34, 114, 172–3
as principles of positive law, 217–18
and principles of adjudicative
preocedure, 216–17
relation of, 208, 214, 216–20
Provine, Doris, Maire, 268, 275
Przeworski, Adam, 81
public reason
content of, 169, 187, 196, 233
disanalogy with legal reason, 204–5
public reasoning, 18, 78, 169–70,
222
public spheres, 83, 207, 212, 226, 242,
313–14, 331, 338–9
formal, 241, 313, 330
informal, 226, 313, 330
punishment, criminal, 186, 189–90
three strikes rule, 190

racial minorties, 197
Radin, Jane, 103
Railton, Peter, 11
Rawls, John, 18–19, 23, 50, 64, 65, 78,
79, 104, 112, 131, 132, 133, 142,
164, 166–72, 175–6, 177, 178,
180, 187, 192, 194, 196, 201–6,
213, 217, 222, 233, 255, 259, 328
Raz, Joseph, 84, 86, 87
reflective equilibrium, 18, 121, 135
regulatory capture, 269, 297
Rehg, William, 229
Rehnquist, Justice William H., 188,
189, 193
religious freedom, 186, 187–9, 218
see also constitutionalism and
religious neutrality
republicanism, 50, 85, 104, 236, 262,
336
rights, 49–50, 60–2
see also constitutionalism and
rights; democracy and rights
fundamental, 99, 100, 304, 306
historical expansion of, 62
individual liberty, 186, 194, 225,
232–5, 316
justification and status of, 50, 99–100,
108, 126, 225, 231–5

legal, 225, 235
political participation, 225, 232, 304,
316
private autonomy versus public
autonomy, 101
social and environment, 232
violations of, 239
Riker, William H., 65
Roosevelt, Franklin D., 302
Rosenbaum, Alan S., 14
Rosenberg, Gerald, 40, 203
Rosenfeld, Michael, 88, 96
Rostow, Eugene V., 180
Rousseau, Jean-Jacques, 49, 52–3, 71,
73, 75, 77, 107, 109, 111, 112, 115,
116, 120, 121–2, 133, 138, 143,
157, 214, 231, 236, 239, 250, 262,
268, 335, 336
Rubenfeld, Jed, 183
rule of law, 85–8, 97, 208, 217
see also constitutionalism and rule
of law
and arbitrary state power, 86
internal morality of, 87, 212, 229,
256, 280
as regulative ideal, 88
values of, 86–7, 94, 153, 211
Ryfe, David, 72, 338

Sager, Lawrence, 120, 183, 291
Saward, Michael, 82
Scalia, Justice Antonin, 43, 135, 201,
279
Schauer, Frederick, 266–9, 297, 302
Schumpeter, Joseph, 33, 81, 82
separation of powers, 245, 250, 255–6,
275, 279, 289
see also judicial review of separation of
powers; Supreme Court of the
United States and separation of
powers
Shapiro, Martin 93, 258, 264
skepticism, moral, 16–17
slavery, 61, 62
social contract theory, 133, 135–8
dilemma of, 137
Solum, Lawrence B., 10
Souter, Justice David H., 22, 193

South Africa, 280
Spaeth, Harold J., 28
Spain, 284, 291, 294, 307
  Tribunal Constitucional, 276, 291
Spector, Horacio, 180, 293, 334
standing, doctrine of, 218
state coercive power, 4–5, 16, 18,
  33–65, 71, 76, 81, 86, 97, 127, 229,
  313, 328
  see also oppression, fact of
state sovereign immunity, doctrine of,
  211
Stewart, Justice Potter, 199
Stone, Justice Harlan Fiske, 45, 311
Strauss, David A., 85, 91, 262
suicide, physician-assisted, 186, 193–5
Sunstein, Cass R., 52, 105, 151, 162,
  165, 192, 258, 307, 315, 320, 321
Supreme Court of the United States,
  3, 24, 6, 8, 9, 15, 19, 21, 22, 26,
  164, 185, 215, 244, 247, 261, 276,
  277, 282, 283–4, 286, 287, 289,
  308
  and appellate oversight, 209, 210,
  282
  cases and controversies limit, 205,
  209, 210, 288, 290
  and common laws methods, 209
  different functions of, 26–7
  and federalism, 209, 210
  rarity of constitutional review by, 28,
  187, 283
  and separation of powers, 211, 219
  and "Washington bar," 290
Sweden, 40
Sweet, Alec Stone, 93, 181, 258, 259,
  260, 264, 268, 269, 274, 275, 276,
  280–1, 284–5, 288, 289, 291, 307,
  312, 317
Switzerland, 24, 40

Tate, Neal, 280
Thayer, James Bradley, 32
Thomas, Justice Clarence, 189
Thomas, George, 96, 302
trans-national law, 29
Tribe, Lawrence H., 49

Tullis, Jeffery K., 305
Tushnet, Mark, 10, 96, 302, 312

United Kingdom, 24, 25, 90, 93, 96,
  119, 145, 209, 262, 297, 298, 305,
  308, 310, 330
  Human Rights Act of 1998, 297, 299,
  309
U.S. Constitution, 47, 107, 307
  Article I, 24
  Article V, 53, 90
  Bill of Rights, 50, 60, 114, 210
  Commerce Clause, 211
  entrenchment of, 91–2
  ratification of, 48
  1st Amendment, 44, 79, 189
  4th Amendment, 79
  8th Amendment, 44, 190, 191
  9th Amendment, 44
  13th Amendment, 48, 50, 53, 61
  14th Amendment, 43, 44, 48, 50, 53,
  61, 199, 200, 206, 210, 241, 305,
  308
  15th Amendment, 48, 50, 53, 61,
  199
  17th Amendment, 199
  18th Amendment, 340
  19th Amendment, 63, 199
  21st Amendment, 340
U.S. Declaration of Independence, 199
U.S. Electoral College, 200
U.S. electoral system, changes in, 260
U.S. Senate, 200
utilitarianism, 50, 234

Vallinder, Thorsten, 280

Waldron, Jeremy, 15, 41, 57, 73, 75,
  86, 102, 104, 119, 124–9, 130, 136,
  138, 139, 140, 141–61, 162, 179,
  180, 204, 209, 223, 230, 242, 254,
  255, 258, 263, 267, 269, 279, 280
Walker, Neil, 96
Warren, Justice Earl, 21, 199–200
Whittington, Keith E., 96, 97, 102, 302
Wittgenstein, Ludwig, 43
Wolin, Sheldon, 166

Table of Cases

Supreme Court of the United States:

Baker v. Carr 369 U.S. 186 (1962), 198–9
Brown v. Board of Education 347 U.S. 483 (1954), 11, 21, 42, 261
Bush v. Gore 531 U.S. 98 (2000), 201
City of Boerne v. Flores 521 U.S. 507 (1997), 308
Colegrove v. Green 328 U.S. 549 (1946), 198–9
Cooper v. Aaron 358 U.S. 1 (1958), 22
Davis v. Bandemer 478 U.S. 109 (1986), 200
Dred Scott v. Sandford 60 U.S. 393 (1857), 11, 28, 61
Elk Grove Unified School District et al. v. Newdow et al., 542 U.S. 1 (2004), 187–9, 210, 218
Gray v. Sanders 372 U.S. 368 (1963), 199
Griswold v. Connecticut 381 U.S. 479 (1965), 42
Lawrence et al. v. Texas, 539 U.S. 558 (2003), 194
Lochner v. New York 198 U.S. 45 (1905), 11, 20
Lockyer v. Andrade 538 U.S. 63 (2003), 189–93, 210, 211, 218
Luther v. Borden 48 U.S. 1 (1849), 199
Marbury v. Madison 5 U.S. 137 (1803), 11, 21, 28, 38, 246, 264
McCulloch v. Maryland 17 U.S. 316 (1819), 11
Miranda v. Arizona 384 U.S. 436 (1966), 42
Planned Parenthood v. Casey 505 U.S. 833 (1922), 22
Plessy v. Ferguson 163 U.S. 537 (1895), 11
Reynolds v. Sims 377 U.S. 533 (1964), 197, 199–200
Roe v. Wade 410 U.S. 113 (1973), 42, 118, 119, 261
Romer, Governor of Colorado et al. v. Evans et al., 517 U.S. 620 (1996), 194
Solem v. Helm 463 U.S. 277 (1983), 191
United States V. Carolene Products Co., 304 U.S. 144 (1938), 45, 128, 311
Vacco v. Quill 521 U.S. 793 (1997), 193–5, 218
Vieth et al. v. Jubelirer, 541 U.S. 267 (2004), 198, 201
Washington v. Glucksberg 521 U.S. 702 (1997), 193–5, 218

German Bundesverfassungsgericht:

Lüth (*BverfGE* 1958, volume 8 page 51), 294